JIMMY CARTER

and the Birth of the
Marathon Media Campaign

MEDIA AND PUBLIC AFFAIRS
Robert Mann, Series Editor

JIMMY CARTER

and the Birth of the
Marathon Media Campaign

AMBER ROESSNER

Louisiana State University Press   Baton Rouge

Published with the assistance of the V. Ray Cardozier Fund

Published by Louisiana State University Press
Copyright © 2020 by Louisiana State University Press
All rights reserved
Manufactured in the United States of America
First printing

Designer: Barbara Neely Bourgoyne
Typeface: Ingeborg
Printer and binder: Sheridan Books

Library of Congress Cataloging-in-Publication Data
Names: Roessner, Amber, 1980– author.
Title: Jimmy Carter and the birth of the marathon media campaign / Amber Roessner.
Description: Baton Rouge : Louisiana State University Press, [2020] | Series:
   Media and public affairs | Includes bibliographical references and index.
Identifiers: LCCN 2019052426 (print) | LCCN 2019052427 (ebook) | ISBN 978-0-8071-7079-3
   (cloth) | ISBN 978-0-8071-7360-2 (pdf) | ISBN 978-0-8071-7361-9 (epub)
Subjects: LCSH: Carter, Jimmy, 1924– | Presidents—United States—Election—1976. |
   United States—Politics and government—1974–1977.
Classification: LCC E868 .R64 2020 (print) | LCC E868 (ebook) | DDC 973.926092—dc23
LC record available at https://lccn.loc.gov/2019052426
LC ebook record available at https://lccn.loc.gov/2019052427

To Joseph and the children of his generation, in hopes that you will demand honest leaders, who represent the people's interest; muckraking journalists, who value truth over profits and partisanship; and a society that privileges civil discourse over rancor.

CONTENTS

Illustrations follow page 110

PREFACE

Plugging In and Tuning Out the Election Night Stalemate

Teletypes chattered in the background as the camera zoomed in. "Well, the first election returns are in," the anchorman said. "Gerald Ford, zero. Jimmy Carter, zero."[1] NBC's *Saturday Night Live* Weekend Update host Chevy Chase was parodying the election night specials that millions would plug into the following Tuesday. Chase underscored the claims of news analysts: voter turnout for the 1976 U.S. presidential election was expected to be light, and the race was too close to call.[2] Discerning truth in satire, Ford and Carter cast their votes near dawn on election day so that the news media might circulate images of them engaged in their civic duty.[3] Presidential candidates in the age of consensus showbiz politics operated based on the common-sense logic that "political reality rests in political images," and they hoped footage might combat apathy by inspiring reciprocal actions.[4] They failed to understand the most poignant insight from Chase's news update: in the bicentennial campaign, the disenchanted tuned out political imagecraft from the stumblebum and lustful politician.[5]

Despite widespread apathy, newspaper headlines encouraged readers to vote the network of their choice to watch returns trickle in for the neck-and-neck battle.[6] Analysts predicted the new rules in American politics might seize, once and for all, from political elites the power of the people to determine the leader of the free world. "It may be one of those years where the machines can't tell us that readily who won," CBS News consultant Peter Hart told *Wall Street Journal* reporter Michael Connor. "This year we may give the election back to the people, and keep them up all night waiting for answers." Influenced by his sources, Connor suggested the election would be a media event rivaled only by *Monday Night Football* and urged his audience of roughly 1.5 million readers to "stock up on beer and pretzels."[7]

Analysts accurately identified interest in the outcome and the stakes of the election—the health of the two-party system, the performance of the fourth estate, and civic engagement in a participatory democracy—but predictions of increased public participation were flawed.[8] New rules in American politics temporarily wrested much control over the nomination process from party bosses, but power was *not* transferred solely to the people. The Quiet Revolution, triggered by McGovern-Fraser Commission (1969–72) and Mikulski Commission (1972–73) reforms, was not televised, but it did create a systemic rupture further privileging consensus showbiz politics. Post-1968 reforms appeared to place the nomination in the public's hands by instituting candidate-bound delegates and doubling the number of state primaries, but influence in great measure shifted from traditional party leaders to *new* elites of mass communication who with modern machines constructed images based on public opinion to speak to the masses.[9] Moreover, after the passage of the Federal Election Campaign Act of 1974 (FECA), which limited campaign financing to a fraction of what was spent in prior elections, presidential contenders increasingly turned to mass media for cost-effective national exposure, and elite political reporters, "the relatively small group of individuals 'representing news organizations with a commitment to coverage of national politics year in and year out,'" anxiously stumbled into their commanding role as kingmakers in modern U.S. politics.[10]

Post-reform presidential campaigning was "a whole new ballgame," New York mayor John Lindsay observed, and underdogs enjoyed a competitive edge in a cultural climate favoring antiestablishment outsiders.[11] Victors under the new system proved most successful at negotiating shifting conditions, but media celebrities reaped the greatest rewards. As the leader of the "not ready for primetime players," for instance, Chase gained celebrity status and considerable influence with an audience of 22 million mostly young, male Americans, and on election eve he illustrated two lingering realities: campaign reporters remained in the competitive business of calling political contests for a nation obsessed with odds and statistics, and winners under the new rules remained uncertain.[12] In the end, as reports indicated, projecting victors in the presidential race (*and* the corresponding campaign reporting contest) was a challenging task, but each party and their respective consultants believed they knew the secret to success—celebrity infotainment.[13]

Declaring victory for network executives meant delivering election night specials designed to boost standings in pivotal ratings wars, which determined advertising revenue and directly contributed to their financial viability.[14] To produce the spectacle they believed viewers expected, the Big Three networks funneled an estimated record $10 million into "mobiliz[ing] a small army of 9,000 people" to report and interpret election results.[15] Gaining the competitive edge required incorporating the latest technological tools—satellites, color video mini-cameras, computerized data, and elaborate Chyron electronic maps—to offer high-quality coverage delivered by trusted celebrity news teams and analysts. The most crucial factor, however, remained the same as always in the news business—getting it *first,* but also getting it *right.*[16]

Election night represented a special opportunity for ABC News president Bill Sheehan and *ABC Evening News* producer Bill Lord to recast their perennial underdog newscast through the art of infotainment. Since mid-century, presidential candidates had shifted to razzle-dazzle campaigns to spellbind potential voters, and incoming news executives hoped to similarly mesmerize audiences with star power.[17] Thus, in advance of the media event, they hired celebrity anchor Barbara Walters and signed two famous analysts from the modern class of political power brokers—journalist Theodore "Teddy" White and pollster-turned-consultant Lou Harris.[18] News divisions once relied on the traditional political establishment (incumbents, party bosses, and special interest group leaders) to serve as conduits of information to the elite postwar news establishment. In other words, chummy Washington correspondents and columnists depended on conventional sources from their exclusive circles. But the ascendancy of primary showbiz politics transformed traditional roles.[19] Hence, White and Harris cashed in on their celebrity insider status and weighed in on returns alongside ABC's celebrity news team.

During the first segment of ABC's *Political Spirit of '76,* Walters first turned to White, the journalist who "revolutionized the art of political reporting" with his *The Making of the President* series, posing the question on many minds: would the election be a "squeaker" or a "landslide"?[20] Wearing his signature wire-rimmed glasses to read notes at a nearby desk, White did not offer a definitive prediction, instead extending a prescient observation: "This campaign has revolved around character and personality more than any other in recent American history, and the direction of power is hidden in their character and in their personalities so . . . we are left with the same mystery that we began the year."[21]

White's reluctance to prognosticate stemmed not from his characteristic style, but from his uncharacteristic absence from the trail in 1976. After offering a comprehensive, backstage look at four presidential races, contributing to a surge in professional and public interest in his new brand of insider reporting, he grew weary of the "mechanical," behind-the-scenes campaign chronicles produced by his host of imitators.[22] Consequently, he staggered away, confounded by persistent industry demands for inside accounts and character examinations. Nevertheless, his assessment was apt: the rise of new politics left journalists mystified by the search to apprehend the real source of power hidden behind a politician's enigmatic masks.[23] Accordingly, while practicing their new-and-improved style of campaign journalism, the consensus-minded pack, consumed with fashionable character probes, struggled to peel back layers of Carter's political persona, to weigh in proportion incongruent elements of the public and private man, and to comprehend how his many mediated faces mirrored fissures in a Democratic Party searching for a cohesive identity and a winning message.[24]

Ensconced in early returns data from Kentucky and Indiana minutes later, Harris instead exuded confidence in his ability to predict and interpret outcomes.[25] Harris told veteran hard news correspondent Howard Smith that early projections suggested the election was a stalemate with potential to hold the attention of engaged observers, and acknowledged the manifestation of malaise that perceptive analysts predicted prior to primary season.[26] As returns poured in, he recognized that, despite reforms designed to inspire greater civic participation by creating a more transparent, inclusive electoral process, voter apathy had intensified amid cynicism over "media-driven performative politics," disillusionment over credibility crises in American culture, and lingering antiestablishment impulses.[27]

After engaging in final acts of imagecraft in an extraordinary marathon campaign, Ford and Carter discovered that analyst predictions were prescient: in an election cycle favoring antiestablishment outsiders, long-shot contenders claimed unexpected victories.[28] Tapping into conventional sources to scoop broadcast rivals, United Press International issued a newsflash at 2:57 a.m.—Carter wins presidency. Network consultants, under pressure to avoid repeating recent mistakes, hurried to confirm the results.[29] Again outpacing industry leader CBS, NBC News anchor John Chancellor shared the culmination of Carter's meteoric rise with his remaining audience thirty-four minutes later.[30] "It just came over television. Mississippi just put me over," Carter exclaimed to Governor Cliff Finch, who called to inform the president-elect that the Charlie Daniels Band's anthem proved prophetic.[31] In the moment of redneck chic, the backwoods region that party regulars considered abandoning aligned solidly behind Carter's unlikely coalition of self-identifying political underdogs—African Americans, blue-collar workers, ethnic white descendants, evangelicals, and women.[32]

With news he captured the necessary 270 electoral college votes ringing in his ears, Carter celebrated the victorious end to his four-year journey with family and staff. Elite frontline reporters hailed the peanut farmer from Plains as a media genius in the days ahead for staging an unprecedented political miracle.[33] As Pulitzer Prize-winning journalist David Halberstam observed, Carter "more than any other candidate this year has sensed and adapted to modern communications and national mood."[34] He rose from obscurity to claim his place in the White House by harnessing members of the new political elite "with access to the devices and channels of mass publicity," who constructed a candidate-centered campaign that deployed appealing moderate images designed for his nonconventional coalition of special interest factions forged in the long decade of the 1960s.[35]

Carter sought to thank supporters and pledged to make America "great . . . again" in a ten-minute message of unity offered by live feed to network audiences, but millions had already tuned out.[36] When he stepped from the stage, ABC News correspondent Sam Donaldson extended his hand and offered words of congratulations, but the president-elect ignored the gesture. Confronted with someone he deemed responsible for his thirty-point slide in the polls—and with it, the ruling mandate he believed necessary to enact significant change—his "bemused contempt" toward frontline reporters hardened into disdain, and "he was ready for a fight."[37] To solidify his mandate from the American public, Carter and his staff intended to orchestrate a permanent campaign designed to outmaneuver elite reporters by deploying everyman imagecraft through controlled channels and negotiating mediated images through stringent news management techniques.[38]

However, Washington-based reporters, who recognized that "covering Carter [was] like playing chess with Bobby Fischer," were determined not to be outsmarted by the peanut farmer from Plains.[39] And, in time, Carter's staff discovered that manipulating frontline reporters, key architects determining image and, by extension, a substantive degree of political power in the White House, proved far more difficult than expected in an adversarial milieu, and the image of credible, competent reform that Carter and his staff meticulously constructed fractured along the same fault lines as his fragile coalition.[40]

ACKNOWLEDGMENTS

This decade-long intellectual journey—lasting longer than Carter's campaign and presidency combined—involved analysis of thousands of media texts produced between 1968 and 1980, thousands of documents located in hundreds of archival boxes, and dozens of in-depth interviews with Jimmy Carter's 1976 campaign staff and frontline reporters.

Archival travel is expensive, and I received generous financial support from the American Journalism Historians Association's 2011 Joseph McKerns Research Grant Award; *American Journalism*'s 2014 Rising Scholar Award; Emory University's 2015 MARBL Fellowship; and the University of Tennessee's 2015 Professional Development Award, 2017 Chancellor's Grant, and the College of Communication and Information Dean's Summer Research Fund. Along the way, I encountered unsung heroes of all histories—archivists (in particular, Keith Shuler at the Jimmy Carter Presidential Library and Scotty Kirkland at the Alabama Department of Archives and History) who extended invaluable guidance and support. Likewise, research assistants, including Denae D'Arcy, Natalie Manayeva, Jackie Cameron, Lindsey Bier, Monique Freemon, and Lexie Little, offered crucial assistance.

Thanks to Jimmy Carter Presidential Library Director of Research Steven Hochman for encouraging President Carter to take a few minutes to chat with an unknown scholar from Winder, Georgia, and to President Carter and members of his campaign staff, including issues specialist Stuart Eizenstat, press aide Rex Granum, television advisor Barry Jagoda, advertising specialist Gerald Rafshoon, and campaign aide Greg Schneiders, and frontline reporters, including David Alpern, Tom Brokaw, Eleanor Clift, Stanley Cloud, Sam Donaldson, Brooks Jackson, Carl Leubsdorf, Walter Mears, Lynne Olson, Wes Pippert, Bob Schieffer, Curtis Wilkie, Jules Witcover, Judy Woodruff, and Pulitzer Prize-winning editorial cartoonists Tony Auth and Paul Szep, who generously contributed time and perspectives, an accurate attribution being their only promised reward. Though, as one participant noted, memories fade with time, these interviews added a rich layer of context to my analysis, and keeping in mind Donaldson's reminder that any producer can make their subject sound like a sage or the village idiot, I have sought, above all, to quote each individual accurately and in context.

I was fortunate to have the opportunity to work out key arguments based on instrumental feedback from mentors, colleagues, and supportive audiences in a variety of forums. Brian Creech generously read and commented on this entire manuscript, and I'm eternally indebted for his brilliant insights. Janice Hume, Jay Hamilton, Karen Russell, and Kristin English, mentors and friends from my days at the University of Georgia, read portions of early drafts and extended advice, support, and encouragement.

Along the way, other historians and cultural studies scholars, including Steve Ash, Jim Baughman, Kristen Block, Kathryn Brownell, Dan Feller, Ernie Freeberg, Joshua Hodge, David Greenberg, Mark Hulsether, Bob Hutton, Ann Jefferson, Zachary Lechner, Kevin Lerner, Will Mari, Matthew Pressman, and Michael Stamm and conference reviewers, participants, moderators, and respondents in sessions at the American Historical Association, the American Journalism Historians Association, the Association for Education in Journalism and Mass Communication, the International Communication Association, the International Association for Literary Journalism Studies, the National Communication Association, and the Southern American Studies Association shared feedback and suggested important interventions. LSU Press series editor Robert Mann, its editorial staff, and Kathryn Brownell also proposed important manuscript revisions contributing to my intervention into modern U.S. political history.

Nonetheless, without support from family and friends this book might never have materialized. My parents always have been among my strongest supporters, and they continued down that path over the last decade, offering not only words of encouragement but also childcare when my research took me far from home. Thanks to my husband, David, for putting up with me when my thoughts were elsewhere—namely, on Jimmy Carter, his staff, and prominent journalists of the 1970s—and to my sweet son, Joseph, who with his grin that wins puts a smile on my face each day. I love you all, and without your encouragement I never could have completed this marathon journey.

JIMMY CARTER

and the Birth of the
Marathon Media Campaign

Introduction

Time's "Miracle" Man

Jimmy Carter's piercing blue eyes gazed out from the cover of Henry Luce's legacy newsmagazine as middle managers perused headlines at the Eastern Lobby Shop in New York's Pan Am Building, elite intellectuals lingered near Harvard Square's Out of Town News, and University of Georgia coeds streaked past Barnett's Newsstand in Athens on January 3, 1977.[1] "Just a year ago, he was walking up to men and women who did not know that he existed, shaking their hands and drawling, 'I'm Jimmy Carter, and I'm going to be your next President,'" *Time* staff acknowledged in the cover story's lede. "The notion seemed preposterous," but the "outsider . . . defied expectations" and prevailed, achieving "a political miracle."[2]

Since 1927, when Luce established *Time*'s special issue, newsworthy politicians and celebrities often entered neck-and-neck races for the coveted man of the year designation, but editor-in-chief Hedley Donovan, managing editor Henry Grunwald, Washington bureau chief Hugh Sidey, and other *Time* staff settled on a clear decision when deliberating over the fate of their special issue in the late fall, citing the peanut farmer's "impressive rise," "the great anticipation" surrounding his presidency, and "the new phase he mark[ed] in American life."[3] Though the decade was later characterized as a mere bridge between cultural revolts of the 1960s and corporate takeovers of the 1980s, *Time* staff offered an apt assessment—the 1970s were a period of transformation in American politics and journalism that determined the present moment.[4] Moreover, these prominent political actors and preliminary historians shrewdly recognized that "Carter was a natural choice" for their profitable commemorative issue "because his rise to power was 'one of the most astonishing in the history of the Republic.'"[5]

1

News of the special issue brought joy to the hearts of the news-making "whiz kids" who fashioned Carter's "miracle" through an intentional image-craft strategy involving modified showbiz campaign approaches designed to frame words, sounds, and images embodied in the peanut farmer-physicist for president's candidacy. Moreover, they welcomed *Time* correspondents back to Plains, Georgia (population 683), one of the main scenes for Carter's trendy, down-home southern campaign designed to simultaneously tap into cultural desires for sincere authenticity in U.S. politicians and the New South, cravings that manifested themselves in popular films such as Michael Ritchie's *The Candidate* (1972) and Robert Altman's *Nashville* (1975).[6]

In anticipation of the special issue, Grunwald commissioned the cover to James Browning Wyeth, a contemporary American realist painter who had previously captured presidential portraits of John Kennedy and Richard Nixon. Inspired by patriarch N. C. Wyeth, he encouraged Carter to pose out-doors before ploughed pastureland and the Plains water tower, which bore the image of an American flag.[7] The ensuing portrait offered a rendering of the peanut farmer, who promised a "government as good as its people," clad in the working man's denim informality, a bricolage constructed by campaign image merchants. With this scene, the candidate's stage managers sought to signify Carter's pastoral roots—the nation's nostalgic site of inno-cence lost to the post-industrial sheen that the Democratic Party's savior symbolically promised to resurrect.[8]

Nearby this site in late December, *Time* staff writers Stanley Cloud and Bonnie Angela, alongside Sidey and chief of correspondents Murray Gart, interviewed the president-elect in his ranch home, and though Carter's im-agecraft advisors once again were on hand to serve as chief liaisons between frontline reporters and their audiences by controlling access, managing rapport, and negotiating mediated images, these commanding reporters, weary of attempts to sell the presidency after recent scandals, peppered Carter with questions about his plans to implement an open administra-tion.[9] Accordingly, after acknowledging his media genius as the "candidate of the 1970s" in the cover story, they promptly turned to the vogue mode of adversarial, watchdog journalism in reporting on the president-elect's transition operations.[10]

Hence, as Carter's press staff examined the special issue more closely, they encountered the recurring adverse theme that had haunted their per-sonal media campaign since its opening stages.[11] "He is complex and sometimes contradictory," *Time* staff appraised Carter's enigmatic qualities. "His creed combines traditionally antithetical elements of help-the-deprived populism and deny-thyself fiscal conservatism."[12] Moreover, as Carter's advisors continued to scour news clips, they discovered they were the butt of the joke in humorist Art Buchwald's most recent syndicated column. As prudent students of post-1968 reforms, Carter's staff had exploited free and paid national exposure surrounding their personal campaign in the preceding months, but as Buchwald quipped, many Americans now suffered from "the Carter syndrome," an overdose of *Time*'s Man of the Year. Amid his permanent campaign their malaise would worsen in the years to come.[13]

★ ★ ★

In their special issue analysis, *Time* staff acknowledged that Carter's salient grassroots media campaign had sparked one of the most astonishing "political miracle[s]" in the nation's history.[14] And though they and their intellectual successors recognized that Carter's "impressive rise" signaled a new phase in American life, they neglected to thoroughly examine (1) the definitive shift from a party system ruled predominantly by urban machines and party bosses to a primary system dominated by mass media and (2) the increased significance of the negotiation of political images in the fortunes of permanent campaigns for the White House.[15] Recognizing these omissions, this book probes how shifting conditions in American politics and journalism contributed to the performances of unexpected winners and losers in the bicentennial campaign and considers how these individuals helped determine existing conditions in American presidential politics and campaign journalism.

This book tells the story of a transformative moment in American politics and journalism by examining *Time*'s 1976 "miracle" man through a representational and relational analysis of media texts, memory texts, and archival documents surrounding the negotiation of political images by presidential aspirants, campaign consultants, frontline reporters, and various publics involved in the bicentennial campaign.[16] The book follows seven primary arguments:

- After the midcentury shift toward primary showbiz politics, presidential candidates increasingly depended on a new class of campaign workers—political consultants, skilled image merchants (in other words, pollsters, public relations consultants, advertising specialists, and television advisors) who capitalized on the visual authority of mass media to sell campaigns to special interest groups and individual constituents.[17] This emerging rank of campaign operatives worked alongside traditional campaign personnel, such as press secretaries (media liaisons who served as intermediaries between frontline reporters, their sources, and their audiences), and together, their prevailing perceptions reshaped ideas about presidential power and political reality moving forward.

- Though most presidential aspirants in the 1976 election cycle accepted the primary rule in "new politics" (images did not simply communicate messages to the masses; images spoke power, transforming political reality), Carter and his advisors most adeptly exploited new kingmakers under the reformed system of showbiz politics—wunderkind political consultants, chic celebrities, and horse race-obsessed frontline reporters, who amplified the antiestablishment outsider's salient personal campaign in the mass media.[18]

- In an era marked by crises of confidence in the executive branch and the fourth estate, the relatively unknown southern governor rose to power by evoking the Nixon-inspired antithesis of Kennedy's winning brand—a personal, (un)celebrity campaign that capitalized on sincere messages of moral reform and authentic images of the triumphant underdog, resonant appeals for Americans who increasingly distrusted the political establishment's slick, Madison Avenue-inspired campaigns masking corrupt presidential actors.[19]

- Though Carter's consultants effectively tapped into the pulse of the American public through tools of new politics, their personal campaign failed to resonate with a vital audience, the bicentennial campaign's principal power brokers—the pseudo-celebrity frontline news pack. Collectively annoyed with Nixon-inspired media management techniques and influenced by the trend to privilege investigative journalism, these frontline reporters relentlessly deconstructed political imagecraft, probed the candidate's character, and offered cultural shorthand to convey their critique—the adverse image of an enigmatic, opportunistic politician, which was symptomatic of the changing nature of liberalism and attempts by the Democratic Party's rising star to develop a winning brand.

- Despite increasing scrutiny from frontline reporters and opposition from party regulars, the front-running dark horse endured to become the semi-consensual nominee and underdog victor by negotiating adverse images and attacking the establishment, and subsequently he established new rules of primary politics.

- Amid slick, populist-inspired campaigns and unrelenting coverage of the presidential horse race, many eligible voters, cynical of American politics and the news media, dropped out of the revolutionary electoral process, and malaise ensued while media critics, inspired by misplaced nostalgia, lamented the decline of a "golden age" of issues-based campaign coverage that informed enlightened voters who freely engaged in the democratic process—a moment that never existed.

- Through an ingenious grassroots media campaign, Carter and his advisors staged the peanut farmer's miraculous rise. But amid an emerging adversarial climate fueled by establishment opponents and elite reporters practicing a penetrating mode of journalistic deconstruction, they failed to translate their permanent campaign into a successful ruling mandate in the White House. Nevertheless, amid the rise of identity politics and the fragmentation of mass media, Carter's political heirs learned important lessons from his failures in media relations and redesigned the media presidency for savvy political actors.[20]

This book considers the construction, negotiation, and consumption of *Time*'s "miracle" man, a political outsider who rose to the presidency in a transformational moment in American politics and journalism. Along the way, the narrative privileges certain individuals, media, and moments while others remain more obscured—the choice of a cultural historian, who intends to avoid the "cartographer's folly."[21] In the final analysis, though many cultural observers dismissed Carter's campaign and presidency as the final chapter of Watergate, this book reveals that his "miraculous" rise in the bicentennial campaign signaled a new chapter in American politics and journalism, a seminal transition prompted by a seismic rupture that still reverberates today.[22]

1

Introducing Jimmy Who

(De)Constructing Showbiz Politics

Atlanta-based advertising specialist Gerald Rafshoon nearly skidded off the road during the country-and-western singer's refrain (crooned to the catchy tune of "The Ballad of Davy Crockett"): "Jimmy Carter is his name, Jimmy Carter is his name, Jimmy Carter is his name, number one for Governor."[1] He pulled into a gas station moments later and called the *Atlanta Constitution*'s progressive columnist Hal Gulliver, a supporter of the little-known peanut farmer in Georgia's 1966 gubernatorial race. Recognizing the idea for the kitschy jingle as a cheap throwback to Democrat Hubert Humphrey's 1960 campaign, an outdated mode in the rapidly advancing world of showbiz politics, Rafshoon grumbled, "Your friend Jimmy Carter needs a lot of help," and he agreed to meet the state senator and his advisors the following Monday at the Dinkler Motor Hotel.[2]

Amid growing cynicism over slick, Madison Avenue-produced spots from disingenuous political actors, Rafshoon recommended harnessing the cultural craze for inside glimpses into campaigns, manifesting itself over the prior decade in popular appeal for Theodore White's *The Making of the President* series and Robert Drew's *Primary* documentary, with cinéma-vérité political advertisements. Convinced by the logic of modified showbiz politics, Carter invested his remaining $78,000 budget into Rafshoon and his spots. Aided by this savvy imagecraft strategy that increased name recognition among voters and combated attacks from Democratic opponents, such as former Georgia governor Ellis Arnall, who mockingly referred to the moderate politician as "Jimmy Who," the peanut farmer's campaign evolved into a "big sensation."[3]

But, despite Carter's Kennedyesque appeal, the longshot failed to win the

Democratic nomination; nonetheless, encouraged by persistent supporters, he vowed he would emerge victorious next time. Truth be told, Jimmy
Carter had not lost, his campaign manager Brooks Pennington proclaimed,
because now "they don't say, 'Jimmy Who?' They say, 'Jimmy When?'"[4] When
Jimmy commenced subsequent campaigns, trusted consultants relied on
evolving principles of showbiz politics to tap into the public's growing distrust of American politicians and media, and this "indelible context" framed
Carter's campaign.[5]

★ ★ ★

Informed by his experience as an advertising director with Twentieth Century Fox, Rafshoon was intimately familiar with the myth world of semi-
ological signs French literary critic Roland Barthes deciphered a decade
prior.[6] He recognized that presidential actors increasingly relied on showbiz
studio apparatuses—laundry soap advertisers, publicity men, copywriters,
and photographers—to sell themselves and their mythic messages to the
electorate.[7] Furthermore, he comprehended, as did industry colleagues, the
decades-long cultural craze to gain a backstage glimpse into the private
lives of actors and even regular Joes that sociologist Erving Goffman had
described in his award-winning book five years prior, and amid emerging
distrust of staged political campaigns, he apprehended the popularity of
candid-style documentaries in political advertising.[8] But, in the final analysis, he recommended the type of imagecraft and news-making strategies that
social historian Daniel Boorstin indicted in his 1962 bestseller as "replica[s]
of reality" contributing to the "reshaping of our very concept of truth."[9]

Influenced by cultural anxieties previously expressed by media critics,
such as Will Irwin, Walter Lippmann, and the Frankfurt School, Boorstin
traced the flood of pseudo-events, what he described as planned promotional spectacles designed to be reproduced in media, and the coinciding
culture of celebrity, manifesting themselves in mid-twentieth-century
worlds of Hollywood, business, and politics, to the transition from news
gathering to news making that developed alongside the mid-nineteenth
century's graphic revolution.[10] As Boorstin, his contemporaries, and subsequent scholars explained, following the development by media innovators of
a commercial news model and new media technologies that rapidly altered
the form of content and accelerated the rate of news transmission, news

workers, imagining audiences that craved information about the private lives of the famous, traded news as a commodity and engaged in round-the-clock production and transmission of "candid" images.[11] With more space to fill and pressure to fill it quickly, professional reporters, increasingly practicing a detached brand of journalism, came to rely on manufactured news in the form of interviews, press conferences, and news leaks from official sources facilitated by public relations and advertising professionals. Thus, by the midcentury, as Boorstin decried, "the vivid [mediated] image came to overshadow pale reality," and the culture of celebrity and the flood of pseudo-events constructed by newsmakers occupied center stage in public discourse, even in the world of U.S. politics.[12]

That image came to define presidential politics hardly should have shocked midcentury political historians.[13] Amid the rising tide of sensational and fake news prompting public cries to access "information . . . not from a careless or reckless press, but from the president himself," Theodore Roosevelt introduced the nation to the "public presidency."[14] But, still lacking a channel to speak directly to the American public, Roosevelt extended William McKinley's model of press relations and constructed a "bully pulpit" to influence the Washington press through emerging professional public relations strategies designed to actively mold public opinion.[15] His successors continued to influence coverage through enhanced showbiz-inspired, newsmaking techniques, such as regular press conferences with the White House press corp, but they also increasingly accessed means to speak directly to the American public through new mass-media technologies.[16]

Amid this backdrop, successful political actors proved most adept at constructing pseudo-events and negotiating image amid moments of disruption that changed the rules of strategic political communication, and image became "one of the most common—and ambiguous—terms" in modern culture, but the concept was not vague to the rising class of campaign consultants who recognized television as an emerging force in American politics at midcentury.[17] These imagecraft specialists, as cultural critic Neil Postman contended, banked on selling the aura of authenticity in presidential politics and, amid the shift from party to primary-television politics during the postwar age of consensus, created politician-gods in the image of the mass electorate.[18]

★ ★ ★

Discovering the power of mass media early in his political career, aspiring presidential actor Estes Kefauver certainly comprehended this prerequisite and fashioned his grassroots media campaign for the White House to appeal to the average American. At the encouragement of *Washington Post* publisher Philip Graham, the U.S. senator from Madisonville, Tennessee, sought to exploit the fame and prestige that he gained through his fifteen-month, fourteen-stop "televised road show," featuring his national probe into organized crime, to promote his underdog campaign for the 1952 Democratic nomination.[19] Despite sustaining ridicule from the small circle of elite political reporters, who mocked "the Don Quixote from Tennessee" for daring to challenge an incumbent, Kefauver's personal campaign attracted enough grassroots support and media coverage to propel him to victory in the New Hampshire primary and to compel President Harry Truman, who denounced primaries as "eye-wash," to announce he would not seek reelection amid lagging public support.[20] Donning his signature coonskin cap, the dark horse frontrunner claimed eleven additional primary victories, but at the convention, party insiders, infuriated over the Kefauver Committee's allegations of corrupt politicians, denied him the nomination.[21] Ultimately, Kefauver's failed media campaign demonstrated the lingering pre-reform power of political bosses and the pervasive cultural anxieties around primary-television politics, captured by Senator John Kennedy in his 1959 *TV Guide* essay: though television afforded political actors with a tool to expose deception and dishonesty, the medium might be misused by demagogues seeking to manipulate the masses.[22]

Though shrewd presidential aspirants recognized power in the new medium and sought to harness television to exploit the latest tools of showbiz politics, disinclined adopters, such as Democratic nominee Adlai Stevenson, bristled at "the idea that you can merchandise candidates for high office like breakfast cereal."[23] Nevertheless, after encountering coverage of public backlash when "Mr. Republican" Robert Taft, like a machine politician, engaged in closed-door, pre-convention meetings and "blacked out TV," Stevenson reluctantly agreed to thirty-minute spots during the general election campaign.[24] But televised appeals from the unenthusiastic participant in primary-television politics frustrated some Americans, who chafed at interruptions to their favorite television programs.[25]

Stevenson's opponent Dwight Eisenhower grudgingly harnessed tools of showbiz politics at his campaign's outset. Moreover, after surviving the disastrous live broadcast of his campaign kickoff, what his advisor Robert Montgomery referred to as the "Abilene debacle," he welcomed Hollywood professionals, advertising specialists, and television advisors into his inner circle. They designed a meticulously constructed campaign that intimately synced Ike's image and his message into spots, such as "Eisenhower Answers America," which were designed to resonate with average American voters.[26]

In advance of this moment, media critics, such as Dwight MacDonald and David Riesman, warned against the influence of commercial forces in presidential politics that encouraged manufacturing glamorized candidates to sell to the American public. Yet, despite their admonitions, as conservative writer Phyllis Schlafly charged, the 1952 presidential campaign represented a critical juncture when new kingmakers specializing in imagecraft and news-making initiated the displacement of political bosses.[27] And, moving forward, the most successful presidential actors were the shrewdest at exploiting tools of showbiz politics; moreover, as Riesman forewarned, blinded by glamour, some voters failed to act in their own self-interest, and apathy materialized among spectators of American politics.[28]

Despite sustained criticism over Eisenhower's showbiz campaign from critics, including Stevenson's advisor George Ball, the iconic American general secured a landslide victory. Once in office, he institutionalized showbiz techniques in presidential politics by retaining imagecraft consultants, establishing a prototype for the White House Office of Communications, introducing televised press conferences, and privileging his primary-television reelection campaign over the whistle-stop tour.[29] Moreover, amid the backdrop of the Cold War and emergent hierarchal institutions, "the TV president" controlled the flow of information to elite reporters—and by extension their American audiences—through secrecy and news management techniques. When he encountered adverse coverage from elite Washington journalists, he turned to television to circumvent the "liberal establishment"—as conservative media activists increasingly referred to "biased" reporters at top-circulating newspapers and magazines—and to speak directly to the American people, tricks of the trade Vice President Dick Nixon and subsequent presidential actors emulated, and elite Washington journalists became increasingly suspicious of their displacement by newscasters and cynical over presidential efforts to manipulate coverage.[30]

★ ★ ★

Amid increasing anxiety over political manipulation accompanying showbiz-inspired campaigns in "mass society" and distrust in institutions after live coverage of congressional hearings (i.e., Estes Kefauver's 1950–51 organized crime and 1954 comic book committees, Senator Joseph McCarthy's 1953–54 committee hearings, and the 1959 television quiz show and radio payola scandal hearings) that uncovered corruption and bias in business, politics, the mass media, and even collegiate athletics and left cultural observers wondering whether America was "a nation of liars and cheats," Theodore White, an unemployed, authorized fly-on-the-wall reporter stood amid the handful of passive, consensus-style Cold War campaign chroniclers ready to offer a nation obsessed with celebrity an insider's look at the 1960 presidential campaign.[31] After nearly two decades as a foreign and political correspondent at Henry Luce's interpretative newsmagazine *Time,* the progressive journal of opinion *The New Republic,* and Max Ascoli's highbrow political journal *The Reporter, Collier*'s national political correspondent planned to expose shifting conditions in American presidential politics with his "The Making of the President—1956." But amid financial competition over advertising dollars from television, the legacy muckraking magazine folded, and White waited until the next election cycle to offer the world his transformative account of presidential politics.[32] "The idea was to follow the campaign from beginning to end," he explained. "It would be written as a novel is written . . . early candidates vanish in the primaries until only two final jousters struggle for the prize in November."[33]

Primed to unearth intimate details and weave interpretative insights about social forces influencing national politics into his literary narrative, and recognizing that "the beginning" of the campaign never ended for Nixon, Stevenson, and the rising stars of the Democratic Party, White documented the first stirrings of presidential aspirants as they conspired with advisors and sought national exposure to their political feats and the announcement of their candidacies.[34] But, despite his ambitious intent, he was not on hand for seminal moments during the invisible primaries—such as the real commencement of Kennedy's campaign when his father, Joseph, proclaimed: "We're going to sell Jack like soap flakes."[35] Nor was he present to witness the image-conscious candidate on "his first unofficial campaign trip," a Sunday-afternoon picnic organized by Nebraska's Democratic national committee chair, Bernard Boyle, in August 1959.[36] But he did observe the finished product—"the Omaha profile," campaign photographer

Jacques Lowe's heroic image of the underdog celebrity candidate arrayed in sunlight and flanked by adoring Democrats, reporters, and photographers that donned campaign buttons and bumper stickers during the primaries and draped the walls of the Los Angeles Memorial Sports Arena during the 1960 Democratic National Convention.[37]

Amid this telegenic backdrop to Kennedy's campaign, White and fellow Luce media-empire journeyman Robert Drew sought a close-range vantage point to offer audiences an inside look that the small circle of consensus-style campaign chroniclers never afforded them. Granted the necessary access in Wisconsin, they placed the primary campaign for public appeal into focus and exposed backstage maneuvers in presidential politics through their candid images.[38] "For John F. Kennedy and Hubert Humphrey," White wrote, "there was no other than the primary way to the Convention. If they could not at the primaries prove their strength in the hearts of Americans, the Party bosses would cut their hearts out in the back rooms of Los Angeles."[39] Through the lens and the printed word, these image-minded journalists deconstructed competing strategies deployed to appeal to three pre-reform primary audiences: local delegates, national audiences, and party bosses, and though both candidates engaged in personal and public media campaigns, the veteran journalists emphasized the stark contrast in Kennedy's public media campaign, featuring the political celebrity amid throngs of adoring fans at big-city rallies that Boorstin deconstructed as pseudo-events, and Humphrey's traditional small-town, personal campaign, involving old-fashioned chitchat and grassroots handshaking.[40] As Barthes presciently suggested, all political actors increasingly harnessed mythic messages to connect with their electorates, but at the end of the day, as Humphrey explained to White, he was like "a corner grocer running against a chain store," and despite Kennedy's indecisive win in Wisconsin, Washington's elite consensus-minded journalists framed Humphrey's moral victory as a loss.[41]

When "Superman [Came] to the Supermarket," as *Esquire* freelance writer Norman Mailer described the political superstar's arrival at the DNC in literary reportage that helped define the New Journalism, network cameras could not adequately capture the scene at the Biltmore Hotel, the Democratic Party, and national news headquarters. Amid the comings and goings of competing reporters, political actors, and celebrities, obscured backroom discussions, and the onslaught of curious onlookers who clamored for one

moment of fame, cultural observers deconstructed the new political landscape through an interpretative lens.[42] And, though they captured backstage maneuvers, such as the influence of elite Georgetown news-makers,
like Graham, and the rising power of image on the front stage of American
politics, mesmerized reporters, distracted by the glitz of celebrity politics,
failed to offer penetrating critiques of Kennedy's political machinations and
to deconstruct chummy, symbiotic relationships among political actors that
created potential for reportorial blind spots.[43]

As commentators conveyed, Kennedy and the Democratic Party deployed
the glamour of Hollywood-inspired appeals to entertain audiences, and they
continued to exploit showbiz tactics against Nixon in the general election
campaign.[44] Amid the backdrop of Kennedy's Rat Pack-endorsed media
campaign, the DNC's advertising agency Guild, Bascom and Bonfigli and
Kennedy's personal advertising specialist Jack Denove developed catchy jin-
gles and one-minute spots focused on party themes, including the ground-
breaking attack ad "Nixon's Experience," which, with the skill of CBS News
broadcaster Edward Murrow, deployed film of Eisenhower stumped by a
reporter's query into Nixon's influence in the administration.[45] Though these
advertisements appear monochromatic compared to ones that followed,
they overshadowed the dull and mundane spots devised by BBDO executives and micromanaged by Nixon—overconfident from the success of his
direct appeal to the American public in his 1952 "Checkers" address, which
mitigated investigative reports of a political slush fund with his appealing
confession of only ever taking one improper gift: a small cocker spaniel.[46]

When advertising budgets deteriorated, Kennedy turned to free media,
such as regular appearances on broadcast news and entertainment programs and to what Boorstin referred to as campaign pseudo-events, in particular the Great Debates.[47] In the moment, consensus-minded campaign
reporters overlooked the significance of this phenomenon, and the first
installment of the joint appearances orchestrated by NBC News president
Robert Sarnoff as a one-time exemption to the Federal Communication
Act's equal-time rule failed to garner advance notice in the nation's news
media.[48] But after audiences tuned in to the media spectacle featuring the
self-confident, suntanned political celebrity passionately addressing party
themes alongside his sweaty, pallid competitor, donning "Lazy Shave" and
resolved to debate the issues, they expressed mixed opinions about the win-

ner. Those who listened in felt certain Nixon had won, while those watching the spectacle unfold on their screens believed Kennedy was the victor.[49]

Moreover, cultural observers conveyed mixed reviews of the staged political performances, cast into sharp relief by White's and Boorstin's reactions.[50] White—and ironically even Lippmann—praised the "revolutionary" debates as a testament to "American genius," celebrating television's power to unpackage politicians counseled by public relations and advertising advisors, but Boorstin decried the medium's trivialization of presidential politics into a "quiz-show spectacular" and warned of the self-fulfilling prophecy of pseudo-events.[51] "If we test Presidential candidates by their talents on TV quiz performances, we will, of course, chose presidents precisely for these qualities," Boorstin presciently contended. "In a democracy, reality tends to conform to the pseudo-event. Nature imitates art."[52] But, despite his warning, political consultants collectively placed their faith in media theorist Marshall McLuhan's axiom, and if "the medium [was] the message," the potential appeal of a telegenic political celebrity who mastered the aural-visual medium was inconceivable.[53] Hence, amid collective memory of the influence of image in Kennedy's victorious performance in the 1960 campaign, the place of campaign consultants was cemented, and as common-sense political logic increasingly stressed the power of image to govern reality, pseudo-events, as Boorstin bemoaned, came to define presidential politics.[54]

Kennedy's advisors certainly understood this phenomenon, but as a former correspondent for Hearst newspapers, Kennedy also recognized the importance of cultivating close-knit relationships with elite Georgetown newsmakers, such as Graham, Lippmann, dean of Washington-based reporters Arthur Krock, syndicated columnist Joseph Alsop, and *Newsweek* Washington bureau chief Ben Bradlee, in promoting positive national coverage of his presidency. Though his efforts to appeal to lingering tendencies of "personal journalism" proved successful early in his administration, they provided fodder for conservative media activists, such as book publisher Henry Regenry, radio host Clarence Manion, *National Review* editor William F. Buckley Jr., and *Human Events* correspondents, who claimed liberals infiltrated every postwar American institution and warned that Kennedy's administration, who "walked in lockstep" with establishment media, might pack the Federal Communication Commission and deploy the fairness doctrine, the policy constructed to ensure broadcasters devoted time to the discussion of issues relevant to public interest, to silence conservatives—an attack that echoed in mainstream media in the coming years.[55]

Conservative critics were right to be concerned about political actors exploiting the fairness doctrine to muzzle expression. In the 1950s and 1960s the doctrine was deployed to stifle alternative voices from the right *and* left. But those critics were wrong about an invisible liberal cabal in U.S. politics and news media, as demonstrated by unraveling chummy relationships during the Cuban Missile Crisis amid conflicting professional interests and government secrecy, news management, and misinformation.[56] As Kennedy and his successors learned, though journalists bristled at secrecy and news management, they revolted amid detection of government distortions. "As long as officials merely didn't tell the whole truth," elite *New York Times* reporter James Reston wrote, "very few of us complained," but amid government lies, former chums, such as Krock, attacked.[57] And in preparation for his reelection campaign, Kennedy's inside circle resumed the imagecraft techniques that contributed to their election, granting close-range access to well-respected and amicable image-makers, such as White, Drew, and photographer Cecil Stoughton.

After Kennedy's assassination in November 1963, newsmakers repurposed these images to craft Camelot. Against a backdrop of romanticized narratives about America's King Arthur and his court of admiring reporters, new political actors entered the stage, and though they differed in their commitment to Kennedy's "New Frontier," most failed to interrogate collective memory surrounding Kennedy's media relations.[58] Amid this emergent class of rising political stars, a little-known peanut farmer from Plains, who had fought corrupt political bosses with aid from amicable reporters to win his first term as a Georgia state senator a year prior, remained committed to advancing economic vitality in the Peach State through better education and good government. But he increasingly cast his eyes toward the national political stage as the long, turbulent decade of the 1960s unfolded.[59]

★ ★ ★

As Johnson took the oath of office, he revealed his commitment to extending Kennedy's foreign and domestic policies, as well as his imagecraft and news management techniques, but after masterfully deploying negative advertising to fend off conservative challenger Barry Goldwater in the 1964 presidential campaign, Johnson and all political actors encountered the national discord that had bubbled under the surface for years—frustrated demands for social justice; public cynicism over showbiz campaigns; general disillusionment with government misinformation and news management; grassroots dissatisfaction with establishment political actors; progressive disenchantment with consensus-inducing corporate, commercial forces; conservative attacks to the liberal establishment; and journalistic anxieties over competing mediums and modes.[60] Though cultural unrest manifested itself around every facet of American life, from dinner table conversations and newsroom debates to campus sit-ins and protests in the streets, the emerging credibility crises in politics and journalism came into the starkest relief around the Vietnam War and the 1968 presidential campaign.

Amid heightened Cold War tensions abroad and escalated involvement in Vietnam in the mid-1960s, a younger generation of skeptical reporters, such as *New York Herald-Tribune* Washington bureau chief David Wise, *New York Times* foreign reporter Neil Sheehan, and CBS News war correspondent Morley Safer, observed a gap between the Johnson administration's words and deeds, and supplied images that conflicted with official government accounts.[61] Despite threats from the Johnson administration and contradictory reports from elite veterans, these brave journalists exposed the "credibility gap" in the Johnson administration and reminded a generation of Americans that words from national leaders did not always reflect lived reality at home or abroad. Amid continued disparities between official government accounts and ground reports, war correspondents and eventually the elite Washington press corps embraced the phrase "credibility gap" as a shorthand quip about Johnson's eroding credibility among national reporters and American audiences, who increasingly questioned the commitment of all institutional leaders to the public good, but especially doubted Johnson's veracity about the war.[62]

An avid news surveyor, Johnson recoiled at media reporting that undermined his credibility, and he responded with more hostile news management efforts and a public relations campaign emphasizing progress in Vietnam. "No President ever worked harder to cajole, control, and neutralize the news media," historian Erik Barnouw wrote, aptly describing Johnson's news monitoring and hot-and-cold press relations.[63] Amid his continued deployment of strong-arm tactics with the most trusted names in news, his press relations deteriorated. When CBS News anchor Walter Cronkite witnessed for himself the disparity between General William Westmoreland's claims that American troops were winning the war and live images of the Vietcong's devastating Tet Offensive in January 1968, he determined, like his predecessor Edward Murrow had during McCarthy's communist witch hunts, that years of detached reporting, biased toward official sources, failed to offer American audiences an accurate picture of reality. Momentarily forsaking the industry-preferred method of objectivity, he underscored the recent wave of bloody images and bleak news analyses, pronouncing: "It seems now more certain than ever that the bloody experience of Vietnam is to end in a stalemate."[64]

Though Johnson likely never uttered the words: "if I've lost Cronkite, I've lost middle America," he was well aware of the shift in news coverage and public opinion around the war. Nonetheless, he remained steadfast in his campaign, reminding his audiences that Americans must persevere in Vietnam.[65] Behind Johnson's statement of resolve, however, his administration was in chaos amid headlines less than a fortnight later that revealed that the antiwar challenger Senator Eugene McCarthy unseated the incumbent in the New Hampshire primary; that polling indicators suggested an "uphill struggle" in the upcoming Wisconsin primary; and that New York's Senator Robert F. Kennedy announced his candidacy.[66] After monitoring bleak news and polling data, Johnson requested time from networks for a television address on March 31. Shocking even his closest advisors, he announced to the world that he would not seek reelection. Hence, as Chicago mayor Richard Daley feared, the Democratic Party splintered against the backdrop of the Vietnam War and violent domestic upheavals on the trail.[67]

★ ★ ★

Shortly after the release of the pre-Tet Gallup Poll revealing approximately 50 percent of Americans disapproved of Johnson's handling of war efforts, Republican presidential aspirant Richard Nixon, an unlikely political actor determined never to taste defeat again, arrived on the scene with his top-notch showbiz team, including image-minded campaign manager H. R. Haldeman, J. Walter Thompson Agency advertising specialists Harry Treleaven and Ron Ziegler; CBS News veteran Frank Shakespeare; and television producer Roger Ailes, ready to stage his political comeback with a shrewd image makeover and meticulously crafted messages.[68] After the bitter defeat by Kennedy in the 1960 presidential election and by Pat Brown in the 1962 California gubernatorial race, ABC News broadcast Nixon's political obituary. But hat in hand, he now expressed regret for his career-long combative relationship with elite reporters, originating in adversarial coverage of his involvement in the House Un-American Activities Committee in 1948 and allegations he was the beneficiary of a secret slush fund in 1952. With aid from his showbiz team during the invisible primaries, he repositioned himself as the top Republican presidential hopeful—ahead of liberal favorite John Rockefeller's stalking horse George Romney and the conservative darling, California governor and former Hollywood B-film actor Ronald Reagan.[69]

Recognizing that Lippmann and consensus-minded colleagues marveled over a more "mature, mellow," "New Nixon," his consultants tapped into resonant campaign themes—restoring credibility to the presidency and the reinstitution of stability and traditional values amid national chaos over freedom struggles at home and abroad—prior to his light-hearted opening remarks to the burgeoning Teddy White-inspired campaign pack in New Hampshire. "Gentlemen, this is *not* my last press conference," he quipped before brazenly insisting to the establishment that "the decisive winner of the primaries will and should be nominated."[70] Despite humorous overtures, elite political reporters still considered Nixon to be the joke. Privileging profit-driven news values, they emphasized conflict and drama in the Democratic race instead of Nixon's convincing victories in the New Hampshire and Wisconsin primaries.[71]

After the success of White's bestselling books, *The Making of the President, 1960 and 1964,* Nixon's advisors well understood the consensus-style pack's desire for insider accounts and its increasing power in primary showbiz politics to "ruin [a candidate's] chances before he even reached the primaries."[72] But, after perceived snubs and recognition of the dubiousness of transforming media relations, they limited access with Nixon to brief "three-bump" interviews en route to manufactured campaign pseudo-events, where the news pack, collectively craving a backstage pass to strategy sessions, were cordoned off to screen viewings of Nixon's center-stage performances.[73] Moreover, after convincing Nixon that television was "not a gimmick," they sold him to American audiences through appearances on news and entertainment programs, where, heeding the general consensus, he bemoaned obsession with image over substance in presidential politics before delivering scripted lines on hit programs, such as Rowan and Martin's *Laugh-In*. And, still reluctant to inject critical analysis into news pieces amid emerging critiques of "establishment bias," frontline reporters privately commiserated about limited access while filing detached reports about his campaign appearances.[74]

Former Alabama governor George Wallace joined Nixon on the front stage of American politics, and after reviewing new Gallup Poll data ranking "crime and lawlessness" as the most pressing domestic issue, he preached a similar message of law and order. In 1964, the arch-segregationist southern Democrat had brazenly opposed Johnson with his politics of rage. However, recognizing the limitations of segregationist stances and directly challenging the incumbency, he established the American Independent Party, which triumphantly obtained the necessary 100,000 signatures to place his name on California's ballot. Amid violent riots and protests after the assassinations of Martin Luther King Jr. on April 4 and Kennedy on June 5, Wallace's backlash campaign gained traction, evidenced by packed rallies, national news exposure, and enough grassroots support from those fed up with the liberal status quo to place his name on ballots in all fifty states.[75] Though his campaign ultimately proved unsuccessful amid shrewd imagecraft of establishment politicians, his law-and-order appeal gained popularity on the trail, and his populist, antiestablishment campaign, as regional actors recognized, established "the template for American conservatism."[76]

All political actors well understood one of the paramount campaign issues—eroding trust in establishment institutions. Moreover, as they and the masses that they mobilized recognized, the credibility gap now extended to all areas of American life, including, amid the backdrop of entertainment and news scandals in the prior decade, images on their television sets.[77] Though political actors recognized this widening credibility gap, they struggled to exploit the phenomenon to their advantage. Liberal antiwar protestors, for instance, comprehended the power of the mass media to define collective reality in politics, but after reading McLuhan's seminal work critiquing television's "unreality," they faced a strategic conundrum: how could they harness the medium without trivializing their message?[78] On this point, Nixon and his staff could commiserate: they hoped to take political advantage of the credibility gap, but amid lingering doubts of the candidate's sincerity, they focused on their showbiz campaign. However, during this moment of mounting distrust in political imagecraft, their "fake" presidential campaign became the butt of comedian Pat Paulsen's news parody on CBS's popular *Smothers Brothers Comedy Hour.*[79]

Frustrations over staged productions from establishment sources coalesced that summer as political actors engaged in struggles over the collective vision of the nation's future and divisive party conventions.[80] Network cameras caught the eruption of chaos when gunfire from an assassin's bullet rang out at a Los Angeles rally after Kennedy's victory in the California primary on June 5, and cameras continued to roll in Chicago on August 28 when, as ABC News reported, protests of more than 20,000 Yippie demonstrators, chanting "hell, no, we won't go" in collective dissent against the war, poverty, and racism, "distracted attention" from the DNC and "provoked violence" from nearly 25,000 armed men in uniform during the "Battle of Michigan Avenue."[81]

As demonstrators intoned, the whole world *was* watching, and they remained glued to their sets as networks interrupted live convention broadcasts with recorded footage from countercultural protests devolving into what some observers called a police riot. News anchors followed the developing story, framing the emerging aggression toward antiwar delegates as a product of the outside hostilities before refocusing on the violence spilling over on the convention floor. Though network anchors and correspondents critiqued "thugs" that attempted to interfere with the "free flow of information" and bemoaned the emergence of a police state, many cultural commentators, including author Theodore White, cast blame on networks for coverage producing a political spectacle that was damaging to American democracy.[82] Amid this contentious climate, Kennedy's delegates split their support among remaining candidates and contributed to the nomination on the first ballot of Humphrey, the establishment leader who circumvented primary campaigning.

Though Wallace's third-party, law-and-order crusade received a post-convention bump from the civil unrest, Nixon's campaign benefited most from resentment toward liberal protesters and the political establishment.[83] Invoking sentiments that proved foundational to Democratic senator George McGovern's railing cry for reform, Nixon told primary crowds that the party establishment could not deny the people their choice for the nomination. And, as the campaign progressed, his imagecraft advisors billed Nixon as a moderate voice that could unite the party, and the Republican nominee delivered words many most wanted to hear—he promised to restore trust in government and order and greatness to the nation. Nixon and his advisors recognized that in the modern presidential campaign "concern for image must rank with concern for substance," and his stage-managed campaign and resonant messages carried him to a general election victory over the liberal establishment and fringe third-party candidates.[84]

★ ★ ★

During the 1968 campaign, Nixon promised to temper the credibility gap by engaging in open communication with the American public, but amid his disdain for elite Washington reporters who "distorted" his messages, the Nixon administration established the White House Office of Communications to develop the official message and to facilitate opportunities for Nixon to circumvent liberal establishment media by cultivating reporters beyond the Beltway and "going public" with presidential messages through televised addresses.[85] Elite reporters initially expressed concern that director Herb Klein might act as an "information czar," limiting the free flow of information from governmental bodies, but Klein's reassuring opening statement about the organization's commitment to transparency and his goodwill gestures during Nixon's first hundred days alleviated many concerns of the Washington press corps. Moreover, even as Nixon reduced his official interactions with national reporters to the lowest level of any modern presidency and engaged in the secret expansion of wars he promised to end, he enjoyed the most positive coverage of any president since Roosevelt.[86]

However, Nixon's breech of campaign promises would not stay secret for long. On May 9, the *New York Times* published Pentagon correspondent William Beecher's dispatch revealing American B-52 bombers' secret raids over Cambodia, and all hell broke loose.[87] Furious over the "serious security breech," Nixon responded by engaging in secret, illegal wiretapping of staff members and elite reporters to discover leaks in his administration, and he finalized plans to go to war with New Left radicals and his longtime enemy—the press (his shorthand term for what many conservatives now called the liberal establishment media).[88]

But elite Washington reporters already were under attack. Amid criticism over fake news, sensational stories, and propaganda, detached journalism had emerged as standard professional practice at newswires, mass-circulating dailies, and weekly newsmagazines. But by midcentury, critics from the right *and* left denounced the consolidation of big media into a few hands, elite fraternities of reporters, and the bias of objective reporting, which privileged official sources and offered interpretative analyses amid competitive pressures from news broadcasters.[89] These exterior assaults over industry practices had surfaced in newsrooms over the prior decade, but amid debates over attacks to their credibility, national reporters also encountered a threat to their legitimacy that left them spiraling in an identity crisis. After the October release of Joseph McGinnis's *The Selling of the President,* many veteran reporters experienced shame for missing the story of the 1968 campaign. Through unauthorized fly-on-the-wall reporting intoned with the critical voice of Boorstin and McLuhan, McGinnis exposed Nixon's staged "con game," and though many elite political reporters praised his volume as a "masterpiece," they endured collective embarrassment for their failure to expose Nixon's imagecraft and news management techniques.[90] Amid this critical discourse inside newsrooms, they encountered another damaging round of attacks from the Nixon administration.

After the summer of 1969, Nixon unleashed Vice President Spiro Agnew to assault radical antiwar demonstrators as "impudent snobs" and "misfits" in speeches delivered to audiences of elite Washington reporters, who were biased toward objectivity. However, when analysts, primed to engage in adversarial deconstruction of media management after the release of McGinnis's *The Selling of the President,* offered unfavorable reviews of Nixon's "great silent majority" address in November, the president, frustrated by his foiled effort to speak directly to the American public through controlled channels, refocused Agnew's attacks on news broadcasters, the "tiny, enclosed fraternity of privileged men elected by no one," and "irresponsible" establishment news companies, such as the *New York Times* and *Washington Post.* As Nixon's administration transitioned from privately shutting out national reporters to publicly attacking them, they hoped strategic confrontations might keep elite reporters in check. Though many progressive journalists shared Agnew's critique of big media, insular reporters, and objective reporting's over-reliance on official sources, the move escalated a long-brewing war.[91]

★ ★ ★

Georgia state senator Jimmy Carter was no stranger to war with the establishment press. During his failed 1966 gubernatorial bid, Carter had bemoaned the "cool" treatment he encountered from elite Georgia journalists, such as *Atlanta Constitution* editor Reg Murphy and reporter Bill Shipp, who collectively bristled at his news management techniques, including his denials of statements and angry missives to editors demanding retractions after claims he was misquoted.[92] Nevertheless, recognizing "image is the reality," an emergent truth in American politics, he succeeded in slyly planting a Camelot-inspired profile with a sympathetic *Columbus Ledger-Inquirer Magazine* reporter.[93] However, despite attracting attention from the nation's paper of record with his moderate statements, Kennedyesque looks, and (left unsaid) polished imagecraft, Carter suffered a bitter defeat to Georgia's Democratic Party establishment, and amid the backdrop of national chaos in 1968 he resolved to develop the grin that wins by taking a page directly from Nixon's presidential playbook, designs his advisors returned to during his bicentennial presidential campaign.

Amid the backdrop of Nixon's expanded wars, Carter and his senior strategic advisors, lawyer Charles Kirbo, businessman Bert Lance, campaign director Hamilton Jordan, and full-time driver/part-time political advisor Jody Powell joined imagecraft specialists, such as Rafshoon, pollster William Hamilton, press secretary Bill Pope, issues specialist Stuart Eizenstat, and strategic advisor Jack Watson, in developing a well-organized, antiestablishment campaign pairing direct grassroots appeals with down-home, "conservative, progressive" media messages attacking elite political actors and promising "a good, clean, honest government" delivered from an "honest citizen who could be trusted."[94] Despite establishing nonideological stances on sixty-five substantive issues, Carter's centrist campaign stressed "evasiveness and vague semantics," the winning language in Georgia politics, a conservative state where the majority of voters supported Wallace's and Nixon's earlier campaigns.[95]

Encouraged by a fall 1968 straw poll indicating he could win the 1970 gubernatorial race, Carter traveled to more than three hundred local communities, but as he later admitted to the state's elite reporters, he was not strictly selling peanuts during the invisible primaries—he was selling himself as a down-home peanut farmer to plain folk, local reporters, and establishment leaders, such as Coca-Cola's chief executive officer, Robert Woodruff.[96] Before Carter commenced his official campaign, photographer

Charles Rafshoon captured the grinning peanut farmer admiring his prized crop, publicity stills designed to appeal to voters who felt alienated from government, and after declaring his candidacy on April 3, 1970, Carter delivered his first attack against elite, establishment actors who profited from public service.[97]

Confiding in many of his underground liberal supporters, "you won't like my campaign, but you will like my administration," Carter and his Sumter County surrogates, clutching their field manual, *Carter '70: The Difference Is You,* embarked on a public, statewide grassroots media campaign involving stops in each of Georgia's 159 counties and a handshake, a smile, and a brief introduction of the people's candidate, who was "basically a redneck."[98] "I'm Jimmy Carter, and I'm running for Governor," the born-again candidate, who had honed grassroots skills while canvasing for Christ in Pennsylvania in the spring of 1968, greeted plain folk with his signature underdog line before disclosing his Wallace-inspired campaign promises—his crusade to improve education, build roads, and reestablish law and order—to "Nixon's forgotten man."[99]

Though the wealthy peanut broker and his elite, liberal opponent, former Georgia governor Carl Sanders, shared more in common than was politically advantageous to admit, Carter and his advisors focused on constructing the peanut farmer's image in direct opposition to Sanders. "Some images have to be projected regarding Carl Sanders," Carter scribbled on a legal pad in a precampaign memo that later fell into the hands of a probing reporter from the *Columbus Ledger-Inquirer.* "More liberal . . . pretty boy . . . nouveau riche . . . excluded George Wallace from the state. . . . You can see some of these are conflicting, but right now, we just need to collect all these rough ideas we can. Later we can start driving a wedge between me and him."[100] After these early strategic negotiations, Carter debuted his series of staged attacks—symbolically exposing Sanders as a papered-over liberal at their campaign kickoff and unveiling an attack advertisement targeting "Cufflinks" Carl Sanders, the "limousine liberal," amid the backdrop of country clubs, "where big-money boys play cards, drink cocktails, and raise money for their candidate: Carl Sanders."[101] When not assaulting Sanders, Carter waged war on the state's establishment press, especially the *Atlanta Constitution* for its "profane" portrait of him.[102]

Behind the scenes of what was characterized by *Atlanta Constitution* political editor Bill Shipp as the Peach State's "first modern media campaign,"

Carter's advisors deployed dirty tricks reminiscent of Johnson's 1948 senate campaign.[103] Though Carter's personal views on race were progressive, he had remained silent as a political actor when the African American freedom struggle arrived in southwest Georgia, and now his staff engaged in clandestine race-baiting tactics. While Carter publicly denounced Sanders for refusing to invite Wallace to speak in the state, his staff secretly reproduced and distributed an image of the part owner of the Atlanta Hawks showering African American star guard Lou Hudson in champagne and financed radio advertisements for the underdog African American candidate C. B. King.[104]

By borrowing pages from the playbooks of establishment presidential actors, Carter's campaign delivered what the *Americus Times-Recorder* hailed as a "stunning upset" over the establishment "press, power structure" in September 1970, and after winning over establishment leaders, such as Woodruff, former governors Ernest Vandiver and Marvin Griffin, and U.S. Senators Richard B. Russell and Herman Talmadge, and waging and encountering vicious attack campaigns centering on the reality of images, the wealthy, "conservative progressive" defeated Sanders in a runoff and cruised to a general election victory over Republican nominee Hal Suit by uniting the state's conservative Wallace supporters with his earlier young, liberal coalition.[105]

★ ★ ★

With ambitions of a higher office in mind, Carter delivered on his secret campaign promise during his January 1971 inaugural address. "The time for racial discrimination is over," he told broader audiences, seizing the key aesthetic moment with an intriguing newspeg for elite national reporters.[106] Much as he and his imagecraft advisors hoped, his twelve-minute speech attracted attention from the nation's establishment press. "Carter, like the South, is . . . an enigma and contradiction," a correspondent for the nation's paper of record described Carter's liberal turn after his "conservative progressive" gubernatorial campaign.[107]

In a journalistic milieu governed by groupthink, other elite reporters grappled with the progressive shift in a new generation of southern leaders, like Carter, and after a nudge from a prominent Atlanta-based national advertiser, *Time* editor-in-chief Hedley Donovan offered the ambitious politician the exposure he craved: in May 1971, the image of Jimmy Carter, draped in a background of the Confederate and American flags, greeted national audiences and beckoned "Dixie Whistles a Different Tune."[108] Inside, *Time* staff broke with tradition, quoting from Governor James Earl Carter's poignant inaugural address in the lede. "I say to you quite frankly that the time for racial discrimination is over." In the "shadow of monuments . . . to Confederate soldiers, of the political captains of a demagogic past," Carter spoke at last "a promise so long coming," they wrote, describing the paradoxical tableau and alluding to *Atlanta Constitution* editor Henry Grady's long-deferred commitment to the New South before framing Carter as the most prominent of an emerging class of southern politicians who "whistle[d] a different tune"—progressive leaders eager to repent from sins of the past and "embrace Civil Rights."[109] But, echoing the *Times,* staff writers offered the harbinger of a troubling enigmatic image that followed Carter throughout his future political journey. "Straddling this varied state is Governor Jimmy Carter, a South Georgia peanut farmer who is both a product and a destroyer of old myths. Soft-voiced, assured, looking eerily like John Kennedy from certain angles, Carter is a man as contradictory as Georgia itself . . ." *Time* staff observed.[110]

After arriving at the governor's mansion, Carter and his imagecraft apparatus hoped to cultivate Carter's national image as a moderate, progressive leader by appointing more minorities to office than his predecessors, reorganizing the state government into three super agencies, introducing fiscal conservatism through zero-based budgeting, and improving the state's education, transportation, criminal justice, and mental health systems. He and his staff negotiated this ambitious political agenda amid increased attacks from enemies in the Peach State. Bristling at the governor's presidential imagecraft and news management techniques and his political patronage toward chummy local reporters and publishers, elite state reporters amplified attacks from Carter's adversaries, such as Lieutenant Governor Lester Maddox, who summed up the sentiment of frustrated pro-Wallace conservatives, who elected Carter: "When I put my pennies into a peanut machine, I don't expect bubble gum, and neither do the people."[111] Nonetheless, this shift in public opinion did not dishearten Carter and his staff, who took the governor's appeals directly to the people and, recognizing limited opportunities in state politics, cast their eyes on a higher office during the 1972 campaign.[112]

2

Post-Reform Blueprint for the Marathon Campaign

Weeks into his term, Georgia governor Jimmy Carter planted a bug in friendly *Atlanta Constitution* political editor Bill Shipp's ear—a southerner deserved the Democratic Party's nomination in the next presidential election cycle.[1] Amid a country still in chaos from domestic conflicts, foreign wars, and mounting cynicism over new evidence of government secrecy and lies revealed in the Pentagon Papers, Carter recognized that the party of Thomas Jefferson and Andrew Jackson was in a transitional moment.[2] Though national campaign reporters acknowledged that gunfire at a Laurel, Maryland, shopping center the following spring terminated the greatest chance for a southerner to end up on the 1972 Democratic ticket, Carter angled for the number two spot as a crowded field of sixteen Democratic candidates made stops in Atlanta during primary season.[3]

As the declared leader of the Stop McGovern movement, Carter found himself on the DNC's national stage preparing to deliver the nominating speech for Senator Henry "Scoop" Jackson in mid-July—the object of derision of the post-reform, semi-consensual nominee George McGovern and the subject of an "objective" interview with an NBC News correspondent.[4] Though the dramatic discord of the Stop McGovern movement attracted attention from national news media, Carter's speech fell flat, garnering only nominal notice.[5] After enduring scornful disregard toward his attempts at a party power grab, Carter and his advisors nevertheless retained the sense he was better qualified to lead the nation than the men who paraded through the governor's mansion in the spring of 1972.[6] Thus, while Nixon and the Committee to Reelect the President (CREP) engaged in dirty tricks, illegal activities, and subterfuge behind the facade of the White House's Rose Garden and McGovern's general election campaign collapsed before its official launch amid intensive probes from elite, frontline reporters, Carter's advisors developed a post-reform blueprint for the marathon campaign, launched the first phase of their invisible campaign, and planned to announce their candidacy for the bicentennial presidential race. With assistance from new kingmakers in presidential politics, Carter's desire to see a southerner on the ticket manifested itself in his own nomination in 1976.[7]

★ ★ ★

Under new guidelines instituted through post-1968 reforms, political actors recognized that the nomination campaign was a "whole new ballgame," but unknown to elite political reporters, one candidate gained the competitive edge in the off-season.[8] As the chief architect of Democratic Party reforms, South Dakota's Senator George McGovern exploited the new rules of the game to construct a grassroots organization, emphasizing his credibility, during the invisible campaign in primary states with a history of attracting widespread news media attention, such as Wisconsin, and favoring progressivism, such as California.[9]

Nevertheless, polling at less than 3 percent in January 1972 after announcing his candidacy the prior year, McGovern remained off the radar of the consensus-minded campaign pack, who instead focused attention on the probable frontrunner, Maine's Senator Ed Muskie, and the media darling, New York mayor John Lindsay. In advance of the New Hampshire primary on March 7, campaign reporters reasoned that Muskie, hailing from a neighboring state, should deliver at least 50 percent of the vote to demonstrate his organizational strength moving forward.[10] But Muskie's support eroded amid Nixon's dirty tricks, partisan attacks in William Loeb's *Manchester Union Leader,* and the consensus-minded pack's assessment that he cracked under pressure, "breaking into tears" while defending his wife from Loeb's assaults.[11] When returns trickled in, elite political reporters scored McGovern, the second-place finisher, as the victor, concluding Muskie "must do very well [in the Florida primary] to keep his candidacy moving—a win or a very strong second showing. Anything less and he might be disastrously damaged."[12]

Elite political journalists, such as R. W. Apple Jr. (of the *New York Times*) and David Broder (of the *Washington Post*), and rank-and-file professional campaign reporters, who traveled, dined, drank, and golfed together, had long engaged in what psychologist Irving Janis referred to as groupthink. Based on this consensus-based mentality and industry pressures, they often echoed wire-reporter newspegs in their detached stories and interpretative analyses.[13] However, their ledes revealed an altered style after the 1964 campaign, when the AP told its increasingly college-educated campaign reporters, mirroring their "middle-class, middle-income, middle-age" audiences: "When Teddy White's book comes out, there shouldn't be one single story in that book that we haven't reported ourselves."[14] Thereafter, frontline campaign reporters, situated at mainstream outlets, suffered from the "Teddy White syndrome," the behind-the-scenes reportorial practice that undermined the presidential chances of unfortunate early frontrunners, such as Muskie.[15] By the 1972 campaign, even White feared he had created a monster, telling long-form campaign journalist Tim Crouse, "Who gives a fuck if the guy had milk and Total for breakfast?"[16]

Narrative-style New Journalists, such as Crouse, and other members of the campaign's journalistic vanguard, including muckrakers and advocacy journalists, situated at alternative news sites, such as *Rolling Stone, Ebony, Berkley Barb,* (*More*), and Top Value Television, increasingly joined detached campaign reporters on the trail in 1972, where, inspired by recent presidential relations, Agnew's attacks, and Joe McGinnis's tell-all campaign book, they sketched impressions about the shifting milieu.[17] As their fly-on-the-wall reporting suggested, the selling of the president transformed the collective mentality of rank-and-file reporters, and during the 1972 primaries they collectively griped about closed-access campaigns, probed frontrunners on the trail, and on occasion, "tired of taking bullshit from Nixon and Agnew," lashed out at campaign actors. But amid collective fears of new attacks about biased reporting, the tone of detached campaign reporting remained largely the same.[18] However, granting (as *New York Times* book critic Dwight Garner suggested) that McGinnis's behind-the-scenes exposé made White's insider accounts look "wan and dated," New Journalists, such as Crouse and Perry, contributed to the campaign canon by documenting the evolving us and them mentality on the trail through literary-inspired, long-form reportage, and in the coming years professional campaign reporters, inspired to deliver imagined audiences in the 'Me' Decade what they were said to crave, probed each candidate's authenticity through candid acts of deconstruction.[19]

In the interim, however, reporters documenting the 1972 campaign collectively turned their attention toward the Sunshine State in advance of the Florida primary on March 14, where, despite showbiz-inspired campaign pseudo-events and "trust Muskie" appeals, "Big Ed" finished a distant third behind "reformed" arch-segregationist George Wallace, who enjoyed widespread support based on his busing stance, and party regular Hubert Humphrey.[20] Moving into the Wisconsin primary on April 4, consensus-minded campaign reporters indicated the Democratic race was up for grabs—a contest between McGovern, Wallace, and Humphrey likely to be decided by a brokered convention. But, based on the mastery of the new rules and new politics, McGovern's progressive, grassroots campaign defeated Wallace and Humphrey in Wisconsin, prompting consensus-minded reporters to label him the clear frontrunner. With Wallace and his campaign seriously wounded by a would-be assassin's bullet on May 15, McGovern rode media momentum "right down to California, for the final shoot-out with Humphrey."[21] Moreover, in the progressive Golden State, McGovern survived reportorial probes into his credibility and Humphrey's attacks on issues stances, undermining perceptions of his authenticity, and when the dust settled, most campaign observers concurred his nomination was inevitable.[22]

After McGovern's narrow victory in the winner-take-all California primary on June 6, elite frontline reporters planned to take a few days off from the trail before the campaign's biggest media event, but as they packed their bags for Miami, the site of both party conventions, they read the first details of the June 17 break-in at the DNC headquarters in Associated Press bulletins and the *Washington Post*.[23] However, after Nixon's press secretary Ronald Ziegler told the White House Press Corp that the Nixon administration had no connection to the "third-rate burglary," most consensus-minded reporters wrote off the bizarre incident and concentrated on news that the Washington Credentials Committee had assigned delegate seating in proportion to votes cast for each Democratic candidate in the California primary.[24] McGovern's status as the likely nominee was in jeopardy, and according to one party source the folks gathering at the DNC "look[ed] like a bunch of people standing around before they jump off a cliff."[25]

At the convention, network teams and news reporters focused on a consensus-style newspeg—discord, featuring balanced packages biased toward drama and conflict surrounding the Stop McGovern movement—but they largely missed the first session's biggest news story, a parliamentary maneuver surrounding the seating of South Carolina delegates that over-determined McGovern's nomination.[26] With the Stop McGovern movement dead in its tracks, Carter's nominating speech attracted little notice from elite frontline reporters, but Carter and his advisors walked away from the convention with new resolve that a moderate leader from the South deserved the party's nomination, and they secretly discussed his future ambitions.[27] "The old politicians who think that once McGovern is defeated, it will be politics as usual are dead wrong and do not understand the social forces at work in the country," Carter's advisor Peter Bourne predicted, aptly recognizing forces manifesting themselves in popular culture texts, such as Fletcher Knebel's novel *Dark Horse* and the comedy-drama *The Candidate,* starring Robert Redford.[28] And, based on 1972 presidential playbooks, they roughed out a post-reform blueprint for the marathon campaign, but as long-form journalists suggested, elite reporters missed the bicentennial campaign's invisible opening chapter.[29]

As Nixon continued his Rose Garden strategy, elite reporters instead concentrated on the only campaign in town. Thus, while McGovern and his advisors retreated to the Black Hills to plot his general election campaign, much of the pack caught up on their rest, but the most enterprising reporters engaged in probes into the personal background of McGovern's running mate, Missouri's Senator Thomas Eagleton. Though many elite reporters were aware of Eagleton's history of alcohol abuse, the pack suffered collective shock to learn more about his mental health history at an official press conference (scheduled on July 25 ahead of the Knight newspaper chain's exposé), which included Eagleton's disclosure that he suffered from severe bouts of depression that had prompted three hospitalizations and two rounds of electroshock therapy. Though McGovern's staff released a statement that he was "1,000 percent with Eagleton," influenced by news editorials biased against "a nut for vice president," McGovern waivered in his support, suggesting Eagleton might withdraw, and campaign reporters acknowledged that the primary candidate, who banked on an image that he was "more open, more accessible, more attuned to issues and more idealistic than other candidates," revealed himself to be a "calculating tactician."[30] Those following the *Washington Post*'s 1972 campaign encountered a banner headline surrounding Eagleton's disclosure the following day, but only studious readers noticed another pertinent campaign story ("Bug Suspect Got Campaign Funds") under Bob Woodward and Carl Bernstein's joint byline.[31]

Amid Nixon's increasing paranoia with the Watergate cover-up, he and his staff remained committed to their fall campaign to intimidate and discredit the *Post*'s investigative team and to limit news media access to Nixon's front-stage performances at the Miami Beach Convention Center and the White House. Despite McGovern's protests of news media bias in the form of one-sided campaign coverage, elite frontline reporters struggled to gain a close vantage point to deconstruct Nixon's public relations campaign. Still collectively reluctant to engage in critical analyses lest they come under further attack for bias, they focused on the most newsworthy official developments—Nixon's coronation, McGovern's lost credibility, and peace talks in Vietnam. And though a small circle of investigative reporters, including the CBS Evening News team, joined Woodward and Bernstein in their probe of Watergate in October, Nixon's news that "peace is at hand" ushered in his landslide victory over McGovern.[32]

★ ★ ★

On November 6, 1972, one day before Nixon secured his landslide victory over McGovern, Jordan and Rafshoon delivered their brain trust's seventy-page, post-reform blueprint for the marathon campaign designed to "set forth in a logical fashion some specific thoughts and recommendations on [Carter's] national effort."[33] Before describing Carter's potential rivals in Wallace and Senator Edward Kennedy and explaining how the campaign's imagecraft apparatus might tap into prevailing public opinion to construct Carter's image as a moral reformer and his promise to restore the people's faith in government, Jordan debriefed Carter on the 1972 campaign. Instead of "inspir[ing] the trust and confidence of the American people at a time in our history when we are hungry for moral leadership," Nixon "adopted a smug attitude refusing to discuss the Watergate incident" and focused the public's attention on "McGovern's liberalism and the Eagleton affair," he contended. Moreover, by focusing on divisive issues, such as abortion, amnesty, and welfare, McGovern missed an opportunity to connect with voters on the theme of restoring trust in government. Determined to learn from the 1972 campaign playbook, Carter's advisors recommended tapping into the mood of the nation with a post-reform, (un)celebrity campaign focused on one primary theme—bringing moral reform to Washington. "Perhaps the strongest feeling in this country today is the general distrust and disallusionment [*sic*] of government and politicians at all levels," Jordan wrote. "The desire and thirst for strong moral leadership in this nation was not satisfied."[34]

In order to satisfy national desires, Carter and his advisors, testifying to the common-sense logic of the mid-1970s, believed he must develop a winning national image through available media channels.[35] Though Carter was known nationally as a "one of several bright and promising young governors," Jordan admitted they were naive to believe favorable coverage of the governor's inauguration established Carter as a "national political figure." Rafshoon concurred: as governor, Carter gained national exposure as "the man who said the time for racial discrimination was over," but Carter's "Kennedy smile" and "Wallace-type populism sans the racism" was not enough.[36] "Infect[ing] . . . other regions with the Jimmy Carter 'good-guy' populism," Rafshoon recognized, required more than grassroots "handshaking": "He will also have to convince press, public, and politicians that he knows how to run a government (and that he has the record to prove this)." To that end, Rafshoon designed a four-phase, year-by-year publicity plan to craft a "heavyweight image," involving projecting the "Carter [gubernatorial] record" in 1973, developing himself as a party leader in 1974, constructing Carter as a Democratic leader traveling the nation with solutions to the country's problems in 1975, and manufacturing the Carter presidential brand in 1976.[37]

Initiating a publicity plan was the first step in crafting the image of the antiestablishment Washington outsider, preaching a message of moral reform, but Jordan realized the plan alone would not ensure positive national exposure: "It is necessary that we begin immediately to generate favorable stories in the national press. Stories in the *New York Times* and the *Washington Post* do not just happen, but have to be carefully planned and planted." He believed the key to positive coverage was developing rapport with elite reporters, and showing them, and by extension their audiences, how Carter's success as governor might be extended to the national stage.[38]

With this relatively naive understanding of mid-1970s political journalism in mind, Jordan supplied Carter with a list of six important regional reporters, including the *Atlanta Constitution*'s Hal Gulliver and Cox Broadcasting's Leonard Reinsch, and eighteen elite newsmakers, including *Washington Post* publisher Katherine Graham and veteran reporter David Broder, *New York Times* senior columnists Tom Wicker and James Reston, *Los Angeles*

Times Washington bureau chief Jack Nelson, and conservative syndicated columnists William F. Buckley Jr., Robert Novak, and Rowland Evans.[39] "You can find ample excuses for contacting them," Jordan coached, "writing them a note complimenting them on an article or a column and asking that they come to see you when convenient. Some people like Tom Wicker or Mrs. Katherine Graham are significant enough to spend an evening or a leisurely weekend with."[40] Jordan suggested that Carter take advantage of the lingering Cold War era's white-tie journalism.[41]

Jordan realized Carter would not look forward to this task, so he attempted to drive home the significance. "Like it or not," he asserted, spouting mainstream conservative logic, "there exists in fact an Eastern liberal news establishment which has tremendous influence in this country all out of proportion to its actual audience. The view of this small group of opinion makers . . . are noted and imitated by other columnists and newspapers throughout the country and the world. Their recognition and acceptance of your candidacy as a viable force with some chance of success could establish you as a serious contender worthy of financial support. . . . They also could have an equally adverse effect, dismissing your effort as being regional or an effort to secure a second spot on the ticket."[42]

Based on his knowledge of post-reform showbiz politics, Jordan suggested that Carter garner attention from leading news- and opinion-makers by making introductions through his cousin Don Carter's press contacts, reviewing national stories daily to provide current events fodder for potential interactions with the Washington/New York-based elite, generating stories in trade magazines that elite reporters might incorporate as source material in coverage, writing a political biography or a column series on pertinent political issues, scheduling appearances on network talk shows to speak directly to the American public, and hiring a first-class speechwriter and polishing his public speaking skills to ensure positive treatment in local, regional, and national coverage.[43]

Though Jordan acknowledged that the task would not be easy in the shifting political milieu, Carter and his advisors quickly discovered that it was nearly impossible amid elite, consensus-minded reporters, who were reluctant to maintain chummy relationships with political actors and more inclined to engage in an adversarial, probing mode of campaign reportage. "My generation discovered, because of the lies of the Vietnam War and because of the lies and the conduct of the Nixon Administration, that we shouldn't be social friends," ABC News chief Watergate correspondent Sam Donaldson recalled. "It's very hard to have a good social friend . . . and then have to report that they are lying and thieving."[44]

Nonetheless, Jordan believed Carter had one advantage as a political actor: he was a southerner, and many elite reporters were "Southerners by birth . . . and harbor a strong, subconscious desire to see the South move beyond the George Wallace era." Other advisors remained unconvinced by this logic. Washington-based campaign advisor Peter Bourne, for instance, warned of "prejudice against a Southerner on the national ticket . . . that still persist[ed]" among otherwise "open and reasonable people" in the northeast and California. To combat southern stereotypes, he recommended Carter present himself as an anomaly.[45] Carter's southern roots ultimately proved to be a mixed blessing for his presidential ambitions. His imagecraft staff banked on cultural affinity for the New South with their down-home (un)celebrity campaign, but regional bias lingered in coverage.[46]

Though Carter's campaign soon discovered that currying favor with elite reporters, even southern-bred ones, proved a challenge in the existing milieu, Jordan presciently recognized the importance of staging a grassroots media campaign at sites of early political contests: "As you know, New Hampshire's primary has traditionally been the place where sure winners have stumbled and the dark horses . . . have established themselves as serious contenders. . . . New Hampshire is a small state which is rural and independent and given to the kind of personal campaign effort that you and your family are capable of waging."[47] Moreover, he aptly predicted that prominent national journalists would take "an exaggerated interest" in these contests: "We would do well to understand the very special and powerful role the press plays in interpreting the primary results for the rest of the nation."[48] Jordan recognized the influence of elite, consensus-minded reporters stationed at mainstream media outlets who framed political winners and the power of momentum to deflect establishment dismissal of the New South son's regional candidacy.

★ ★ ★

Over the next two years, the governor and his advisors engaged in an invisible campaign for the nation's highest office, involving testing campaign themes, developing an appealing image designed to attract national exposure, and laying political groundwork for a state-by-state grassroots media campaign. Harnessing his status as an emerging leader of New South governors, Carter beta-tested two primary themes—his antiestablishment crusade and his populist brand of "benevolent conservatism"—before the National Press Club in Washington, D.C., in early February 1973, but elite reporters, unaccustomed to encountering presidential appeals in advance of an election year, offered the relatively unknown governor passing coverage.[49] As *Los Angeles Times* Washington bureau chief Jack Nelson, a member of the inside circle of elite political reporters aware of Carter's presidential ambitions, told Bourne several days later: "Your biggest problem is not going to be whether anyone knows Jimmy Carter is running for president; it's whether anyone gives a damn."[50]

Though widespread national exposure initially eluded Carter, he landed a platform the following month that served as the national launching pad for his presidential campaign when Democratic Party chairman Robert Strauss appointed him as the DNC's honorary chairman. In the role, Carter not only gained an image among the Washington establishment as a promising party leader, but he and his advisors also developed key political contacts and insights into critical national issues.[51] Moreover, in the party leadership position, Carter gained a national forum to denounce Nixon's corruption and to preach an exceptional message of moral reform.[52] Recognizing that many Democratic politicians were saying all "the same things" about Watergate, Jordan encouraged Carter to craft a positive message around the "sad and tragic" break-in scandal: "[Watergate] was a confirmation of our democratic system of government that people in high places who violate the law can be caught, prosecuted and held accountable for their actions. At its very worst, Watergate showed people in high places deliberately violating the Constitution they were sworn to uphold. At its very best, Watergate demonstrated that a strong and independent news media exercising its freedom of speech, the American people not satisfied with denials from the White House, and an independent Congress exercising its investigative prerogatives, all worked successfully to counter the abuse of power by a few."[53] At Jordan's urging, Carter exploited Watergate to his advantage from his new position by cautiously condemning the sitting president, lauding the Democratic Party, and constructing his image as an antiestablishment reformer.[54]

While developing a reputation as one of the nation's leading governors and an emerging moderate party leader, Carter encountered other opportunities to enhance his presidential qualifications. In May, for instance, he gained experience in international relations when New York governor Nelson Rockefeller recommended him for the Trilateral Commission, an entity designed to initiate relations between key opinion leaders in North America, Western Europe, and Japan. In this role, Carter curried favor with key foreign policy experts, such as Zbigniew Brzezinski and Cyrus Vance, and gained access to elite reporters, such as *Time* editor-in-chief Hedley Donovan and CBS president Arthur Taylor.[55]

By December 1973, while Nixon maintained his innocence in the Watergate case, Carter negotiated sporadic coverage from elite political reporters, but he also managed to gain unexpected national exposure.[56] On Thursday, December 13, he appeared on CBS's popular game show *What's My Line?* From the opening moments, Carter's appearance elicited laughs from the studio audience, as the witty actress Arlene Francis asked if his "service [had] to do with women," to which Carter uncharacteristically retorted, "Yes, it certainly does . . . but not enough." Movie critic Gene Shalit eventually guessed Carter was a governor, but in the end, reaction from panelists, who struggled to identify Carter, reflected the sentiment of the general public, who remained largely unaware of the Georgia governor until he launched his official campaign the following December.[57]

In the interim, Carter continued to consider how to construct a successful presidential campaign. Based on Bourne's recommendation, he pored over Gary Hart's *Right from the Start: A Chronicle of the McGovern Campaign,* and heeding lessons from McGovern's early successes in the primaries and failures in the general election campaign, his advisors considered it, alongside James David Barber's *Presidential Character* (1972) and Crouse's *Boys on the Bus* (1973), a primary source for their post-reform campaign how-to guide.[58] While reflecting on these works, he faithfully followed Jordan's campaign blueprint focusing on developing a positive national image through personal interactions with elite reporters and a grassroots media campaign across the Peach State.[59] "The strategy was to get to know the press," Rafshoon explained to one reporter. "We knew your names, even if you didn't know ours."[60] Elite campaign reporters were hardly surprised by the first strategy, but most failed to probe Carter's early grassroots media campaign, which served two primary purposes beyond enhancing Carter's public approval in Georgia: it provided an opportunity for Carter's image-craft apparatus to collect raw footage of Carter interacting with everyday

Americans, material they incorporated into their bicentennial advertising campaign, and it served as a template for Carter's grassroots media strategy in Iowa and New Hampshire.[61]

Carter continued his grassroots media campaign the following spring at the University of Georgia's Law Day event, where he captured the attention of gonzo journalist Hunter S. Thompson while delivering closing remarks at a ceremony honoring former Secretary of State Dean Rusk.[62] Quoting liberally from theologian Reinhold Niebuhr and folk musician Bob Dylan, the governor upstaged event keynote speaker Ted Kennedy with his thirty-minute critique on the criminal justice system's failure to administer social justice. "I've seen the proud statement of an attorney general, who protects his boss, and now brags on the fact that . . . he came out 'clean' . . ." Carter said, referring to sins of John Mitchell and the Nixon administration. "I think our people demand more than that. I believe that everyone in this room . . . ought to remember the oath that Thomas Jefferson and others took . . . to preserve justice and equity."[63] Thereafter, Thompson told influential cronies that he never heard "a sustained piece of political oratory that impressed me more."[64]

After these developments, Carter enjoyed a wave of positive national exposure. On June 2, 1974, he appeared with five other governors on NBC's *Meet the Press,* featuring moderator Lawrence Spivak and a panel of elite political reporters, including the *Washington Post*'s David Broder, the *Washington Star*'s Jack Germond, the *New York Times*'s Christopher Lydon, and NBC News correspondent Tom Pettit. When asked about the country's best interests in light of the Watergate scandal, Carter impressed Spivak with his polished response: "I believe that the impeachment proceedings is the best one to follow now because it is much more stable; it is a constitutional provision and also it might and probably will result in much more effective presentation of the evidence so that the people will trust the final judgment if the President is guilty."[65]

When *New York Times* editorial writer William Shannon engaged in early presidential horse race prognostications the next month, he included Carter alongside eight others as potential Democratic presidential candidates, observing that the relatively unknown candidate impressed "small audiences with his charm and his skill in defining the issues."[66] Though Shannon's prediction was apt, his words were ironic, considering that his colleagues critiqued Carter in the coming months for "fuzzy" issues stances.

Nevertheless, Shannon's early coverage of the 1976 presidential race was an anomaly; for now, most headlines concentrated on news that the House Judiciary Committee had passed the first three articles of impeachment against Nixon, charging him with obstruction of justice, and rumors of his impending resignation.

★ ★ ★

In the days following Gerald Ford's assumption of the presidency and his controversial pardon of Nixon, Carter, in his role as Democratic national campaign chairman, engaged in a vigorous public campaign for Democratic candidates running in midterm elections in the fall of 1974, culminating with the party's Watergate Babies regaining majorities in the House and Senate. But behind the scenes, informed by reformed showbiz politics' common-sense logic, he and his advisors considered political timing and theatrical backdrops as they refined plans to launch his presidential campaign.[67] Though they sought to capitalize on national exposure that the Georgia governor might earn from announcing his candidacy first, they recognized that they might encounter critiques of grandstanding if they announced prior to the party's mini-convention in Kansas City in early December.[68] This in mind, they settled on an informal launch at the event, involving the circulation of a ten-page glossy brochure promoting Carter as "Georgia's Governor for a New Political Season" and private conversations with amicable, elite political reporters, such as the *Washington Star*'s Jack Germond and the *Baltimore Sun*'s Carl Leubsdorf Jr., followed by a formal launch the following week. After briefly considering issuing the formal announcement from Plains, a site conveying "the image of the non-politician from rural America," Carter's imagecraft advisors settled on an informal announcement to the National Press Club in Washington, D.C., headquarters for the nation's establishment political gatekeepers and news agenda-setters, before his formal announcement to a partisan crowd at the Atlanta Civic Center on December 12.[69]

Master plan in place, they negotiated logistical arrangements with assistance from Peach State supporters and amicable political reporters, such as Spivak and Nelson, and they drafted their primary campaign script.[70] "What you say, and how you say it, will be scrutinized by every key political analyst in the country," Carter's aide Jack Burris reminded the presidential aspirant in mid-September after unveiling extensive preparation steps and an initial speech draft, including an account of Carter's accomplishments as governor, America's "new reality," and major themes and issues from the environment to health care that should be addressed. The "speech should be the essence of Jimmy Carter and what you stand for," he explained. "Every line of every paragraph needs to be substantive and thought provoking. It should combine wit with seriousness, idealism with pragmatism, vision with reality, and above all convince people that you are to be reckoned with."[71] Burris cautioned Carter against characteristic last-minute preparations: "Drafts should be written now. . . . Your delivery on every point needs to be carefully timed and phrased, and the speech probably needs to be practiced several times with Jerry Rafshoon and perhaps video-taped for your review."[72] Moreover, Carter should be prepared to negotiate queries from elite political reporters about his presidential qualifications and whether Americans were ready for a southern president, he contended. "I think your responses to these [potential] questions should also be drafted . . . and circulated to your advisors," he coached. "The answers should be fairly short, covered point by point, and be very clear. Often I've noticed that in your response to a reporter's question, you answer more questions than he might have asked. This tends to cut off other reporters, and you end up blowing your whole ball game on one question."[73]

After receiving the memorandum, like a studious student, Carter underlined in red ink portions he deemed most important, including Burris's critiques of his past performances. Moreover, he composed a list of action items—at the top he included a reminder to review announcement speeches from John and Robert Kennedy. Nonetheless, Carter neglected to undertake preparation as quickly as his advisors hoped, and in late October Burris followed with another memo, reminding him "in less than eight weeks, you will make [a] presidential announcement speech. . . . In order for your announcement to be successful, many decisions have to be made now . . . to ensure good attendance, press coverage, and maximum exposure."[74] Burris also included advice on how to solve internal communication concerns and suggestions for the campaign's formal organizational structure, and he attached a sample agenda. In coming days, as logistical arrangements were finalized, Carter developed several handwritten drafts based on extensive feedback from Jordan, Rafshoon, Powell, and Eizenstat and prepared to deliver one of the most important speeches of his life.[75]

"I am a farmer, an engineer, a businessman, a planner, a scientist, a governor, and a Christian," Carter said, introducing himself to the nation's most
influential presidential power brokers and their mass audiences on December 12 as the second candidate to enter the 1976 presidential marathon.[76]
"Recently, we have discovered that our trust has been betrayed. The veils of
secrecy have seemed to thicken around Washington."[77] With that line, Carter and his advisors tapped into the mood of the nation and delivered the
most poignant promise in the bicentennial campaign—"a government that
is honest and competent, with clear purpose and strong leadership [that]
can work with the American people to meet the challenges of the present
and the future." Carter concluded with a rhetorical question, inspired by his
mentor, Admiral Hyman Rickover: "Why not the best?"[78]

Though Carter's resonant appeal prompted one *New York Times* reporter
to hail the "Southern-style Kennedy," most elite political reporters wrote
off his longshot candidacy as a regional nonstarter with "token coverage."[79]
Closer to home, *Atlanta Constitution* editor Reg Murphy treated Carter's announcement as a joke—"Jimmy Who Is Running for WHAT?" he mocked.[80]
In the coming days, Carter and his advisors staged a compelling grassroots
media campaign to attract attention from the establishment news media,
and elite reporters, such as Leubsdorf, sought to untangle just who Jimmy
really was.[81] "The day before he announced . . . Carter was basically an
unknown candidate," Leubsdorf recalled. "I think of all of the stories that
I ever covered in politics his rise was the most stunning. It was the most
uncommon. It was something that could only have happened, I think, when
it did, in the aftermath of Vietnam and Watergate."[82]

★ ★ ★

Jimmy Carter and his advisors possessed a keen awareness of the power
of image in American politics since the nascent moments of his political
career. In an age of credibility crises, they understood that political power
resonated from authentic sources: echoes of stump speeches, subtle imper-
fections of candid photographs; personal anecdotes from grassroots supporters; crackling endorsements from folksy, regional celebrities; smudged
news columns; unpolished cinéma-vérité spots; and pronouncements from
"the most trusted man in news." During Carter's invisible campaign they
developed their post-reform blueprint for a marathon presidential race

and prepared to harness the newest talent, technologies, and techniques, from Caddell's polling data to Rafshoon's cinéma-vérité spots, to deliver a grassroots media campaign featuring candid images of their chic, down-home, (un)celebrity candidate. Now, as Carter's term as governor drew to a close, they turned their collective efforts toward appealing to elite political reporters, a task that proved more challenging than they recognized in a post-Watergate world.

3

Rockin', Down-Home, Grassroots Media Campaign and the (In)visible Primaries

Elite *New York Times* political journalist R. W. Apple Jr. fired off a speculative lede to his interpretative news analysis based on five days of reporting around the bicentennial campaign's kickoff event: "Former Gov. Jimmy Carter appears to have taken a surprising but solid lead in the contest for Iowa's 47 delegates to the Democratic National Convention next year."[1] In the days leading up to the Jefferson-Jackson Day Dinner in Ames on October 25, 1975, "Johnny Apple," as his friends in the business called him, assessed the progress of Democratic hopefuls by interviewing approximately fifty Iowans from all walks of life and consulting the *Des Moines Register*'s straw poll and their correspondent James Flansburg's reporting.[2] As the subsequent headline indicated, Apple determined that the dark horse outpaced the crowded field of nine declared candidates "as the campaign's first test approache[d]."[3]

Prior to post-1968 reforms, Ames was not on the map of most presidential aspirants or consensus-minded campaign chroniclers, but after the unexpectedly strong showing of Democrat George McGovern in Iowa during the 1972 election cycle, Carter and his advisors recognized the precinct caucuses as an opportunity to gain grassroots support and early national media exposure.[4] And, grasping that the world of showbiz politics "is theater," Carter's campaign staged a political coup d'état at the fundraiser orchestrated as a media event by Democratic state party chairman Tom Whitney, thereby capturing attention from "America's most powerful political reporter," who decided to pay careful consideration to early political indicators instead of establishment endorsements to ensure that he and his colleagues were not surprised by the rise of another dark horse.[5]

Based on evidence from his sources, Apple offered incisive analysis about Carter's increasing strength as a frontrunner in the Hawkeye State. Though he conceded that the outsider's "presidential aspirations have been considered laughable by many Washington experts," he acknowledged facts from the ground: the former Georgia governor claimed 23 percent of the vote, defeating his nearest rival, the write-in establishment leader Hubert Humphrey, by more than 10 percentage points, and in the process he encouraged further "foundations of strong organizations in New Hampshire and Florida."[6] "What is evident is that Mr. Carter, working from Atlanta rather than Washington, has made dramatic progress while attention [from elite political journalists] was focused on the scramble for liberal primacy among Mr. [Mo] Udall [U.S. representative from Arizona], Mr. [Birch] Bayh [U.S. senator from Indiana], Mr. [Fred] Harris [U.S. senator from Oklahoma], and Mr. [Sargent] Shriver [founding director of the Peace Corps]," Apple apprised before offering evidence of the source of Carter's popular appeal, quotes from state legislators and county chairpersons acknowledging his outsider status and an anecdote from a rural farmer stressing his grassroots campaign's personal touch.[7] Afterward, as literary journalist Timothy Crouse had suggested four years prior, the unimaginative national news pack "peered over [Apple's] shoulder again." As a consequence of peer pressure and groupthink, his message rang throughout the land.[8]

Apple's apt analysis captured the progress of the grassroots campaign in Iowa. Nevertheless, though he and his buddies from the bus were more focused on the nascent stage of the campaign than ever before, they ultimately missed the lede to Carter's dramatic rise in the (in)visible primaries, the increasingly important time period between a candidate's announcement and the election year's first nominating contest, in which contenders clamored for endorsements, grassroots support, fundraising contributions, and national media attention to boost name recognition and to distinguish themselves from the field.[9] Since endorsements from party regulars lagged for the Washington outsider, Carter and his campaign staff focused on alternative routes to his party's nomination, establishing grassroots support, banking contributions fueled by regional celebrity fundraisers, and attracting local coverage to generate national media exposure.

Hence, after officially announcing his candidacy on December 12, 1974, Carter, his family, and staff only paused for a moment over the holidays before hitting the road to shake hands and introduce Jimmy Who to farmers, factory workers, housewives, journalists, business moguls, and political power brokers in small communities and urban centers throughout the United States. As Apple acknowledged, elite political reporters obsessed with speculative news coverage about probable frontrunners initially transfixed their attention on a crowded field of well-known party regulars. Nevertheless, Carter and his staff faithfully heeded their post-reform campaign blueprint.[10] Billing himself as a progressive leader from the down-home New South,[11] the peanut farmer from Plains traveled across the country, hobnobbing with influential power brokers of showbiz politics and pedaling his antiestablishment message of moral reform to grassroots leaders in Iowa, New Hampshire, and Florida. Under the new rules of U.S. politics, the "Ramblin' Man" achieved success by incorporating his showbiz-inspired grassroots media campaign to garner electoral name recognition that accompanied national news media exposure, and future presidential aspirants followed his lead in the coming years, while party regulars late to recognize modern techniques of presidential politics struggled to survive.

★ ★ ★

On Wednesday, January 15, 1975, Carter and press secretary Jody Powell boarded a jet plane bound for the Beltway to attract the national coverage that had eluded the former Georgia governor since his announcement a little more than a month prior.[12] Carter's staff planned the overnight trip so the relatively unknown candidate could appear on NBC's *Today Show* the following day, but Washington-based campaign advisors Peter and Mary Bourne arranged a small fundraising dinner held in Carter's honor by party insider Bardyl Tirana, the Princeton-educated lawyer and former aide to Bobby Kennedy, and scheduled a meeting with the *Washington Post*'s editorial board, where the candidate explained his campaign strategy.[13] In response to these initial efforts, however, elite political reporters rebuffed the outsider's media queries with sneers and silence.

Recognizing that the establishment news failed to greet with seriousness the candidacy of the New South governor who "whistled a different tune," Carter's campaign persisted and exploited any chance to curry favor with media contacts to garner positive coverage.[14] As Carter traversed the nation on his grassroots media campaign, he continued to plead his case to national reporters, primarily in editorial board meetings at mass-circulating newspapers and magazines located in major metropolitan cities, but he also sought attention from local reporters in rural towns, mid-sized media markets, and urban hubs along the trail through his decentralized publicity strategy.[15]

When opportunities for local media appearances shortly materialized, Carter exploited them to voice concerns that elite national reporters were not taking seriously his candidacy inspired by Kennedy's outsider strategy and taken straight from the pages of Theodore White's *The Making of the President, 1960.*[16] Influenced by regional prejudice against the South, these key national political gatekeepers and news agenda-setters wrote off his campaign as a regional candidacy, the peanut farmer-physicist for president confided to Rollin Post, a leading Bay Area political journalist, on KOED's *Newsroom,* the current events program that Powell recommended due to its popularity among politicians and the intelligencia.[17] The outsider's brazen echo of the mainstream conservative critique of the establishment news media provided evidence of his campaign's emerging us-versus-them posturing, but it was not far from the truth: only two elite political reporters, the *Washington Star*'s national editor and syndicated columnist Jack Germond and the *St. Louis Post-Dispatch*'s Washington-based political correspondent Tom Ottenad, had determined that the nascent stage of the southerner's antiestablishment bid was newsworthy enough to follow on a regular basis.[18]

After wielding his antiestablishment media critique inspired by recent predecessors,[19] Carter returned to the trail, but contrary to popular memory, he did not commence his grassroots campaign on the snow-packed streets of Iowa or New Hampshire, the bicentennial campaign's first contests. Instead, he and his imagecraft apparatus crisscrossed the nation, traveling to Kentucky, Arizona, Florida, California, South Carolina, Wisconsin, New Jersey, and New York to solicit support at meetings with local and state Democratic leaders, to shake hands at campaign pseudo-events, and to attract media attention.[20] Though these events did not result in immediate national exposure, they often provided key opportunities to cull rapport with elite political reporters, which, as Carter's critique indicated, was a necessary move to cultivate exposure from national political gatekeepers and news agenda-setters.[21]

Moreover, after scrutinizing McGovern's 1972 campaign, Carter's staff also recognized the wisdom of hustling to broadcast their populist messages at early sites of political action likely to attract national news media attention. In mid-February, Carter and Powell traveled across New Hampshire with stops in Concord, Manchester, and Nashua to meet state party leaders and to canvass for support from local citizens. Once again, Carter's campaign exploited any media exchanges, recording interviews with local radio stations and making introductions with small-town publishers.[22] Likewise, at month's end in Iowa, Carter and Powell zigzagged across the state to Ames, Sioux City, and Des Moines, meeting with state party leaders, attending pseudo-events held in the candidate's honor, appearing on panel programs on local stations, and addressing the *Des Moines Register*'s editorial board.[23]

"At first [however, even local reporters] ignored me because I was not on their radar screen," Carter contended. "They didn't even know I was alive." Carter and his advisors longed to harness the image-amplifying power of local news coverage, but when opportunities were not immediately forthcoming, they were willing to accept any sort of media exposure. "One night, Jody came in, and told me I was going to be on TV the next morning. I couldn't believe it. Jody wouldn't tell me what it was—it was a cooking show, and on our way to the TV station, he asked me if I remembered any recipes. Luckily, I remembered one [favorite fish-fry recipe]."[24]

This small victory in mind, the presidential aspirant trudged on through snow, on occasion struggling to find hands to shake. At a Des Moines hotel reception, Carter recalled that, other than his staff and event organizers, "I think there were only three other people."[25] At such stops, he eagerly looked "for somebody with a notebook, and somebody with a tape-recorder would be the epitome of excitement."[26] Moreover, after persistently scouring crowds for reporters, they encountered the *Des Moines Register*'s chief political correspondent, and the unknown political outsider succeeded in currying Flansburg's favor. "Seldom has a candidate without a fabled name made such a fast and favorable impression on Iowans," he applauded.[27]

"The *Des Moines Register* became more important [to us] than the *Washington Post*," Powell recalled.[28] "I would suspect that we concentrate more heavily on local media than anybody else does, if for no other reason than . . . the national media . . . is not there for us." Carter's staff hoped a decentralized approach might prompt increased national exposure, but in the interim, as the *Atlanta Constitution* noted in February, one barrier remained: Carter's ability to make news in one rural town did not easily translate into coverage in another area.[29]

Amid persistent struggles to attract and transform local coverage into something more, advertising guru Gerald Rafshoon directed the documentation of Carter's personal campaign, collecting footage of bleak initial efforts of the lone candidate alongside snapshots of Carter's caravan of unpaid Peach State volunteers.[30] In all, Rafshoon and his crew gathered more than 100,000 feet of film and photographs of the peanut farmer's quaint grassroots campaign to weave through Carter's primary materials. The best shots resurfaced in advertising spots the following year and offered a cinematic introduction for the Democratic Party's nominee.[31]

In the interim, as campaign director Hamilton Jordan's sophisticated delegate calculus demanded, based on post-1968 reforms establishing candidate-bound delegates and federal matching funds, Carter campaigned in all fifty states, spending the majority of his time in Florida, where he had to defeat southern son George Wallace's stalwart campaign; the Northeast, where he laid groundwork for party leader Ted Kennedy's defeat, if necessary; and national media hubs, such as New York, Chicago, and Los Angeles, where he hoped to garner exposure to increase his name recognition.[32]

Despite the continued drought in national coverage, the Carter campaign's grassroots efforts reaped gradual rewards: his campaign yielded support among a segment of East Coast intellectuals, scheduled additional editorial board meetings at prominent media outlets, and garnered positive local trail coverage.[33] Carter recruited "some campaign volunteers at the Democratic Youth Caucus convention in Eau Claire . . . [and] had received a 40-second standing ovation at the end of a speech to the Wisconsin Jaycees in Madison," *Milwaukee Journal* staff writer Leon Hughes reported.[34] But, despite increasing acknowledgments in mid-circulating newspapers, challenges remained. After editorial board meetings, it was not uncommon to hear responses similar to those of *Philadelphia Inquirer* editorial cartoonist Tony Auth, who wondered aloud—"Is this guy for real?"[35] But, instead of struggling to convert nonbelievers, Carter's imagecraft apparatus renewed efforts toward increasing the candidate's national name recognition through his decentralized strategy, which involved gaining free local media, gleaning positive coverage from grassroots efforts and campaign pseudo-events, and currying favor with elite political reporters.[36]

★ ★ ★

Many candidates recognized that elite political reporters were more attuned to the (in)visible primaries after the post-1968 reforms.[37] But, while
leading establishment candidates, adhering to brokered convention strategies, intended to attract national attention toward fledgling campaigns by
making news in the halls of Congress, Carter's imagecraft team continued
to perfect their original plan, which combined primary, showbiz-infused
techniques initiated by party underdogs since midcentury with a Kennedy/
Nixon-inspired local media strategy.[38] These schemas in mind, they developed branding materials to enhance Carter's image as an antiestablishment
moral reformer; concentrated grassroots efforts at early political sites,
which promised to attract intense media scrutiny; and harnessed popular
regional celebrities to enhance grassroots support, fundraising initiatives,
and national attention.

   After completing the requisite background reading, including Crouse's
Boys on the Bus, Jordan and other campaign architects realized that they
needed to refine the candidate's image to fit the needs of the moment.[39]
Jordan recognized that Carter's current grassroots appeal derived from his
"personal attractiveness, his character, and his intelligence," but he believed,
moving forward, that the staff should stress to public opinion leaders, especially elite national reporters, who served as "chief conduits of political
information to the public," the qualities proven to garner positive press,
such as the Renaissance man's diverse background and innovative gubernatorial record.[40] Jordan also reminded staff of his two-step primary plan
to attract national media attention: build personal relationships with elite
reporters and stress the legitimacy of Carter's antiestablishment campaign.

   With this original directive in mind, Powell and press assistant Betty
Rainwater produced essential publicity materials needed to promote the
dark horse candidate as a promising alternative to more well-established
party figures to potential supporters and reporters.[41] Though Carter's campaign projected an antiestablishment brand, his press staff modeled publicity materials, including campaign manuals, advance guides, and press releases, after recent showbiz-inspired presidential campaigns.[42] Informed by
successful public relations techniques of presidential actors, such as Nixon,
they scrutinized emergent coverage through Burrelle's Clipping Service, and
as Carter's grassroots strategy attracted positive local reporting, Rainwater
culled and catalogued stories for her campaign reference guide, and she
later published many repurposed positive clips in the campaign's newsletter,

The Carter News, which was distributed to prominent national reporters and potential supporters across the country.[43]

When elite reporters continued to ignore the outsider's campaign, Carter and his advisors redoubled their energies at early political sites. On hiatus from his graduate studies in political science at Berkeley, Carter's twenty-four-year-old delegate coordinator, Rick Hutcheson, encouraged Jordan to enhance efforts in Iowa by selecting a diverse range of county chairpersons; organizing another trip to off-the-beaten-path cities, such as Waterloo and Cedar Falls; and implementing direct mail marketing for more rural areas.[44] Jordan heeded Hutcheson's advice. Recognizing that the state's precinct caucuses might be framed as a major media event due to their status as the bicentennial campaign's first political test, he shifted Carter's attention back toward Iowa. Neglected by leading contenders, the state offered favorable grassroots support and local coverage to the peanut farmer from Plains.[45] Consequently, Carter's staff scheduled a whirlwind personal campaign through Davenport, Des Moines, Dubuque, and Muscatine, and after additional nudging from national field director Timothy Kraft, the campaign established a permanent presence in Iowa, what he later referred to as a "horse-and-buggy operation" functioning with a meager "$18,000 [shoestring] budget."[46]

Jordan's "magna carta," as campaign reporter Kandy Stroud famously referred to it, offered a shrewd blueprint for the outsider's rise from obscurity to the White House, but the campaign director was not a seer.[47] Consequently, informed by certitude that Kennedy would not enter the race and news that the Massachusetts and Vermont primaries would intervene in the succession of the New Hampshire and Florida contests, he modified Carter's primary plan in June 1975, emphasizing the reprioritization of fundraising and the exploitation of favorable media modes and frames, especially local broadcasts of his antiestablishment appeals.[48]

In prior election cycles, presidential aspirants had relied on a few wealthy backers to fund their campaigns, but in order to receive federal matching funds, post-reform candidates needed to amass a multitude of moderate contributors willing to support their campaigns with small donations of at least $250.[49] Though the new legislation was most inclined to benefit the unknown outsider's campaign, Jordan recognized that his staff needed a reminder of the new stakes in the game.[50] "Fundraising has got to be the continuing priority of the campaign," he stressed, acknowledging that political efforts, including those of the imagecraft apparatus, and financial needs were "truly . . . inseparable."[51]

Recognizing these intertwined objectives, Carter's staff recommended harnessing the power of celebrity endorsements.[52] Since midcentury, presidential aspirants had relied on Hollywood star power and Madison Avenue advertising and public relations techniques, and now, based on Hutcheson's suggestion, Jordan suggested amplifying support from leading New South political actors, such as prominent African American U.S. Representative Andrew Young and Capricorn Records cofounder Phil Walden, designed to boost Carter's standing among special interest groups essential to the outsider's emerging coalition.[53] Young's support might enhance Carter's image as a progressive southerner among northern liberals and African Americans, who were empowered to engage in their civic duty after the passage of the Voting Rights Act of 1965, and endorsements from Walden and his hip Southern Rock acts were designed to bolster Carter's appeal among new college-age voters. As early local coverage indicated, Carter's grassroots campaign gained ground with these special interest groups, and in the coming months the campaign continued to reach out to targeted communities through tools of showbiz politics.[54]

Moreover, Jordan recommended the continued exploitation of favorable tendencies in news media coverage. He recognized that the post-reform role of national reporters involved interpreting political contests for audiences and predicted their inclination to revert to their horse race bias by deliberating on progress in the presidential race when explaining contest outcomes.[55] "We would do well to understand the very special and powerful role the press plays in interpreting the primary results for the rest of the nation," Jordan wrote. "What is actually accomplished in New Hampshire is less important than how the press interprets it for the nation. Handled properly, a defeat can be interpreted as a holding action and a mediocre showing as a victory."[56] Heartened by his progress, Carter temporarily disregarded this insight at a Beltway event, where he delivered the emergent standard political line, promising to finish no less than second in Iowa, New Hampshire, and Florida, but Jordan warned against foolhardy overconfidence in such posturing, and he reiterated the importance of exploiting establishment news media's expectations.[57] "We must keep in mind the fact that our performance in the early caucuses and primaries will be measured against arbitrary standards established by us for the press and influenced in large part by our own claims and statements along the way," Jordan warned, cautioning Carter to eliminate the term winning from his "public political vocabulary."[58]

★ ★ ★

As *Los Angeles Times* reporter Robert Shogan avowed, elite political reporters, who once scoffed at the presidential chances of the little-known peanut farmer-physicist, could not discount Carter's candidacy in the summer of 1975.[59] Carter's campaign generated a steady stream of positive press in local and regional newspapers, and in the year of the Washington outsider, the antiestablishment candidate who campaigned six days a week might have a chance, they begrudgingly conceded.[60] Nevertheless, many elite reporters admitted they were at a disadvantage in covering Carter. Shogan, for instance, returned to his reporting notebooks months after their first meeting in 1974, and the pages were blank. "It suddenly occurred to me that here was a man determined to make it to the White House who had said nothing I felt obliged to record," he wrote.[61] Consequently, many elite reporters focused attention on the "epic struggle" between more well-known candidates in the Democratic field, which liberal contender might beat Wallace, and whether Humphrey or Kennedy would reconsider and enter the race.

Despite lagging national coverage and low name recognition, Carter's campaign, influenced by regulations involved in campaign finance reform, persisted with minor modifications to garner grassroots support and favorable coverage.[62] Consequently, Carter campaigned at sites of early political action, stumping in Iowa, New Hampshire, and Florida on consecutive visits, and traveling to Chicago, the nation's midwestern media hub, to engage in meetings with mainstream political pundits and editorial board members of minority magazine giants *Ebony* and *Jet,* two remaining mass channels of communication to reach newly enfranchised African American audiences with his progressive record on race.[63]

Moreover, he and his staff persevered in their laborious attempts to cull rapport with elite reporters. Prior efforts with dean of political reporters David Broder and his colleagues had prompted laughable results,[64] but now the elite, intellectual reporter offered Jordan key strategic advice, which the campaign director passed on to Carter and his staff:

I spent a couple of hours with David Broder in Washington. He said that his initial judgment about your being a "regional candidate" was wrong and that he was surprised with the progress that you had made this year. He thinks that someone will emerge from the early primaries as a "new face" and does not ascribe to the "brokered convention theory." He thinks that the key to winning the Democratic nomination is a candidate's ability to develop an intensity factor among their supporters, and that this year in the absence of a burning issue which a candidate can use to generate the intensity required, that personal qualities are very important. He outlined for me the coverage that the *Post* has planned for Fall and I have conveyed this info to Jody. He thinks that our strategy is sound and says that regardless of what people say, New Hampshire will still be very important as a first benchmark of voter attitude. He says that he continues to hear good things about you from the local press people and national press that have traveled with you.[65]

Words from the influential power broker provided precious reassurance to Carter's campaign that the organizational plan first outlined in the "magna carta" was viable and offered key tactical advice for a national media strategy moving forward.[66] After such rapport-building sessions, Powell often followed up with letters of gratitude, such as he extended to New York-based syndicated columnist Jimmy Breslin, who often considered how events impacted the common man. "I enjoyed the chance to meet you and chat briefly in D.C.," Powell wrote. "Us poor ole country boys need all the insight we can get into the vagaries of New York politics."[67]

In the coming days, Carter's campaign labors generated a groundswell of free local and regional exposure that, in turn, commanded attention from prominent national reporters by exploiting favorable news modes and frames, especially campaign journalism's horse race bias and the salient underdog frame.[68] In mid-July, for instance, the *Florida Times-Union and Journal*'s Washington correspondent, Jayne Brumley, reached out to local and state party leaders, such as Senator Richard Stone, to assess Carter's progress in the Florida primary. In the final analysis, she contended, despite the Carter campaign's unprecedented efforts, his odds of defeating Wallace were slim.[69] Carter's staff, however, was not disappointed with the underdog label. Instead, modeling the strategy used for his second gubernatorial bid, they exploited the media's horse race bias and manipulated the framing of expectations to their advantage.[70] Consequently, they presented Carter as a progressive alternative to Wallace. Suggesting that Wallace's success threatened to fracture the Democratic Party and undermine the presidential ambitions of other contenders, they encouraged liberal candidates not to contest the Florida primary. Moreover, they harnessed media expectations of Carter as an underdog, recognizing that if they managed to defeat Wallace, they could suggest Carter had developed an upsurge of popular support, but should they encounter defeat, they could insist the Washington outsider had experienced bias from the establishment news media.

By late summer, Carter discovered that his grassroots media campaign had gained its first indication of national legitimacy, and at a late August press conference in Washington, D.C., he announced news of the first triumph of his antiestablishment outsider campaign: qualifying for federal matching funds in the new age of campaign finance reform. "The day when one or two people could bankroll a candidate through the early stages of a campaign is gone forever. . . . The raising of funds has been a city by city, step by step process, and I have enjoyed it thoroughly," he said. Amid his us-versus-them posturing, the peanut farmer from Plains reveled in his success to national reporters, stressing his nationwide journey to more than 175 cities and towns in forty states.[71]

Carter and his press staff sought to amplify the announcement by illuminating his antiestablishment candidacy in the nation's paper of record. Acknowledging his emerging legitimacy, the *New York Times* published the former Georgia governor's letter to the editor on September 5.[72] In "Why I Am Running," Carter explained that, after concerned citizens reached out to him with anxieties about the ailing nation, he had offered himself—a Washington outsider—as the best solution to restore America to greatness. Following the sign of Carter's legitimacy and conforming to the cue of the industry leader, national newsmagazines, such as *U.S. News and World Report* and *Time,* indicated that Carter was a viable candidate before deliberating on his primary strategy and overall chances.[73] According to consensus-minded accounts from frontline reporters, Carter's campaign remained a longshot, but evidence indicated the underdog was making important strides in gaining grassroots support and national exposure. After hearing news that Carter had finished first in Iowa's off-year caucuses, the campaign's imagecraft apparatus expanded its efforts to enhance his media schedule and harnessed national exposure to project their candidate's luminary, Kennedyesque qualities—his attractive smile, his charming young family, his hip celebrity pals, and his popular antiestablishment message.[74]

★ ★ ★

After observing unanticipated coverage of the inconsequential, off-year Iowa caucuses, Whitney convinced elite political reporters that the Democratic Party's next major fundraising dinner was an early predictor of the 1976 presidential contest.[75] Intent on exploiting the expanded role of frontline reporters as political power brokers, Flansburg aided Whitney's endeavor, encouraging the *Des Moines Register* to sponsor a straw poll that might "show important differences among the candidates' organizations."[76] Hence, interested parties staged a political spectacle, complete with a credible straw poll and speeches from all candidates contesting the Iowa caucuses, for the consumption of elite political reporters.

Moreover, despite limited news budgets for the (in)visible primaries, national political correspondents, eager for an early presidential barometer, focused attention on Ames as "an early line on the 1976 contenders."[77] "You grasp at straws in this business, and if you can detect the slightest straw in the wind or any reaction to a candidate, it can be helpful in the early stages," ABC News correspondent Frank Reynolds reported, explaining the consensus-minded rationale surrounding the value of early predictors.[78] Furthermore, Whitney ensured that presidential kingmakers returned in ensuing years by staging an event with "all the trappings of a political convention, with booths set up at the back of the arena for each of the hopefuls, and time set aside . . . to man the booths, shake hands, and answer questions."[79]

Although other candidates, recognizing potential in the Jefferson-Jackson Day Dinner to bolster early grassroots efforts in the Hawkeye State, accepted invitations to the speaking engagement and organized private fundraising events, Carter's imagecraft apparatus appreciated the event as a showcase of strength for elite political reporters, who influenced the national news agenda through their dominant echo-chamber. This apt supposition in mind, Powell's staff crafted a news release touting Carter's first-place finish in the September 22 "trial runs" and encouraged national reporters to observe his progress at upcoming Iowa events.[80] Moreover, heeding strategic advice from Jordan and Kraft, Carter's state organizational machine made plans to swing the poll in his favor by packing pennywise supporters into the balcony, the $2 cheap seats of the $25-a-plate dinner venue.[81] Consequently, Carter's imagecraft apparatus outmaneuvered early frontrunners by claiming 23.4 percent of the straw-poll vote at the event, keynoted by McGovern, the chief engineer of party reforms.[82]

As the supervisor of the *Des Moines Register*'s straw poll, Flansburg planned to be first to deliver the Iowa progress report, but speculation from the nation's top political reporter overshadowed the local journalist's page-one story, "Carter Tops Democratic Straw Poll—Other Candidates Trail Far Behind."[83] After describing Carter's "surprising but solid lead," Apple reported the results from the *Register*'s straw poll, provided insight into Carter's Iowa machine, offered local reaction to the peanut farmer's "personal touch," and analyzed the former governor's dinner speech.[84] Apple also addressed the strengths of other candidates, but in the final analysis he recognized that Carter "maximized McGovern's playbook" in Iowa.[85] And, though he acknowledged it remained unclear whether the Washington outsider's campaign might maintain his appeal with "rank-and-file voters. . . . [or] whether a victory here would translate into momentum in other states," he focused on Carter in his inverted pyramid-style analysis and constructed him as the party's frontrunner in Iowa precinct caucuses.[86] Moreover, much as Crouse suggested, the national pack echoed his lede, a political reality the brash news hustler well understood.[87]

As *New Yorker* journalist Elizabeth Drew aptly contended, critiquing Apple's news judgment and the New York/Washington echo-chamber, the story "was itself a political event, prompting other newspapers stories that Carter was doing well in Iowa, and then more news-magazine and television coverage for Carter than might otherwise have been his share."[88] Although it is impossible to determine the exact impact of the piece, it is fair to say that Apple's article prompted a ripple effect in early coverage of the Democratic field, and Carter's campaign enjoyed amplified coverage in national news media.[89]

Though Apple's name was absent from the campaign's "magna carta," Carter's advisors recognized the potential of Apple and his buddies from the bus to wield tremendous influence on the bicentennial campaign.[90] When attempts to curry favor from these emerging kingmakers lagged, Carter's campaign staged a grassroots political spectacle that stressed the legitimacy of his antiestablishment appeal. By managing press expectations and over-performing in this early presidential showcase, Carter's campaign gained additional attention from elite, consensus-minded national reporters, anxious to cover the dark horse lest anyone cry foul. In the coming days, they harnessed further tools of showbiz politics to increase national name recognition and appeal through entertaining images of the "Ramblin' Man['s]" down-home campaign.

★ ★ ★

Carter did not slow down to pore over positive press; instead, he practiced his speed-reading skills as he perused clips en route to his next major campaign stop—Atlanta's Fox Theatre, where Capricorn Records' Marshall Tucker Band was scheduled to headline his campaign's sold-out benefit concert.[91] Amid continued struggles to attract widespread donations necessitated by campaign finance reform, Carter convinced Walden, a major political power broker in the record industry cultivated through the governor's 1971 "Stop and Listen Tour," to encourage his antiestablishment acts to launch a series of benefit concerts from Atlanta's former movie palace.[92] Consequently, the Marshall Tucker Band posed for obligatory photo-ops at a pre-show reception for the former Georgia governor and applauded when Carter introduced them onstage: "Tonight is the night for music, not politics. I want to say just four things: (1) I'm running for president. (2) I don't intend to lose. (3) I need your support. (4) I'd like to introduce you to my friends, the Marshall Tucker Band."[93]

Though other candidates sought to exploit celebrity endorsements, Carter benefited most from his deft deployment of showbiz politics in the new age of campaign finance reform.[94] Celebrity benefit concerts bolstered Carter's appeal with Southern Rock fans, enhanced fundraising and volunteer efforts, and prompted additional national coverage.[95] Images of Carter schmoozing with Marshall Tucker's lead guitarist, Toy Caldwell, and his bandmate George McCorkle, the composer of the band's hit "Fire on the Mountain," rematerialized in the form of enhanced grassroots support and attention from national reporters.[96]

These new signals of legitimacy prompted pseudo-celebrity journalists, such as *The Making of the President* author Teddy White and gonzo journalist Hunter S. Thompson, to check into Carter's chic campaign. After more than two years of attempts to attract attention from this influential crowd, Carter's staff recognized the magnitude of his accomplishment. "Theodore White, yes, that's right, *the* Theodore White, would like 30 minutes with JC next time he is in New York City. Mr. White is not yet ready to go out on the campaign trail, so it must be in New York City," Rainwater wrote Powell in early November.[97] Later in the month, Thompson penned Carter a letter in his signature style, assuring his friend he would catch up with him in New Hampshire and Florida.[98] After jesting about the possibility of a "Humphrey-Thompson" ticket, the famed purveyor of New Journalism informed Carter that many elite agenda-setters from the New York/Washington echo chamber now considered him to be the early frontrunner in the contest for the Democratic nomination and offered the candidate some friendly advice: he should appear alongside Wallace as often as possible to secure victory in Florida. In exchange for the goods, Thompson requested a "gaggle of favors," including Carter's help in securing a convertible and a ground-floor room at the Royal Biscayne for his Florida primary coverage. Carter's staff could not accommodate Thompson's request, but they did offer the celebrity frontline reporters something increasingly more important—access to the celebrity candidate after his early victories.

Despite increased attention from elite reporters, Carter's closest advisors reminded him that the personal media campaign still had a "long way to go and we cannot let up."[99] In the ensuing days, Carter continued to preach his grassroots message in rural Iowa and New York, where the "front runner among the dark horses," as the *Times* dubbed him, attracted more attention from campaign agenda-setters, including broadcast correspondents and newsmagazine reporters.[100] During Carter's late-November trip to New York, for instance, ABC *Evening News* coanchor Harry Reasoner interviewed the candidate, while special events producer Jeff Gralnick considered how to integrate him into the network's primary plans.[101] Later, Carter convened with influential editorial boards, while *Newsweek*'s Eleanor Clift and *Time*'s Stanley Cloud angled with his press staff for close-range campaign access to generate insights for their Teddy White/Joe McGinnis-inspired insider accounts.[102]

He immediately followed this grassroots media blitz with an appearance in Providence, Rhode Island, at the second in a series of celebrity benefit concerts. After the reception at Royal Roost Restaurant in La Salle Square and a thirty-minute news conference at the Civic Center, Carter was escorted backstage, where he greeted event emcee and celebrity broadcaster Geraldo Rivera and members of the Allman Brothers Band before striding onstage. And, after delivering an ad-libbed version of his standard campaign line in his southern twang—"I'd like to say one thing. My name is Jimmy Carter, and I'm running for President. I'd like to introduce you to my friends, the Allman Brothers," he slipped backstage to visit Grinderswitch, the lesser-known Capricorn act hoping to gain visibility from the fundraising concert.[103]

In advance of the event, Carter's press staff issued a release, acknowledging that the first fundraising effort by the popular Allman Brothers Band was "especially important to Carter in the early primary states" and expressing Carter's gratitude to his "friends in the entertainment industry."[104] Stripped of spin, the release offered prophetic insight into the importance of celebrity fundraisers in post-reform politics. Carter later acknowledged that the benefit concert, which netted approximately $60,000, plus matching federal funds, kept him in the race: "The Allman Brothers basically put us in the White House."[105]

After breaking bread with families on Thanksgiving Day, Carter's staff sought to harness attention from national reporters into free exposure that might further increase Carter's name recognition and bolster his image by accepting an invitation to appear on CBS's *Face the Nation*.[106] Carter was not the only candidate on the Sunday morning talk show circuit that day, but he was the best at exploiting media expectations. And, while Udall, a favorite among reporters and the liberal darling who campaigned extensively in Iowa and New Hampshire, underscored the necessity of finishing strong in at least two of the first four campaign tests due to the constraints of campaign finance reform, Carter heeded Jordan's advice, instead emphasizing his underdog status and his antiestablishment message.[107]

Though the Washington outsider proved the eventual unintended beneficiary of campaign finance reform, Carter and his staff wisely remained silent to network personalities about the burden of reform, including their latest challenge: though they recognized the image-enhancing power of clever advertising campaigns, they lacked sufficient funds to saturate media markets with Rafshoon's novel five-minute cinéma-vérité spots. Consequently, they turned once more to what proved to be one of the most effective tools in their campaign arsenal, the popular appeal of celebrity star power, and they planned "Georgia Loves Jimmy Carter," a celebrity-fueled fundraising telethon for early February, to attract fundraising dollars for the next phase of their primary campaign—paid media blitzes in New Hampshire and Florida.[108]

★ ★ ★

Carter's campaign encountered mostly positive coverage of grassroots efforts during the (in)visible primaries, but it now confronted increased scrutiny from consensus-minded frontline reporters and unappealing media frames, which coalesced into an enigmatic media label that haunted Carter in the bicentennial campaign and beyond. To combat adverse coverage depicting unsanctioned images, Carter's imagecraft apparatus harnessed prominent news management tools tested by their predecessors in the age of showbiz politics.

During the (in)visible primaries, local and regional reporters often depicted Carter as "an energetic candidate who intends to take his campaign to all the states," but increasingly, news coverage included disclaimers, such as the one appearing in the Wilmington, Delaware, *Evening Journal*'s house editorial on November 5: "Gov. Carter is a many-faceted individual and which facet is prominent depends on where he is at any given moment. In rural areas, he is the Georgia peanut farmer. Among professional people, he is the nuclear engineer and accomplished politician. Among business people, he is the successful administrator who tamed his state's bureaucracy."[109] Moving forward, Carter's staff worried that consensus-minded establishment reporters might amplify the unsanctioned image.

Moreover, as "the frontrunner among the dark horses," Carter endured increased scrutiny from elite political reporters that autumn.[110] Carter's staff plotted to attract attention in national newsmagazines, but now they were dissatisfied with how *Newsweek* staff appraised Carter's chances to earn the Democratic nomination. Carter's only hope was a brokered convention, they contended under the subhead "Whistling Dixie."[111] Carter's press staff had not voiced frustration over the reference to Dixie when it appeared emblazoned over Carter's head on *Time*'s May 1971 cover, but now they charged that the *Newsweek* headline denigrated the South and that their reporting dismissed Carter as a regional candidate.[112] Though they may have ruffled a few feathers with their unfashionable news management technique, Carter and his press staff offered an apt critique. "Frankly, the people in New York and Washington didn't give him great odds of getting the nomination," Clift admitted.[113] And, in a forthcoming *Newsweek* issue, she and her colleague Tom Mathews conceded that Carter "succeeded in making Democrats [and, left unsaid, national reporters] who once dismissed him as a regional nonstarter look twice." But, still displeased, Carter's staff complained again of regional bias when national reporters included derisive remarks from one veteran politician, who compared the former governor to a South Georgia snapping turtle, "stubbornly toiling and pushing ahead," and from one former campaign aide, who likened Carter to Nixon.[114]

Despite Carter's grumblings, the latter comparison was not completely unfounded. By exploiting tools of showbiz politics first harnessed by Eisenhower, Kennedy, and *Nixon,* Carter attracted coveted national coverage with celebrity endorsements from the most popular antiestablishment acts in Southern Rock, but as the projected frontrunner moving into Iowa, Carter now endured premature scrutiny to those symbiotic relationships in national forums. Though alternative monthly *Rolling Stone* reporter Art Harris documented the new campaign trend to seize exposure from celebrity endorsements and fundraisers, he focused his attention on dissecting the symbiotic alliance between Carter and Walden, tracing origins of their cordial relationship to the governor's 1971 "Stop and Listen Tour" and documenting shared motives. As an influential political power broker, Walden convinced other record executives and artists on his label to promote the peanut farmer from Plains and to participate in fundraisers on his behalf in hopes that as Carter advanced he would advocate for copyright and antipiracy laws. "Carter had treated multimillionaire Walden like a good ol' boy—with respect," Harris wrote. "Now that Carter requires a good deal of money and loyalty to boost his name recognition and glamorize his persona of soft-spoken sincerity, Walden has not forgotten." Accordingly, instead of sporting William Jennings Bryan's cross of gold, the record mogul wore a "green Jimmy Carter for President button."[115] Rainwater, initially encouraged by the hip forum's attention to the celebrity connection, scribbled a reminder to "get [the] original for [the] good file," but Carter and his staff soon discovered that when it came to free media not all publicity was good publicity.[116]

To counter scrutiny and negative frames, Carter's staff deployed tools of showbiz politics, debuting their campaign autobiography and first paid media spots. Through *Why Not the Best,* Carter and his aides sought to capitalize on the peanut farmer's chic, down-home sensibility.[117] Consequently, with assistance from *Atlanta Constitution* associate editor Hal Gulliver, Carter emulated the model suggested in James David Barber's *Presidential Character* (1972), and in an accessible tone and unpolished style he spun the yarn of his idyllic childhood in Plains; his education at the U.S. Naval Academy; his marriage and the birth of his sons and daughter, Amy; his stint in the navy's nuclear submarine program; his return home after the death of his father, Earl; and his early political career inspired by reform-oriented altruism. In a postmodern age governed by reformed showbiz politics, many establishment political consultants and reporters believed the selling of presidential candidates occurred on the screen, but Carter proved them wrong, exploiting print media to craft an unassuming, straightforward autobiography designed to meet the demands of the times by chronicling his rural origins, his strong Protestant upbringing, his military training, his loyalty to family, his transition into political leadership, and his desire to restore America to greatness after the national traumas of Vietnam and Watergate.[118] When big-name New York publishers, such as Little, Brown, rejected the manuscript idea, Carter turned to Broadman Press, a conservative, faith-based "inspirational literature" publisher, and turning down royalty checks, he negotiated an extensive publicity campaign, including full-page advertisements in the nation's top-circulating newspapers and newsmagazines. Though it was not widely acclaimed, Carter's autobiography managed to capture and harness many of the qualities of the popular, folksy television show *The Waltons,* and as his grassroots media campaign gained traction, average Americans and celebrities endorsed the hip volume as required reading, and more than a million folks, including frontline reporters, plucked up the bestseller along the trail.[119] As historian Douglas Brinkley noted, Carter's "inspired work . . . transcended the tired campaign-book genre" and revived the necessity of crafting campaign autobiographies in the age of reformed showbiz politics.[120]

Carter's imagecraft apparatus further countered enigmatic images from emerging adversaries, including the establishment news media, by complementing the release of his campaign autobiography with the aura of "truthful cinema." Carter's authentic "politics of amazing grace" resonated with Rafshoon as he reviewed film collected on the trail.[121] "I'll never lie to you. I'll never make a misleading statement. I want to be as good and as honest and as decent and as full of love and competent and compassionate as are the American people. I'll never lie to you. If I do, don't vote for me. Read the papers. Watch the television. Listen to the radio. If I lie, I will not deserve your trust." Rafshoon recalled that this was his a-ha moment. "I turned to our editors and said, 'You know, if anybody can spend five minutes with Jimmy Carter, they're going to vote for him. Let's do five-minute spots.'"[122] Accordingly, in two- and five-minute cinéma-vérité spots, bankrolled by federal matching funds stimulated from benefit concerts headlined by prominent Southern Rock artists, Carter's imagecraft apparatus projected B-roll footage of the populist peanut farmer from Plains hand-sifting his prized crop and shaking hands with average Americans along the trail while campaign surrogates, including the peanut farmer's wife, his mother, and his most faithful supporters, shared folksy anecdotes and the moral reformer promised never to "tell a lie" in his voiceovers.[123] With their Teddy White/ Robert Drew-inspired bricolage of the Kennedy/Humphrey 1960 primary campaigns, Carter's imagecraft apparatus sought to deliver an authentic appeal to enhance the legitimacy of the dark horse candidate's chic, down-home persona and antiestablishment message, and as one scholar later observed, "the medium matched the message perfectly."[124] Consequently, as *New York Times* media critic Joseph Lelyveld indicated, the commercials succeeded in convincing many Iowans that they were CBS documentaries about the rise of the dark horse candidate.[125]

★ ★ ★

By December 1975, evidence mounted that Carter's grassroots media campaign had paid dividends in his national name recognition rates. As Mathews and Clift reported to *Newsweek* readers, most Americans had never heard of Jimmy Carter a year prior, but now approximately one out of two citizens were familiar with the peanut farmer from Plains.[126] Recognizing their progress, Carter's imagecraft apparatus sought to control his emerging political brand through campaign autobiographies and paid media blitzes.[127] But they continued to discover that anticipated strengths, such as his nuanced background, might become liabilities when, amid increased scrutiny, trail reporters dubbed their Renaissance man as a "contradiction in terms."[128]

Despite looming challenges, as the Iowa caucuses approached, Carter and his caravan blitzed the state and harnessed subsequent national attention to gain the edge over establishment party candidates.[129] But, with the eyes of national reporters now squarely on Iowa, all contenders ramped up their personal campaigns.[130] Despite these grassroots efforts, *new* political power brokers played a prominent role in determining the fate of political actors. Under the new rules of U.S. politics, masters of "the devices and channels of mass publicity" increasingly influenced contest outcomes that determined the next nominee.[131]

Within the new system, frontline reporters claimed a more visible role, acting as "talent scouts" for audiences during the (in)visible primaries.[132] Elite journalists long prided themselves on their influential role as the fourth branch of government, and they were determined to learn from mistakes of the recent past. In advance of the 1976 presidential campaign, they promised to concentrate on issues instead of campaign pseudo-events and to forgo the horse race mode for precision journalism, but despite these commitments, during the campaign's nascent stages elite political reporters lapsed into the sweeping horse race narrative to prognosticate on political winners and losers.[133]

On the eve of Iowa precinct caucuses in January 1976, Apple traded his detached press badge for the odds-making devices of a Vegas bookie. In his page-one *Times* story on January 19, he ranked Carter atop his list of Democratic hopefuls. Though he acknowledged early media perceptions influenced outcomes, he persisted in reporting the expectations game, only hedging to admit his "early calculations were highly speculative."[134] Until the Jefferson-Jackson Day Dinner, Carter's candidacy was a brief footnote in the national coverage of the (in)visible primaries, which instead focused on speculation about probable frontrunners in the absence of party leaders, such as Humphrey and Kennedy. But Apple's analyses marked a shift in journalistic attention to early polling indicators of projected leaders and contributed to increased coverage of Carter's grassroots efforts and the construction of the Washington outsider as the frontrunner in Iowa by consensus-minded frontline reporters, the bicentennial campaign's key kingmakers. As Drew suggested, Apple's stories—what some fellow reporters critiqued as speculative "puff pieces"—and echoing national coverage afforded Carter the edge in Iowa and by extension the Democratic primaries.[135] However, Apple's stories elicited one potential downside for Carter's presidential ambitions, as Jordan acknowledged: "After that poll . . . we *had* to win Iowa."[136]

Though Carter and his advisors needed to manage expectations in the aftermath of Apple's analyses, they were thrilled to receive the positive coverage they had sought since crafting their initial media strategy in November 1972. After skillfully maneuvering to gain national exposure to increase name recognition through news media, Carter's imagecraft apparatus—the campaign's organizational, publicity, and advertising machinery producing the words, sounds, and images contributing to the candidate's official political persona, and the personnel who served as liaisons with political journalists and the general public by controlling access, managing rapport, and negotiating mediated images—sought to seize the advantages that early national coverage afforded, most importantly consensus advancement of Carter's persona as a victorious, antiestablishment underdog. On the eve of the Iowa caucuses, while other political actors made last-ditch efforts around the state, they intended to amplify this image by stationing Carter in the nation's top media hub to await the outcome of the bicentennial campaign's first political contest. From that strategic site, Carter relished his emerging status as the Democratic frontrunner. "I remember one of the turning points in the campaign was when [Johnny Apple] wrote an article in the top headlines in the front page of the *New York Times* saying Carter was leading in Iowa," he recalled.[137] In the coming days, Carter and his imagecraft apparatus recognized that they had perceptively tapped into the mood of the nation as the down-home "Ramblin' Man," but amid the shifting milieu in American journalism, they discovered that the pious political actor struggled in his personal campaign with the nation's most important kingmakers, frontline reporters.

4

Man to Beat

Antiestablishment Underdog Exploits Horse Race Bias

"Hard to believe," Carter mumbled as he munched a cheeseburger in his Orlando suite. Elite *New York Times* reporter R. W. Apple Jr. had framed the peanut farmer-physicist for president as the man to beat in advance of the Iowa precinct caucuses, but despite coalescing conjecture from frontline reporters in the rush to judge the bicentennial horse race, Carter had remained the antiestablishment underdog until this moment in the eyes of more cautious veterans.[1] Nevertheless, inspired by a page from Theodore White's *The Making of the President, 1960,* his imagecraft apparatus exploited this political reality when they staged a limited-access pseudo-event on the night of the Florida primary for the benefit of the most prominent campaign agenda-setters in the 1976 cycle—CBS News anchor Walter Cronkite and campaign canon-inspired frontline pool reporters.[2]

News cameras captured the scene as Carter and his surrogates huddled around media sets to bear witness to the peanut farmer's fate, and as if on cue, they delivered flawless backstage performances to audiences of elite campaign reporters—and, by extension, their American audiences. Eight-year-old Amy, the veteran politicker, joyously clapped her hands to news of favorable incoming returns, and minutes later campaign director Hamilton Jordan belted out a rebel yell and offered press aide Betty Rainwater an exuberant embrace when industry leader CBS News, feeling competitive pressures, projected the former Georgia governor as the victor an hour after polls closed. Downstairs in the hotel lobby, Carter's campaign staff placed long distance calls to loved ones. "Did you hear?" they asked as campaign reporters listened in.[3]

"This finishes [George] Wallace, that stinker," Miss Lillian exclaimed to an

AP reporter when she heard news over the local Plains radio station. "I was praying, but I didn't expect him to beat Wallace."[4] As Carter's beloved mother attested, many consensus-minded observers had considered the antiestablishment underdog's campaign a longshot weeks earlier, but heeding the cautionary tale of 1972 Democratic frontrunner Ed Muskie, who "lost" after failing to meet expectations of elite reporters, her son's staff cunningly deployed expectations to their advantage to construct a victor against all odds.[5]

Longshot presidential contenders of the last two decades had harnessed national exposure accompanying victories in key primary contests, but after George McGovern's rise in the 1972 election cycle amid a climate of reform, Carter's advisors recognized the enhanced status of frontline reporters as visible presidential power brokers and sought to take advantage of their expanded role in determining winners in political contests that now decided the party nomination's outcome.[6] After exploiting their grassroots media campaign for national exposure in the (in)visible primaries, Carter and his advisors continued to take advantage of favorable media modes and frames during the primary season.

And, though they struggled to handle unanticipated challenges, such as the emergence of an enigmatic label amid intense scrutiny from national reporters and lagging funds to counter adverse images with their showbiz-inspired campaign, they succeeded in harnessing the psychological advantage accompanying national coverage of early victories to become the man to beat after the Florida primary and in establishing a new campaign blueprint, including the strategy of sequence, for future presidential aspirants.[7] But, while new political power brokers focused on these campaign battles, their audiences missed the emerging election story—political apathy.[8]

★ ★ ★

Since midcentury, imagecraft apparatuses had orchestrated campaign pseudo-events to attract national exposure toward their candidacies, but now party insiders and campaign strategists staged limited-access events for the benefit of primary gatekeepers and agenda-setters.[9] Prior to the Iowa precinct caucuses in January, for instance, Democratic state party chairman Tom Whitney had recognized, after McGovern's dark horse rise four years prior, that post-reform frontline reporters were prone to pay closer attention to the bicentennial campaign's first political contest, and he sought to forever engrain the state in national political conversations by constructing a limited-access pseudo-event to magnify attention from elite reporters.[10]

Inspired by media spectacles accompanying party conventions and election night, Whitney organized the state caucus return headquarters at the Des Moines Hilton with up-to-the-minute returns from each of Iowa's ninety-nine counties and party sources to offer analysis for campaign reporters on hand. And, though cost-conscious network executives did not erect special studios or anchor booths for the emerging political showcase, they stationed producers, cameramen, crewmembers, and correspondents, alongside print news colleagues to offer live coverage of the bicentennial campaign's first hard news event.[11]

Exploiting showbiz tools, "the P. T. Barnum of electoral politics" choreographed the type of pseudo-news event Daniel Boorstin described in *The Image* (1961)—a meticulously orchestrated happening designed to be reported and reproduced, and party insiders, elite reporters, and presidential contenders on site enacted dramatic, front-stage performances from well-prepared scripts.[12] Whitney even offered a postmodern touch to raise funds for the state party—a media-watching event organized for local spectators willing to cough up $10 each to watch celebrity correspondents deliver the live story as the dramatic action unfolded, and the studio audience, in turn, clamored for just one moment in the national spotlight as cameras panned to crowd shots at the return headquarters. Each political actor gained a modicum of influence, power, prestige, and, in some cases, financial reward from the symbiotic pseudo-event.

After concluding intense eleventh-hour blitzes, early favorites, such as Birch Bayh and Mo Udall, exploited free exposure at the site of political action that evening, but eager to avoid being viewed "in a goldfish bowl," yet nevertheless hoping to amplify attention from the strong finish, Carter's imagecraft apparatus stationed him in New York, the nation's top media market, to interpret results to celebrity correspondents and their vast network audiences the following morning.[13] Powell facilitated the media tour after Apple placed Carter atop his list of projected frontrunners in Iowa, and news outlets that once had dismissed the dark horse candidate made every effort to secure interviews with the rising star, who they increasingly positioned as the frontrunner for the Democratic nomination.[14]

The strategic maneuver proved an immediate success. Carter made "the rounds on all the morning shows," and much as his imagecraft apparatus intended, informed by newswire bulletins, consensus-minded correspondents declared him the victor, asking him to interpret the Iowa results.[15] By nightfall, Cronkite, "the most trusted man in America," echoed earlier reports: "The Iowa voters have spoken, and for the Democrats, what they said was 'Jimmy Carter.'"[16] Though 37.1 percent of the fifty thousand caucus delegates still were uncommitted, NBC News correspondent Charles Quinn emphasized the symbolic importance of Carter's victory: "The candidates were really not after delegates here in Iowa. What they were after was a boost—some momentum to carry them into the primary battles ahead, and a big boost is exactly what Jimmy Carter got here."[17]

As Cronkite's colleague Roger Mudd assessed, Carter "was the clear winner in this psychologically important test,"[18] but the commentator and his colleagues, blinded by the industry's horse race bias, missed the more important angle—Carter's campaign manipulated elite daily reporting modes and frames to secure an important victory, and now they staged a triumphant media tour to amplify the appealing image of the victorious underdog, which gained resonance in contemporary American culture.[19] Moreover, this strategic maneuver signaled the campaign's shift to a more centralized, controlled media strategy that sought to harness free exposure, a transformation that eventually grated the nerves of many pack members.

As one chronicler contended: "Television had brought Jimmy Carter to the nation,"[20] transforming the peanut farmer-physicist for president into "an instant media star," and his imagecraft apparatus took advantage of network news to amplify his political persona as a triumphant dark horse and to deliver a salient message of moral reform to the American public. When the dust settled from his staged victory lap, Carter had received five times as much post-caucus broadcast coverage as his competitors, and the dominant medium had delivered a conclusive message inspired by the sports page— Carter was the "big winner" in Iowa and the frontrunner moving forward into New Hampshire.[21] Cultural observers claimed that "Carter put Iowa on the map" for all future presidential aspirants.[22] In reality, political insiders and campaign chroniclers elevated the status of the Iowa caucus for their mutual benefit, but for the moment, they were content to credit the victory to the longshot dark horse.

Witnesses to the 1976 campaign contended that the longshot candidacy was a "natural" sensation "for the early primaries. . . . making good news copy." Carter "fill[ed] a vacuum" in American politics, one Washington insider explained to *New Yorker* journalist Elizabeth Drew, and his "style, image, and message . . . met the needs of the media."[23] In the final analysis, as the insightful source suggested, all reporters yearned for a sensational story, and influenced by pressure to offer decisive analysis to compete with breaking news delivered by broadcast correspondents, many elite print journalists constructed narratives that exploited the drama of the horse race and projected Carter as the underdog frontrunner.[24]

Despite criticism from political scientist James David Barber and industry leader David Broder, who warned that the horse race mode was not necessarily reflective of reality, many elite campaign reporters, succumbing to deadline pressures and profit-driven news values, painted Carter as the frontrunner in the Democratic race.[25] "Former Gov. Jimmy Carter of Georgia found himself widely regarded today as a major contender for the Democratic Presidential nomination as late reports from last night's Iowa precinct caucuses gave him a solid victory," Apple explained in his summary lede.[26] Though he cautioned readers that it remained to be seen how Carter might fare in upcoming primary states, such as New Hampshire, based on evidence gleaned from precinct caucuses and early reaction from party insiders, such as DNC chairman Robert Strauss, he stressed that Carter "would be a major factor in 1976." The consensus-minded pack again echoed Apple's lede. For instance, one UPI correspondent observed that Carter "bolted to a fast start in the Democratic presidential race" following his "lopsided win."[27] Though the UPI story acknowledged that this preliminary step in the state's delegate-selection process was largely "symbolic," the wire reporter amplified the most powerful, but problematic, aspect of the horse race mode— frames of political winners and losers.

After deadline pressures faded, more cautious veteran reporters acknowledged that Iowa was not the landslide victory that many sensational daily reporters initially suggested. Though the consensus-minded pack, pressured by deadlines and profit-driven, drama-ridden news values, stressed that Carter defeated Bayh by a margin of two to one with more than 27 percent of the vote, more responsible reporters noted that fewer than fifty thousand Iowans participated in the precinct caucuses' first round, and more than 37 percent of these delegates were uncommitted.[28] Moving forward, the *Christian Science Monitor*'s Washington bureau chief, Godfrey Sperling Jr., encouraged readers not to be "too influenced by the headlines that doubtless will be hailing each new primary as a great victory or a great failure." Grappling with campaign journalism's post-reform vetting role, he maintained that elite political reporters were not cigar-smoking fat cats wielding undue power, but products of an industry that valued drama, conflict, and novelty. Under these systemic conditions, they were prone to "lose . . . perspective and read too much importance into what takes place." The conundrum, Sperling admitted, was the potential for these "on-the-scene interpretations of election results [to] take on a life of their own. . . . That is they sometimes become the 'reality.'"[29]

As Sperling incisively indicated, early contests represented critical political junctures, intervals at which candidates, such as Carter, fought on the ground for votes and delegates, but they also signaled moments of message negotiation, when campaign strategists and trail reporters clashed over who controlled the narrative and its determinant impression on constructions of image and truth. In the final analysis, introspective frontline reporters agreed on one important fact: the news media's frontrunner frame offered Carter's campaign a tremendous "psychological advantage," but the characterization also placed a heavy burden on Carter's staff as they struggled to manage media expectations and scrutiny moving forward.[30]

★ ★ ★

With the mushrooming pack trailing their grassroots campaign through New Hampshire, Carter and his advisors encountered new queries from horse race-obsessed frontline reporters about expectations greeting the emergent frontrunner. "There's only two choices," Carter brashly explained after shaking hands with potential voters outside a Manchester shoe factory on January 20: "Either you're a front-runner or a loser."[31] Acting in accordance with the campaign's earlier strategy, Carter projected a more cautious attitude at a press conference later in the day: "One state's results out of 50 is certainly a premature basis on which to predicate who is and who isn't a front-runner in the final election."[32] Recognizing the continued necessity of managing speculation, Carter's strategic posturing concerning overriding expectations "haunting" his campaign less than a week later suggested a strategic intervention. "[The frontrunner label] does put extraordinary expectations on me," he told the AP in Keene, New Hampshire, "I don't know what to do."[33] Based on Carter's comments, influential *New York Times* political columnist Tom Wicker reflected on campaign reporters' enhanced post-reform role and potential consequences of their horse race mode: "If he does not do as well . . . as the press perception suggests that he will do, his campaign could be badly damaged."[34]

As McGovern's candidacy demonstrated, frontline reporters biased toward prevailing news values and modes that privileged the drama of the presidential horse race were prone to analyze the dark horse's triumph, but after the presidential credibility crises in the prior decade, they believed readers demanded additional scrutiny of frontrunners, including intensive character examinations.[35] "The electorate was interested in character in 1976—not surprising, in light of the fact that voters had bought experience at the expense of character in 1968 and 1972. . . . The press, too, no doubt in large measure because it had been burned so badly by [Richard M.] Nixon, was taking an extra-close look at character," well-respected *Washington Post* veteran political reporter Jules Witcover wrote, justifying magnified probes toward all candidates and the intense scrutiny frontrunners encountered.[36]

The dark horse's "sudden rise" prompted frontline reporters to immediately examine the former Georgia governor's antiestablishment campaign, his issues stances, and his background.[37] For instance, the morning after many pro-life delegates pledged their support for Carter in Iowa, CBS *Morning News* anchor Bruce Morton broached possible contradictions in Carter's stance on abortion, and the following day a *Christian Science Monitor* reporter appraised the alternative partisan news media's mounting skepticism toward Carter's candor.[38] Based on his experience covering McGovern in the 1972 election cycle, the *Baltimore Sun*'s Washington correspondent, Carl Leubsdorf, explained the intense scrutiny Carter encountered as the dark horse frontrunner: elite national reporters largely had ignored the antiestablishment underdog's unconventional campaign in the (in)visible primaries, and Carter had "bask[ed] in the uncritical glow of local newspaper and television coverage" as his grassroots media campaign in Iowa and elsewhere earned "support and favorable [local] press." "Now that is over," Leubsdorf aptly contended.[39]

Even before Leubsdorf placed the finishing touches on his column, elite newsmagazine writers, such as *Newsweek* staff writers Tom Mathews and Eleanor Clift, conferred on the new mode of coverage accompanying the emergent frontrunner's campaign. And, after reviewing "the state of [Carter's] plans and organization in Florida" and "points of contradiction and controversy" surrounding his campaign, they jotted down handwritten notes about

Carter's "haziness" on issues, such as amnesty and abortion, which signaled that he was an "expedient politician," alongside a quote from Jordan, who told frontline reporters "if [Carter] can't stand up to this type of scrutiny, he doesn't deserve to be president."[40] Post-reform media scrutiny constituted a new strategic condition that Carter's advisors confronted as they assembled their primary imagecraft apparatus.[41]

Many observers of the bicentennial campaign concurred with the assessment of one well-respected *Atlantic Monthly* correspondent—Carter's advisors possessed a relatively sophisticated understanding of the national news media. More than any presidential candidate since Kennedy, Carter had studied "the inner workings of the press," and based on insights gleaned from required readings and personal experience, Carter and his advisors had recognized that assembling a skilled imagecraft team would be vital to their efforts to effectively negotiate increased scrutiny from elite reporters at establishment news media outlets.[42] Consequently, as funds for their long-shot campaign materialized, they hired three instrumental staff members—campaign aide Greg Schneiders, press director Rex Granum, and television advisor Barry Jagoda.[43]

With Schneiders taking over in the role of utility player on the trail, Powell managed media relations and appearances with assistance from Rainwater, Granum, and Jagoda.[44] Each new hire provided vital support, but as the bicentennial campaign became an increasingly important news story, Jagoda offered invaluable advice about how to exploit favorable tendencies across news media.[45] "The differences between the people who are involved in magazine, periodical journalism and wire service journalism or daily journalism and television journalism are profound because their decision-making processes are very different, the assumptions are different," he recognized, encouraging Carter's advisors to meet each medium's specialized needs.[46]

Based on personal experiences and examinations of post-reform presidential politics in the 1972 primaries, Carter's advisors anticipated enhanced scrutiny from elite reporters comparable to that accompanying McGovern's dark horse rise. Hence, Powell warned of anticipated inspections and attempted to construct a campaign panopticon to isolate and mitigate coverage that might threaten Carter's meticulously constructed political persona. "As the campaign progresses, Jimmy Carter will undergo tough and legitimate scrutiny of his position on the issues, his record as Governor of Georgia, his campaign for Governor and his present campaign. This is as it should be," Powell wrote, admitting that Carter garnered "accurate and balanced" treatment during the (in)visible primaries. But he acknowledged shifting conditions and warned his imagecraft team to be wary of adversarial activist media and partisan coverage that "lacks substance and truth," citing recent clips from conservative columnists Rowland Evans and Robert Novak.[47]

Despite continued efforts to develop cozy relationships with elite reporters and pundits, at this critical juncture the campaign regarded prominent political journalists, such as Broder and conservative columnists Evans and Novak, as emerging enemies. This view was based on the journalists' recent probing analyses.[48] Though Carter's advisors were prepared for investigative scrutiny, they exacerbated tensions with adversarial partisan pundits and cynical frontline reporters, who were leery of Nixon-inspired media strategies, with their aggressive news management techniques, which included memos of admonishment and attached line-by-line rebuttals.[49] Moving forward, they struggled to negotiate the barrage of en vogue investigative scrutiny from cynical veterans and antiestablishment-minded newcomers at mainstream and alternative media sources and the ferocity of political attacks from adversarial partisan pundits, who collectively harbored deep distrust toward all political actors and skepticism toward the motives of southern politicians.

★ ★ ★

Leubsdorf's recent analysis was revelatory—"After a year in which [Carter] was helped by a virtual free media ride, [he] now may be damaged even more by 'revisionist' reporting that will tend to tear down his earlier image." He contended that the peanut famer-physicist for president's "non-political image" might be replaced by the vision of an opportunistic politician "who evades and reverses himself at least as much as the others."[50] In the coming days, despite Powell's warnings, the scrutiny and salvo of political attacks continued as consensus-minded frontline reporters deconstructed Carter's rockin', down-home image and asserted that his warm smile bore the Ultrabrightened glisten of a "Janus-faced politician."[51]

While Powell and his staff considered strategic efforts to manage adverse coverage from elite regulars, they encountered a barrage of scrutiny from an unforeseen source—investigative freelance correspondents yearning for career advancement, the stable of regular content producers for national magazines. Nevertheless, a familiar foe, former *Atlanta Constitution* editor Reg Murphy, delivered the first major threat to Carter's candidacy, an assault to his credibility, in the traditional progressive journal of opinion *New Republic*'s mid-February profile, "The New Jimmy Carter."[52] As the title suggested, in a style inspired by Joe McGinnis, the elite state reporter, seeking to advance his career with the national freelance assignment, deconstructed Carter's Nixon-inspired brand of showbiz politics, claiming that his image-craft apparatus manufactured the "charming Populist reformer with an impeccable reputation." "To Georgians, the idea of Carter as a presidential candidate is hilarious . . . ," Murphy pounced. "Plastic surgeons have made him a national figure. The boys on the bus haven't had a chance to look into his background and administration yet. When they do, they won't be quite as tempted to produce a papier-mâché mask because political campaigns aren't covered that way anymore—thank goodness."[53]

Murphy's piece signaled the first wave of fashionable deconstructions by magazine freelancers who interrogated the authenticity of Carter's political persona and the credibility of his claims, but the characterization by the old foe was tame when compared to the one unveiled by a recent Yale Law School graduate. In "Jimmy Carter's Pathetic Lies," *Harper's Magazine* contributor Steven Brill engaged in a James Barber/Joe McGinnis-inspired character analysis of a "real-life enlightened Southerner."[54] Inspired by seminal texts in the campaign canon and his distrust of politicians, especially those of southern descent, the twenty-five-year-old freelancer critiqued Carter's candor in the six thousand-word, seven-page magazine piece.

Relying on material gleaned from campaign insiders, such as advertising specialist Gerald Rafshoon, who admitted "the *People* picture of [Carter] shoveling peanuts was a phony," Brill scrutinized the sincerity of Carter's grassroots media campaign and revealed his meticulously cultivated heroic image as a hardworking peanut farmer "was brass" before exposing "dirty tricks" from his 1970 gubernatorial bid, exaggerated claims about his public record, and fuzzy campaign promises. In the final analysis, his act of journalistic deconstruction branded the wealthy peanut broker/nuclear engineer as a serial liar masquerading as a "salt-of-the-earth peanut farmer"/ nuclear physicist for president. "His is the most sincerely insincere, politically antipolitical, and slickly unslick campaign of the year," Brill concluded of the candidate's manufactured authenticity. "Using an image that is a hybrid of honest, simple Abe Lincoln and charming, idealistic John Kennedy, he has packaged himself to take the idol-seekers for a long ride."[55]

Despite ambitions to jumpstart his career with the investigative exposé, the novice was naive if he believed for a second that he might scoop competitive, frontline reporters. Southern-born campaign reporter Curtis Wilkie heard whispers about Brill's forthcoming probe when he commenced primary coverage in November, and at the urging of crusading editor Tom Winship, who claimed the helm of his family-owned newspaper in 1965, the *Boston Globe* published news of Brill's unflattering profile, including the most troubling assertions—the "Machiavellian ploy" involved in Carter's 1970 gubernatorial campaign and his "high regard for Alabama Governor George C. Wallace"—and, to maintain objective balance, early efforts from Carter's staff to mitigate damage.[56]

As Wilkie acknowledged, Powell requested an advance copy of Brill's piece from *Harper's* editor Lewis Lapham, and behind the scenes, the press secretary managed the campaign's first public relations crisis by supervising the development of a twenty-two-page rebuttal to be circulated to working news media.[57] "This memorandum has been compiled in the limited time available to us after we were able to obtain a copy of the article," Powell opened before launching into hard data. "There were 21 current sources used in the piece. We have contacted most of them over the past 3 days. Our findings were that the writer misquoted his sources at least 13 times and seriously distorted his sources in at least 8 instances." Powell provided his line-by-line refutation before offering a news supplement—positive coverage of Carter's public record in local and regional newspapers, such as the *Atlanta Journal.*[58]

Powell's quick-thinking, strategic political communication prompted approximately one hundred newspapers to publish rebuttal excerpts, alongside Carter's official statement—Brill's "very, very vicious" article was a "collection of lies, distortions and half truths"—and commentary from campaign surrogates, who protested the "garbage" and labeled Brill as a "liberal hit-man" or a "political hatchet-man."[59] Influenced by this public relations strategy, well-respected political journalists, such as the *Washington Star's* Jack Germond, defended the former governor, calling Brill's piece the "latest round in what has become a liberal assault on Carter perhaps unmatched in harshness and intensity in any presidential campaign of the postwar period."[60] Moreover, the strategic intervention prompted other news media outlets to examine the emergent negative tone in coverage toward the front-runner.[61] Subsequently, many accounts condemned Brill for his "hatchet job"; criticized partisan transgressors, such as Evans and Novak and left-leaning *Village Voice* columnist Alexander Cockburn, for misrepresenting Carter's campaign; and attempted to locate the sources of attacks.[62] Many concurred the main culprit was the novel brand of adversarial campaign reporting that materialized after recent credibility crises in American politics and journalism.[63] McGovern, the recent frontrunner most accustomed to encountering post-reform media scrutiny, suggested that Powell's nascent Nixon-inspired crisis management techniques ensured that Brill's piece was "a popgun not a bombshell."[64]

But popgun fire still smarted, consensus-minded campaign reporters aptly suggested when evaluating the damage inflicted. Some crusading newspapers, such as the *Globe,* offered primary placement to the sensational story while burying news of the candidate's progress in the presidential horse race, *New York Times* ombudsman Joseph Lelyveld suggested, neglecting to turn his microscope inward.[65] Adversarial reporters, such as his southern-born colleague Jim Wooten, were biased against strident news management techniques, and Powell's aggressive rebuttal prompted them to engage in a new brand of combative transparency, offering readers a glimpse inside raw private exchanges with the candidate. "'I've read it,' Mr. Carter growled, his eyes turning cold in the glare of the television lamps. 'He said he was coming down to gut us, and he has had a close association with our opponents. What else could you expect?' Then he moved toward the door, . . . the smile had magically reappeared," Wooten wrote, demonstrating Carter's vulnerability as frontrunner.[66]

Moreover, as *Texas Monthly* editor James Fallows asserted, sensational character profiles prompted an echo effect in the media landscape.[67] Birch Bayh and U.S. Senator Henry "Scoop" Jackson's opposition campaigns in New York and Florida distributed copies of Brill's piece to attack Carter's authenticity, while other political enemies took to the air to ignite a new wave of attacks.[68] "TV news, in particular, often acts as a *Reader's Digest* of what the magazines have been printing," Fallows astutely maintained, and only a fortnight after news of Brill's piece broke, Cronkite introduced a news package about the latest assaults facing the frontrunner: "It's axiomatic that when you are out in front, you become a target. Jimmy Carter . . . now finds himself a target, and old campaign rhetoric and old political enemies are haunting him."[69] Subsequently, CBS News correspondent Ed Rabel unveiled his investigation into Carter's alleged inconsistencies: "Judging by appearances, he is still the same man that he was a year ago . . . but for Jimmy Carter the presidential campaign isn't the same any more. Carter's victory in the Iowa caucus proved to be a mixed blessing focusing attention on him, but also offering him a share of notoriety."[70]

Rabel's story offered a fitting illustration of that "mixed blessing," featuring promotional quality B-roll of Carter engulfed by admiring throngs at a campaign rally juxtaposed with tape of former Georgia governor Lester Maddox, a forthcoming third-party presidential contender, who lambasted his longtime political enemy: "Jimmy Carter is a fraud; he's a total fraud."[71] To maintain objective balance, Rabel offered interview footage with Carter, who rebutted Maddox's claims: "Everybody in Georgia that knows about politics has always understood that Lester Maddox and Jimmy Carter have been bitter political opponents." However, conforming to the era's investigative impulse, the hard-hitting watchdog reporter interrupted: "But you didn't disavow Maddox or Wallace." "That's right," Carter replied. "George Wallace was not running for anything in 1970." Rabel interjected once more: "Some people are saying that it was a racist campaign. . . ." "I don't believe that anybody has ever insinuated that," Carter retorted. "I never have seen anybody claim that I ran a racist campaign or ever made a racist remark." "How would you characterize the campaign to win the primary election," Rabel countered. "Well, obviously successful," Carter replied with a smile.[72]

Though Rabel privileged fairness and balance as a broadcast correspondent, practicing the industry-standard objective journalism, his reporting perpetuated opposition attacks and inquiries into Carter's candor. "The questions being raised about Jimmy Carter have caused his campaign to be bombarded with charges that he is playing fast and loose with the truth . . . that he is intentionally deceptive. . . . Even Carter supporters have privately begun to grill him intensely on where he stands, and Carter's staff people have spent much of their time recently defending their man. Publicly, at least, Carter doesn't seem to be worried," Rabel explained before producers cut to the package's final sound bite. "It's a compliment that I am now the subject of scrutiny. . . . it hasn't caused me to lose any sleep," Carter confidently contended.[73]

Carter's assertion belied the anxiety that the media-anointed frontrunner and his advisors bore from this in-fashion wave of interrogation to his public record and private life. After studying the new rules of U.S. politics, they recognized they would confront probes similar to those encountered by Muskie and McGovern's 1972 primary campaigns, but after their extensive efforts to curry favor with elite reporters, they were unprepared for the intensity of the examinations offered by adversarial journalists more intent to vet character in the aftermath of the presidential abuses in the Johnson and Nixon administrations.[74] Furthermore, though their moderate Democratic campaign expected attacks from liberal and conservative columnists, right-wing activist media, and lingering partisan newspapers, such as William Loeb's *Manchester Union-Leader,* they encountered unanticipated assaults from adversarial editorial cartoonists, such as the *Globe*'s Pulitzer Prize-winner Paul Szep, and left-leaning alternative forums, such as the *Village Voice.*[75] For instance, based on a *New York Times*/CBS News poll indicating the frontrunner's strategic, nonideological message was "equally favored by liberals, conservatives and moderates," Szep roughed out "Three Versions of Jimmy Carter," his satirical parody critiquing the candidate's credibility in the adverse fashion Carter's advisors feared—projecting the image of an enigmatic, opportunistic politician and disingenuous huckster.[76]

Despite unexpectedly harsh criticism toward the candidate, who like his party was struggling to find a winning message, Carter heeded his campaign strategy and told reporters that if he could not "answer the detailed questions that are put to me in a reasonable way, then I don't deserve to be President."[77] But, internally, an us-versus-them mentality developed. Moreover, to combat continued scrutiny and an emergent adverse, enigmatic image, his advisors focused on sustaining his grassroots media campaign by generating a massive volume of donations through nontraditional forums, a new necessity in the age of campaign finance reform.

★ ★ ★

In a post-reform landscape, presidential candidates depended on free media from grassroots media campaigns in Iowa, but moving forward, as finances allowed, they gradually turned to one of the primary tools of showbiz politics—Madison Avenue-inspired personal advertising campaigns—to cover more ground in advance of successive caucuses and primaries. This reality was not lost on veteran reporters, who analyzed the trend in presidential campaigns.[78]

"The TV spot is to the Florida primary what the handshake was to New Hampshire: an absolute necessity," Mudd explained. "Because the distances are so great here, the politicians are relying on television and radio ads to cover the ground, and the media expenditures for this 4-week campaign will easily exceed a million dollars."[79] Mudd's primary source, premier political filmmaker Charles Guggenheim, explained that expensive television spots were now the "primary advertising vehicle" for presidential campaigns. "It's an expensive business . . . but we are stuck with it," Mudd chimed in with his discerning assessment of the post-reform political landscape.[80]

Comprehending growing resentment toward increasingly slick, negative spots in a post-reform campaign climate, Carter's imagecraft apparatus incorporated five-minute cinéma-vérité spots through limited broadcast blitzes in Iowa and New Hampshire. These were financed by campaign contributions generated through celebrity endorsements and benefit concerts in the (in)visible primaries, but now the campaign navigated two emerging challenges to its shrewd primary plan—resistance by some broadcast affiliates, such as NBC's WBZ-TV in Boston, to airing the campaign's lengthy spots and dwindling funds to purchase expensive television time. The former challenge threatened Carter's hidden secret for the New Hampshire and Massachusetts primaries, broadcasting spots featuring his grassroots media campaign in the regional media hub of Boston to reach voters in both states, and Rafshoon navigated the hurdle by immediately filing a complaint with the FCC.[81] To negotiate the second challenge, Carter's staff returned to a proven showbiz tactic—celebrity endorsements. But they waged their fundraising drive through a relatively unorthodox primary campaign channel, the celebrity campaign fundraising telethon.[82]

Jordan was apt in his earlier assessment that in the age of campaign finance reform fundraising was key to a candidate's success since it contributed directly to the effectiveness of the campaign's imagecraft.[83] With this in mind, Carter's staff planned to broadcast "Georgia Loves Jimmy Carter," a five-hour Valentine's Day fundraising telethon featuring national celebrities, ranging from comedian Pat Paulsen to Southern Rock singer-songwriter Gregg Allman and "King of Soul" James Brown, from Atlanta's WAGA studios to Georgia's six major markets.[84] Extending the (in)visible primary fundraising strategy, Carter's campaign advised local supporters to purchase $25 tickets to join the live studio audience or $10 tickets to attend television-watching parties across the state.[85]

Building on party tradition, Carter's staff engaged in a tactic perhaps only envisioned by literary journalist Norman Mailer—they incorporated political patronage into celebrity telethons.[86] Under the direction of Jack Watson and S. Stephen Selig III, Carter's Atlanta headquarters delivered strict instructions on how to host telethon-watching parties to television party captains selected the prior fall. Keeping in mind that elite national reporters likely would cover the event, party captains were expected to stay on theme, to raise at least $1,000 each, and to call in expected contributions. In exchange, they received an autographed copy of Carter's bestselling campaign autobiography, *Why Not the Best,* and a Jimmy Carter telethon t-shirt.[87] Though the primary purpose for the event was to raise money for media blitzes in New Hampshire and Florida, Carter's staff also sought to establish an effective state organization in advance of Georgia's May 4 primary.

In the end, the celebrity telethon was a success. Carter's campaign raised approximately $250,000 from contributions and ticket sales generated from one hundred television-watching parties and one thousand supporters in the studio audience, but celebrity endorsements and performances also inspired a new wave of volunteers and tons of free media. "It was a great outpouring," Carter told one reporter after the event, neglecting to mention that the incoming contributions would finance the penny-pinching campaign's last-minute grassroots canvasing efforts and media blitzes in New Hampshire and Florida.[88]

As one elite former newswire reporter reminded readers, Carter hoped to influence primary voters as they weighed choices in two key early contests and to "generate momentum" and a "psychological advantage" moving ahead.[89] But, quickly recognizing the limits of his grassroots media campaign, Carter's imagecraft advisors turned to the tools of showbiz politics to finance an advertising blitz promoting their personal campaign. Consequently, as families in New Hampshire and Florida clicked on the tube after dinner, many encountered two of the Carter campaign's standard thirty-second primary spots exploiting the down-home, antiestablishment underdog's salient message of moral reform.[90] Inspired by earlier underdog campaigns, the innovative spots featured telegenic footage of the peanut farmer from Plains inspecting his prized crop and addressing supporters at a campaign rally timed to optimistic, populist-infused voiceovers and the primary campaign's signature tagline, "Jimmy Carter: A Leader, For a Change."[91] They capitalized on pairing authentic images with two central campaign themes: the New South leader's commitment to the working man and the Washington outsider's pledge for reform. However, as campaign advisors and trail reporters soon discovered, many voters, cynical of consensus-minded appeals, were no longer interested in listening to Hollywood-inspired spots, even Carter's (un)celebrity campaign.

★ ★ ★

While most frontline reporters, situated at mainstream news outlets (i.e., the Big Three networks, daily newspapers, and weekly newsmagazines) with mass audiences, remained fixated on handicapping the bicentennial horse race and scrutinizing emerging frontrunners in advance of the New Hampshire primary, *Washington Post* ombudsman Charles Seib warned his audience that the campaign pack was "missing the election story."[92] Consensus-minded reporters covering early campaign efforts in Nashua and St. Petersburg were so caught up in anointing frontrunners that they failed to review the latest polling data, which suggested that, despite reforms designed to create a more transparent, inclusive electoral process, voters were cynical over recent showbiz campaigns and presidential abuses, and thus were relatively apathetic about the upcoming election. *Wall Street Journal* political reporter Al Hunt isolated the trend toward apathy after the Iowa caucuses, acknowledging the key implication: "huge numbers of Americans think it doesn't matter who wins the presidency."[93] But, biased toward profit-driven news values, most frontline reporters and the scholars trailing them focused on the drama of the next leg of the horse race, leaving only invested observers to weigh in on one of the most significant trends in presidential politics.[94]

One such individual, Lothar H. Wedekind of Annandale, Virginia, a graduate teaching assistant and master's candidate at American University in Washington, D.C., crafted a letter to the editor to the *Washington Post* praising Seib's news analysis and further critiquing a presidential "horserace handicapped by the media."[95] Though "loss of confidence in the political 'system'" was the most pressing concern, post-reform political reporting remained tethered to the profit-driven horse race mode, which constructed presidential politics as an overblown spectacle, a sporting contest featuring hundreds of reporters "on the sidelines" shadowing every movement of the candidates while "up in the stands, more than 40 per cent of voters haven't bothered to show up for the race."[96]

As *Post* editor Philip Geyelin recognized, Wedekind's extension of Seib's critique remained true in advance of the New Hampshire primary. When the modern New Hampshire primary emerged during the 1952 campaign cycle, only a handful of elite national reporters covered the "beauty contest" on the path to brokered party conventions, but after White exposed the significance of media attention from primaries in Kennedy's dark horse rise eight years later, prominent political reporters trained their eyes on early contests.[97] Moreover, in a post-reform presidential landscape, news industry experts recognized that early contests gained new significance in the nomination selection process, and as media executives funneled money and resources into covering what political experts still deemed to be the first significant campaign contest, the New Hampshire primary evolved into a media circus.

Accordingly, producers and editors stationed celebrity reporters at the center of the political stage, and two weeks in advance of the primaries frontline reporters, such as NBC News correspondent Tom Pettit, offered audiences news packages about the still crowded field of Democratic contenders and their two-fold objective: to establish a "clear-cut [national] identity and to avoid finishing way behind the others."[98] By the day of the New Hampshire primary, "the Sheraton Wayfarer teemed with newsmen and activity," trail reporter Kandy Stroud observed in her account inspired by the campaign canon. "David Brinkley swaggered by to do his radio cuts. Tom Brokaw dashed about. . . . Word had it that Walter Cronkite was downtown standing in line for election night credentials just like everyone else. NBC public relations officials circled a twenty-five-foot table pasting names on twenty type-writers that would be manned by reporters whose news operations had purchased NBC's computer election services."[99] Though those election news services discovered low turnout rates, consensus-minded campaign reporters, privileging profit-driven news values, remained unduly obsessed with leaders in the horse race.[100]

As Academy Award-winning screenwriter Paddy Chayefsky underscored in the 1976 film *Network,* cultural observers discovered that many Americans were "mad as hell." But despite their rage, most still tuned into network coverage of the sports spectacle-inspired New Hampshire primary.[101] Those that did witnessed accounts inflating the significance of New Hampshire's delegate share, but aptly noting its new role as a "psychological spring-board" in the party nomination process.[102] And though elite political reporters, such as Broder, cautioned those on the trail to avoid premature speculation about leaders in early contests, cultural forces and industry pressures prompted many to interpret the early campaign barometer.[103] The Big Three networks reported more than one hundred stories on the New Hampshire primary, and in the aftermath, despite Carter's slim six-point victory over Udall, network correspondents, constrained by pre-campaign guidelines, declared the contest a clear victory for Carter, one that might propel the frontrunner to his party's nomination.

As Pettit pronounced, Carter was now "the man to beat," and the consensus assessment by the campaign pack prompted immediate advantages in the age of reformed showbiz politics.[104] Carter enjoyed a "major boost in the only area that makes the New Hampshire primary worth the effort: national television and the press," *Baltimore Sun* rookie reporter Adam Clymer aptly expounded.[105] Subsequent coverage affirmed this fact to Carter's imagecraft advisors, and a personal exchange with a prominent national reporter suggested other strategic advantages. "After Carter won in New Hampshire, he and I were getting ready to drive over to *CBS News,* and there was a knock on our window. . . . it was Jim Wooten of the *New York Times* and he said, 'Governor Carter, I think you just won the Democratic nomination,'" Jagoda recalled. As Carter's campaign moved forward in upcoming caucuses and primaries, his imagecraft apparatus capitalized on this pervasive industry assessment and prevailing tendencies of campaign journalism—in particular, the post-reform definition of a political winner and news media's bias toward drama.[106]

Until this juncture, based on advice from his imagecraft team, Carter had attempted to curry favor with elite national reporters, but now the campaign initiated a strategic transition to a more controlled, centralized media operation customary of establishment politicians, which prioritized celebrity reporters with a broad reach and limited time with adversarial journalists. Recognizing that breaking news broadcast by industry leader CBS influenced summary news ledes for even the most influential print reporters, Carter's press staff established a news media pecking order: Walter Cronkite before Harry Reasoner, network correspondents before newspaper reporters. Apple before Wilkie. "[Carter] was hot . . . [news organizations] just had to take what they got on Carter," Rafshoon recalled. "I got a kind of kick in New Hampshire listening to a guy from ABC arguing with Jody that he had been double-crossed. I can remember a year earlier if we could have a two-minute shot with ABC, we'd have flown out of Georgia, gone up there, waited. . . . [there was] a feeling of satisfaction that now it's a case of 'rationing' his time to national media."[107]

Moving forward, Carter was not compelled to cozy up to campaign reporters he deemed as emerging adversarial enemies, as several trail reporters testified. "[On] the day of the New Hampshire primary, . . . the networks planned to accompany Carter to New York for some event. . . . But Jody Powell forgot to tell the reporters assigned to Carter that Carter's charter only had six seats. Three were allocated for the press and two were already filled. 'You'll have to flip a coin to see who gets the third seat,' Powell announced."[108] ABC News correspondent Sam Donaldson secured the coveted seat. "A general impression emerged [among reporters] that the Carter people, like other campaigns, opened and closed access depending on what they thought worked in their favor," broadcast correspondent Judy Woodruff contended, and trail reporters constrained by these emerging conditions developed deep resentment toward Carter that manifested itself in an emerging us-versus-them mentality and ensuing adversarial coverage.[109]

As the burgeoning campaign pack collectively turned their attention toward the frontrunner, mutual animosity surfaced. Amid increased scrutiny at center-stage, the irritated frontrunner critiqued the establishment news media for interfering in his personal campaign. "Can you move over," Carter barked at a network cameraman impeding his rush-hour, handshaking efforts on a busy Boston corner before, inspired by his political predecessors, brazenly confiding to a fundraiser crowd about the toll the news media inflicted on his personal campaign: "You lose that intimacy with the people. . . . It's almost impossible to maintain an intimacy with them."[110]

Despite Carter's salvo, newshounds, influenced by competitive industry pressures, now collectively crowded in to engage in fashionable deconstruction of the campaign's front- and backstage maneuvers and to gain insight into Jimmy Carter, the private man. Exceptional frontline reporters had engaged in similar acts throughout the course of the twentieth century, but in the wake of recent presidential abuses, campaign canon-inspired reporters privileged character examinations motivated by cultural anxieties and probed the moral and ethical standards for presidential leadership at the root of their query through the empirical tools at their disposal—analysis of primary campaign materials, such as stump speeches, position papers, and public opinion polls, and investigative queries into contextual sources offering insight into Carter's public record and private life.[111]

Constrained by the tight deadlines involved in daily coverage, trail reporters turned first to analysis of stump speeches, position papers, and public opinion polls, and they immediately substantiated Brill's criticism of Carter's "fuzzy" campaign promises. For instance, cognizant of opposition attacks leveled at the "waffling" candidate, Apple scrutinized recent results from a *New York Times*/CBS News poll, determined that the fuzziness charge stemmed from the candidate's effort to appeal to a wide swath of voters by standing "squarely in the middle of the ideological spectrum," and warned his audience that Carter's "ability to reconcile seemingly contradictory viewpoints" might wane moving forward.[112] Apple's analysis was prophetic. Carter's equivocating stances on social issues, such as abortion, ultimately contributed to eroding support that coincided with the fracturing of his coalition and the subsequent rise of the Religious Right.[113]

During the intervening period, elite, frontline reporters assigned to cover Carter's campaign moved forward with investigative probes into state archival documents and community sources that might offer insights into his character and presidential potential. As these intense, time-consuming examinations unfolded, they offered on-the-spot deconstructions of Carter's brand of showbiz politics. Echoing Brill, consensus-minded reporters collectively warned that in a presidential landscape determined by the "survival of the slickest," Carter donned "many faces" to attract voters from a two-party system in electoral chaos.[114] "Underneath [Carter's] Ultra-Brightened smile, the Super-Held sandy gray hair . . . [and] the pleasing drawl," Clift and Goldman concluded after their initial examination, "[Carter was a] country slicker [with a] gift for big-time politicking."[115] Faced with this new barrage of scrutiny and the coalescing of an adverse enigmatic image, the moral reform candidate harbored deep resentment toward his adversaries and, operating in a post-reform campaign landscape, continued to respond with assaults against the establishment, vindicating his nuanced campaign by contending that "old categories no longer work[ed]" and brazenly alleging the establishment news media engaged in "erroneous . . . distortions."[116] In the short term, Carter's assault to the establishment proved effective.

★ ★ ★

On the eve of the Florida primary, campaign newsmakers temporarily cast aside concerns about the conundrum of Jimmy Who. Instead, they shared a singular focus—progress in the presidential horse race. Though many elite political reporters at mainstream networks, dailies, and weeklies billed Carter as the frontrunner after victories in the Iowa caucuses and New Hampshire primary, at least one veteran remained unconvinced after Carter's defeats in the South Carolina caucuses and Massachusetts primary, suggesting that "Wallace [was] still the man to beat in Florida."[117]

Leubsdorf's assessment reminded Carter and his staff that the key to maintaining their status "as a serious, viable candidate depend[ed] to a large extent on . . . convinc[ing] the working press that [Carter could]—in fact—win the Democratic nomination," and after recent setbacks, they strategically repositioned media expectations, framing Florida as a must-win for the former Georgia governor.[118] Since the campaign's nascent stages, Carter's staff had recognized that a "serious national effort by George Wallace in 1976 could preempt [Carter's] candidacy," and with these sustained efforts in mind, they remained focused on their innovative grassroots media campaign, which involved scheduling their thirty-fifth official visit to the Sunshine State, managing canvassing efforts by their primary surrogates—the Peanut Brigade—and saturating Floridians with their cinéma-vérité spots.[119]

Anecdotal evidence and polling data suggested that after persevering through twelve- to sixteen-hour days on the trail to promote the peanut farmer as a viable southern populist candidate, the "more responsible alternative" to Wallace, Carter's campaign had made inroads in the Sunshine State.[120] "I've seen him on television," said nurse Ann Ford, "and he seems more sincere than the others."[121] Recorded sentiments from like-minded Floridians represented the fruits of Carter's grassroots media candidacy. "[By Florida], Carter had it all down to a science," *Time* staff writer Stanley Cloud recalled. "He would hand out brochures with one hand and shake hands with the other. He would look each voter in the eye, talk to them, and . . . make a contact each time."[122] Precision trail reporting proved prescient. In what the news media framed as a dramatic triumph, Carter delivered devastating blows to Wallace's and Jackson's campaigns, a win his advisors had deemed necessary in their first strategic memorandum.[123] As Carter's son Chip recalled: "Iowa turned the corner, but Florida kept us going."[124]

During the (in)visible and early primary seasons, Carter and his staff labored tirelessly to gain national name recognition and to construct their media brand as a triumphant underdog, and they largely succeeded. As Witcover noted in his 1976 campaign biography, "the political prize in the early [contests] of 1976 was not delegates, but acceptance—by the media, by the other politicians, and to a lesser extent by the public—of the seriousness of the candidacies."[125] Carter and his advisors recognized this new post-reform rule of U.S. politics and, for future contenders, established a primary strategy of sequence that capitalized on "big mo [momentum]" from news media.[126]

In Florida's aftermath, one veteran campaign reporter at a popular mainstream daily observed that the days of Jimmy Who were over, and Carter's advisors framed the front-running dark horse as the presumptive nominee.[127] Both assessments were premature.[128] Though the once little-known politician no longer combatted a negligible name recognition rate, as the media-anointed frontrunner, he and his advisors negotiated scrutiny from frontline reporters searching to uncover who Jimmy Carter really was. And moving beyond the Sunshine State, the campaign was forced to clarify Carter's issues stances, to combat misinformation surrounding his southern roots and faith, and to renegotiate favorable relations and images with establishment news reporters amid a coalescing Stop Carter movement.[129]

5

Front-Running Dark Horse Encounters Resistance

While Carter prepared for "the biggest test" of the primary season, fellow Georgian Jack Davis, a founding cartoonist for the popular satirical magazine *MAD,* roughed out several cover art samples for *Time* editor-in-chief Hedley Donovan.[1] At the behest of prominent national advertiser Coca-Cola president J. Paul Austin, Donovan had offered Carter his first major national exposure by featuring him on a May 1971 cover as the "New South" leader who "whistled a different tune," and almost five years later he focused the March 8, 1976, cover story on the front-running dark horse in advance of Florida's "showdown."[2] Detached editors posed the query revealed in the cover line: "Who is Jimmy Carter and why do they love/hate him?" Inside, staff writers, such as Stanley Cloud, decreed in characteristic *Time*speak that Carter was "not just peanuts"; he was a serious frontrunner.[3] *Time*'s interpretative, synthesis-minded staff writers, inspired by political scientist James David Barber's call for character assessments and author Teddy White's and Joe McGinnis's backstage accounts, sought to uncover Carter's true nature and to reveal the techniques of "the men behind a front runner."[4] Recognizing the adversarial political milieu, Davis sketched the grinning candidate with a straw hat and a handful of peanuts, straddling a perplexed Democratic donkey forced to a halt by Wallace, Jackson, and Udall as Humphrey, the interested establishment leader craving one last brokered convention, glared at his foil.[5] To assist him in permanently damaging Wallace's campaign, Carter convinced several Democratic candidates not to contest Florida, but now, as Davis captured, everyone sought to obstruct the New South son's path to the nomination.[6] *Time*'s cover reflected the intense scrutiny Carter encountered as frontrunner and portended the resistance he faced from the coalescing Stop Carter movement.[7]

Carter and his staff discovered the path to the nomination was more challenging than anticipated in the ensuing days as they combatted attacks from opponents in the Anybody But Carter (ABC) movement and endured intense scrutiny from frontline reporters determined to ensure that Carter did not share personal qualities or the news management techniques of recent presidents.[8] Under these conditions, Carter's campaign negotiated an adverse enigmatic image, one painted by adversarial editorial cartoonists, partisan pundits with activist agendas, and elite reporters practicing a fashionable brand of horse race-biased investigative probes—frontline campaign journalists with whom they once attempted to cultivate rapport. As expected, media commentators and activists deconstructed images and messages of all presidential candidates, but the frontrunner encountered intense scrutiny from consensus-minded campaign reporters intent on exposing the political background, personal roots, and religious faith of the southern phenom.[9] Both parties committed mistakes as they encountered pressure from competition along the trail, but after the polls closed in the last primaries, they all contemplated Carter's survival, the resonance of his "politics of amazing grace," and the words of gonzo journalist Hunter S. Thompson, who urged voters to take "the great leap of faith."[10]

★ ★ ★

After scrutinizing the details of post-1968 reforms and the 1972 Democratic primaries, Carter's staff presciently anticipated that better-than-expected performances in Iowa, New Hampshire, and Florida would translate into momentum in the form of increased national media exposure and fundraising opportunities.[11] "The idea that the machine was everywhere was just not true. The Carter campaign ran on momentum, and the momentum from Iowa, New Hampshire, and Florida was enormous," former *Baltimore Sun* trail reporter Carl Leubsdorf said, recalling Carter's paradigm-shifting primary campaign strategy of sequence.[12]

To harness momentum, Carter's staff transitioned in early March to phase two of their primary strategy, which relied on "30–60 day campaigns that [were] heavily dependent on . . . national momentum, media and our

ability to impose a campaign structure on a state that had previously received very little attention."[13] Campaign director Hamilton Jordan's strategic memorandum outlined details about delegate allocation and tracking
strategies; plans for priming surveys that served as blueprints for ten-day
paid media blitzes intended to add depth to Carter's national image; tactics for handling lingering opponents, such as Wallace, Udall, and Jackson,
and newcomers, such as California governor Jerry Brown; and preliminary
convention organization and vice presidential vetting procedures.[14] Jordan,
at first glance, appeared to cover the strategic bases, but he neglected one
area: the impact of national exposure from free media on Carter's image.

While considering the primary's second phase, Carter and his staff did not
sufficiently predict the intense scrutiny frontrunners encountered, nor did
they envision the coalescing ABC movement mounted by the party establishment.[15] A more methodical analysis of campaign literature or a moment
of introspection might have forewarned them of these developments.[16] Relatively uncritical consensus accounts of favorite-son campaigns and nominations determined at brokered conventions were routine in the era of
smoke-filled rooms, but in a political mediascape defined by the apotheosis
of primary showbiz strategies, frontline reporters anxiously claimed more
responsibility for vetting candidates as a part of their public service watchdog role. Leading candidates, in turn, discovered that heightened media
expectations for flawless performances, greater poll margins, and increased
fundraising goals accompanied the status.[17]

Despite warnings of these conditions from campaign consultants, all
frontrunners after the 1960 campaign struggled to withstand constant media scrutiny, but early pack leaders were particularly vulnerable to intense
inspection. Opponents and reporters in this climate pounced on imper-
fections, including scandals, policy inconsistencies, and verbal gaffes, and
public opinion of the degree of error signaled to a campaign immediate
collapse, such as Democrat Ed Muskie encountered after his tearful rebuke
over intense media scrutiny in the 1972 primaries, or the challenge of an
establishment opposition movement threatening a contested convention,
such as Democratic nominee George McGovern endured at Carter's hands
at the 1972 DNC.[18]

Carter and his staff took advantage of the relatively uncritical coverage
afforded to the dark horse candidate in the (in)visible primaries while early
frontrunners, such as Bayh, Wallace, and Jackson, suffered through intense

media scrutiny, but after the Florida primary Carter also encountered un-intended consequences of the frontrunner label.[19] Material effects included a new wave of external pressures on Carter's imagecraft apparatus, which was forced to navigate increased requests from frontline reporters for information about the candidate's private life, his background, and his political record and to negotiate adverse images of an enigmatic, opportunistic politician. Mediated interrogations of Carter's political persona, spurred by the reflexive determination to avoid mistakes of the past, most notably the failure to properly scrutinize the "new Nixon," created a material, strategic obstacle for Carter's imagecraft apparatus, one requiring altered news management strategies, publicity materials, and advertising campaigns, demands they did not adequately forecast at the campaign's outset.

In the end, however, Carter and future candidates discovered that while media scrutiny of frontrunners triggered a narrowing effect in the polls, party reforms limited the effectiveness of establishment-fueled, stop-candidate movements mounted after the early primaries and reduced the likelihood of brokered conventions. By monitoring public opinion to determine campaign strategy, an outsider candidate in a crowded field instead could seize media-fueled momentum generated by early victories to become the frontrunner, who then benefited from a bandwagon effect, transforming themselves into the semi-consensual nominee.[20]

★ ★ ★

Carter and his staff only celebrated their seminal victory over Wallace for an evening; the following morning they boarded a plane bound for Illinois, the site of their next major political test.[21] Before negotiating the hastily planned six-stop, twelve-hour tour through southern Illinois coordinated after wunderkind pollster Patrick Caddell's Cambridge Survey Research data indicated undecided voters remained widespread in the region, Carter delivered a press conference at the Chicago O'Hare Airport.[22] The antiestablishment candidate told campaign reporters he was not directly challenging Chicago's Mayor Richard Daley for delegates committed to favorite son Adlai Stevenson because such an attempt was "hopeless"; instead, he sought to win up-for-grab delegates to prove his victory over Wallace in Florida was no fluke and to provide evidence that he could carry a northern industrial state.[23] Carter's posturing with establishment frontline reporters authenticated his claim that he was a political outsider, and though he contended that he was not directly challenging the establishment, his message and his primary strategy was a direct challenge to the old system, a reality the political elite well understood.

When they embarked on the blitz, Carter and his staff, conscious of McGovern's criticism of 1972 campaign reporting, expected continuing coverage of what Caddell termed the "beauty contest," a technologically enhanced form of horse race analysis accompanying U.S. presidential elections for more than a century.[24] Instead, they encountered a more incisive, adversarial mode of horse race journalism focusing intense scrutiny on how Carter was faring day to day, his performance in key events, the effectiveness of his political strategies, and the suitability of his issues stances.[25] Aware of their enhanced vetting role after party reforms, frontline reporters, in recompense for sins of the past, focused special attention on investigating the frontrunner's positions and personality.[26]

Attuned to hot button issues of the last election cycle, pack reporter Sean Toolan delivered this sort of reporting when he observed the uncharacteristic "chorus of hisses and boos" greeting Carter when he announced his position on amnesty for draft dodgers at his third campaign stop. Though Carter's position was unpopular with this particular crowd, his advisors suggested the promise to offer "blanket pardons" to Vietnam War draft evaders would placate many constituents.[27] Politicians, since Kennedy's 1960 campaign, had engaged in analogous priming strategies to promote popular policies to enhance their image, but Carter's staff, implementing Caddell's polling data and Stuart Eizenstat's issues research, now constructed nuanced positions designed to appeal to the broadest swath of voters, even on controversial issues, such as amnesty, and after reviewing issues materials and consulting public opinion polling, which indicated that approximately half of Americans approved of conditional amnesty with two years of alternative service, they settled on their campaign strategy to pardon draft dodgers.[28] And, though Toolan acknowledged the crowd's reaction to the Carter campaign's unveiling of his stance, the trail reporter neglected to dissect the political strategy involved in the nuanced position.

Despite their efforts, in this climate of establishment resistance and media scrutiny, as elite *New York Times* political reporter R. W. Apple Jr. forewarned, Carter's complex stances prompted opponents to denounce his credibility as a flip-flopping politician and journalists to critique his rhetorically facile positions.[29] To combat sustained criticisms and to "convince voters" he was "not fuzzy on the issues," Carter accepted on March 16, the day of the Illinois primary, an interview with *Washington Post* editors and reporters, who, committed to rectifying mistakes of the last election cycle, intended to probe Carter about his position on a wide variety of issues.[30] However, despite symbiotic motives, neither party satisfied detractors and criticisms of "fuzzy" stances and issue-devoid coverage lingered.[31]

★ ★ ★

After Carter defeated Wallace and minor candidates Sargent Shriver and Fred Harris to mark his fourth primary victory, despite emerging challenges to his candidacy, consensus journalists confirmed Carter was "the man to beat," but despite Carter's posturing of a two-man race, his "impressive victory" did not result in a winnowed field.[32] Instead, evidence continued to suggest the materialization of the brokered convention analysts predicted as the party establishment mounted a Stop Carter movement through the latest entrants into the presidential race, Brown and Senator Frank Church of Idaho.[33]

These developments prompted dean of political reporters David Broder to deploy horse race journalism, a reportorial mode he often denounced, to explain the intent of "the latest entrants in Democratic presidential derby" to test "their legs for future races" and to critique the power of horse race coverage to trim "political roster(s)" and to act as a "psychological springboard" for victors.[34] Contrary to Broder's assessment, however, Church and Brown desired more than a test case; they sought a path to the nomination under the new rules of American politics. Broder may have erred on this point, but his analysis of horse race journalism was spot-on. As fresh faces in the race, Church and Brown encountered relatively uncritical treatment, comparable to the early coverage of the peanut farmer from Plains, while, as frontrunner, Carter faced a new brand of inquiry.[35]

Frontline reporters were no longer solely chronicling campaign events, nor were they simply engaged in backstage deconstructions. Though critics claimed campaign reporters suffered from "the Teddy White syndrome" of over-probing the candidates' private lives, in reality they practiced an incisive, adversarial brand of campaign reporting inspired by exposure to the deconstruction of Nixon's imagecraft in *The Selling of the President*

(1969), revelations of presidential corruption by investigative journalists during the Johnson and Nixon administrations, and recommendations for character assessments by political scientist James David Barber.[36] After years of encountering sophisticated imagecraft, news management techniques, and attacks toward the news media, campaign reporters were not only conscious of these tactics, they were collectively committed to a more penetrating mode of campaign reporting involving pack probes of a presidential contender's background and character.[37] Before the emergence of a frontrunner, veterans, still reeling from their failure to thoroughly scrutinize the "new Nixon," dissected showbiz-inspired imagecraft techniques deployed by all candidates, but with the materialization of a frontrunner, with a single-minded absorption, they shifted focus to the close inspection of the public and private lives of the prime candidates to expose valid indicators of character.[38] When they focused on the front-running dark horse, they concentrated their attention on remaining areas of concern after early journalistic inspections of his southern roots, his faith, and his strategic appeals.[39]

Anxieties over Carter's ancestry nagged frontline reporters. For a generation, many political reporters gained their mentality about people of the region from two sources: required reading on the South, in particular, W. J. Cash's *Mind of the South* (1941), which offered binary images of a "proud, brave, honorable" people inclined toward "violence, intolerance, aversion, and suspicion toward new ideas," and their personal involvement in the region, which for many included brief stints of ground reporting surrounding the civil rights movement and the rise of arch-segregationist George Wallace as a serious presidential contender in the long decade of the 1960s.[40] Since these experiences shaped their understanding of the region, many consensus-minded campaign reporters shared a collective understanding of the South as being a backward region scarred by racism and ruled by romantic, hedonistic impulses.[41] Influenced by this collective mind-set, they greeted constructions of a Henry Grady-inspired "New South" with logical skepticism and scrutinized Carter's background to ensure he was not a closet racist and to gain insight into the influence of his mysterious "old-time religion."[42]

Though some perceptive frontline reporters observed the religious tenor of Carter's stump speeches during the (in)visible primaries, campaign reporters did not focus their attention on Carter's faith until they detected audience disapproval for what Jordan called Carter's "weirdo factor"—his evangelical Baptist fundamentalism. Practicing a campaign canon-inspired brand of reporting, they pinpointed conflicting strategic logics within Carter's campaign and documented campaign staff requests for Carter to tone down the religious rhetoric.[43]

As these perceptive reporters detected, Carter's staff recognized that evangelical fundamentalism had largely receded from mainstream American culture after the 1925 Scopes Trial, and though they understood approximately 60 percent of Americans identified loosely as Christian, they were concerned that Carter's pronouncement of a close personal relationship with Jesus Christ might generate a Jesus-freak image, which could alienate broad swaths of the voters they hoped to attract.[44] Carter, however, agreed with evangelical politicians, such as Wallace, Democratic governor Reubin Askew, and Republican Congress members John Anderson, Margaret Chase Smith, and Nelson Rockefeller, who testified that politics and religion could mix. From the evangelical left, Carter hoped to tap into the emerging conservative mood in the nation and to harness a coalescing religious bloc of born-again voters with his message of love and social justice.[45] His faith in this emerging coalition in mind, he refused to temper the religious overtones in his message despite staff advice.[46]

Elite reporters shining a light on Carter's "old-time religion" initially settled on references to his faith as a metaphor for his message. *Newsweek* staff writers Peter Goldman and Eleanor Clift, for instance, examined Carter's rise through his "politics of piety" in early March, and syndicated columnists, such as Richard Reeves, chimed in with commentary on Carter's strategic moral message.[47] Reeves contended that the masterful campaigner recognized that the political crisis was a "spiritual crisis, and that more symbolic communication is the best way to reach Americans drifting in an atmosphere saturated with instant communications."[48] Comparing Carter to Gandhi, Reeves considered the symbolic language of Carter's politics of love—"the symbolism of Christianity and the land" included in frequent campaign speeches about faith, family, and farming. Reeves, however, believed the antiestablishment candidate's "calculated inoffensiveness" might become a stumbling block, particularly with Washington insiders and elite reporters, who critiqued the southerner as a phony even while acknowledging he was the smartest politician they ever had encountered.[49] Moreover, many reporters and some voters were troubled by the "idea of a highly sophisticated

51-year-old man sounding like a thinking man's Billy Sunday." Reeves had a point, as Carter discovered when trail reporters zeroed in on the issue.

Carter's faith attracted minimal attention from campaign reporters until the *Washington Post's* Myra MacPherson interviewed Carter's evangelist sister Ruth Stapleton in advance of the North Carolina primary. Only then did they recognize its profound influence on his life. Stapleton had campaigned extensively on her brother's behalf through her faith-based network, and when asked about Carter's faith, she described his decision to accept Christ after his gubernatorial defeat a decade prior. *Post* editors, considering the dramatic narrative of a weeping, born-again conversion controversial after recent campaigns, asked veteran political reporter Jules Witcover to fact-check the story. Carter confirmed all details, sans the tears, en route to a reception in Winston-Salem, adding: "I spent more time on my knees in the four years I was governor . . . than I did in all the rest of my life."[50] Though Carter took great pains to assure Witcover that the conversion experience was not "mystical," but instead was "a typical experience among Christians," his response attracted the consensus-minded pack's scrutiny.[51] Probing reporters peppered Carter with questions about his faith after the reception and again the following day at a press conference in Wake Forest.

As his staff feared, Carter's off-the-cuff comments about faith became a potential liability. "It was fairly late in the [primary] campaign before it was said I was a born-again Christian," Carter recalled. "Some reporters . . . elevated the born-again part as some kind of strange, mysterious sect that receive their orders from heaven every morning. . . . They completely distorted that."[52] UPI reporter Wes Pippert agreed: "The press engaged in a pretty superficial examination of Carter's faith."[53] Pippert characterized much coverage as comparable to initial superficial reports offered by NBC *Nightly News* anchor John Chancellor, who reported that millions shared Carter's mountaintop conversion experience. Moving forward, Carter and his staff discovered that his evangelical faith and the political mobilization of like-minded Christians would be both a blessing and a curse for their political fortunes.[54]

For now, the consensus-minded pack focused on probing Carter's foreign love language, and though Carter confirmed that he strictly adhered to the fundamental Baptist belief in the separation of church and state, frontline reporters became consumed with the influence of his born-again faith on his ability to govern.[55] In "The Spirit that Moves Jimmy," for instance, conservative syndicated columnist George Will acknowledged parallel trepidation over Carter's and Kennedy's faiths. Will concluded that anxiety was triggered by potential for willy-nilly decision-making. "Every politician believes in God, or at least in the currency," he wrote, but apprehension over Carter's faith stemmed from his level of piousness. "There is a Washington doctrine about the appropriate way to pray," he acknowledged. "Prayer is fine if done in moderation. . . . But Carter prays in church, and even while at home and while campaigning, for Pete's sake." Will asserted that this tendency was disconcerting to frontline reporters and potential voters not because it belied lack of "intellectual seriousness and emotional balance," but because it meant Carter was unlike the average politician, who has "no spiritual process more complex than calculation—politicians who can be trusted to obey the First Commandment (revised): Thou shalt worship naught but the Gallup Poll." Will and like-minded souls were distressed over the idea of a politician who "might occasionally doubt the axiom, vox popull, vox del ('the voice of the people is the voice of God.')."[56] They did not consider that Carter was attuned to the voice of God *and* the people in 1976.

Broder did not doubt that Carter listened to the voice of the people. While covering the last five presidential campaigns, he had witnessed the ascendancy of candidate-centered campaigns that discerned voter preferences through public opinion polls.[57] Though he was not privy to Caddell's cutting-edge strategy of targeting voters at the precinct level, Broder recognized modern priming tactics through inconsistencies in Carter's stump speeches. After having observed these techniques deployed to unethical ends in the last administration, he was concerned about the frontrunner's "uncommon precision" at enunciating unclear positions and the "risk in nominating a man whose support is as thin [and] whose views are as unexamined . . . as Carter's."[58] This in mind, he articulated his apprehensions over the "deliberate deception[s]" of the candidate who promised to "never tell a lie" in news commentaries.

After encountering deceptions of previous administrations and Carter's truth-in-politics claims, Broder and his colleagues incisively inspected Carter's campaign to vet his credibility, but his nuanced background and complex issues stances prompted them to construct Carter as an enigmatic, opportunistic politician.[59] These industry leaders recommitted to forgoing horse race journalism in the ensuing days so they might more thoroughly scrutinize the presidential candidates' personalities and positions, but institutional pressures to conform to the horse race system remained and contributed to unforced errors by leading journalistic and presidential contenders that damaged perceptions of their credibility.[60]

★ ★ ★

Despite Broder's warnings about the dangers of horse race journalism, the dean himself was not immune from competitive pressures to engage in the mode and subsequent miscalculations. He and Witcover, conscious of the trend to embrace "objective," data-based journalism after attacks of biased news reporting from the political right *and* left, adapted nonrandom sampling techniques to gain a sense of voter attitudes about the candidates and the issues.[61] However, after spending "hours and days door knocking" in Wisconsin, the historically pivotal primary state, they succumbed to pressure to predict outcomes in the presidential horse race. Broder reported that Carter and Ford were headed for "comfortable victories." They were not.[62]

Carter made tremendous strides in the Badger State due to efforts of field operator Phil Wise, but not enough to pull off a landslide victory.[63] To the contrary, upon first glance at exit polls, prominent political scientist and elections analyst Richard M. "Dick" Scammon suggested that Udall carried the state. His assessment prompted NBC, determined to be first to declare the next victor in the primaries, to interrupt its hit Tuesday primetime program *The City of Angels* before the first commercial break with Chancellor's news bulletin of Udall's victory.[64] Faith in the projection contributed to the story's mishandling by several morning newspapers.[65] *Milwaukee Sentinel* staff, for instance, proclaimed "Carter Upset by Udall; Ford Easily Beats Reagan" in a front-page banner headline.[66] Although *Sentinel* editors corrected the mistake by the day's final edition—amending the headline to read "Carter Edges Out Udall" and including a bulletin that described the incoming voter tally that contributed to Carter's narrow victory, they could not strip the early edition from newsstands in time to keep Carter from enjoying a moment shared by his political hero Harry Truman. Smiling in celebration, he held a copy of the erring edition above his head. An AP photographer snapped a photograph of the staged moment, and the image of the victorious antiestablishment underdog circulated around the globe, helping to solidify Carter's assertion that he would be the Democratic nominee despite the efforts of a Stop Carter movement.[67] Carter celebrated another development that morning: in addition to edging past Udall, he surged ahead of Ford in the latest head-to-head Gallup Poll. But unforeseen challenges loomed.

★ ★ ★

Political journalists were not the only ones who committed unforced errors in early April. Responding to competitive pressures to win the New York and Pennsylvania primaries by bringing northern blue-collar, white ethnic voters into his fold, Carter attempted to harness Nixon's "white ethnic strategy," a primarily symbolic effort to respond to insecurities about unfavorable government policies erected in response to the civil rights movement, but Carter's initial efforts to embrace new ethnicity prompted him to commit a verbal blunder, which threatened to undermine his image as a progressive, populist reformer.[68]

After receiving materials from Catholic cleric and social justice activist Monsignor Geno Baroni, the president of the National Center for Urban Ethnic Affairs, Eizenstat and other staff members encouraged Carter to articulate a stance in support of the conservation of ethnic neighborhoods through a direct challenge to the Department of Housing and Urban Development's dispersal policy. Carter, however, botched the directive and fumbled badly in an interview with *New York Daily News* reporter Sam Roberts. In response to the query about his position on government policies to finance low-income, scatter-site housing in the suburbs, Carter said: "I see nothing wrong with ethnic purity being maintained. I would not force racial integration on a neighborhood by government action. But I would not permit discrimination against a family moving into the neighborhood."[69]

Roberts did not find the quote to be particularly newsworthy, and it appeared after the jump in graf thirteen of the page 34 story in the Sunday edition on April 2. However, Carter's deployment of the phrase "ethnic purity" troubled CBS News political editor Marty Plissner, and he pressed his colleague Ed Rabel to have Carter clarify his statement. At a press conference in South Bend, Indiana, four days later, Rabel questioned Carter "with regard to the integration question," and Carter responded at length: "I'm not going to use the Federal Government's authority to deliberately

circumvent the natural inclination of people to live in ethnically homog-
enous neighborhoods, [but] any exclusion of a family because of race or
ethnic background, I would strongly oppose."[70] Carter repeatedly declared
his support for federal and state open-housing laws, but his use of the term
"ethnic purity" and his assertion that he opposed government programs
that would "inject black families into a white neighborhood just to create
some sort of integration" astounded campaign reporters, who as a pack
continued their collective efforts to deconstruct the racial undertones of
Carter's comments.[71]

Despite warnings from staff who recognized the inflammatory nature of
his language and the potential harm it could inflict on a southern candidate
running on his progressive civil rights record, Carter maintained his position in the short term, and consensus-minded reporters announced that
the frontrunner had committed his "first big mistake."[72] They demanded
clarification over his assertion that government should "refrain from trying
deliberately to alter the ethnic composition of residential neighborhoods."[73]
They reached out to his supporters in African American communities and
to his opponents for reaction.[74] When approached by network correspondents, campaign advisor Andrew Young admitted that Carter's comments
were a "disaster."[75] "Either he'll repent, or it will cost him the nomination.
. . . I can't defend him on this," he said. Udall concurred. He told frontline
reporters that Carter's remarks were part of an intentional effort to secure
voters from Wallace by practicing the "politics of racial division . . . preaching 'ethnic purity' and voluntary busing on the white side of town and soul
brother on the black side of town."[76] Many campaign reporters agreed and,
in pieces of news analysis and commentary in mainstream and alternative
forums, asserted Carter offered code words designed to court Pennsylvania's
conservative, ethnic voting blocs in areas such as Philadelphia's Polish community. In Johnson Publishing Company's *Jet* magazine, for instance, staff
writers reported extensively on the response of national African American
leaders to the campaign controversy and echoed suggestions of Carter's critics, such as Georgia state representative Hosea Williams, to their national
African American audience: "Blacks should not forgive Carter . . . [who]
purposely made the 'slip' to lure the 'polack' vote."[77]

Behind the scenes, Carter's campaign was in chaos. Some staff members
were "disturbed" by his statements, and recognizing from the outpouring
of complaints through telephone calls, telegrams, memos, and news clips

that he had alienated members of his African American base, they were concerned over what the remarks might mean for Carter's presidential ambitions.[78] Although his closest advisors, including Rosalynn and Charles Kirbo, encouraged Carter to apologize, he insisted it was a misunderstanding.[79] Nonetheless, while he considered these entreaties, his press staff engaged in damage control by drafting a paragraph-by-paragraph response. Moreover, once Carter admitted his error, they crafted a press release including his confession about his "unfortunate choice of words," his progressive stance on racial issues while governor, and his continued support from the African American community, and they organized a press conference in Philadelphia to issue the public apology.[80] Despite these nascent crisis management efforts, Carter's gaffe took on a symbolic life of its own in a political mediascape biased toward campaign controversies.

Although the national media widely covered Carter's delayed confession, the public apology did not produce the desired outcome because of lingering saturation media coverage. Balanced news stories amplified voices of frustrated supporters who insisted Carter should apologize and opponents who claimed Carter's comments were nefarious. As NBC News correspondent Robert Hager aptly explained: "So far Carter's run an almost flawless campaign, but his ethnic purity comment could be trouble. His opponents are already taking advantage of it."[81] Moreover, after thoroughly scrutinizing Carter's confession, some adversarial-minded reporters implied that the frontrunner was disingenuous. Rabel, for instance, observed that Carter expressed regret "for using the words ethnic purity to describe his feelings, but not for the thoughts expressed."[82] Consensus-minded frontline reporters agreed that the incident would "haunt Democratic presidential candidate Jimmy Carter."[83] They understood that Carter's critics would continue to broach the incident that tapped into fears about the frontrunner's southern background and opportunistic political strategies.

Telegenic images of Carter at staged pseudo-events and analysis of his narrow victory in Wisconsin momentarily tempered critical voices. For instance, ABC news anchor Howard Smith's commentary on Carter's performance in the primaries nullified much of the blowback from Sam Donaldson's report.[84] "Yesterday, I said that Tuesday's double-header primaries slowed Jimmy Carter's bandwagon," Smith continued, speculating, "I wonder now, if considering the circumstances, they didn't speed it up some. He campaigned only one month in Wisconsin compared to Udall's one year. He spent little; Udall spent a small fortune . . . giving him [Carter] the image of someone who licked the establishment . . . the kind of image that might do him wonders in future primaries. The way he won helped—at the last minute . . . making the media, who projected his defeat and are widely considered part of the establishment, look rather foolish. . . . His defeat [in New York] does nothing to change the results of the latest Gallup Poll, which say that in the General Election, he is the only candidate who can defeat Ford."[85]

Images of Carter's victory in Wisconsin momentarily overshadowed his "ethnic purity" gaffe, but chic, watchdog reporters remained unsatisfied by Carter's justification and his defensive posturing, and they continued to interrogate the New South son's remarks. The following day, Donaldson asked Carter in a press conference if the term "ethnic purity" was almost "Hitlerian."[86] Moreover, some national reporters remained adamant that Carter's gaffe was not an unforced error at all, but rather a strategic attempt to gain the Polish vote in Pennsylvania's urban centers.[87] They contended that the mistake might cost him the nomination. "Was this one of those fatal slips that can destroy a candidate?" *Time* pondered.[88]

To combat conjecture that Carter engaged in politics of racial division, his public relations staff enlisted African American leader Jesse Hill to arrange a rally for the beleaguered candidate on April 13.[89] Carter's staff "pulled out all of the stops," Witcover reported, enlisting Martin Luther King Sr. to assure the nation that he was with Carter "all the way."[90] Influential political reporters conceded that Carter's staff staged a successful intervention, and media mention of the gaffe in ensuing days diminished. In the end, the "ethnic purity" incident revealed new tendencies of watchdog trail reporters, who offered saturation media coverage of the semantics of Carter's blunder rather than analysis of his strategic stance on the complex policy issue, and the attitude of Carter's press staff, who "viewed the entire episode [as] a ritualistic test of strength between Carter and the press rather than a search for Carter's real position on racial issues."[91]

★ ★ ★

Carter experienced a new mode of adversarial examination prior front-runners had not encountered, and perceptive reporters observed that under intense scrutiny the prime candidate struggled to remain cordial with frontline reporters amid the emerging us-versus-them milieu. "He does not seem to take kindly to close questioning, to being challenged," *New Yorker* journalist Elizabeth Drew wrote. "In his fatigue, he is unable to cover his feelings. Carter does not have a particularly good relationship with much of the press that covers him regularly. . . . Much of the press is suspicious of his style and put off by his evasions and worried about his self-righteousness."[92]

Recognizing the sustained scrutiny and emerging mutual disaffection, Carter's imagecraft apparatus exploited one of Nixon's most effective news management techniques: they limited direct media access to the candidate. In the short term, the strategy was effective, but they did not adequately anticipate their decision's lingering unintended effects. After encountering more than a decade of limited and closed press operations, frontline reporters chafed at the shift in strategy and quipped in tones reminiscent of trail reporters covering Nixon's 1968 campaign: "Even when he is accessible, he is inaccessible."[93] For the moment, the consensus-minded pack was content to laugh at the running joke that spoke to Carter's authenticity and to offer more intense scrutiny to the frontrunner, but in the coming months they attacked Carter's credibility when he broke promises of open press access.

Carter's staff, in the hiatus, recognized that "the fuzzy issue had caught up with Carter."[94] Caddell's latest polling data revealed that the public's leading negative perception of the candidate was his "wishy-washy" stances, "which inevitably unchecked will lead to perceptions of Carter as 'untrustworthy' and 'dishonest,'" the curse of doom in this milieu.[95] Based on data, which suggested the fuzzy label was contributing to soft support for Carter in Pennsylvania and beyond, Caddell issued a memo insisting "issue themes" were the "area of the campaign . . . in need of the most attention."[96] Caddell's assessment prompted Carter's imagecraft apparatus to implement strategic modifications to negotiate his adverse media image as an enigmatic, opportunistic politician and to resist additional media scrutiny.

To combat criticism that his positions straddled political lines, Carter and his staff attempted to circumvent critics by "going public" with his issues stances through a new advertising campaign in advance of the Pennsylvania primary on April 27.[97] "People said Carter wasn't talking about the issues," Rafshoon recalled. "So I re-cut [our ads] to say, 'Jimmy Carter on the issue of welfare . . . Jimmy Carter on the issue of foreign policy . . . ' [and included] a new tag, 'If you agree with Jimmy Carter on this issue, vote for him.'"[98] The thirty-second spots were simple, but effective. As Rafshoon explained, they included the text "Jimmy Carter on the issue of . . . ," before

Carter, casually dressed and lounging in his backyard, discussed his position on a particular issue and offered a segue to the relevant tag, read by the narrator: "If you agree [about said issue], vote for Jimmy Carter. A leader, for a change."[99] "That was it," Rafshoon acknowledged. "So next time Caddell does the poll, 'Oh, he's talking about the issues.'"[100] Evidence suggested that Carter's advertising shifted pubic opinion, but Carter's critics remained unconvinced, and media scrutiny continued unabated.[101]

Appreciating this reality, Carter's imagecraft apparatus staged an intervention with journalists. Carter granted additional group interviews with national news outlets to clarify his stances, but he also resorted to alternative strategies gleaned from recent campaigns.[102] "When I came down off this ladder from my campaign plane," Carter recalled, "there would be people that would come from my own campaign. They would ask me, 'Governor Carter what are you going to do about welfare, what are you going to do about education, what are you going to do about the environment, what are you going to do about defense spending?' I would turn around and answer their questions, and they would record it, and we used that in our commercials. So, it looked like it was completely extemporary, which it was as far as my answers were concerned, but the questions were staged."[103] Carter's imagecraft apparatus effectively incorporated controlled media, as Caddell's latest polling results indicated, but the success of their free media strategy at this point was debatable. Despite attempts to convince frontline journalists that his positions were well-defined, the charge lingered and attacks from critics in the Stop Carter movement kept coming.

Network correspondents dutifully reported the persistent critique and assault in advance of the Pennsylvania primary. "Here in Pennsylvania . . . the name of the game is stop Jimmy Carter," CBS News correspondent Ed Bradley reported before exploring efforts to suppress the Carter vote by Stop Carter opponents—candidate Henry "Scoop" Jackson, Mayor Frank Rizzo, and elite leaders of the AFL-CIO, "who dislike Carter because they say his record is anti-labor."[104] NBC News correspondent Don Oliver concluded that Carter's support was soft: "That means that some of the folks who like Jimmy Carter may not actually like him enough to get out and vote."[105]

Carter's campaign answered these challenges by attempting to shore up grassroots support and, in one their shrewdest staged moves of the primaries, by constructing the ABC movement as a relic of the boss system.

Carter waved his copy of a local Philadelphia newspaper in the air at a press conference in mid-April. With the front-page headline "Stop-Carter Alliance Is Formed" visible to cameras, he asserted: "I'm not going to yield anything to the political bosses. . . . I am letting the voters know that I belong to them, and not to the party bosses."[106] Carter and his imagecraft apparatus continued to implement this winning strategy until after the final primary battle, when an endorsement from an old party boss contributed to the dismantling of the Stop Carter movement, and future consultants to outsider candidates learned the efficacy of sustained antiestablishment attacks in the primary campaign.

★ ★ ★

Despite these material challenges, strategies contributing to Carter's early victories were successful in Pennsylvania's "three-man showdown." To supplement paid media blitzes, Carter made himself known to Keystone State residents much as he had before, through his grassroots media campaign. He was just a regular American, Carter told those suspicious of his southern heritage in light of recent remarks. Carter and his Peanut Brigade campaigned from dawn to dusk before cameras, shaking hands outside the Bethlehem Steel Mill in Johnstown, rallying African American voters at the Carnegie Library in Pittsburgh, and granting local media interviews across the state.

Pennsylvania was "being Carterized," and his antiestablishment, moralistic appeal resonated with voters.[107] After sustaining establishment resistance and media scrutiny, Carter's grassroots media efforts once again were greeted with positive coverage, and the outcome surpassed the candidate's expectations as he gained 37 percent of the popular vote and more than sixty delegates, nearly more than Udall and Jackson combined. "When the results were in, Scoop Jackson became the seventh Democratic contender to abandon this year's race. And Hubert Humphrey, poised and ready to take one last fling at the presidency, thought again, choked back some tears, and got out of Jimmy Carter's way," *Atlantic Monthly* reported.[108]

But *Atlantic Monthly*'s narrative synthesis did not reveal the whole story. After Pennsylvania, Carter's campaign still encountered unanticipated challenges—such as the resignation of speechwriter Robert Shrum amid allegations that Carter "was manipulative and deceitful."[109] They still faced media critics, who continued their search for the real Jimmy Carter amid increasing frustration with restricted access that accompanied Carter's victory in Pennsylvania. They endured the ABC movement, which persisted with a degree of success behind the efforts of Church and Brown in northern and western states.[110] In the end, however, the establishment's challenge failed on June 8, when the former Georgia governor secured enough delegates with his victory in Ohio and pledged support from Wallace, Daley, and Stevenson to become the presumptive, semi-consensual nominee.[111]

In the postmortem, campaign reporters and scholars observed that no single candidate emerged early enough to genuinely challenge the centrist Carter—a socially moderate, fiscally conservative candidate who exploited the new rules of American politics to win pluralities of African American, southern, and working-class voters, but the truth was more complicated.[112] After enduring intense media scrutiny as the frontrunner, Carter's staff effectively deployed news management strategies to construct a post-reform mantra—the establishment cannot deny the people's choice for the nomination—and to harness horse race coverage by controlling media expectations about outcomes, by placing the candidate in locations where he expected victory, and by exploiting the spectacle of staged pseudo-events.[113]

Before the June 8 primaries in Ohio, New Jersey, and California, for instance, Carter staged campaign pseudo-events more frequently in Ohio, where he was expected to deliver a strong showing, and shaped news reports and analyses by proclaiming his post-reform mantra and convincing power brokers that regardless of other outcomes, a win in Ohio would transform him into the presumptive nominee. His strategy convinced establishment figures that it would be dangerous to resist further. On the eve of the primaries, for instance, Daley held a press conference telling establishment reporters that, should Carter win Ohio, "he'll walk in under his own power." Carter fared well in Ohio as expected, and based on Daley's influence and comments from Democratic opponents, key network news sources declared Carter's nomination a foregone conclusion.[114]

The end result was live coverage possessing the telegenic qualities of campaign advertising. On June 9, Bradley offered viewers B-roll of Carter's victory rally with images of the presumptive nominee waving the infamous *Milwaukee Sentinel* as his adoring crowd chanted "We're number one" alongside his tightly scripted standup:

A confident Jimmy Carter had predicted all along that it would end this way, and last night's strong showing made it clear to the last of the doubters, touching off a chain reaction that virtually assures Carter a first-ballot nomination. . . . This day should end all talk about momentum. If it wasn't clear before it should be now that the Carter Express has left the station, but in the interest of national unity, Jimmy Carter has indicated that he'll make a few more stops on down the line to pick up those that missed the train . . . And now 16 and 1/2 months after he started they no longer ask, Jimmy Who.[115]

In the final analysis, Carter was crowned as the presumptive nominee not only because of the resonance of his antiestablishment message of reform amid the nation's credibility crises, but also because of the begrudged backing that he gained from journalism's Watergate Babies, the new generation of antiestablishment reporters who, engaged in a symbiotic relationship with the candidate, hitched their journalistic carts to the horse of a peanut farmer from Plains.[116] Along the way, both parties committed unforced errors that undermined credible images they sought to project—a progressive populist reformer and vigilant watchdog reporters. Nevertheless, forthcoming presidential aspirants learned important lessons from their performances. Future contenders understood that increased media scrutiny and establishment resistance often accompanied "big mo," and though the intensity of these challenges often provoked mistakes, front-runners who maintained popular support could withstand these tests and transform themselves into the semi-consensual nominee.[117]

★ ★ ★

On June 3, several days before the ABC movement crumbled, a caricature of Jimmy Carter appeared on the biweekly alternative *Rolling Stone's* cover. Alongside a cover line that promoted "Jimmy Carter and the Great Leap of Faith," literary journalist Hunter S. Thompson's profile of the New South's leader, strode a beaming Carter donning a white robe and a Confederate flag draped across his shoulder at the pinnacle of the mount like Jesus with a host of disciples from Humphrey to Gregg Allman following behind.[118] Inside, Thompson conceded that "a vote for Carter requires a certain leap of faith, but on the evidence, I don't mind taking it."[119]

With Thompson's glowing cover story, *Rolling Stone* offered Carter something of an endorsement, which served him well with newly enfranchised college-age voters, and publisher Jann Wenner, a Carter supporter, followed up the issue with a celebratory bash given in honor of Carter's staff at the DNC in mid-July. Thompson found himself briefly on the outside looking in that night, but he did not appear to mind.[120] With his long-form, fly-on-the-wall reporting, he struck a blow to the establishment, and with his leap of faith, the celebrity journalist contributed to the rise of the antiestablishment, moral reformer.

Carter confounded Thompson and other key kingmakers in the ensuing days as he entered into a more adversarial relationship with elite reporters from mainstream media outlets, belittling individual reporters, complaining about adverse coverage, and confronting an establishment system he deemed biased. He watched his cultural appeal fade as frontline reporters continued their fashionable probe into the "fuzzy" imagecraft of an enigmatic candidate. Many consensus-minded campaign reporters maintained that they engaged in such inquiries as a national safeguard, but Carter's faithful claimed media attack dogs foamed at the mouth after Vietnam and Watergate.[121] Neither party was completely inaccurate, as *Chicago Tribune* rookie campaign reporter Eleanor Randolph explained: "The Nixon Presidency helped create a whole breed of political journalists, who appeared in great numbers in 1976 to explain the character of Presidential candidates. It was a kind of Teddy White-ism gone wild. . . . Yet for all of us out there trying to explain what kind of person Jimmy Carter was, most of us didn't or couldn't and opted to call him an enigma."[122]

Many frontline reporters struggled to deconstruct authentic sources of power behind Carter's political persona, but his image as an enigmatic politician lingered as a journalistic signifier for his complex imagecraft apparatus and as the industry's collective shorthand for shared antipathy for Carter. "Maybe it was better to say that Carter was an enigma than to say directly, in the middle of the campaign, that he wasn't a particularly nice guy," Randolph conceded. In the final analysis, Carter's rapport with frontline reporters contributed to his rise, but as he and future presidential aspirants learned, it also signaled his demise. "Handling the press is part of the process of campaigning and of governing," *New Yorker* journalist Elizabeth Drew wrote, and Carter and his imagecraft apparatus struggled with this task in the coming days.[123]

Figure 1. The candidate and his wife, Rosalynn, watched in triumph as networks declared James Earl Carter Jr. the thirty-ninth president of the United States. (Photo credit: Charles Rafshoon Photography. This image is archived in the Charles Rafshoon Photograph Collection, Stuart A. Rose Manuscript, Archives, and Rare Books Library, Emory University.)

Figure 2. In advance of Carter's second gubernatorial bid, advertising specialist Gerald Rafshoon and his brother Charles, members of the candidate's nascent imagecraft apparatus, collected footage of the populist peanut farmer from Plains. (Photo credit: Charles Rafshoon Photography. This image is archived in the Charles Rafshoon Photograph Collection, Stuart A. Rose Manuscript, Archives, and Rare Books Library, Emory University.)

Figure 3. "I am a farmer, an engineer, a businessman, a planner, a scientist, a governor, and a Christian," Carter said, introducing himself to elite reporters—and their audiences—at the National Press Club in Washington, D.C., on December 12, 1974, during his 1976 presidential campaign kickoff. After the post-1968 reforms, pseudo-celebrity campaign reporters became key kingmakers under the new rules of U.S. politics. (Photo credit: Charles Rafshoon Photography. This image is archived in the Charles Rafshoon Photograph Collection, Stuart A. Rose Manuscript, Archives, and Rare Books Library, Emory University.)

Figure 4. As Carter's daughter, Amy, cheered incoming broadcast returns, one pool reporter duly noted personal reactions to news of Carter's Florida primary victory during the campaign's staged news event. (Photo credit: Charles Rafshoon Photography. This image is archived in the Charles Rafshoon Photograph Collection, Stuart A. Rose Manuscript, Archives, and Rare Books Library, Emory University.)

Figure 5. Network cameras only caught glimpses of the party redeemer as he mean-dered through New York's Madison Square Garden. "This is as well-staged of an en-trance for a nominee as I have seen in a number of conventions," NBC News anchor John Chancellor told his audience. Carter traveled an unexpected route, much as he had in the primaries, walking among the people, through rows of standing delegates, before he mounted the national stage, forgoing the chance to shake Chicago mayor Richard Daley's hand, en route to accepting his party's nomination. (Photo credit: Charles Rafshoon Photography. This image is archived in the Charles Rafshoon Pho-tograph Collection, Stuart A. Rose Manuscript, Archives, and Rare Books Library, Emory University.)

Figure 6. Carter's campaign saturated news media with resonant images, such as the one above, prior to the general election campaign, but many pack reporters shared the mentality of Pulitzer Prize-winning campaign journalist Walter Mears: Carter's "garment-bag, living-room-couch kind of politics [was a success] . . . but his staying power was very much in doubt even as he won the nomination." This suspicion and other nagging uncertainties about the New South's redeemer was on the minds of trail reporters as the nominee reunited with his faithful followers in Plains. (Photo credit: Charles Rafshoon Photography. This image is archived in the Charles Rafshoon Photograph Collection, Stuart A. Rose Manuscript, Archives, and Rare Books Library, Emory University.)

6

Party Redeemer Choreographs Made-for-Television "Love-In"

Network cameras only caught a glimpse of the party redeemer as he meandered through the crowd at the DNC in New York.[1] "This is as well staged of an entrance . . . as I have seen in a number of conventions," NBC News anchor John Chancellor observed.[2] Since 1952, when networks initiated live national coverage, Chancellor had watched from the floor and then the anchor's booth as both parties transitioned from producing conventions to scripting coronations, and he recognized a staged affair when he encountered one.[3]

Carter and his staff, alongside DNC chairman Robert Strauss, had studied past convention outcomes and recognized the opportunity to exploit a controlled media event.[4] They understood that the establishment news media, guided by professional values, chased down controversy, but conflict in the form of backroom deals, intraparty battles, and protests did not serve the nominee nor the party well.[5] Prior to the convention, Carter's staff had learned to harness television's melodramatic bias to their favor at pseudo-events with scripted displays and manufactured drama, and they now sought help from Strauss and party leaders to orchestrate a made-for-television "love-in."[6] All interested parties recognized that staging a display of unity was essential for the party's future.[7]

Recalling press criticism over Nixon's "coronation" at the 1972 RNC, Carter's imagecraft apparatus avoided the appearance of an overdone production and abandoned the plan for Carter to materialize before a spotlight in the darkened arena.[8] The former Georgia governor instead took an unexpected route, much as he had in the primaries, walking among the people, through rows of standing delegates, before he mounted the national stage, forgoing the chance to shake Chicago mayor Richard Daley's hand, en route to accepting his party's nomination.[9]

Amid mounting frustration with Carter and pressure from the industry vanguard to deconstruct political maneuvering, Chancellor acknowledged the scripted entry. Though Carter's efforts at undetected imagecraft were futile, media revelation of the staged entrance marked a momentary setback in an otherwise well-choreographed performance. Carter's campaign had adeptly negotiated the changing conditions of American politics, and now they established new rules for party conventions in the age of the candidate-centered campaign. Despite the campaign pack's collective desire to engage in fashionable, investigative probes, Carter's campaign exploited a favorable political milieu, dominated by party longings for victory and news industry fears over attacks of biased reporting, with presidential imagecraft and news management techniques that privileged new media and positive frames to dictate convention business. Based on their success, the business of both parties came to revolve around the production of unified media events designed to project the nominee-centered brand.

★ ★ ★

Party conventions encountered a decades-long evolution in the twentieth century, from limited-circulating, interpersonal politics of party bosses and machines to live, mass-mediated politics of candidate-centered campaigns.[10] Prior to this seismic shift, the proceedings revolved around traditional party business, including platform debates and multiple-ballot selections of favorite-son nominees, but the rise of primary showbiz politics transformed the business of the party to the construction of symbolic, nominee-driven productions designed for public consumption through channels of mass media.[11]

With the transition to primary showbiz politics in motion, the age of candidate-centered campaigns and party productions blossomed with the emergence of television in postwar America.[12] Savvy politicians translated classic stump speeches to conversational chats designed to appeal to living room audiences, and leading political parties scrambled to take advantage of the technological capacity to broadcast live proceedings across the nation.[13] Despite increasing skepticism over political propaganda and criticism over vacuous excesses of the new medium, print and radio journalists partnered with network camera crews to offer audiences consensus-style reports and interpretative commentary about the staged spectacle.[14] All parties involved recognized what the trade press observed: live broadcast coverage transformed "Convention Hall into 'a gigantic goldfish bowl.'"[15] Triumphant nominees and parties in this new landscape learned to construct entertaining images that exploited mass media, and top-notch reporters discovered that audiences craved a new brand of behind-the-scenes political journalism inspired by former *Time* reporter Theodore White.[16]

Although both major parties understood the benefits of producing a media spectacle that conformed to the demands of television with brief speeches and primetime sessions and exploiting network coverage to their advantage with uniform campaign themes and patriotic displays in appealing geographic host cities, they struggled to convey unity from national conventions amid the further fracturing of national divides by domestic conflicts, foreign wars, and political assassinations.[17] National audiences first witnessed political chaos unfolding at San Francisco's Cow Palace in 1964, where Barry Goldwater's insurgent conservatives battled entrenched "Wall Street Republicans" promoting a moderate brand of consensus politics.[18] Four years later, after Lyndon Johnson's announcement that he would not seek reelection and the assassinations of Martin Luther King Jr. and Bobby Kennedy, the American public watched the Democratic Party splinter and collapse into political turbulence, civil unrest, and violence in Chicago.[19] "The center was not holding," as New Journalist Joan Didion presciently observed in 1967, and both parties struggled to project harmonious images in the face of social and political ruptures.[20]

Richard Nixon proved the most successful political actor amid the rubble of the two-party system in the late 1960s. Adopting Madison Avenue strategies made famous by Dwight Eisenhower and John Kennedy, Nixon's talented, behind-the-scenes imagecraft apparatus developed a "new Nixon," a trustworthy everyman who mocked political showmanship while exploiting celebrity and entertainment impulses of mass-mediated politics. After "Nixon's miracle" in 1968, his imagecraft team launched a permanent campaign to control media narratives with a "razzle-dazzle strategy." The outcome was Nixon's "coronation" in 1972, a well-scripted, professional production featuring Hollywood celebrities, such as Sammy Davis Jr., and tightly scheduled, (un)spontaneous eruptions of party unity, such as the rehearsed chants of "four more years" delivered by Nixon Youth.[21] Nixon's showbiz strategy certainly was not "new," but it was well-attuned to changing conditions in American politics and news media.

The encounter with showbiz impulses had transformed the rules of American politics since midcentury, and through an exhaustive look at convention history, Carter and his staff adapted lessons drawn from the 1972 party conventions to the political realities of the moment. In choreographing a "Carterized" coronation, they defied scholarly logic, which asserted that only an incumbent without significant opposition could orchestrate a harmonious affair.[22] Post-1968 reforms altered the function of political parties in American life by temporarily diminishing the influence of traditional elites and transforming nominating conventions from instrumental events to symbolic rituals. And, after Carter's much-acclaimed success in promoting his unified brand at the 1976 DNC, the business of party conventions further shifted to legitimizing the nominee, demonstrating harmony, and extending the nominee's party-stamped brand in advance of the general election.[23]

★ ★ ★

Campaign director Hamilton Jordan acknowledged that Carter's status as the presumptive nominee placed a special burden on the campaign. Elite reporters, practicing a fashionable mode of political deconstruction, concentrated their full attention on Carter, and based on recent history, they expected an "efficient and professional" convention.[24] To meet expectations and to take full advantage of free media exposure accompanying the political spectacle, Jordan coordinated with Strauss, party leaders, and staff to keep intraparty friction behind the scenes, to manage and exploit coverage, and to construct a smooth script for the convention. Bearing the 1972 party conventions in mind, all entities were committed to ensuring that "primetime viewing audiences saw the most interesting and positive parts of the Convention."[25]

Jordan understood that the first and most important step in keeping intraparty friction offstage involved negotiating a moderate platform when the Democratic Platform Committee convened on June 15. To that end, he tasked issues advisor Stuart Eizenstat with finalizing a controversy-free platform that might unite the party.[26] It was a daunting assignment that involved addressing controversial issues, such as amnesty and bussing, in a manner that aligned with Carter's moderate positions, mitigated intraparty strife, and avoided controversial buzzwords that might derail the general election campaign. "[My mission] involved preserving the unity of the party—but *not* at the expense of taking positions that would have been disastrous to us in the general election," Eizenstat recalled.[27] His efforts culminated with widespread support for the adoption of "A New Beginning," Carter's platform, which promised transparent, compassionate, and competent government, but also satisfied demands for full employment and tax reforms from party liberals.[28]

Momentary victory in hand, Jordan shifted focus to developing a convention organization strategy that adeptly managed imagecraft when he convened with top advisors at St. Simons Island in mid-June.[29] Based on insights gleaned from McGovern's and Nixon's 1972 convention press operations, they established a news management operation that could "react quickly to swift-changing developments" with a control room for media gatekeeping at Carter's convention headquarters and command trailers for managing floor operations.[30] As a decoy to deflect attention away from their sophisticated imagecraft apparatus, Carter's campaign erected faux headquarters in the Americana Hotel's Albert Hall with offices for top campaign figureheads, who instead were stationed at authentic sites of political action—inside the gatekeeping suite and command trailers or on the convention floor.[31]

Carter's press staff designed polished media materials to encourage positive coverage in the coming days. For traditional working media, they produced a sleek convention press kit featuring biographical sketches and photographs of Carter's family, an issues booklet, a convention schedule, and a New York City guide.[32] They also established two convention news channels for nontraditional audiences: the *Carter Campaign News Service* offered nominee-branded convention releases and favorable national reports and editorials to local community newspapers, alternative news outlets, and trade publications, and the *Jimmy Carter Convention News* newsletter presented convention delegates with Carter-related releases designed to "give the appearance that the Carter campaign is the only 'game in town.'"[33] Carter's press staff, inspired by Nixon's news management techniques, intended to facilitate positive coverage by guiding working media to pro-candidate newspegs, feeding positive stories to alternative news outlets, and promoting candidate-driven news to delegates and party leaders.

Carter's staff also unveiled to working media the nation's first public vice presidential vetting process in advance of the convention. First outlined by Jordan in a confidential memo in April and refined at the St. Simons Island conference, the protocol was part authentic strategy, part publicity stunt inspired from the pages of White's *The Making of the President* series.[34] After the 1972 DNC, Carter's closest advisors, alongside millions of Americans, watched the derailment of McGovern's general election campaign as news reports disclosed that his running mate, Thomas Eagleton, suffered from severe bouts of depression, and now, determined to avoid a similar stumbling block, Jordan and his aides formed an ad hoc committee of distinguished Americans tasked with establishing a pool of qualified vice presidential candidates to be interviewed and vetted by Carter and his staff. But Carter's strategy afforded an additional benefit—good, free press. Under the guise of avoiding another Eagleton debacle, Carter's team devised a plan designed simultaneously to capture media attention with a heightened sense of drama and to invite public praise for replacing behind-the-scenes maneuvering with a transparent process. Formalizing a page from Kennedy's playbook as described in White's *The Making of the President, 1960,* Carter and his staff commenced interviews with prospective vice presidential nominees in early July, seeking advice from prominent journalists at informal meetings and releasing details about the process through regular press conferences, but they remained silent about the final selection, promising not to release the identity of their pick until the appropriate time at the convention.[35]

Further implementing techniques of showbiz politics, Carter's image-craft apparatus enlisted assistance from the entertainment industry to produce the first fifteen-minute biographical documentary to introduce a DNC nominee.[36] Advertising guru Gerald Rafshoon tasked Magus Films owner Roger "Rod" Goodwin, who produced twenty-eight commercials for Carter's primary campaign, including five-minute cinema-vérité documentaries and more traditional thirty- and sixty-second spots, with revealing a new, lighter side of the nominee. With assistance from film editor Ed Keen, narrator E. G. Marshall, and various writers, cinematographers, and production assistants, Goodwin incorporated popular elements from past advertisements, including stock footage of Carter's campaign debut at the National Press Club and his door-to-door handshaking efforts in New Hampshire with new features, such as candid, man-on-the-street interviews about Carter's sex appeal.[37] But, he reserved his facelift to Carter's image for the film's climax, where he shrewdly incorporated the unexpected—a progression of political cartoons, drawn by popular editorial cartoonists, such as Herb Block of the *Washington Post,* which featured Reagan and Ford struggling to wear Jimmy's winning grin and an exasperated Rosalynn, beckoning her beaming husband to "cut it out and go to sleep." Commentators praised Goodwin's integration of humorous elements to engage in image repair without inflicting additional criticism on the nominee.[38]

Carter's staff also managed unexpected developments that might undermine a harmonious image. Rumors circulated of escalating frustrations with representation among African American and women's rights leaders,[39] and amid concerns over the potential eruption of divisive floor demonstrations, Carter's campaign liaisons Ben Brown and Patt Derrian scheduled meetings with Carter and influential leaders of both groups.[40] Carter's willingness to meet, his promises to include African Americans and women in major decision-making areas in his administration, and his commitment to support the Equal Rights Amendment and equal opportunities in the workplace, contributed temporarily to the deescalation of tensions between these key social movement-driven special interest groups and the Democratic Party and won over even the most cynical activists. *Feminine Mystique* author Betty Friedan told campaign reporter Kandy Stroud that she was "moved to tears by Carter. He made a commitment to us in such a substantive way that unless he's an absolute liar, he'll be doing something for women."[41] While Carter's staff negotiated unexpected challenges, elite reporters encountered crises of their own—a crisis of consciousness surrounding primary coverage and a resource crisis triggered by the dramatic rise in costs associated with convention coverage. They also engaged in final logistical preparations to offer behind-the-scenes, gavel-to-gavel coverage of a drama-driven media event.

★ ★ ★

Elite reporters recommitted themselves to covering substantive campaign issues and to thoroughly vetting politicians in the spring, but as a pre-convention conversation among *Washington Post* veteran David Broder and the *Democratic Review* editorial staff revealed, frontline reporters underperformed.[42] Broder attributed the former failure to resource limitations. "It's very difficult to slow down long enough to get the background papers,

the clips, the policy statements and so on," he explained, failing to acknowledge that many campaign staffs offered these media materials on the trail.
As for the latter concern, Broder offered a mixed assessment:

> At the beginning of this year . . . there was the desire to focus on the back-
> grounds, the records, and the reputations of the candidates. That desire had
> two sources—one, the chagrin that a lot of us felt about all of the nonsense
> we'd written about the 'new Nixon' instead of exploring what it was that was
> consistent in his pattern of personality and the way in which he reacted to
> political challenges. Secondly, I think that the work that was done by David
> Barber in his *Presidential Character,* and the individual meetings that he had
> between '72 and '76 with individual political reporters, made us realize how
> important our work could be in laying out the candidates' records and repu-
> tations.[43]

Moreover, Broder asserted that the consensus-minded campaign pack
committed other miscues, such as falling prey to the Teddy White syndrome,
relying too heavily on early poll results in reporting, and generally succumbing to professional flaws, including adhering to unbridled objectivity.
"[The blind commitment to objectivity] is a very serious problem, because
it does require that you take seriously in quite literal terms things that could
perfectly well be described as utter nonsense," Broder explained.[44] In the
final analysis, Broder was left with the "impression that [Carter was] still a
relative stranger to the people who will be voting in the general elections."
Despite numerous in-depth personality profiles, elite reporters failed to
offer a nuanced sketch of the enigmatic candidate or the sources of power
behind his rise. Left unsaid was the news industry's undiagnosed failure to
recognize the underlying paradoxes embedded in the many mediated faces
deliberately donned by the party's dark horse to attract a new coalition of
social movement-driven special interest groups.

Phil Stanford, a freelancer based in Washington, D.C., shared Broder's
sentiment. Stanford crafted a Capitol Hill News Service *Citizen's Guide* profile on Carter during primary season, and now he pondered whether the
furor unleashed by the *Harper's Magazine* exposé obscured important questions.[45] He reminded *Columbia Journalism Review* readers that although
Steven Brill's profile was not the first, the best, or the hardest-hitting piece,
it raised significant uncertainties about Carter's past that still needed to be

considered. Brill's mistakes—the use of unverifiable quotations, the over-interpretation of facts, and misplaced emphasis—overshadowed justifiable concerns about Carter's 1970 gubernatorial campaign, his claims of reorganizing Georgia's bureaucracy, and his issues stances. More investigative probing was necessary, Stanford suggested.

In the short term, however, most news workers were unconcerned with reflexivity and focused instead on a resource crisis triggered by inflation. Management at the AP, *Washington Post,* and other major outlets complained about soaring costs associated with convention coverage, including a 300 percent hike in telephone costs, and encouraged Carter's staff to intervene on their behalf.[46] As complaints from news media organizations escalated, Carter's staff encouraged Strauss to negotiate a rate reduction with convention contractors. Some costs declined after Strauss's intervention; nonetheless, many news organizations sought alternative arrangements. The Hearst newspaper chain, for instance, decided to rent 1,700 square feet of temporary office space at the Statler Hilton.[47] All national media outlets, but in particular the networks, begrudgingly invested necessary funds, which far exceeded party staging costs, to cover the convention. They understood that convention coverage would not recoup their investment directly, but it might enhance their prestige, sparking an increase in audience shares and advertising dollars.[48] The resource crisis did not alter convention coverage substantively, but it did further reduce the access and time necessary for the most probing journalism, further privileging ritualized, consensus coverage.[49]

Nonetheless, these constraints did not prevent frontline reporters from stationing themselves to cover one of the biggest political spectacles of the year, and the nation's most reflexive journalists contended that the scene was far removed from ones accompanying recent conventions in Chicago and Miami.[50] Delegates no longer were dressed in love beads and scowls as they debated acid, abortion, and amnesty; instead, they donned Pucci dresses and powdered noses, attire befitting a White House gala.[51] Gone were scenes of bloody protests and violent floor fights. The divisiveness of the past was replaced by a spirit of unity inspired by Nixon, one that prompted Broder to pronounce the wounds of the past healed.[52]

While reporters considered the context surrounding the 1976 DNC, the presumptive nominee and his staff transitioned from convention planning to participating in what Jordan admitted was one of the most important

weeks of Carter's candidacy, with millions anticipated to watch his acceptance speech.[53] Many elite reporters realized that under the system of primary showbiz politics the once all-important convention, where political
bosses engaged in backroom bargaining over the crowning of the next nominee, had devolved into an empty political spectacle.[54] Some came to the
revelation that the 1976 DNC was orchestrated not by the party chairman
or the networks, but by Carter's campaign.[55] The consensus-minded pack
covering the "Carterized" coronation watched as past conflicts transformed
into the staged drama of reconciliation.[56] Gone was unrehearsed political
theater; in its place was a love-in choreographed by Carter and his imagecraft apparatus.[57]

★ ★ ★

Consensus-minded campaign reporters initiated round-the-clock coverage
of Carter and his entourage when they arrived at LaGuardia Airport. Over
the next twenty-four hours, amid the tightly-scripted schedule orchestrated
for the benefit of Teddy White-inspired campaign reporters, many frontline
journalists, limited by obscured vantage points and industry fears of new
attacks of media bias, reverted to consensus-style campaign chronicles.[58]
Constrained by these forces, even the more fashionable probing reporters engaged in a reserved brand of campaign canon-inspired coverage that
characterized much late-primary reporting. Carter, the enigmatic candidate
known for his sermon-like speeches, engaged in a paradoxical day marked
by tensions bound up in the sharp contrasts of his rural origins and the
urban trappings of the Democratic establishment, they reported. Depending on the mood and ideological leanings of the reporter and news source,
the peanut farmer from Plains either stuck out or seemed quite at home in
his new surroundings, but tempered by fears of attacks that might further
erode journalistic credibility, most campaign reporters controlled their chic,
adversarial impulses.[59]

After inheriting an unpopular assignment at the campaign's outset, many
frontline reporters, predisposed to favor underdogs and biased toward
antiestablishment sentiment, initially warmed to the front-running dark
horse during primary season, recognizing that their journalistic fortunes
climbed with the candidate's presidential chances.[60] Even as relations with
the fuzzy, hot-and-cold candidate cooled, chic, antiestablishment reporters

supplied tempered coverage amid management demands to privilege their commitment to professionalism and unbridled objectivity during a period of lingering attacks over biased reporting and heightened public distrust of journalism.[61] Hence, critique of Carter the candidate primarily was relegated to opinion pages or alternative news outlets, where columnists with ideological leanings and media activists engaged in adversarial deconstruction consistent with their skepticism over Carter's moderate political posturing and their cynicism toward his imagecraft.[62]

As the convention approached, however, the consensus-minded pack's attitude toward the presumptive nominee shifted. Many frontline reporters voiced collective frustration with Carter's volatile rapport with trail reporters and suspicion over his polished imagecraft and sophisticated news management techniques, qualities they associated with Nixon. Rookie *Los Angeles Times* political reporter George Skelton aptly summed up the emerging frustration in his lede of July 12: "There was a time this year when Jimmy Carter would have driven 100 miles to be interviewed by a small town newspaper reporter. Now, a newsman must fill out a written application to interview a member of his staff."[63] Carter's imagecraft apparatus now stressed the importance of scheduling time for magazine cover shoots and interviews with network celebrities and star reporters, such as White and Thompson, but otherwise sought to limit the overexposed semi-consensual nominee's media commitments.[64] Many working journalists resented the abrupt shift in the outsider's press strategy. Some marginalized reporters, such as Kandy Stroud, fought their way into limited-access events, but others labored in vain to gain an audience with Carter.[65]

Even sympathetic, high-profile reporters, such as Thompson, struggled to connect with the leery semi-consensual nominee as the convention approached. Thompson, for instance, outlined his rationale for an interview: "I've agreed to do another long Rolling Stone article on Campaign '76 . . . and since I can't count on the convention itself to generate the kind of adrenaline-action that I need to get me to the typewriter for another long bout with political journalism, it occurred to me tonight that the sanest . . . potentially meaningful thing that I could do . . . would be to sit down with you . . . and have another one of our more or less 'annual tape talks.'"[66] Thompson recalled that the moment marked the first time he "ever asked for flat-out preferential treatment as a journalist": "Jody Powell says there are a hell of a lot of journalists who want private time with the next president; he has a long list of requests or even demands in some cases . . . but my feeling is Fuck Them; where were they when there were no lines at Jimmy Carter's door? . . . I don't see any need to 'be fair' when it comes to the National Press. . . . And besides that I've been sitting out on a very uncomfortable limb . . . for the past year, while Carter was using my name at campaign appearances."[67] Some critics pointed to such admissions as grounds to reject New Journalism,[68] but Thompson's reasoning appealed to Carter's staff, who scheduled the requested interview. Many other less fortunate reporters by contrast found themselves, increasingly frustrated, on the outside looking in and more inclined to wield an en vogue adversarial brand of journalism moving forward.[69]

★ ★ ★

"The buzzword for this year's Democratic Convention is 'dull' . . . but political conventions, by definition, are not dull," *New Yorker* reporter Elizabeth Drew wrote, acknowledging the general assessment of the consensus-minded pack before addressing the dangers of their tunnel vision.[70] Drew's critique was spot-on, but that did not alter the political reality. "Strauss was determined to have . . . the most boring convention in the history of politics," CBS News reporter Bob Schieffer recalled. "But, that's what they wanted . . . the last thing they wanted was another 1968 . . . or '72."[71]

Dull was the word consensus-minded reporters settled on, and whether that was a blessing or a curse depended on the eye of the beholder.[72] For party leaders, delegates, and the average American, the lack of controversy signaled "how far the nation and its majority party [had] come in healing the divisions that vexed them so terribly in recent years," but for network news teams the lack of conflict represented a significant challenge.[73] Networks were committed to their vested interest of "keeping the affair alive," commentators such as Joseph Lelyveld of the *New York Times* perceptively contended. Though Carter and the Democratic Party hoped to "keep the nation glued to the television screen" for four days with a post-1960s message of unity, the networks needed to manufacture drama to secure high Nielsen ratings that might appease advertisers.[74] Broder understood that a dull convention was not a particularly positive development for print journalists either.[75] This in mind, he encouraged readers to ignore speculation that the convention would be "a yawn. A prime-time bore." Only those who evaluated their "television fare by the number of corpses displayed each half-hour and by the ingenuity of the script-writers in arranging it for their disposal" would be bored, he contended. "For those here and across the country who have a sense of history and a love of this land and its system of self-government, this has to be a fascinating moment," signaling the promise of post-1968 reforms.[76]

Whether inspired by civic duty or simple curiosity, many Americans flipped on the opening night coverage.[77] Those who tuned in witnessed a night of made-for-television oratory and symbolism with a montage of familiar faces.[78] And, in the absence of controversy, network anchors and correspondents speculated on potential for conflict. "A half hour before the opening gavel, Dan Rather of CBS was already reporting from the floor in minatory tones: 'Walter, there's bad blood in this California delegation, and that could mean trouble for Jimmy Carter.'" Earlier, Cronkite had warned viewers that the proceedings might not be "sweetness and light" and sounded almost hopeful that a floor fight might be breaking out, according to media critics, who, on occasion, still lapsed into attacks on the credibility of broadcast news.[79] Despite grumblings of anchors wishing for conflict, cameras captured images of delegates chatting. Fearing the masses might indeed tune out a "prime-time bore," producers appealed to human-interest appetites by cutting away from convention formalities to offer interviews with party leaders, delegates, and Carter's family, who were stationed nearby.[80]

News media sought narratives that both adhered to their professional values and attracted audiences with drama, but in the absence of controversy, they largely conformed to Carter's script, emphasizing the unity absent from past conventions. Nonetheless, they still sought to illustrate that they retained the power to present a well-choreographed convention as a snoozefest or an inspiration—a framing potential evident in media juxtaposition of the DNC's keynote speakers.[81] Cameras focused on yawning delegates during Senator John Glenn's lackluster speech and on entranced gazes when Barbara Jordan, the first African American congresswoman from the Deep South, spoke of "an American dream that need not be forever deferred."[82]

★ ★ ★

Absence of drama lingered. Private meetings with Carter assuaged mild threats of conflict over equal rights, and the second session featured a parade of party leaders—Daley, Humphrey, McGovern, and Wallace—unified in their celebration of Carter's "politics of joy."[83] In lieu of a contentious platform debate, moments of authentic drama that networks craved, audiences witnessed tightly scripted speeches choreographed by Strauss and Carter's imagecraft apparatus to symbolize "a kind of unity and strength through diversity." This type of contrived drama was more conducive to the narrative syntheses of print reporters.[84]

After days of chronicling convention activities, the news pack transitioned to the art of deconstruction made famous by practitioners of New Journalism, but for the moment McGinnis's Nixon-inspired adversarial teeth were absent from most accounts by consensus-minded frontline reporters, who sought to remain above reproach for biased coverage.[85] Instead, prominent national political reporters seized on the opportunity to capture the climatic scene, a tableau of unity meticulously constructed by Carter's imagecraft apparatus and consented to by a party establishment in search of a winning formula. As leading political journalist R. W. Apple Jr. wrote: "There was someone black—Coretta Scott King, the widow of the civil rights leader—and someone brown—Dr. Graciela Olivarez from New Mexico. There was someone from Maine and someone from Florida and someone from California. . . ."[86]

The consensus-minded pack praised proceedings that oozed unity, but the well-orchestrated political theater failed to hold its audience. "Humphrey had talked too long, dissipating the warmth of his welcome and seemed to freeze the smile on Mrs. Onassis' face," one consensus-minded journalist observed. Even the anchors seemed bored.[87] Nielsen released early survey results the next day, indicating that the convention lost more than half its traditional audience and signaling disinterest with primary showbiz politics.[88] Research of pollsters and reporters suggested that apathy over the nomination process stemmed from cynicism with American journalism and politics, but it also portended looming discord bound up in Carter's fragile coalition rooted in region, religion, and identity politics.[89] In frustrated boredom, many Americans switched over to Major League Baseball's All-Star Game on ABC, which featured a cameo appearance by President Gerald Ford.

As lingering audiences witnessed, cameras remained trained on those closest to the presumptive nominee during the third session.[90] Given advance notice that the Ohio delegation would deliver delegates Jimmy needed for the nomination, Rosalynn stood to her feet, waved to the crowd, and hugged her sons when Christine Gitlin, the chairperson of the Ohio delegation said: "I am proud and honored . . . to cast in the spirit of unity, love, and victory in November, 132 votes for Jimmy Carter."[91] Cameras caught the emotional—if not, postmodern—moment as Carter, absent from the convention hall following party tradition, witnessed his own nomination on television. His imagecraft apparatus delivered manufactured melodrama staged for the benefit of White-inspired campaign reporters, and as the only hope of real excitement evaporated, crews submissively saturated audiences with the "Carterized" convention.[92]

Amicable, image-conscious frontline print reporters, invited into Carter's suite to witness the reaction to his nomination, instead captured the most interesting scenes of the night. "The scene at the climatic moment when Ohio cast its votes was strangely subdued," Apple observed. "Mr. Carter smiled, but it was not the famous campaign grin of the last several months. Then he leaned over to his seventy-eight-year-old mother and embraced her tightly."[93] These elite, consensus-minded political power brokers placed the moment into historical context: Jimmy Who's miraculous rise—beginning in the snow and ice of Iowa and New Hampshire—was one of the most dramatic in American history, and his nomination marked a moment of national reconciliation with the Deep South, which had not seen a major party nominee since Zachary Taylor in 1848.[94] The party redeemer restored order to a divisive party.

Consensus-minded reporters agreed that it was a well-choreographed coronation, but Carter and his imagecraft apparatus—not party leaders or network anchors—controlled the level of drama.[95] As if to demonstrate this point once more, Carter unveiled his running mate choice at a "slickly produced" press conference the next morning before the final convention session, and as intended, Walter Mondale's introduction to his ticket was controversy-free, accompanied only by the manufactured drama of anticipation and human-interest storylines.[96]

Later an audience of millions witnessed live coverage of the fifteen-minute biopic "Jimmy Who" at the final session.[97] Some critics condemned networks for offering Carter a "free commercial" by broadcasting the film.[98] But many begrudgingly admitted that they did not have much choice. "Like all films that are shown at political conventions, this one presents the three networks with a tricky problem. If they don't show it, they are stuck in a darkened hall with a quarter of an hour to fill; in this case, they also miss part of the introduction of the candidate."[99] This in mind, networks reluctantly showed portions of the film.

Biased toward superficial emotion, they also carried the five-minute ovation that followed as Carter took an unusual route through the venue to the podium.[100] Cameras panned from the beaming nominee to the jubilant crowd of twenty thousand delegates on Madison Square Garden's convention floor. One camera lingered for a moment on a close-up of a dancing delegate, waving a makeshift message—"Give the Smiling Man a Chance." The peanut farmer from Plains prepared for his crowning moment with a swig of water before flashing his hallmark grin and delivering the signature opening line from his well-tested campaign script: "My name is Jimmy Carter, and I'm running for President."[101] During the well-received, forty-minute acceptance speech, one Caddell's polls revealed prompted a positive rating by 78 percent of Americans, he told a nation "shaken by a tragic war abroad and by scandals and broken promises at home" that he sensed a "new mood in America." He reminded his audience of the party's proud legacy and stressed the potential to heal national wounds by heeding his campaign message. "I have spoken many times of love, but love must be aggressively translated into simple justice," the party redeemer said, offering an invocation to the multitudes.[102] Networks likewise transmitted the emotional closing moments of the convention—a moving benediction from Rev. Martin Luther King Sr. and a chorus of "We Shall Overcome" sung from the stage by a diverse mix of party leaders who linked arms to symbolize unity.[103] Faces on the stage reflected Carter's fragile coalition, alongside the last vestige of the New Deal party elite, and suggested the lengths that conflicted leaders went in search of a winning formula.[104]

Elite reporters interviewed Carter, his entourage, and party leaders, typed up their consensus-minded campaign chronicles of the "Carterized" coronation, and phoned in accounts to editors at news outlets across the nation.[105] Cameras captured live images of the nominee addressing the crowd, and print journalists translated these scenes into a narrative synthesis, a tableau of love and unity, borrowing from powerful imagery of peaceful hippie gatherings and Protestant revivals. Newspaper reporters included full transcripts of the speech and excerpts of key lines, such as Carter's pledge to toil for "an America that lives up to the majesty of our Constitution and the simple decency of our people."[106] Consensus-minded pack reporters recounted observations of "a cheering crowd swelled by [Carter's] jubilant supporters and youthful volunteers" and acknowledged resounding themes that "marked [Carter's] dramatic rise to national political leadership."[107] Moreover, they echoed Carter's benediction to the American people: "Love must be aggressively translated into simple justice."[108]

These messages reverberated in newsmagazines. On July 19, *Newsweek* devoted a special issue to Carter's nomination, providing insight into, among other subjects, the regional intricacies of the campaign and its "Southern mystique."[109] Observing that Carter's nomination marked the first of a Deep South candidate since 1848, *Newsweek* reporters contended the event was the final chapter in U.S. reconstruction and crafted the story of southern restoration and American reconciliation. "Carter's impending nomination for President," *Newsweek* staff writers reported, "marked an extraordinary turn in American political history—the triumph of a backwater Southern outsider in a game dominated almost entirely by Yankees since Appomattox. . . . The Georgia peanut farmer has skillfully applied and extended the South's traditional sense of place, family and community to national politics." Carter "engineer[ed] the beginnings of a new politics," a brand of moderate-progressive populism forged from his winning coalition united around region, religion, and identity politics, they wrote. Carter's "God-is-my-copilot campaign" inspired elite consensus-minded reporters to praise the "politics of amazing grace" and to construct the New South's leader as the savior of the Democratic Party.[110]

In the final analysis, consensus-minded print reporters decreed that Carter orchestrated a week-long "love-in."[111] Comparing the born-again, Southern Baptist politician to a tent revival evangelist, they proclaimed that Carter's "politics of amazing grace" delivered unity to the Democratic flock, redemption to the "prodigal South," and healing to those scarred by past wounds.[112] "One could almost hear shouts of 'Hallelujah,'" *Time* professed.[113]

★ ★ ★

Consensus-minded reporters marveled at the well-orchestrated political event, acknowledging stark contrasts between divisive past conventions and the unified display. The political spectacle, however, was not orchestrated by party leaders, delegates, protesters, or even the networks. Carter and his imagecraft apparatus, keeping in mind lessons learned from the 1972 party conventions, masterfully choreographed a harmonious media event. Borrowing from Nixon's playbook, they convinced party leaders and delegates to project unity for the party's benefit, and they exploited national coverage to broadcast their scripted drama. The convention was "Carterized," the consensus-minded pack aptly reported, and the result was a "yawnfest," an obstacle for networks who yearned for the televisual drama that past conflict-ridden conventions offered, but a blessing for a campaign staff who succeeded in offering viewers nominee-driven images of Carter's America. All parties now recognized the necessity of coalescing in harmony behind the candidate-driven brand in order to exploit free exposure and propel themselves to an election day victory. After more than a quarter-century of live national convention broadcasts, networks also understood the value of a strong reciprocal relationship with the parties, and in the future they continued to primarily adhere to the party script in an effort to attract as many viewers as possible with live, dramatic programming that might garner prestige for their news divisions.[114] Hence, the nature of party conventions were transformed from public showcases of intraparty debates over platforms and nominees to nominee-branded, made-for-television displays of harmony.

But the victory for Carter, the Democratic Party, and the networks was short-lived. In the process of projecting staged unity, all parties contributed to growing apathy and cynicism over presidential politics. Although primary politics promised to democratize the nominating process, party conventions by accounts from some observers became less democratic. Forces of showbiz politics and the rise of new political power brokers contributed to the great paradox. "[Television] seems to be making conventions less democratic," one mid-1960s observer wrote. The sociologist misidentified television as the culprit; instead, it was forces of showbiz politics amplified by live network broadcasts that contributed to "greater effort by political leaders to keep the battle in the hotel rooms and the caucuses, away from the eyes of the public."[115] As the promise of greater transparency and inclusivity evaporated after the post-1968 reforms, some Americans tuned out convention noise and checked out of national politics.[116] Moreover, identifying the trend of reduced ratings and acknowledging that authentic political drama shifted to the primary season, networks eliminated gavel-to-gavel coverage four years later.[117]

★ ★ ★

In the coming days, as contractors broke down the stage at Madison Square Garden, celebrity kingmakers, such as Norman Mailer and Andy Warhol, joined the traveling press in "the tiny hamlet of Plains" to witness the backdrop to the film "Jimmy Who."[118] In "Peanutville, U.S.A.," the consensus-minded pack chronicled movements of Carter, his family, and his staff and deconstructed the nominee from another world, "where the creeping kudzu gives way to fragrant honeysuckle."[119] Elite reporters reflected on their powerful role in the shifting political environment prior to the convention, and they now grappled with this newfound power.[120] Until this juncture, Carter had experienced a remarkable degree of success with frontline reporters due to their reliance on horse race narratives celebrating dark horse victors, their vested interest in his triumph, and their renewed commitment to professionalism and objectivity in a moment of journalistic crisis. But as the crowned nominee of the Democratic establishment deploying polished presidential imagecraft and news management strategies, Carter encountered an increasingly adversarial mode of campaign reporting, one that involved investigative probes and adversarial transparency deployed by a consensus-minded pack, who was influenced by a chic, antiestablishment logic and profit-driven forms, that reified the emerging us-versus-them mentality in political communication.[121] "Up until the Democratic Convention, I would say I got very fair coverage, because I was kind of a curiosity," Carter recalled. "But I would say that after I became the nominee, the news media were much more incisive and much more critical, and in general, from my perspective, much more negative."[122]

7

The Battle to Control the
New South Nominee's Narrative

Bemused with the consensus-minded pack's passive lede about the Democratic party's savior, *Baltimore Sun* veteran trail reporter Carl Leubsdorf sketched the nominee donning a beard, long hair, and priestly robes. "J. C. can save America," Leubsdorf captioned the drawing before affixing it to Carter's United Airlines charter bulkhead. Photographers snapped dozens of images of the candidate next to his "Glorified Self," prompting *Time* staff writer Stanley Cloud to mumble, "he's going to be furious when he finds out."[1]

Failing to notice the nearby mocking image, Carter engaged in an impromptu press conference. Asked about his speech's tone, he responded that it shifted between "the liberal and conservative" but was "populist." "Are you saying you're a populist," one contrarian reporter asked as several others giggled at the unwitting nominee. Annoyed with continued probes, Carter replied, "Yes," before another campaign watchdog pressed him to refine his stance on populism's definition. "I don't want to be in a position where I have to define it," Carter said before storming off in frustration over cooling press relations and continued inspection of his "fuzzy" political postures.[2] Carter later dispatched a press aide to remove Leubsdorf's sketch, but antiestablishment frontline reporters, the nation's increasingly commanding political kingmakers, had already captured impressions of the Democratic nominee's "weirdo factor."[3]

Amid this emerging us-versus-them mentality, Carter and his image-craft apparatus shrewdly exploited the potential for the party convention to be a controlled media event by staging a "made-for-television" lovefest, but less than twenty-four hours later they encountered an uncontrollable, prying pack intent on continued scrutiny and scorn to Carter's political persona. They sought to restrain the increasingly adversarial impulses of elite reporters from establishment media outlets and to add depth to Carter's image as an antiestablishment moral reformer and budding statesman through a staged interregnum in their official campaign, a strategic retreat to Plains, a controlled environment designed to afford staff space to finalize general election strategies and to provide campaign reporters, engaged in fashionable probes, with an idyllic southern sanctuary to explore. Conscious of Gerald Ford's Rose Garden strategy, Carter's staff hoped to harness the semi-controlled media environment to tap into collective nostalgia for pastoral small-town America and the cultural craze for the New South. They instead encountered hazards similar to those that greeted McGovern on his summer retreat to South Dakota's Black Hills in 1972. Antiestablishment watchdogs resented sophisticated imagecraft and spin control, and they redoubled their efforts to inspect Carter's stances and investigate lingering concerns over the New South nominee's politics of race and religion. Nonetheless, despite the consensus-minded pack's emerging antipathy toward the candidate and the correspondents' desire to embrace campaign canon-inspired reporting, many initially were reluctant to engage in adversarial transparency due to fear of another wave of media bias attacks.

"Jimmy Carter had struck a chord with the American people," NBC News correspondent Tom Brokaw recalled. "He was a Washington outsider, a church-going man, a farmer."[4] Carter's campaign saturated the news media with these resonant images prior to the general election campaign, but many consensus-minded trail reporters shared the mentality of Pulitzer Prize-winning campaign newswire reporter Walter Mears: Carter's "garment-bag, living-room-couch kind of politics [was a success] . . . but his staying power was very much in doubt even as he won the nomination."[5] This suspicion and other nagging uncertainties about the New South's redeemer was on the minds of traveling reporters as the nominee trudged off the plane with his garment bag in hand to reunite with faithful followers in Plains.

★ ★ ★

The period in advance of the traditional Labor Day kickoff to the general election campaign presented post-reform nominees with a new strategic opportunity. Pre-reform nominees engaged in the practice of ceasing official campaign activities in order to organize their general election campaign during the summer lull, but post-reform presidential aspirants commenced general election planning as semi-consensual nominees and were rewarded with additional time for campaign activities.[6] Plagued by one-sided media scrutiny as the presumptive nominee, McGovern's staff failed to recognize this potential strategic advantage and instead sought to harness the post-convention summer interlude to limit media coverage during a working retreat in South Dakota's Black Hills. Instead, as members of Carter's staff witnessed firsthand, McGovern's campaign encountered debilitating scrutiny while favorable coverage greeted Nixon's Rose Garden strategy.[7]

Carter's campaign recognized that future nonincumbents would meet similar one-sided media scrutiny, but they could not combat negative exposure through campaign tours and paid media blitzes due to the constraints of campaign finance reform. Bearing this in mind, Carter and his staff decided to counter a Nixon-inspired Rose Garden strategy by constructing a post-convention stage favorable to the antiestablishment outsider. Searching for such sanctuary, they turned to Carter's hometown, a semi-controlled environment offering space to privately strategize over general election plans and to engage in limited campaign activities that might enhance Carter's image as the Democratic Party's New South redeemer.

Before the first political contest, Carter's staff established his charming hometown as the central backdrop to his campaign. His campaign brochures and advertisements were layered with images of the candidate amid his peanut farm's fence line, the old white and green Seaboard Coastline railroad depot, and the corner store on Main Street.[8] Carter claimed in his autobiography that he was "a Southerner and an American . . . a farmer," and these images offered evidence of his authentically southern, red clay roots and exploited collective nostalgia for a simpler way of life.[9] They signified his central campaign theme: he was a populist-leaning outsider who sought to reform the Washington establishment. After some debate, Carter's imagecraft apparatus decided to launch their campaign from Washington (in order to confront elite reporters situated at establishment media outlets), but they frequently returned to Plains in the days and weeks that followed.[10] Carter claimed the town offered a regenerative escape, but the backdrop's mere presence served to reiterate his central campaign theme to the American public. Carter's imagecraft advisors were so impressed with the small town's ability to signify Carter's antiestablishment status that they selected Plains as the site of his triumphant return and the strategic campaign interlude.[11]

Jordan recognized the necessity of the Plains interlude before the primaries concluded. Intense media scrutiny had overexposed Carter's fresh face to inquiries into enigmatic smiles and nefarious glowers, and returning to his roots might restore the wholesome image of the grin that wins. "I know nothing that will do more to fully restore these qualities to your image than for you to spend a lot of time at home with your family and friends while maintaining a low political profile," he wrote in his confidential May 8 memo.[12] The campaign could renegotiate Carter's image at the strategic site, Jordan explained, offering reporters depth while magnifying strengths and correcting "wrong impressions," such as claims of "fuzziness," before Carter's public persona "hardened."[13]

Based on this strategy, Carter's staff notified frontline reporters that they planned to cease official campaign activities until the traditional general election kickoff on Labor Day due to new federal funding limits.[14] While Carter's staff perfected their general election strategy and initiated long-range issues and transition planning at alternative sites of political action in Atlanta and Washington, D.C., Carter's imagecraft apparatus in Plains orchestrated one of the most sophisticated pseudo-events ever staged. They offered authentic snapshots of Carter's life in his idyllic hometown for frontline reporters and their national audiences. Carter's campaign exploited free media to provide American audiences with images of a God-fearing man teaching Sunday school lessons at Plains Baptist Church, a regular fun-loving Jimmy playing softball, a family man hosting a communal fish fry, and a president-in-waiting in training sessions with foreign policy and domestic affairs experts at "Miss Lillian's Pond House" in the "Walden South."[15] American media consumers were exposed to lucky tourists, such as Jim Quinn, who chatted with Miss Lillian while she patiently signed autographs near the small pot-bellied stove at her son's local headquarters in the old clapboard railroad depot.[16] Everyone who visited Plains that summer wanted to meet the real Jimmy Carter, and consensus-minded, adversarial reporters believed the most effective way to introduce Americans to the authentic man involved close scrutiny of Carter's place of origin.

★ ★ ★

In the days immediately following the DNC, campaign reporters, confined to a limited vantage point, offered relatively uncritical coverage of Carter's summer interlude, settling on the peaceful retreat as the consensus counter-narrative to the RNC free-for-all. "All in all, [early] reporting from Plains was soft and sleepy, like a Southern afternoon," *Washington Post* ombudsman Charles Seib wrote. "It provided a pleasant pastoral counterpoint to the growing frenzy of the Ford-Reagan struggle."[17] Carter and his staff constructed a summer camp-like atmosphere for trail reporters, good-humoredly scheduling leisure-time activities, such as fish fries and softball games between competitive, consensus-minded teams—"Big News" and "The Newstwisters."[18] They supplied reporters with human interest newspegs, inspired by Carter's campaign autobiography, reminding them that young Jimmy once "walked up and down the streets of Plains on a Saturday night selling ice cream. Three scoops for a nickel."[19] In search of a narrative to rival the presidential campaign canon, trail reporters, anxious over a new wave of media bias attacks, in turn, offered passive, consensus-minded probes about the value of Amy Carter's bargain ten-cent lemonade and her father's meetings with experts; his Sunday school messages of love, humility, and social justice; his prowess on the softball mound; and his catch as a pond-draining fisherman. To acquire the more riveting stories that their supervisors claimed audiences craved, they armed themselves with gloves and laced up their cleats; some even resorted to more onerous measures, wading into thigh-deep muddy waters.[20]

Carter's imagecraft apparatus could not have been more pleased with early coverage of the Plains interlude. "The type of publicity we were getting was the best we had gotten during the whole campaign period . . . ," press secretary Jody Powell asserted. "If we could have stayed in Plains until October . . . we would have won by five or ten points."[21] Carter's staff joked that Plains was like a "modern-day Brigadoon . . . that seemed to materialize each morning just as the stream of journalists and tourists turned the corner on the road from Americus."[22] Carter agreed: "It was a magical time."[23] His staff tapped into collective nostalgia for a simpler way of life, discerning reporters observed, offering the American public a "yearned-for past, a chance to satisfy for a few hours at least that nostalgia for the 1920s and '30s that has swept the country in the last couple of years," but Carter's Camelot was fleeting.

Once consensus-minded campaign reporters had established Carter's summer interlude as a peaceful counterpoint to Republican strife, many White/McGinnis-inspired journalists deconstructed Carter's campaign strategy and its imagecraft. "The Carter camp's aim is to create an aura of invincibility and inevitability about Carter's victory next fall," *St. Louis Post-Dispatch* Washington bureau chief Tom Ottenad wrote after an interview with Carter advisor Charles Kirbo. "The surprise plan for Carter to lie low from the end of the convention until the start of the fall campaign . . . is intended principally to develop a new public image of the still little-known Southerner as a man able to meet the demands of the presidency."[24]

In a White-inspired act of reserved deconstruction, *Los Angeles Times* staff writer Kenneth Reich affirmed Ottenad's inside-baseball reporting and asserted that the Plains interlude bolstered the "down-home image" of the "budding statesman."[25] "Every seven days, the televised and written reports emanating from Plains feature the candidate attending church, teaching Sunday school, giving one of the prayers at worship services, greeting the masses of tourists who are now coming here on the steps outside—homely, traditional American scenes that also may be leaving vivid and lasting images in people's minds," he speculated.[26] Reich asserted that Carter's campaign had organized an effective strategy to exploit free media with on-brand imagery that contrasted advantageously with that of the incumbent:

> [Carter's] summer in Plains is an integral part of his long, carefully-calculated presidential campaign, and not even his able advertising chief, Jerry Rafshoon, could do as good a job conveying the images Carter wanted conveyed as the newsmen do day in and day out. . . . The feelings that Carter evokes, the images of peanut-farmer, family-man, devout believer, that had come to be associated with him, seem, in short, to be at the very heart of his unusual bid for the Presidency. The scenes of Plains go hand-in-hand with the central message in the speeches he has delivered throughout the country—that Americans and American government need to return to the old values, and that he is the man who represents them.[27]

While many journalists offered an insider's glimpse into Carter's campaign, at least one journalist sought to avoid the Teddy White syndrome.[28] White typed up a cordial interview request to Powell prior to the convention.[29] He wanted to move past "mechanical questions" about Carter's stances and his "programmatic thinking." Inspired by political scientist

James David Barber, he instead sought Carter's "inner mind" on the history of presidential leadership: "Let him lecture me, as if I were a college freshman in American history, about how he sees the great episodes flowing together."[30]

White's interview request was indicative of a transformation in his political reporting. In late 1975, after publishing *Breach of Faith: The Fall of Richard Nixon,* White expressed personal frustration over his failure to probe the surface of his subjects. He "neither paused nor dug deep enough" to consider his focus, White reflexively lamented before coming to an epiphany: "Identities in politics were connected far more to ideas than to ego. At the core of every great political identity lay an idea—an idea imposed on the leader from his past, which the leader absorbed, changed and then imposed on the others outside."[31]

Based on this perspective, White sought to scrutinize Carter's historical understanding for his final scheduled iteration of *The Making of the President* series. He hoped through the interview to "bring my recounting of twenty years of American politics to a climax in the Carter victory; a triumph of the imagination, planning and, yes, folklore, over some of the most astute rival political figures in modern times." "It's the future that interests me, in this book, more than the past," he confessed. "If I can describe Carter's view of the past twenty years, I can make the next twenty years more comprehensible. For Carter has an opportunity that hasn't happened to a President since Roosevelt—to change the rules of the game."[32]

Faced with new opportunities after the post-1968 reforms, both men struggled to further transform the rules of the game. After the introduction of White's paradigm-shifting brand of campaign reporting in 1960, fashionable political reporters were biased toward acts of deconstruction, and presidential aspirants were inclined to exploit these media impulses. "Teddy White came down to Plains," Carter recalled. "He interviewed me for about two hours, and I gave him all the details about my campaign." At the conclusion of their interview, White and Carter took a look at the other side of the table. "His tape was in a big wad on the floor," Carter remembered. "The tape recorder hadn't worked. I really felt sorry for him, and I said, 'Look we can reschedule.' 'No I'll fix it—I'll fix it,' he said. So, I carried the tape recorder, and he walked out to his car holding the tapes like this [gesturing with outstretched arms]. It was a big bundle of—it looked like straw. I never will forget. He never did wind it up."[33]

The unfortunate incident was a metaphor for White's experience on the trail in 1976, where he encountered circumstances that left him befuddled and "bewildered."[34] White parachuted into a new political mediascape far removed from the relatively deserted, establishment-regulated space he had encountered during the 1956 and 1960 campaigns, and he struggled to gain a secluded vantage point to observe Carter's "inner mind."[35] Frustrated, he walked away from his *The Making of the President, 1976* manuscript, leaving it like his interview with Carter—unfinished. Instead, he offered the American public his commentary as an election night television analyst, his memoir *In Search of History: A Personal Adventure,* and a chapter on Carter's rise in *America in Search of Itself: The Making of the President, 1956–1980.*[36]

★ ★ ★

Cultural observers agreed that Carter's campaign deployed "his story to great effect on the campaign trail" for a season.[37] In the beginning, narratives of an idyllic, slow-paced, kudzu-filled place, where options for entertainment included absorbing pastimes, such as watching peanuts grow, swatting gnats, and counting tourists, bolstered Carter's "down-home image," but the setting for his story produced unintended negative consequences during the dog days of summer when antiestablishment campaign reporters engaged in fashionable deconstructions of Carter's "backwoods Disneyland."[38] Informed by their own experiences and required reading on the region, journalists painted Plains as another world.[39] They wrote of a place, in the words of one *Time* reporter, that was "so archetypically Southern that it is almost parody."[40] "Carter country," these consensus-minded reporters observed, was a place where "twice-born" Southern Baptists dotted the landscape like familiar green-and-white campaign signs and where "some call blacks by another name."[41]

Nagged by lingering anxieties over Carter's politics of region, race, and religion, some veterans interrogated Carter based on W. J. Cash's stereotypical binary presented in *The Mind of the South.* Leubsdorf, for instance, wondered whether Carter was a "'good ole boy' redneck," whose life was "shaped by antagonism to and fear of blacks," or an "aristocratic bourbon," whose financial success depends on blacks." In the final analysis, he concluded Carter was something different altogether—a "complex son of the New South," a tenth-generation farmer of the "red-Georgia soil," born to parents who had more progressive relations with African Americans than most of their neighbors.[42] Other trail watchdogs, who scrutinized Carter's "red-dust beginnings" to better understand the New South redeemer's roots, religion, and racial leanings, came to less glowing conclusions.[43]

These inferences were magnified when Curtis Wilkie and Eleanor Randolph, two antiestablishment campaign reporters, uncovered a story signifying the region's bigoted impulses. "Eleanor Randolph and I caught a ride back from Miss Lillian's pond house one day with a local woman, and as we were passing down that street nearby Jimmy's house, the woman looked over and she said, 'Oh, look, they're tearing that ol' nigger's house down.' Eleanor and I looked at each other and said, 'very interesting.'" When the watchdogs returned to press headquarters at the Best Western in nearby Americus, they engaged in a joint investigation into the displacement of A. Z. Pittman, an elderly African American man, by Carter's campaign apparatus. "[Pittman] had been moved to a housing project," Wilkie recalled. After tracking him down, Wilkie and Randolph engaged in "a heartbreaking interview." "I remember he started crying and telling us how he missed his little pigs he had in his yard and how he was still going over, trying to tend the garden."[44]

When the investigative team reached out to Carter's campaign for comment, his press staff released a statement stressing his blamelessness while acknowledging he was "very sorry" the Pittmans were forced to move.[45] After assessing the nominee's sincerity, the investigative-minded team published stories concurrently in the *Tribune* and the *Globe,* and it "created a furor."[46] Consensus-minded campaign reporters "jumped on the story," and though all parties acknowledged that Carter did not give the order "to raze the structure," the headlines raised suspicions about his commitment to social justice.[47]

Much as Jordan predicted in his May 8 memo, the Plains interlude was a pivotal time for the solidification of Carter's image, and campaign staff was concerned with negative associations over recent coverage of Pittman's displacement. In a moment of fury over perceived unfair coverage, Powell cancelled a scheduled press conference, voiced frustrations to network executives, and lectured trail reporters on press relations at an informal "poolside seminar."[48] Frontline campaign reporters, resentful over manipulative news management techniques recently deployed by corrupt political actors, criticized Carter's campaign for these behavioral patterns.

Reich, for instance, cited reaction to the Pittman incident as an illustration of Carter's unsound press strategy. Though he lauded the candidate for being "more open with the press than most presidential campaigns have been" and for "almost never speak[ing] off the record," he condemned Powell for "his record of rather explosive reactions to critical reports" dating back to Carter's 1970 gubernatorial race. Reich offered other recent examples, such as Powell's twenty-two-page rebuttal over Steven Brill's "The Pathetic Lies of Jimmy Carter," clashes with reporters at the DNC, and decisions to limit access as a means of retribution. He warned that such a policy would "land Powell and Carter himself in quick trouble with the White House press corps if Carter should become President next January."[49]

Carter's staff encountered another crisis on the heels of Reich's indictment. Though Carter said he had "no objection" to their presence, female reporters from the AP and the *Washington Post* were barred access to Carter's forty-five-minute men's Sunday school lesson on August 8. In response, Washington Press Club president Ellen Wadley (of CBS News) offered Powell and Deputy Campaign Director Barbara Blum a scathing rebuke: "It is a matter of grave concern to the membership of the Washington Press Club that two reporters last Sunday were excluded solely on the basis of sex from a press pool covering your Bible Class. . . . Exclusion of reporters from participation in press pools, on the ground of sex or race, denies those reporters an equal opportunity to cover the news."[50] Powell worked quickly to resolve the potential communication crisis that might expose other discriminatory practices within the campaign. He interceded on behalf of reporters and arranged access for *Washington Post* staff writer Helen Dewar and NBC News correspondent Judy Woodruff the following Sunday.[51] "I believe that you will find that the situation has been resolved equitably," he wired Wadley, before informing Blum the situation was rectified.[52]

Carter's press relations "sour[ed]" in August. Most frontline reporters were frustrated over being sequestered in Plains, removed from the niceties and excesses of information available in major political hubs and "reduced to the kind of crumb-gathering that marks the journalistic baby-sitting of presidents." "These were the weeks that tried the souls of the accompanying press corps," Witcover wrote. Dewar agreed, aptly summarizing life during the Plains interlude: "[We] write about or film Carter when he does something newsworthy, which isn't too often. [We] also interview campaign staff members, visiting advisers, friends and neighbors of the candidate and one another. That still leaves much of the day for quiet contemplation or other pastimes."[53] Now, amid the "growing edginess" of Carter's staff, most front-line campaign reporters were "pressed for laughs in Carter country,"[54] and these conditions prompted consensus-minded reporters to transition to a more adversarial, transparent mode.[55]

"Cranky" trail reporters initially buried resentments in code words in daily narratives. From the mound, Carter was a "fierce competitor and a relentless wisecracker," a pitcher willing to "flatten" his third baseman in pursuit of a pop fly. However, they soon shifted to a more adversarial tone. "Relentless on defense, tricky on the mound," Carter, they asserted, played softball like he practiced politics: with a "never-say-die attitude" and a Nixonian flair in pursuit of victory at all costs.[56] Moreover, they recommitted to exposing Carter's news management tactics—making visible the imagecraft strategies at "Camp Carter" and uncovering "icy" relations with traveling reporters.[57] These adversarial narratives competed with more obliging accounts offered by celebrity journalists, such as White and literary journalist Norman Mailer, who parachuted in to deliver a quick take on Carter, the private man.

★ ★ ★

The search for Jimmy Carter took Mailer on the well-trodden path that many political journalists followed, down the eastern seaboard, through Appalachia, and into the Deep South. Each journeyman sought the man "behind Carter's smile," but they delivered character sketches in varying fashions—hard news reporters, such as Mears, strictly adhered to the objective method, but members of the journalistic vanguard, such as Mailer, eschewed objectivity for the sake of literary veracity and cultural candor. Each political journalist was dedicated to crafting a revelatory sketch through psychobiographical analyses in fashion since the 1964 election cycle.[58]

Mailer, like many journalists, engaged with prominent backwoods southern stereotypes made famous in Cash's *Mind of the South* before settling on an idyllic portrait of Plains, a panacea to both the "redneck redolence" of nearby "meaner looking places" and the modern world. "It had the sweet deep green of an old-fashioned town that America all but lost to the Interstates, and the ranch houses, the mobile homes, and the condominiums, the neon strips of the hotted-up truck stops and the static pall of shopping centers," Mailer wrote in his signature long-form style.[59]

In small towns such as Plains, church steeples gave a clue "that the mysterious gentility of American life was present," and it was inside Plains Baptist Church one Sunday morning, alongside two newly admitted female colleagues, that Mailer attempted to gain insight into Carter, the private man. Like other chic, probing reporters, Mailer believed that through "old-time [southern] religion" he had found the key to understanding Carter, but instead he only found more contradictions. In the last analysis, he lamented the flaws of the prominent psychobiographical approach: "It was useless to hope the candidate might be analogous to a Chinese puzzle, where once one piece is pulled loose, or one line of dialogue overheard, all the parts could be removed."[60]

Nevertheless, Mailer came as close to understanding the complexities of the candidate as other journalists who journeyed to Plains before him in search of Jimmy Carter, which is to say a certain mystique remained. That paradox of Jimmy Carter was captured in a simple sentence, which appeared in Mailer's final manuscript, one used to introduce his subject to readers. "Maybe Carter was one of the few people in the world who could look good under fluorescent light," Mailer wrote, returning to the moment when he first peered into the eyes of the candidate who sat across the desk from him under his ranch home's fluorescent glow.[61]

The postmodern glow of the same bulb was visible when celebrity pop artist Andy Warhol snapped images with his signature Polaroid Big Shot later that summer. Warhol's camera came to life as he collected dozens of snapshots of Carter, his kinfolk, and the landscape of rural southwest Georgia to produce a fitting cover image for Mailer's long-form profile, but on Carter's face loomed an expression akin to a scowl.[62] The enigmatic smile greeting Mailer and those journalists who came before him had been present for the benefit of an audience of supporters and reporters the day prior when Warhol accompanied Carter to the fifth annual Capricorn Records company picnic.[63] But now, as Warhol engaged in his Big Shot shuffle, the clumsy shimmy of half-steps forward and back necessary to focus the affordable, rigid-bodied camera designed for close-range portraiture, the struggles of modern campaigning washed over Carter's face.[64]

Warhol followed his artistic gathering ritual with an intensive culling process to find an image that would serve as the basis for his distinctive portraiture. He settled on the glaring image, remarkable for its uncharacteristic glower, not because it represented mounting tensions in Carter's campaign, burdened by financial constraints and an emerging adversarial relationship with frontline reporters, but instead for its ability to signify the candidate's seriousness.[65] In the final analysis, the cover image, which was characteristic of Warhol's distinctive style of painted portraiture, was mechanically reproduced with an ironic cover line describing Mailer's attempts to "look behind Carter's smile" emblazoned upon it. It would circulate to thousands of readers, potential voters who might be persuaded by Mailer's endorsement of Carter as "somewhere within the range of the very good and very decent man he presented himself to be," as someone "he thought he would find himself on Election Day happy to vote for."[66]

★ ★ ★

The expression of the man on the magazine cover and the portrait painted by the words therein were determined by the "period in Plains," which both Carter's staff and trail reporters agreed were some of the most important moments of his campaign.[67] "We interacted with him and his family on a level that, you know, certainly hasn't been done since (and not much before)," Olson asserted. "I don't know that they planned that. I mean, that . . . The Carter campaign . . . They didn't know what they were doing. . . . this was all new for them . . . And, it was really good . . . you really felt you knew [Carter] a little bit . . . during that kind of special magic time that we had that summer, he did open up."[68] As Olson indicated, Carter's strategists largely succeeded in presenting the nation with a picturesque candidate from the small-town New South, a place so many citizens yearned to know that summer.[69]

By summer's waning days, however, as Olson acknowledged, circumstances shifted. Frustrated and fashionable antiestablishment veteran and rookie reporters rejected their symbiotic relationship with the candidate that they believed had succumbed to the establishment. Cynical over Carter's sophisticated imagecraft maneuvers and indignant over manipulative news management techniques, they collectively transitioned from derisive code words to transparent coverage with an adversarial tone. When the candidate's face peered out from the cover of the *New York Times Magazine,* hailing folks passing by newsstands in big cities and small towns, like Plains, Carter's smile faded amid his growing animosity toward the press.[70] In ensuing days, the consensus-minded pack, practicing a fashionable brand of adversarial watchdog journalism, painted Carter in unfamiliar hues, magnifying cracks in the patina of his smile.[71] In many respects, the ninety-minute, winding drive from Carter's summer headquarters in Plains to the site of his general election kickoff in Warm Springs, Georgia, signaled the end of Carter's honeymoon with elite reporters. His relationship with the establishment news media continued to rupture in the coming months, and the split caused his Mr. Nice Guy image to crumble. The wan image that emerged as chic, adversarial watchdogs sought to understand the mystery behind Carter's smile followed him throughout the general election campaign and into the White House.[72] In the future, candidates constrained by campaign finance reforms still engaged in working retreats during the summer lull, but the savviest recognized that traveling media with extra time on their hands focused on any lingering concerns about a candidate's character, and thus sought to minimize damage from their scrutiny by limiting access to staged photo-ops and more recently by assaulting news media.[73]

8

Lusting in My Heart for Jack Kennedy and Bob Woodward

Before Jimmy Carter strode onto the front porch of Franklin Roosevelt's Little White House for his nontraditional Labor Day kickoff to the general election campaign, he trotted into Plains for a trim of his "Kennedyesque coiffure," *Chicago Tribune* correspondent Eleanor Randolph reported in her lede before subtly weaving in her finer point four grafs later: in early September, Carter and those closest to him were grooming themselves for the launch of their official campaign, and their primary objective was much as it had been in the months prior—crafting and maintaining Carter's image as an honest reformer who yearned to become the people's president.[1] Only one central difference existed: Carter's campaign now engaged in their image-craft on a hostile battleground surrounded by consensus-minded campaign watchdogs practicing a fashionable brand of adversarial transparency and an incumbent president assaulting opponent positions from the safety of the Rose Garden.

Randolph's reporting provided evidence of the new political terrain. Inspired by recent additions to the campaign canon, the chic, antiestablishment correspondent had deconstructed Carter's showbiz politics since arriving on the scene, but after encountering an antagonistic candidate who increasingly engaged in adversarial press management tactics and preached an establishment-intoned message, she and her colleagues wielded transparency as a weapon. Journalists within this new landscape transformed routine trips to the barbershop into metaphors designed to expose political imagecraft and maneuvering. Inspired by the investigative techniques of Watergate sleuths Bob Woodward and Carl Bernstein, Randolph also sought out disgruntled staff members who might be willing to confide hidden anxieties about the most well-known unknown man in America. Anonymous aides, in turn, disclosed concerns that Carter's boastfulness might "offend a nation who admires humility in its leaders," and more importantly, their fears that the persona they projected might be overshadowed by the news media's image of a fuzzy candidate.

Carter's staff, as Randolph reported, was perplexed by the adverse mediated specter of an enigmatic politician, which had trailed the campaign since January, and they were hoping to recast Carter's likeness in the tones of heralded Democratic leaders, such as Roosevelt, Harry Truman, and John Kennedy for the general election kickoff. But, seeking to appeal to the broadest swath of constituents, Carter's imagecraft team created the riddle of Jimmy Carter, and as Randolph astutely contended, Carter's brand devolved into a "conciliatory politics gone sour. And whomever it was meant to please, it simply confused instead."[2] To obtain the plurality of primary votes necessary to secure the nomination, Carter claimed the middle ground on a variety of issues, such as abortion, school desegregation, and affordable housing, and Randolph now incisively exposed the polluting of Carter's centrist appeal by concessions made to party liberals in the name of establishing a unified brand that might propel the peanut farmer to a general election victory.[3] The new risk, according to Randolph, was simple: Carter was in danger of undermining his general election campaign theme—that he could supply the leadership Ford lacked—and with it the fifteen-point lead he retained in the polls.

In the days ahead, Carter and his staff attempted to renegotiate the presidential aspirant's persona in the media, drawing on a wide array of historical images to project a bricolage of the renewal of presidential leadership and the restoration of ethical governance to Washington. Their image negotiation attempts, however, nearly were thwarted by a first-order *Playboy* flop, a political controversy of their own making that threatened to undermine all they tirelessly had constructed. The origin of Carter's one-term presidency can be traced to the launch of his general election campaign in Warm Springs, Georgia, his interview with *Playboy* correspondent Robert Scheer, and the sensational coverage of his "lust in my heart" gaffe.[4] Carter's staff constructed a second-order image of a Democratic redeemer, a moral reformer who might restore the nation to greatness. But in the age of credibility crises, they did not anticipate cynicism and antipathy from consensus-minded campaign watchdogs, nor their determination to engage in fashionable deconstructions of the Democratic redeemer's image.[5]

★ ★ ★

Carter and his staff may not have foreseen the transformation in the mood of campaign canon-inspired journalists, but they had divined the telegenic potential of a unified party nominating convention and a summer retreat in Plains to increase momentum in the polls over Ford, the unpopular incumbent who narrowly had claimed his party's nomination over conservative challenger Ronald Reagan a fortnight prior. Carter's staff recognized the weaknesses of their battle-scarred opponent, discredited by his pardon of Nixon, embarrassed by his near defeat from the challenge within his own party, and humiliated by his caricature in popular culture, but as lay scholars of the 1972 presidential campaign, they also understood the exceptional potential that the White House afforded to incumbents to command admiration and consent from constituents.[6]

Ford's campaign staff, conscious of his weakness as a political campaigner, hoped to exploit the presidential persona that the Rose Garden strategy afforded to overcome his near insurmountable thirty-nine-point poll deficit.[7] Despite shrewd strategy, Ford's advisors were realistic about his odds of winning reelection: "If past is indeed prologue, you will lose on November 2."[8] Winning would involve a political miracle, one Ford's advisors claimed faith in, but to succeed, the incumbent of the minority party would need to eliminate a three-to-two gap in support during the general election campaign, something no other candidate in modern U.S. political history ever had managed to accomplish.

Achieving the impossible required more than Rose Garden optics, and with this in mind Ford's staff encouraged "an aggressive media-oriented effort" to shift public opinion about both candidates. The perceptions of middle America, Ford's advisors wrote, were a "reflection of how the TV viewer and newspaper reader 'sees' you." Ford's staff isolated positive and negative public perceptions of both candidates based on polling data and media analyses, and with this information in hand they supplemented their Rose Garden strategy, which avoided overtly partisan campaigning, by scheduling a campaign blitz that incorporated live campaign appearances in multiple media markets with paid advertising two weeks prior to election day to generate maximum media impact. In these venues, they encouraged Ford to project the image of an intelligent leader with a clear vision for the country while attacking Carter as a power-hungry, flip-flopper—the mirror image of the "new Nixon."[9]

Despite meticulous plans to exploit the incumbency, Ford's staff was concerned with the magnitude of Carter's lead and his mastery of new politics. Ford's advisors acknowledged that Caddell's data gave Carter's campaign the capacity to swiftly respond to unexpected developments, an "important tactical" advantage. "On an institutional basis, he is a generation ahead of most other techniques," one memo warned. "No one has yet devised a system for protecting a GOP incumbent from the Caddell-style alienation attack."[10] Ford's advisors offered an astute observation: Caddell's ground-breaking techniques had contributed to the development of the Carter campaign's primary themes and his central promise—to establish "a government as good as the American people."

Caddell's most recent data, however, indicated that Carter's themes had not resonated deeply with all segments of the American public. Put simply, his support was soft. Bearing this in mind, Carter's campaign mastermind, Hamilton Jordan, reminded his staff of the primary objective for the general election campaign. "Our clear and simple goal must be to simply win 270 electoral votes," he contended. "If our projected lead in the Electoral College is commanding and our survey results are solid in mid-October, we can begin to spend an appropriate amount of time and resources trying to win the mandate we will need to bring real and meaningful change to this country."[11] Jordan's message was simple. And, though he did not belabor the point, his strategy primarily remained the same: Carter's campaign must win the image war with the establishment news media. "In the general election," Jordan reminded Carter, "the electorate will be drawing a contrast and making a distinction between you and Gerald Ford based upon a huge amount of knowledge and information supplied by the national news media. Our paid media will serve to reinforce certain themes of your candidacy."[12] Recognizing funding limitations and that recent studies of presidential advertising had revealed the limited effects of image appeals, Carter's image-craft team concentrated on the stagecraft of presidential politics as they designed a general election campaign and kickoff that would emphasize Carter's presidential character—their latest attempt to harness free media and to counter media queries and opposition attacks.

They also considered the efficacy of going on the offensive against the opposition—the incumbent president and the news media biased toward sensational campaign headlines. They had engaged in limited beta-testing of this rebranding strategy during their Plains interlude. For instance, during a rare summer campaign appearance on August 5 in Manchester, New Hampshire, Carter criticized "the Nixon-Ford Administration" for governing with "vetoes not vision . . . scandal not stability . . . and rhetoric not reason."[13] He resumed his uncharacteristically harsh attack of "the Nixon-Ford Administration" later in the month on a four-day, eighteen-stop "non-political" campaign trip to the Midwest and West Coast.

Watchdog trail reporters, practicing a new mainstream brand of journalistic deconstruction inspired by Joe McGinnis, Hunter S. Thompson, and Tim Crouse, noted that Carter's latest attack antics were incongruent with the image that the good-and-decent politician had projected throughout the primary campaign, and Carter's advisors encouraged the candidate to cease personal attacks and to return to his more appealing politics of love.[14] Carter ignored the recommendation in the short term and extended his attack to critique consensus-minded campaign watchdogs consumed with fashionable probes designed to uncover sensational controversies, but elite nonpartisan reporters with antiestablishment instincts stationed at mainstream media outlets, quick to indicate inconsistencies in Carter's political persona, were slow to report his criticisms of the establishment news media.[15]

To supplement tactical assaults on political opponents, Carter's staff hoped to exploit the craze for Teddy White-inspired strategy analyses by planting his fall campaign strategy with an amiable reporter. Despite the recent deterioration in Carter's media relations, his campaign still retained a few friends among campaign reporters, and Carter's press staff offered Jules Witcover, the well-respected veteran political reporter who afforded the first serious coverage to Carter's campaign, key access to instrumental advisors and strategic documents to facilitate his delivery of the first inside-baseball breakdown of Carter's fall campaign. In the final analysis, the candidate's relationship with Witcover and other frontline reporters predetermined access and overdetermined the critical vantage point of trail reporters.

Much as Carter's advisors hoped, Witcover's insider analysis published in the *Washington Post* on September 7 deemed the general election campaign to be well-organized and patterned closely after Carter's primary formula: "start with a Southern base and run everywhere." Witcover stressed the savvy electoral college math governing the run everywhere strategy, but as expected, he also acknowledged some challenges awaiting the presidential contender—most notably, the fact that Carter was no longer an unknown candidate who could amass a string of primary victories on a weekly basis, quickly recovering from any setbacks along the way.[16]

Still dabbling in the safe Teddy White/Joe McGinnis-inspired, industry-preferred brand of campaign journalism, the consensus-style reporter nearly overlooked the nuance in Carter's approach. On the surface, Carter's general election plan appeared to be an extension of traditional grassroots strategies, but instead it was a political illusion that relied on tactics of showbiz politics.[17] Carter's campaign publicly emphasized its grassroots, run everywhere strategy, which paid homage to recent reforms designed to increase civic engagement, but nonetheless, based on polling data, his staff concentrated their schedule in key television markets and promising battleground states. Though Witcover missed this angle, more conscious of new politics infused with showbiz impulses, in lexicon made fashionable in the year's blockbuster *All the President's Men,* he followed the money, duly documenting that though Carter's $6.5 million television advertising budget comprised a considerable portion of his $21.8 million treasury disbursement, it represented a mere fraction of pre-reform budgets. Nonetheless, the insider's analysis ultimately conveyed confidence in the campaign's electoral college math that, if calculated properly, would send Carter and company to the White House.

★ ★ ★

Political tradition and the limitations imposed by campaign finance reforms prevented Carter's staff from campaigning widely in the days immediately following the DNC, but as the traditional Labor Day general election kickoff approached, Carter's staff realized they must stage a spectacular display of support to combat Ford's Nixon-inspired Rose Garden strategy.[18] Since 1948, New Deal politicians had exploited the custom to energize their traditional

party base, in particular union voters, with regular pseudo-events in Detroit's Cadillac Square, but recognizing the erosion of the New Deal coalition
and organized labor in the last two election cycles, Carter's staff sought to
simultaneously galvanize traditional Democratic supporters and to inspire
his new coalition rooted in the South by harnessing the symbolic appeal of
a general election kickoff from Roosevelt's Little White House followed by an
appearance at NASCAR's Southern 500.[19] Jordan hoped to exploit "Southern
regional pride . . . without unnecessarily alienating potential anti-Southern
voters."[20] Recognizing existing regional bias among elite reporters and the
American public, Carter's staff downplayed the perception that his candidacy was "a captive of the Southern states and/or people" but endeavored
to capitalize on national affinity for the chic New South.[21]

Passive Cold War, consensus-style reporters would have duly documented
Carter's saunter up the Little White House's front porch and his subsequent
speech, but the White/McGinnis-inspired consensus-minded pack of the
mid-1970s systematically deconstructed "the simple 27-minute speech,
written by Carter himself, without flourish."[22] Veterans and rookie trail
reporters exposed the Carter campaign's attempt to "dramatize links with
past Democratic heroes for a national news audience."[23] They also transparently reported on the tightrope performance the showbiz politician delivered for his nontraditional coalition on hand and for frontline reporters
to amplify to broader American audiences. "In a thematic speech—laced
with assurances to conservatives that he would not follow Roosevelt's example of vastly expanded government," Broder reported, "Carter stressed
the message that 'a new generation of leadership' is needed to rescue a country he described as 'stagnant, divided and drifting.'"[24] The intellectual veteran exposed the campaign's exploitation of collective nostalgia for party
standard-bearers and the subtle assault of Ford as a good man who, like
his Republican forerunner, Herbert Hoover, could not intervene against
"terrible economic and social ills of our nation."[25] Moreover, one rookie
reporter further accentuated the imagecraft tactics deployed to rebuild "the
old Roosevelt coalition of the South and big cities," observing that a filmmaker producing a blockbuster about politics could not have staged a more
fitting scene.[26] Chic, antiestablishment reporters bristling at how Carter's
campaign repositioned the nominee in overtones of the party establishment
underscored contrasts between Carter's projected images as the party's
"political heir" and Jimmy the "Georgia 'farm boy'" amid the "tableau of

Confederate flags, campers, sunburned faces drinking beer, and shirtless stomachs" accompanying NASCAR's Southern 500.[27]

Carter's general election kickoff marked the launch of a sixteen-day campaign trek through twenty cities in eleven southern, eastern, and midwestern states "laden with other visual elements," Broder warned, and his news colleagues armed themselves with transparency for their sustained efforts to deconstruct his imagecraft displays. On September 9, *Los Angeles Times* veteran Bill Boyarsky frankly described Carter's seething reaction to failures of his advance team in Pennsylvania.[28] "Disgusted with what he obviously considered the incompetence of his crew, the old Navy submarine officer took command of the operation himself," observed Boyarsky, a former AP reporter, who now wielded transparency as a weapon.

Despite the best attempts of Carter's staff to combat the adverse image of a "fuzzy" candidate, suspicious watchdog reporters and adversarial columnists, who remained weary of Carter's media relations and leary of his conflicting campaign images, continued to brand the peanut farmer from Plains as an enigmatic politician. Just a day after Carter launched his official campaign, one reporter from the *Wall Street Journal* was especially quick to label Carter as "the enigmatic man," echoing the consensus refrain. Modeling the en vogue style of New Journalism, Whillmint Boyster ushered his readers into Carter's home with his fly-on-the-wall reportage, offering thick description of the carefree candidate before surreptitiously deconstructing him. "Relaxed—his leg over the arm of his easy chair in the modest living room, he gives the interview an air of a friendly chat," Boyster observed, acknowledging the absence of aides, who might "monitor the conversation [as is] that habitual practice of politicians weary of journalists."[29] Despite the candidate's frankness, for Boyster and others the puzzle of Jimmy Carter remained.

While Carter marched up the eastern seaboard spending money to gain media attention on the trail, Ford only needed to stroll out to the Rose Garden to sign bills into law before reporters and their audiences. Ford engaged in the tactic three times on the first day of the general election campaign, and "the exposure didn't cost Ford's campaign committee a penny," one reporter critiqued.[30] But acknowledgment of the advantages of incumbency was an anomaly, and most mainstream journalists, especially network correspondents constrained by the FCC's equal time rule and fear of retribution from adversarial-minded presidential actors, dutifully reported on bills Ford signed into law and his statement about American relations with Vietnam. In overtones of McGovern's media critique four years prior, Carter's staff disparaged the biased mainstream media for its incongruent campaign coverage, featuring sustained scrutiny and sensational treatment of the unknown candidate juxtaposed with limited examination of Ford's re-election campaign.[31] Continued criticism over the lack of balanced scrutiny prompted many frontline reporters to deconstruct presidential Rose Garden strategies four years later, but for the moment the pack with a single-minded absorption continued character examinations of the little-known Democratic nominee who rose to power in Nixon's long shadow.[32]

★ ★ ★

Since the late 1960s, presidential aspirants had sought to avoid slick, over-done productions that might attract critical media attention and trigger public cynicism. With this in mind, to counter Ford's Rose Garden strat-egy, Carter's imagecraft apparatus turned to the down-home whistle-stop campaign, a popular strategy to deliver campaign messages directly to the people prior to midcentury.[33] During the primary season, Carter's staff had observed widespread media coverage and positive public opinion toward the "Presidential Express," Ford's whistle-stop campaign through Michigan, and they sought to take advantage of the campaign strategy as a pseudo-event exploiting collective nostalgia for Truman's ole-time politics.[34] But Carter's staff did not encounter the positive coverage they sought from the Democratic Whistlestop, which departed New York City's Penn Station early on the morning of August 20 to retrace the first leg of Truman's campaign through the battleground states of New York, New Jersey, and Pennsyl-vania.[35] Instead, aboard their chartered Amtrak, watchdog trail reporters bearing "political dynamite" greeted them.[36]

Influenced by profit-driven professional pressures to deliver fashionable campaign reporting based on perceived audience demand, many White/ McGinnins-inspired trail reporters were prepared to deconstruct the "elabo-rately extensive, two-day 950-mile media event" for what it was, a "nostalgia campaign" designed to steep the candidate in "the finest traditions of his own party," but plans shifted when supervisors instructed them to secure Carter's reaction to an advance release of his "frank discussion of his reli-gious beliefs with *Playboy* magazine."[37] After watching NBC's *Today Show* host Tom Brokaw's exclusive interview with NBC News rookie campaign correspondent Judy Woodruff and *Playboy* correspondent Robert Scheer, profit-minded news editors and producers sensed a dramatic, self-inflicted wound in Carter's strange admission to committing "adultery in his heart many times" and his pious assertion that he would never "take on the same frame of mind that Nixon or Johnson did—lying, cheating, and distorting the truth."[38] Biased toward news values privileging conflict and controversy, the editors and producers scoured the AP bulletin and encouraged correspondents to nail down an exclusive. With Xeroxed copies of excerpts in hand by that afternoon, trail reporters, such as *Times* veteran Charles Mohr, peppered Carter with questions about *Playboy* and treated his confessions as a major campaign controversy.[39] Unaware of the looming firestorm, Carter "brushed their questions aside."[40]

Carter and his staff did not recognize the furor unleashed by his carnal comments to the provocative magazine.[41] Instead, some staff still considered the *Playboy* interview a strategic victory. Since September 1962, when *Playboy* founder Hugh Hefner assigned future Pulitzer Prize-winning writer Alex Haley to interview jazz icon Miles Davis about his thoughts on race, politics, and culture, the publication had emerged as more than a pin-up magazine, and in the mid-1970s well-respected cultural figures, such as newsman Walter Cronkite, Senator George McGovern, and California governor Jerry Brown, had agreed to interviews with the risqué forum. With this in mind months before, prominent staff had encouraged the extensive interview with the hip medium to offset the notion that the candidate was prudish, to shore up his standing with liberal voters in states such as California, and to boost his appeal with newly enfranchised college-age men, the target demographic of the magazine, which circulated to roughly 7 million readers.[42]

"Jody Powell insisted that I do the *Playboy* interview," Carter recalled. "I didn't much want to do it . . . [but we did it] because we could not get much publicity among the young people of America."[43] Powell was sold on the strategic value of the story, carving out extensive time for Scheer amid more than seven hundred post-convention interview requests. "[We] wouldn't do [the interview] if it weren't in our interest," Golson recalled Powell confiding. "It's your readers who are probably predisposed toward Jimmy—but they may not vote at all if they feel uneasy about him."[44] In short, Powell and other interview advocates hoped *Playboy* might stimulate youthful passions similar to the ones *Laugh-In* inspired for Nixon in 1968. These intentions in mind, Powell assured Golson and Scheer that he would encourage Carter to "loosen up" prior to their final session in Plains.[45]

Armed with the knowledge that Carter would "eventually respond directly to a question if you press him hard enough," Scheer returned to the topic mystifying his contemporaries one final time in their last interview.[46] "Both the press and the public seem to have made an issue out of your Baptist beliefs," Scheer observed. "Why do you think this has happened?" When pressed, Carter explained his strongly held religious views in a salty manner: "I'm not unique. There are a lot of people in this country who have the same religious faith. It's not a mysterious or mystical or magical thing." Six questions and some time later, however, Carter grew impatient, interrupting: "I think we've pursued this conversation long enough—if you have another question." Scheer replied that his persistence stemmed from "the moral certainty of so many of [Carter's] statements," and he tenaciously returned to the topic one last time on Carter's front porch after his allotted time expired.

His final probe prompted Carter to launch into a sermon on pride, lust, and lying that came to haunt the candidate. "The thing that's drummed into us all the time is not to be proud, not to be better than anyone else, not to look down on people, but to make ourselves acceptable in God's eyes . . . ," Carter confided in tones of liberal Christianity, trusting he was off the record. "I try not to commit a deliberate sin. I recognize that I'm going to do it anyhow, because I'm human and I'm tempted. . . . I've looked on a lot of women with lust. I've committed adultery in my heart many times." Uninterrupted, he explained in salty language his understanding of Matthew 5:28: "Christ says don't consider yourself better than someone else because one guy screws a whole bunch of women while the other guy is loyal to his wife." Carter concluded his tirade by clenching his fist and gesturing sharply that he would never engage in Johnson's or Nixon's actions.[47]

Carter's controversial comments, as speechwriter Patrick Anderson aptly contended, are best understood as a "rebuke to Scheer and an attempt to have the last word."[48] But the candidate would not be afforded the concluding thought; instead, the nation's increasingly commanding political power brokers—pseudo-celebrity trail reporters and comedians—offered the final word on Carter's earthy religious reflections. Treating his musings as a major miscue, networks offered reports on the fallout over Carter's interview in evening newscasts. On CBS, Cronkite and trail reporter Ed Bradley delivered a comprehensive three-minute package emphasizing the broiling controversy over Carter's impromptu remarks about Christ's teachings, sexual morality, and the misdeeds of former presidents amid the backdrop of his whistle-stop tour, which Bradley suggested was a staged media event designed to "revive memories of past" presidents.[49]

Mohr placed the juicy excerpts into greater context than the AP and broadcast correspondents had done the day prior: "It is clear from the text of the interview that Mr. Carter made these remarks in answer to repeated questions about possible public concern that his religious beliefs might impinge on the private lives of others." Though Carter brushed off Mohr and his colleagues, the *New York Times* reporter managed to unearth a quote from Powell. The interview offered "very good insight" into the presidential candidate, Powell admitted, asserting that Carter's comments indicated his reluctance to "judge others." "I suspect that a salty word or two is not going to be nearly as much concern to the American public as some folks are going to think it is," Powell asserted.[50]

Carter and some staff did not recognize the sensational story's significance, but they gained a sense of the cultural magnitude soon enough. As *New Yorker* correspondent Elizabeth Drew put it: "The *Playboy* interview . . . is the kind of unexpected event that whangs into a campaign and throws everything off balance. It has little to do with the important questions before the country, but there it is, like a big rock that has rolled off the hillside and onto the road."[51] In the coming days, watchdog trail reporters lusting to be the next Bob Woodward (as played by Robert Redford) and still searching for a defect in the presidential contender's character filed hundreds of news stories about Carter's controversial confessions.[52]

Though some religious leaders observed that Carter's comments were "on solid theological ground," the interview proved upsetting to many news sources, including potential voters and prominent persons of faith, such as rising televangelist Jerry Falwell, who claimed the opportunity to testify against Carter. Moreover, news analysts and political pundits criticized Carter and his staff for their lack of discretion for agreeing to an interview with the controversial forum; the use of "what the *New York Times* primly described as 'vulgarisms'" by the pious candidate; and the presidential contender's lack of discernment and style.[53] As political pundit Mary McGrory aptly noted, the real rub was that Carter went "just a little too far, as he often does in trying to make a point that is mainly of interest to him."[54] In the end, many individuals agreed that the interview "should have been an off-the-record conversation with God, not one taped by Playboy."

The brewing *Playboy* controversy constituted the opportunity Ford's advisors had sought since primary season to advance their own evangelical strategy, and in the aftermath Ford's team released a transcript of their recent conversation with evangelical leaders, unveiled a new television advertisement flaunting Ford's faith, and publicized Southern Baptist crusader Billy Graham's visit to the White House.[55] To add insult to injury, the advance release of Carter's comments to *Playboy* managed to overshadow the Democratic Whistlestop, to undercut his general election strategy, and to undermine his double-digit lead in the polls.[56] The interview lent credence to a hand-scribbled note Powell wrote to Carter somewhere along the campaign trail: "Do you have a deep psychological need to step on your best lines?"[57]

★ ★ ★

A similar question might have been posed to Powell and Carter's imagecraft apparatus. They believed they had choreographed a series of media coups with their general election kickoff designed simultaneously to appeal to the Democratic establishment and their New South base, their nostalgia-inspired Democratic Whistlestop orchestrated to pay tribute to party standard-bearers, and their *Playboy* appeal organized to attract the liberal youth vote. They hoped the barrage of synchronized images would shore up Carter's soft support among his broad coalition. But they failed to consider how conflicting images circulated in mainstream channels and to recognize the dangers of misanticipating their campaign montage's timing. In addition to prompting renewed criticism of a "fuzzy" candidate and solidifying an adverse, enigmatic label, the mass projection of contradictory, disjointed images of a wholesome candidate cut from the cloth of the party establishment and a goodtime fellow might clash, as happened when the magazine's relatively routine advance interrupted Carter's whistle-stop. Powell recognized this snag along with the likelihood that Carter's comments might intensify his "weirdo factor" as he read the advance copy delivered to his room at New York's Statler-Hilton one day prior to Scheer's interview with Brokaw.[58] He realized then that the campaign would "catch some shit" in the media.[59] Powell's observation was an understatement: The *Playboy* interview became "Carter's albatross."[60]

Carter might have avoided the debacle altogether had Powell, one of the principal architects of the *Playboy* strategy, better managed surveillance of the interview. Powell was hands-on in the arrangement of the interview's final session, but he did not take advantage of his chance to inspect and expurgate the transcript according to the negotiated provisions.[61] Powell's admitted lapse in oversight created an environment in which Scheer engaged in ineffectual attempts to comply with their agreement. Scheer claimed his calls to Carter's press headquarters went unreturned, but Carter's staff countered that his good-faith efforts were half-hearted.[62]

Powell later admitted to mishandling the story's oversight, but for the moment he and his staff managed damage control for what became one of the most memorable gaffes in U.S. campaign history.[63] Powell's press office issued a statement to frontline reporters, the nation's foremost campaign agenda-setters, downplaying the brewing controversy and instructed Carter-Mondale campaign surrogates to release statements of support.

While on the second leg of the Democratic Whistlestop, Rosalynn explained that she never "worried about Carter committing adultery." "I trust him completely," she told watchdogs, who were concerned Carter's admission signaled a character defect. "I have never had to worry about him at all."[64] She continued to spout this official line over the next few weeks in a number of national and local forums, including NBC's *Meet the Press, U.S. News and World Report,* and the *Tallahassee Democrat,* among others, and she was featured in a new advertising spot touting her husband's virtue and scandal-free existence.[65] "Rosalynn stuck by me," Carter recalled. "She understood the passage . . . just like other devout Christians did. We have heard Jesus' words all our lives, ever since we were three or four years old, and we knew what it meant. But, obviously, the general public didn't. When I said 'lust in my heart' that was a top headline. It looked like I spent my time trying to seduce other women. Rosalynn knew that wasn't true."[66]

Other surrogates used humor to offset the damage. Condoning Carter's behavior with a shrug and a smile, Joan Mondale told reporters that Walter likely committed adultery in his heart many times.[67] En route to an Iowa fundraising event, Carter's son Jack explained he also lusted.[68] Nevertheless, for the moment, Carter remained off the record on the matter.[69] His silence in lieu of an immediate, straightforward apology proved detrimental.[70]

On the eve of the Great Debates' renewal, evidence mounted that report-ers were treating Carter's statement about pride, lust, lying, and political corruption as a major political gaffe indicative of his presidential character and potential leadership flaws, and public opinion polls indicated that po-tential voters were becoming skeptical of the candidate's central promise.[71] Carter was "becoming his own worst enemy," CBS News correspondent Ed Rabel remarked of the emerging national consensus. "Carter's strategy calls for him to appear decent, consistent, and presidential, while portraying Mr. Ford as weak, inconsistent, and unpresidential, but by using earthy language in a *Playboy* magazine interview . . . Carter, his backers agree, seems to be mocking his own strategy," Rabel reported as telegenic footage of Carter's peanut harvest rolled. "The Carter followers are expressing con-cern that by such erratic behavior, he is contributing to the notion that he is fuzzy on the issues and they are counting on the debates as a forum to make himself clear."[72] Ordinarily, Carter's campaign scored media saturation of Plains B-roll on nightly newscasts as a victory since it reinforced Carter's image as a decent working man, but in this instance, words of network correspondents deconstructed Carter's imagecraft efforts and underscored the damage caused by Carter's gaffe.

The first debate installment offered Carter's campaign a momentary re-prieve, but news coverage of the Carter controversy resumed as soon as his plane touched down in Houston for his Texas blitz. Wire reports that Johnson's widow was still "distressed, hurt, and perplexed" over Carter's comments prompted reporters to revisit the story.[73] Instead of claiming re-sponsibility, Carter heaped blame on Scheer for taking his "post-interview" monologue out of context: "The unfortunate juxtaposition of these two names in the *Playboy* article grossly misrepresents the way that I feel about [Johnson]." When pressed by ABC News correspondent Sam Donaldson about his responsibility in the matter, Carter responded: "It was a mistake . . . [but] I thought that the interview was over. The *Playboy* folks were leaving the house."[74]

The press conference marked the first occasion on which Carter publicly addressed his "vulgarisms," but it was his accusation of Scheer's mishan-dling of his remarks and his refusal to accept culpability for his poor choice of words that prompted many cynical, frustrated frontline reporters to take issue with Carter and resuscitate the story. "Reporters, led by the ubiquitous Sam Donaldson, confronted Carter as to the accuracy of the Johnson quote,"

Scheer recalled. "At first [Carter] said it was taken out of context until I rushed back to the press plane for the taped interview, which I played for Donaldson and others. Carter recanted."[75]

The week marked a new low point in the campaign, Jordan recalled. "I just got sick," he told *New York Magazine* in November 1976. "I thought that was it."[76] Jordan was not the only one feeling frustration over the political miscue. Behind the scenes, Carter and his staff were at odds with one another. Carter was frustrated with Powell for persuading him to accept the interview, Anderson recalled, and Powell, for his part, was furious with Donaldson for his treatment of the incident. His anger and frustration boiled over, and he unleashed it on the traveling press aboard *Peanut One.*[77] "Reporters on the back of the plane were going around saying that now Carter had tried to mislead. Distort," *Newsday* reporter Martin Schram recalled in his campaign canon-inspired book, *Running for President 1976: The Carter Campaign.* "And for the press secretary, who had served Carter with dedication for years, it was too much. . . . Now Powell, fuming, went back to the press section of Peanut One and started picking fights. He defended the way Carter handled the Johnson matter, and bristled at the suggestion that Carter had tried to mislead or deceive."[78] "Powell was a very charming person," press aide Rex Granum recalled, "but he could be very sensitive about coverage of Governor Carter, and he was quick to rise to Governor Carter's defense."[79]

Powell's wrath was not without some justification, Schram admitted. Carter had been "victimized in the past by some bad stories," he acknowledged, conceding to the pitfalls of modern campaign journalism.[80] "Everything Jimmy does is examined under a microscope . . . ," Powell told one reporter that afternoon. "Ford sits there hiding in the White House and gets off scot-free." Echoing McGovern's condemnation of media bias in the last election cycle, Powell criticized the establishment news media for their relatively uncritical coverage of Ford's Rose Garden strategy as compared to the intense scrutiny Carter's campaign encountered. Powell recognized that Ford's staff had quietly appropriated Nixon's reelection strategy, and he threatened to take his own page from Nixon's playbook. "Let me tell you right now," he warned. "We don't have to do it this way anymore. We can run a closed operation, too. We can cut off your access to the candidate."[81]

Behind the scenes, Powell and Jordan scrambled to decipher how to correct their miscalculations. After arriving at the Royal Inn Hotel in San

Diego, Powell marched up to Carter's room. As the candidate sat on his bed, Powell paced, acknowledging the hubbub stirred by the Texas press conference. "Nothing can be done about the sort of scrutiny you're under," he told Carter. "But you've got to be very careful not to give them opportunities to jump all over you." They further discussed how to resolve the situation and ultimately settled on an impromptu meeting with frontline reporters later that night. They could not have picked a less opportune option to handle cynical, browbeaten reporters suspicious of sophisticated news management strategies and primed to battle back with transparent exposure.[82]

"Quietly, word was passed," Schram recalled. "Lower-level Carter aides fanned out. 'The governor wants to see you upstairs,' they told approximately one dozen select members of the traveling press," among them Schram, Leubsdorf, Randolph, and Wilkie. "One by one, the reporters walked into a suite furnished like a living room." Powell and Schneiders offered them a cold beer. "Then Carter walked in, shirtsleeves rolled up; he pulled a narrow coffee table over to the wall and sat down, straddling the table, cowboy-like."[83] Carter, in an unusual moment of soft-spoken desperation, acknowledged that some festering problems with news media recently had surfaced and divulged that he hoped to solve them in an off-the-record, closed-door meeting. "By then, Carter loathed those reporters," Anderson contended, "and for him to go to them hat in hand was a measure of how desperate he was."[84] "The reporters glanced at each other," Schram recalled. "Nobody wanted to permit himself to be used, but, on the other hand, it did not seem right to cut Carter off in mid-thought and walk out."[85] Carter continued his impromptu meeting. No one took notes, but reporters present recalled that Carter asked for advice on how to improve relations. "Now the atmosphere seemed clearly awkward," Schram observed. "One reporter interrupted to say that he did not think it was his place to be giving advice to Carter—or to Ford, for that matter."[86] The well-respected veteran added that he would be happy to discuss circumstances contributing to his reporting, but he would not give Carter's staff advice.

Leubsdorf acknowledged that the occasional request for advice, while a rarity, was not an anomaly on the trail in the 1970s. He had experienced a similar scenario with McGovern in March 1971. The unusual nature of the Carter incident involved the scope of the request and the transparent, adversarial accounts following the closed-door meeting. During the height of the Cold War's passive, consensus-minded journalism, reporters either would have entertained the opportunity to offer private advice or simply dismissed the request as an odd hiccup without filing a report, but after being manipulated and exploited by a generation of presidents, cynical reporters resented the request for advice, and those with a fashionable watchdog impulse transparently included the anecdote in accounts for the next news cycle.[87] Some vexed veterans, such as Leubsdorf, cursorily acknowledged Powell's outburst and the "off-the-record session," but chic, antiestablishment reporters, such as Randolph and Wilkie, offered in-depth accounts of Powell's meltdown, the impromptu advice-seeking session, and insight into Carter's collapsing media relations.[88] For instance, Wilkie wondered whether the subsequent decline in press accommodations was punitive in nature: "Telephones set up for them to file stories were placed on foot-high tables in a children's nursery."[89] "When the meeting provided no miracle cure," Anderson explained, "[Carter] proceeded to follow his natural instincts and to see less and less of the national media for the rest of the campaign."[90] As his advisors threatened, he shifted press operations, temporarily appropriating Nixon's bunker mentality, a move that did not go unnoticed or unremarked upon by frontline watchdogs, who countered that they would not tolerate such treatment should Carter make it to the White House.[91]

★ ★ ★

In the final analysis, all those involved in Carter's *Playboy* interview shared one common frustration: the establishment news media's obsession with sensationalistic coverage of Carter's controversial gaffe and its most trivial element—the Southern Baptist's "lust in my heart" admission.[92] "Lust dominated the news for weeks," Scheer lamented, overshadowing remarks on political corruption, issues statements, and flaws in campaign coverage.[93] "This interview is arguably the best known, most widely read, and most frequently quoted of all Carter conversations. . . . Although the interview is extensive and informative, most of the world only remembers that Carter lusted in his heart," Golson admitted.[94]

The collective remorse was apropos. The infamous *Playboy* interview, an insightful Q&A with the nominee, featured thoughtful questions about claims Carter was a fuzzy politician and his nuanced perspective on a wide range of issues, from his faith to his evaluation of the media's performance. When asked about the "fuzzy" charge, for instance, Carter explained that the label stemmed from opposition political strategy, his unpredictable positions, and his refusal to deliver simplistic answers: "I've tried to analyze each question individually; I've taken positions that to me are fair and rational, and sometimes my answers are complicated." In the final session, Carter launched into one of his most complicated answers of the 1976 campaign—"a long, softly spoken monolog [*sic*] that grew in intensity as he made his final points" in response to Scheer's final query about the potential impact of his faith on his presidency. Much to the chagrin of everyone present, however, consensus-minded reporters, biased toward profit-driven news values, focused almost exclusively on Carter's remarks on lust, going so far, some contended, as to take them out of context.[95]

As fortune would have it, Carter also addressed this sensationalistic tendency of the establishment news media in the interview, but his McGovern-inspired tirade against biased campaign coverage was overshadowed by coverage of his controversial comments. The media's negligent omission lent credence to Carter's condemnation of the establishment news media's campaign coverage: "The traveling press have zero interest in any issue unless it's a matter of making a mistake. What they're looking for is a 47-second argument between me and another candidate or something like that. There's nobody in the back of this plane who would ask an issue question unless he thought he could trick me into some crazy statement."

Carter endured intense scrutiny first as the front-running dark horse and subsequently as the antiestablishment nominee turned party poster boy. Though unrelenting examinations stemmed from a variety of factors, most notably elite reporters' understandings of their augmented role in vetting presidential contenders amid post-1968 reforms and their new concentration on character analyses inspired by recent experiences in journalism and presidential politics, Carter was convinced that he encountered more pronounced scrutiny than other candidates due to his southern heritage. "There's still a tendency on the part of some members of the press to treat the South, you know, as a suspect nation," he observed. "There are a few who think that since I am a Southern governor, I must be a secret racist or there's something in a closet somewhere that's going to be revealed to show my true colors."[96]

Constant probing by Scheer and his colleagues about Carter's experience with race and religion substantiated his claims, but, frustrated with this alleged regional bias, he and his staff failed to understand the major source from which the sustained investigations emanated—the chic, adversarial watchdog bias toward political unknowns that emerged among antiestablishment reporters in the long decade of the 1960s. In the absence of this knowledge, Carter and his staff struggled to develop an approach to effectively confront this increasingly vogue mainstream mode. Instead, amid their pervasive us-versus-them mentality, they borrowed press strategies from postwar showbiz politicians: they ostracized and marginalized offending journalists; they transitioned to a more controlled press operation and implemented sophisticated news management strategies that favored channels to speak directly to the American people; and, when under attack, they shifted to a closed-door press strategy reflecting a bunker mentality.[97] And the watchdog press bristled and waited to pounce.

These conditions temporarily resulted in more of the same—prolonged scrutiny and persistent critique to the enigma of Jimmy Carter. In "Jimmy, We Hardly Know Y'All—A Southern Odyssey: Unguarded Moments in the Life, Times and Recent Past of the Most Guarded Presidential Candidate in Recent Decades," Scheer's supplement to the Q&A, the radical reporter offered his reaction to Carter's contention that he was not a "packaged article" and his answer to industry calls for continued scrutiny to the nominee's background. In short, he delivered his own take on existing campaign profiles. He refuted Carter's claims and exposed him as a political actor with one of the best-packaged campaigns in American history.

Behind Plains's "movie-set" backdrop, Carter's staff paraded out his "central casting mother, Miss Lillian," the rest of the family, and the Peanut Brigade for a troupe of political journalists, who remained exasperated with the paradoxes of Jimmy Carter. Scheer endeavored to dig past the mythology of Jimmy Carter, but he remained perplexed by the man:

> The problem is that one's judgments about Carter are necessarily fragmented, because we have no sense of depth of the man, of his experience and his roots. He just came to us a winner. Carter's people are good at their business, so good that they've managed to cover the hard and interesting edges of the man. What we see is the packaging. The young men surrounding Carter let an occasional nugget drop for a particular constituency, then wrap him up again quickly. The manipulation of staged media events along with color results in lopsided opinion polls that will probably carry him to the White House, but when you look closely, you end up confused.[98]

Carter's imagecraft apparatus offered the nation what Jean Baudrillard referred to as second-order simulacra, images hinting at the existence of character qualities designed to appeal to nontraditional special interest groups comprising Carter's coalition. But from differing and on occasion obstructed vantage points, campaign canon-inspired reporters consumed with deconstructing imagecraft struggled to connect with the real, private man and to locate the authentic sources of political power reflected within his presidential persona.[99]

★ ★ ★

To combat the effective Rose Garden approach first implemented during Nixon's 1972 reelection campaign, Carter's imagecraft team developed a general election strategy designed simultaneously to exploit his reputation as an antiestablishment leader with populist impulses alongside the rich legacy of the Democratic Party and to shore up soft support among key special interest groups, including college-age men.[100] But in the cynical climate of the mid-1970s, Carter's general election campaign plans backfired.

Chic, antiestablishment campaign watchdogs incisively deconstructed Carter's unsynchronized projection of conflicting images.[101] In the more cynical environment following the Johnson and Nixon administrations, skeptical journalists applied constant scrutiny to expose inconsistencies embedded in the constructed brand and the authentic man. The image of a party man cloaked in the spoils of the past contradicted those of an antiestablishment, NASCAR-loving populist. Moreover, Carter's extended earthy monologue on lust and corruption in *Playboy* provided evidence of manifold inconsistencies in Carter's brand and its alignment with his authentic self. Carter's hip persona donned to attract the liberal, youth vote did not jibe with the more presidential image designed to appeal to older, moderate voters. Furthermore, his earthy delivery conflicted with the private man that frontline reporters had come to recognize as a pious soul.

The consensus-minded pack believed Carter was a walking contradiction, and his comments both enhanced the "weirdo factor" some advisors hoped to downplay and represented a political miscalculation primed to undermine his favor with social conservatives and party regulars. Within this new political environment, campaign reporters, influenced by the fashionable us-versus-them mentality, perceived an enhanced duty to vet presidential character, but their focus on controversial comments quickly escalated into sensationalized coverage of a political gaffe. Sensationalistic news reporting, in turn, incited mass reaction from pundits, columnists, editorial cartoonists, and letter-to-the-editor writers. Most cultural commentators lampooned Carter's gaffe in the vein of *Los Angeles Times* editorial cartoonist Paul Conrad, who sketched the presidential aspirant lusting after Lady Liberty.[102] However, some anomalous voices came to Carter's defense. For example, letter to the editor writer Jill A. Hackett of Van Nuys, a neighborhood in the San Fernando Valley region of Los Angeles, offered a rare critique of the press coverage of the controversy and endorsed the presidential aspirant, writing, "what healthy, active adult human being doesn't 'lust in his heart.' . . . I'd sooner worry if he didn't!"[103] But voices such as this were uncharacteristic, and overnight, media coverage transformed Carter's political persona into material for sketch comedy spoofs of a lustful politician, images that became embedded in the American imagination and threatened to garner more laughs than those of the bumbling incumbent.[104]

Carter later reflected on why the *Playboy* story took on a life of its own: "You know, I did not want—I did not deliberately inject my religious beliefs into the campaign. I think that when the 'lust in my heart' comments came out, it showed I was not of the high sterling character that had been built up. The *Playboy* interview was a very serious, damaging thing for me. I dropped 15 percentage points in the polls."[105] Carter and his staff believed his *Playboy* remarks contributed to the public opinion tailspin that nearly undermined his presidential aspirations. Contrary to these assertions, recent research indicates that Carter's comments elicited a negligible influence on his standing in the polls; instead, after experiencing a slight surge in public approval after the DNC, Carter's campaign encountered a steady decline throughout the general election campaign, the result of a narrowing effect triggered by constant media scrutiny that challenged many post-reform presidential contenders.[106]

Carter's comments were less damaging than they were unforgettable. The real cost came from America's lingering collective memory of the incident, which lived on in *Saturday Night Live* sketches, and its subsequent impact on his image.[107] In the short term, Carter's political miscue contributed to the unfavorable public impression that he was an unknown commodity. "[*Playboy*] contributed to a concern that people had that they really didn't know who this guy was, and did they really want him to be president,"

Schneiders maintained.[108] Carter concurred, admitting irreparable harm to his campaign in projecting a persona that failed to "complement my previous image."[109] In the long term, however, as some cultural observers acknowledged, Carter's remarks signaled a lack of political judgment and the potential for American audiences to laugh at (and not with) the politician.[110] As Anderson aptly asserted: "In retrospect, it is difficult to overstate the impact of the *Playboy* interview, not only on the campaign, but on Carter's presidency. It destroyed his lead, soured his press relations, threw him on the defensive and his campaign into chaos, and probably cost him the big electoral victory he expected. Moreover, Carter's remarks first raised the possibility to millions of voters that he might be a bit too different, too strange, for them to be comfortable with him for four or eight years. The honeymoon was over."[111] Evidence from the summer of 1976 suggested that the honeymoon was over before it ever began.

By September 1976, amid the pervasive us-versus-them mentality, Carter's relationships with traveling reporters were unraveling quickly. Collectively, the consensus-minded pack was exhausted from Carter's pious tirades and his hot-and-cold manner, and they were suspicious of his campaign pseudo-events. But, more importantly, they were resentful over the moral reform candidate's perceived deceptiveness and his efforts to manipulate press coverage. The *Playboy* episode represented the supreme example of all their frustrations, and in the aftermath, the consensus-minded campaign watchdogs determined to interrogate Carter's second-order image more closely than ever.[112]

9

Contesting Opponents, Debating the Future, and Resisting Malaise

Donning dark suits and dour expressions, Republican incumbent Gerald Ford and former Georgia governor Jimmy Carter appeared as straight-faced puppets propped behind twin podiums in Mike Peters's syndicated cartoon. Wavy static distortion lines appeared inside speech bubbles above their heads, and a sound technician informed viewers "the trouble [was] not in [their] set."[1] Peters cued newspaper readers to consider the twenty-seven-minute technical delay in the first presidential debate, suggesting that the second in the series of so-called "Great Debates" offered more of the same—dead air delivered by wooden political pawns in the age of reformed showbiz politics.[2] Carter's staff encountered Peters's image on the cover of "What the Press Had to Say," the campaign's news summary, as they considered how to negotiate Carter's souring relationship with frontline reporters and emerging political apathy in American culture, a state of affairs that campaign staff and discerning reporters acknowledged contributed to soft support and declining poll figures.[3]

In a new landscape determined by credibility crises in American politics and journalism, post-1968 reforms, and refashioned showbiz politics, both candidates agreed to the renewal of the Great Debates and eleventh-hour campaign blitzes to shore up soft support and to gain ground in the polls. Once on the national stage, however, they encountered antagonistic consensus-minded watchdogs determined to engage in fashionable deconstructions and character examinations and an apathetic public on the verge of malaise. Finance reforms had triggered a permutation of showbiz politics in the 1976 election cycle, and now both campaigns sought to project complimentary political personas through nontraditional modes, such as media pseudo-events, intended to target special interest voters in the most cost-effective manner. Within this landscape, presidential contenders and front-line reporters claimed that substantive coverage of campaign issues was neglected, and all parties heaped scorn upon their adversaries for forsaking the real issues. Carter, for instance, in his infamous *Playboy* interview, condemned journalists for bias toward horse race reporting and gotcha journalism over issues coverage. In retort, elite reporters blamed Carter for running the "least issues-oriented campaign since the nineteenth century."[4] More discerning experts denounced all parties, noting that issues were "lost in the campaign debris."[5] In actuality, all parties constructed a straw man in their criticism of an issue-devoid campaign. Within their resounding critique of the political mediascape, each actor presumed the existence of a golden age of American politics, a moment of pure, wholesome civic debate.[6] Such a moment, of course, never existed. And, in final analysis, mediated finger pointing at culpable parties responsible for the descent into trivial reporting overshadowed the most significant headline on election eve: a host of undecided voters remained apathetic about presidential politics in 1976 and beyond.

★ ★ ★

The precedent for the "Great Debates," the series of joint television appearances by presidential candidates, materialized from a telegram invitation issued by NBC president Robert Sarnoff in the summer of 1960. First John Kennedy and then Richard Nixon, over the objections of his media advisors, promptly accepted Sarnoff's telegram, inspired by a congressional resolution earlier that year to temporarily suspend the equal-time provision, Section 315(a) of the Federal Communications Act of 1934.[7] In advance of the first encounter, all parties underestimated the significance that the debates might have on the 1960 presidential race and the future of general election campaigns, but in the aftermath, most political actors and cultural observers admitted that they transformed the landscape of presidential politics.[8]

In conception, the 1960 presidential debates were an anomaly, a one-time suspension of the equal-time rule, but in practice they prompted the general consensus that presidential debates were valuable media events for political actors and were essential campaign proceedings for the American public. Network executives certainly recognized the potential in presidential debates as political novelties, imbued with drama and conflict, to attract sizeable audiences, and political actors appreciated the potential of free media events to cost-effectively influence public opinion and the presidential race's outcome.[9] Awestricken by the reputation of the 1960 presidential debates, neither Lyndon Johnson nor Nixon sought to revisit the one-time waiver of Section 315(a) in order to cultivate an opportunity to debate opponents in the next three election cycles.[10]

However, with its so-called Aspen ruling in 1975, the FCC removed the equal-time obstacle by concluding that presidential debates were exempt as bona fide news events, covered in their entirety and sponsored by non-broadcast entities, involving qualified major party candidates. The League of Women Voters encouraged both candidates to engage in their sponsored revival of the Great Debates. Trailing by thirty-two points in one poll, the underdog incumbent, at staff urging, decided to issue a debate challenge to Carter in his RNC acceptance speech.[11] "I am eager to go before the people and debate the real issues with Jimmy Carter," Ford challenged the miraculous dark horse, who, encountering soft support from his base, was prepared to offer a similar challenge the next morning.[12] Carter's staff issued a statement that evening, countering with an offer to Ford to engage in a series of debates allowing "tough cross-examination of the candidates by representatives of the news media."[13] In so doing, all parties signaled that they intended to treat the 1960 debates as the model for upcoming media events.

News media personnel also were eager to facilitate the debates' restoration. Thus, while media advisors for both candidates negotiated details with League of Women Voters representatives and network executives, reporters readied themselves to serve as moderators, panelists, and chroniclers of the media events.[14] Passive, consensus-style, Cold War era campaign reporters, practicing strict objectivity and unaware of the event's cultural magnitude, offered subdued coverage prior to the first debate between Kennedy and Nixon, but prior to the 1976 presidential debates reporters offered frenzied media advances that promised the debates would rival *Monday Night Football*'s drama.[15] News producers, avoiding accusations of bias, sought newsworthy general election campaign events comparable to state caucuses and primaries about which to deliver detached campaign analysis, and collective memory of the Great Debates prompted news gatekeepers to suggest their revival was a major story in the bicentennial campaign.[16] This consensus mandate in mind, frontline reporters privileged coverage of the second installment of the Great Debates across media and supplied saturation coverage by chronicling negotiations among campaign staffs, networks, and the League of Women Voters, analyzing the expectations of all parties, deconstructing strategic preparations, handicapping winners and losers, and speculating on the role of the media event in the general election's outcome. Once established in the bicentennial campaign, this narrative line came to define future coverage.[17]

Consensus-minded reporters promised American audiences a drama-filled political novelty in advance of the 1976 presidential debates, but post-debate accounts revealed that many of the 100 million viewers who tuned in widely conceded the greatest drama ensued when both candidates stood motionless like exasperated statues during the twenty-seven-minute sound delay.[18] Although no party scored a major victory, the consensus-minded pack, biased toward horse race journalism but not yet comfortable with their role adjudicating this exceptional news event, declared Ford, the more polished debate performer, to be the slim victor.[19]

While frontline reporters turned their attention back to the trail, Carter's staff shifted to preparations for the next encounter.[20] In particular, they sought to transform how Carter prepared for the crucial media events. They recognized that delivering a polished performance was most critical to Carter's success in a political system permeated by showbiz impulses, and they borrowed a page from Ford's campaign plan by insisting Carter engage in mock debates instead of simply reviewing debate briefing books, as he had before the first event.[21] Prior to these rehearsals, Carter's advisors peppered him with guidance: "Give clear, crisp, decisive, straightforward answers. . . . Your long thoughtful answers may lose the audience and make them believe you are being evasive."[22] Carter needed a wardrobe transformation, one aide suggested, and in the tradition of Franklin Roosevelt, he should repeat key phrases for emphasis. Above all, aides advised Carter to issue a civil attack; he should "keep a cool, polite but vigorous and not deferential demeanor."[23] Based on this counsel, Carter treated the debates as a forum to cautiously attack his opposition, thereby stretching the limits of the civil debate and offering a model for future candidates.[24]

Carter's aides offered suggestions in tandem with advice to rank-and-file campaign workers, who they encouraged to reach out to establishment figures, such as future Speaker of the House Tip O'Neill, who might help the campaign take the offensive.[25] And staff heeded this advice, providing field desk personnel with insight into key themes that Carter intended to ad-dress in the debate, such as "the need for more openness and congressional participation in foreign policy," so they could stress Carter's success to his supporters and local media in the event's immediate aftermath.[26]

Widely regarded by the consensus-minded pack as the victor in the first debate and favored in the second debate focused on foreign policy, Ford and his advisors maintained intense debate preparations.[27] Ford was mindful of new suggestions from his advisors, including David Belin, who reminded the president's team that both campaigns centered on public perceptions of the candidates, not the issues.[28] Nonetheless, Ford's team concentrated on one issue throughout their preparations—how to address the recent Helsinki Accords. National Security Advisor and Secretary of State Henry Kissinger stressed that the United States never had recognized Soviet dom-ination of Eastern Europe, and Ford rehearsed these remarks alongside those of responses to other likely queries.[29] With strategic plans in place, at staff prompting, both candidates the spent final hours vigorously preparing for the second debate, a moment all parties agreed could make or break both men's presidential aspirations.

★ ★ ★

Frontline reporters needed no additional prompting. In advance of the second major media event, they offered saturation news coverage about technical preparations. Some reporters, however, did not miss the oppor-tunity to offer analysis about the potential impact of a verbal miscue in the increasingly close race, and with his more aggressive debate strategy in place, Carter could not resist nudging reporters in this direction. "If one of us makes a mistake," he told ABC News correspondent Sam Donaldson, "that will be damaging."[30] Biased toward sensational, horse race-style cov-erage, campaign reporters and elite political journalists claimed seats at the Palace of Fine Arts in San Francisco or otherwise stationed themselves at the best reportorial vantage point to recap and speculate on round two's winner and loser.[31]

After reviewing briefing books and engaging in full-scale rehearsals, both candidates were primed for their second political showdown. Three minutes before the debate was scheduled to begin, they shook hands, strode across the stage, and perched themselves behind their respective podiums just in time for debate moderator Pauline Frederick of National Public Radio to introduce them to the eager crowd.[32] That evening, the incumbent, the media panelists (*New York Times* associate editor Max Frankel, *Baltimore Sun* diplomatic correspondent Henry L. Trewhitt, and NBC News correspondent Richard Valeriani), and the nation's primetime television audience encountered a "looser, leaner and meaner" Democrat from Georgia in the joint television appearance.[33]

From the opening moments Carter took the offensive, linking Ford to his predecessor and characterizing his administration as a failed presidency, one mostly of style and lacking in substance. It was these attacks, Carter's advisors and some frontline reporters asserted, that created the sense of pressure, contributing to the most memorable moment of the debate— Ford's response to Frankel's inquiry about the influence of the Soviet regime in Eastern Europe. Ford might have used the question as an opportunity to tout the recent success of the Strategic Arms Limitation Talks (SALT I), but instead, he bumbled, "I believe that we have, uh, negotiated with the Soviet Union since I've been president from a position of strength," he maintained, referring to the progress of arms negotiations at the Vladivostok Summit before turning to the case of Eastern Europe. "There is no Soviet domination of Eastern Europe and there never will be under a Ford administration."[34]

Ford's response so shocked Frankel that he interrupted the moderator, who asked for Carter's rebuttal. "I'm sorry, I—could I just follow," interjected the sympathetic editor, who offered Ford a chance to amend his prior statement. "Did I understand you to say, sir, that the Russians are not using Eastern Europe as their own sphere of influence . . . ?" Ford responded by avowing his earlier comments: "I don't believe, uh, Mr. Frankel, that uh, the Yugoslavians consider themselves dominated by the Soviet Union."[35] Failing to acknowledge his momentary miscue, Ford delivered the most memorable mistake of the 1976 Great Debates and committed a verbal gaffe many analysts credited with restoring Carter's lead and supplying a surge of crucial momentum in the general election's final weeks.[36] Carter immediately recognized Ford's misstep and seized the opportunity to pounce: "I would like to see Mr. Ford convince the Polish-Americans and the Czech-Americans and the Hungarian-Americans in this country that those countries don't live under the domination and supervision of the Soviet Union behind the Iron Curtain."[37]

At the news briefing following the debate, Ford's staff committed an equally damaging unforced error. When given the opportunity, they failed to issue a clarification. Ford's press secretary, Ronald Nessen, later admitted his miscalculation:

> After each debate, top Ford campaign and White House aides held a briefing for reporters—what is called a "spin session"—to influence press coverage . . . my deputy, John Carlson, who had watched the debate with the press corps, warned the Ford team that the reporters were in an uproar over the president's answer on Soviet domination. . . . one of us should have phoned the president and told him we were going to clarify his answer. . . . For some reason, none of us made that call. Instead, we faced the press and denied that the president had made a mistake with his answer.[38]

Evidence of the mistake appeared in press conference transcripts. *Washington Post* correspondent Lou Cannon immediately referenced Ford's Eastern Europe remarks with his opening question: "Are there Soviet troops in Poland?" "Yes," responded Assistant to the President for National Security Affairs General Brent Scowcroft. "Do you think that would imply some dominance to Poland?" he followed. "I think that what the President was trying to say is that we do not recognize Soviet dominance of Europe," Scowcroft replied, attempting to clarify the president's response, but when Cannon and another colleague asked if Ford had erred, advisor Dick Cheney refused to admit the miscue: "I understood exactly what he was saying, and I think that the American people will understand exactly what he was saying, too." Cheney concluded by claiming Ford scored well with the American public. "I thought that the closing statements went right to the heart . . . of the debates . . . with respect to foreign policy . . . when he was able to point out that, after two years, we do in fact have peace and that not a single American is fighting anywhere in the world tonight."[39]

As many Americans now expected, both campaigns announced their candidate as the victor, but many reporters remained unconvinced of a clear leader in the debate's aftermath.[40] Several reporters, however, expressed remaining concern over Ford's statement about Eastern Europe, and the consensus-minded pack honed in on the newspeg. "The next day, the uproar gathered steam . . . ," Nessen recalled. "In a private meeting, Cheney and I urged the president to acknowledge his misstatement about Soviet domination of Eastern Europe. He replied in a steely tone, 'I am not inclined to do that.'"[41] Cheney and Nessen encouraged Ford to take a simple, but central, step in image repair and nascent crisis management. However, out of stubbornness, as Ford later admitted, he refused to apologize for what he deemed to be a minor miscue for five days, and the damaging controversy lingered.[42]

Carter's advisors followed the post-debate spin session with an effort to keep Ford's gaffe in the headlines, thereby potentially seizing momentum in public opinion polls. Jordan asked Carter's staff "to react strongly to Ford's performance in the prior evening's debate."[43] They did, articulating his success in language appealing to reporters biased toward the sensational, horse race mode. Rafshoon declared Carter slugged a "home run." "He had Ford on the defensive the whole time," he explained to *Boston Globe* campaign reporter Curtis Wilkie. "Ford showed he had no sensitivity to people of other countries. All he could do was to give out a morass of statistics. Jimmy showed he could think."[44] From the trail, Carter emphasized Ford's "serious blunder," alleging he must have been "brainwashed" in his last trip behind the Iron Curtain.[45]

The controversy persisted as a direct result of the Ford campaign's mismanagement of the communication crisis, the Carter campaign's political attack strategy, and the establishment news media's bias toward sensational stories about political controversies. On October 10, for instance, Ford's campaign manager, Jim Baker, fielded additional questions related to the Eastern Europe gaffe at a press conference aboard Air Force One. Although Baker stressed Ford's surge over Carter in the polls in the last month, reporters remained fixated on the unforced error, even when they were offered data about Carter's continued miscues.[46]

Consensus-minded reporters ultimately pronounced Carter the definitive victor.[47] Defaulting to their horse race bias, the pack announced that Carter delivered "a clear-cut decision." He had "take[n] off the [boxing] gloves in round two" and landed a "knock-out punch."[48] Elite reporters collectively agreed that Carter had achieved one of his central general election goals: he appeared "presidential" beside Ford, but they wondered whether he could retain the image in the coming days.[49] One could see tensions over Carter's political persona manifest themselves in popular culture. During *Saturday Night Live*'s October 16 episode, for instance, portraying a media panelist, Jane Curtin asked Dan Aykroyd (as Carter) if the *Playboy* interview was a mistake: "Do you think you are being too honest with the American people, and do you still lust after women?" Carter (played by Aykroyd) responded: "Well, I don't think there's such a thing as being too honest, uh Ms. Montgomery, and just to prove it I'm going to answer honestly how I feel right now . . . I want to say that you're a very attractive woman, and your hair looks kind of silky and kind of soft and uh, at this moment in my heart, I'm wearing a leather mask and breathing in your ear."[50]

★ ★ ★

In the aftermath of Ford's gaffe, Carter and his staff remained on the offensive, seeking to capitalize on the news that Watergate special prosecutor Charles Ruff was investigating Ford's campaign contributions and allegations by Nixon's former White House counsel John Dean that Ford was aware of Nixon's obstruction of justice before the 1972 election.[51] While vice presidential candidate Walter Mondale linked Ford to the Nixon regime and Watergate, Carter critiqued Ford for his irresponsible comments about Eastern Europe and his mishandling of a racist incident involving Secretary of Agriculture Earl Butz, and his aides condemned the incumbent for his Rose Garden reelection strategy and his deliberate distortions about Carter, including recent fabrications about infidelity and mental health breakdowns.[52] Although polling data suggested that potential voters bristled at negative attacks from the moral reform candidate, assaults from alternative channels proved successful.[53]

Mondale, in particular, became an effective campaign tool.[54] His basic stump speeches stressed Carter's primary campaign theme while simultaneously reminding the American people of the sins of Watergate. "If elected, we pledge to govern only as the people please, honestly, openly, and under the law. . . . One of the most tragic scars in the aftermath of Watergate is the perception today of a double standard in our system of justice," he told trail audiences.[55] Mondale further demonstrated his value to Carter's campaign during the nation's first vice presidential debate when he retorted that Ford's running mate, Bob Dole, "richly earned his reputation as a hatchet man."[56] Consensus-minded reporters conceded, despite Dole's more extensive preparations, that Mondale delivered a decisive victory with his effective one-liners.[57]

★ ★ ★

Behind the scenes, both candidates at their staffs' behest prepared for the last debate, a news event that they recognized as the final opportunity to re-iterate their unique appeals to the American public, to dispel any misinfor-mation regarding their candidacy, and to cautiously attack the opposition. Running low on funds, Carter's staff followed Kennedy's cue and sought to utilize the media pseudo-event as a strategic device to springboard the Democrat into the White House.[58] His advisors contended that the key to Carter's success in the second debate was his ability to direct his answers toward a discussion of his main themes and his willingness to attack Ford on the failures of the Republican platform. They observed that this strategy contributed to Ford's Eastern Europe gaffe, and they hoped Carter might deliver a repeat performance.[59]

This intention in mind, Carter's issues staff, under the direction of Ei-zenstat, pored over news coverage of Carter's performance in the first two debates. They contended that the most thoughtful coverage, interpretative analysis "written at least two days after the [second] debate," acknowledged that Carter was "capable of managing the office of the Presidency." "The leap of faith now required," they asserted, "is that he be perceived as 'Presiden-tial'—a short leap from his last performance." They noted that the only cri-tique of Carter's performance had surfaced around his "substance," not his style, but overall he was portrayed as a "man 'at home with himself,' tough, and possessing a cohesive point of view about foreign affairs."[60] Buttressing this position, Carter's advisors provided the candidate with excerpts from *New York Times* veteran Tom Wicker's recent news analysis and a *St. Louis Post-Dispatch* house editorial. They concluded by suggesting the obvious: Carter should project a presidential persona and avoid gaffes, such as Ford's Eastern Europe miscue.

Carter's debate team also provided the presidential aspirant with a sum-mative briefing book, which included polished answers developed for poten-tial questions about a variety of campaign issues, ranging from campaign contributions to the *Playboy* interview. The briefing book also offered points for Carter to highlight and to dispel, a brief summary of Carter's administra-tion as governor, and a news summary of media panelists' recent coverage.[61] Carter's advisors posed the most prescient counsel related to the *Playboy* ordeal, detailing specific responses for potential questions around the topic that dispelled the notion he was a risky choice because of his poor judgment surrounding the interview.[62] This information in hand, Carter spent hours preparing in the days leading up to the final debate.

Ford, however, devoted less time to debate preparations due to conflicting staff advice. Much of his staff agreed that Ford should only make minor modifications in the style and delivery of his one-liners. Only one advisor—his director of communications, David Gergen—suggested he make a substantive shift. "To win decisively," Gergen advised the president to offer a confident, relaxed delivery of several themes designed to put Carter on the defensive.[63] Forthcoming evidence suggested Ford did not heed this advice.

★ ★ ★

As both candidates prepared to take the stage for a news event that would be broadcast to millions by the networks, polls indicated that the presidential race was a dead heat, and consensus-minded reporters, defaulting to the horse race mode, speculated that the final installment was a must-win. Sensationalistic hype indicated the pseudo-event might be the "deciding factor" in an election promising a razor-thin victory margin and warned that a slight stumble might signal doom to either candidate.

This media speculation in mind, both candidates decided to play it safe by limiting opposition attacks. Carter only once delivered a blow to Ford—a predictable jab over the state of the economy, but otherwise both candidates refused to elicit an assault, even when opportunities to pounce on controversies, such as Watergate and *Playboy,* materialized. Instead, the reserved, poised candidates assured the American public that they were good, decent men who would guide the country down the path to peace and prosperity.[64]

Engaging in now standard political practice, both staffs declared victory on the heels of the media event and agreed that the presidential debates should be "institutionalized in [the] American political system."[65] Enhanced presidential power brokers, consensus-minded frontline reporters, interpreting analysis of the final campaign contest, declared that the last round was "a punchless draw" and admitted that the rather tepid event failed to live up to the predictions that it would rival the drama of *Monday Night Football.*[66] Both candidates, according to the *Chicago Tribune* Press Service's

Washington bureau chief, Jim Squires, appeared relaxed and reserved, but in the final analysis, the 1976 Great Debates left the "story unchanged," with the election too close to call.

Man-on-the-street reporting from Squires and industry colleagues revealed that many viewers found the event to be a primetime bore—the only glimmer of drama emanating from Carter's response to *Washington Post* editorial page staff member Robert Maynard's query about the controversial *Playboy* remarks. Carter's admittance that he had "gone astray" by accepting the interview satisfied at least one viewer, Kathy Choboda, a student at the College of William and Mary, who, alongside her classmates, meticulously deconstructed images of Carter and Ford during the debate for a university assignment. Needless to say, they were not the only ones studying the presidential debates.[67]

To the contrary, as *Wall Street Journal* managing editor Fred Taylor astutely observed at the campaign's outset: "There's the reporter covering the campaign, the reporter covering the reporter covering the campaign, and the sociologist covering the whole damn thing."[68] Alongside the sociologists, social scientists sought to gain a scholarly vantage point for the general election campaign's pivotal event. Scholars immediately recognized the opportunity to continue a promising avenue of research into shifts in voter perceptions of candidate personalities based on media exposure, but contrary to scholarship surrounding the 1960 presidential debates, research revealed that exposure to the media events prompted minimal effects on voter perceptions.[69] Research in 1976 and beyond indicated that exposure to presidential debates tended to yield the greatest influence on undecided swing voters, but otherwise the media events tended to freeze campaigns in place primarily by reinforcing beliefs about individual candidates and only exerting minimal influence on public perception of a candidate's image.[70] Carter learned these lessons firsthand, as his performances moderated his decline in the polls and reinforced voter perceptions about his image as an intelligent and competent leader who was concerned for America's future.[71]

Although both candidates issued media statements proclaiming the presidential debates' civic virtue, media experts and cultural critics expressed skepticism in their value as news events for the public's interest.[72] *New Yorker* journalist Elizabeth Drew, the moderator of the first installment, believed the debates were infotainment spectacles, designed for reporters to speculate over winners and losers and differences in style rather than substantive issues stances.[73] Wicker agreed, but he heaped more scorn on candidates, claiming that instead of lifting the "level of the Presidential campaign by focusing attention on the issues," the mediated pseudo-events afforded both candidates the opportunity to engage in showbiz politics by emphasizing "visual impact, confident mannerisms, slick debating points, exaggerated positions and facile use of evidence."[74] Wicker also clairvoyantly warned that the debates created a space for candidates to be disingenuous by offering "more misrepresentations" and for frontline journalists to damage their professional credibility through their involvement as panelists in the mediated pseudo-events. These two veterans echoed shared sentiments that cultural critics and scholars, such as Jeffery Auer, offered after the 1960 Great Debates: they were "counterfeit" media events.[75]

The 1976 presidential debates also dissatisfied many members of the general public. Hundreds of Americans issued last-minute telegrams and phone calls with queries for Nelson, Maynard, and syndicated columnist Joseph Kraft to direct toward both candidates, but, in the end, based on the discretion of the panelists and the constraints of the forum, most questions remained unasked and unanswered.[76] *Baltimore Sun* correspondent Richard O'Mara summarized the pervasive public reaction toward the debates: "they were dismissed as dull, uninformative, almost soporific." Influenced by nostalgia, he lamented that the revival failed to live up to the original, but nevertheless, despite their shortfalls, that they remained the best means to examine the candidates.[77]

Despite emerging critiques, many public officials agreed that the presidential debates were the most worthwhile prism through which to probe candidates during the general election campaign, and for what it was worth, they also continued to provide a popular source of material to lampoon candidates.[78] *Saturday Night Live* cast members, for instance, offered skits centered on the 1976 Great Debates on three occasions, and though Aykroyd jabbed at Carter for his controversial *Playboy* comments, Chevy Chase inflicted the greatest satirical damage to the president's campaign by bumbling and staging falls with such intensity that they ended in actual injury and remained etched forever in the minds of Americans as emblematic of Ford.[79]

★ ★ ★

In advance of his nomination, Ford's reelection team had divided the general election campaign into three phases—the Rose Garden interlude, the Great Debates, and Operation Over the Top, an eleventh-hour campaign blitz.[80] Ford's staff scheduled the ten-day, twenty-five-city, cross-country trip to immediately follow the final presidential debate, but to "offset the notion [Ford was] writing off the South," his advisors suggested including a southern leg in his itinerary. Thus, on the heels of the debates, recognizing an "opportunity to score major points in Carter's stronghold," they added a stop at the North Carolina State Fair in Raleigh.[81]

Ford's trek into Carter country coincided with the release of his new media campaign designed by political advertising heavyweights Doug Bailey and John Deardourff. When Bailey came onboard before the general election campaign, he was stunned by news that Ford's reelection team lacked a coherent media strategy, but based on his counsel, they wisely reserved much of their advertising budget for a last-ditch, one-two punch involving one-part image repair, one-part political attack.[82] To combat images of the bumbling oaf saturating popular culture, Bailey sought to strengthen the "human" and "leadership" dimensions of Ford's presidential persona by portraying his accomplishments, vision, and compassion. And though he acknowledged that one advertisement could not accomplish every strategic objective, he constructed a masterful spot that even left Rafshoon marveling at its genius forty years later.[83] In "Peace," Ford's seminal general election advertisement, Bailey transformed a sixty-second spot into a cinematic masterpiece, featuring a montage of average Americans—working men, mothers, the elderly, children, and African Americans in rural and urban settings—woven together to Ford's campaign soundtrack and his voice reminding Americans they enjoyed "the most precious gift of all. We are at peace."[84]

The release of Bailey's image-repair chef-d'oeuvre accompanied the broadcasting of a series of political attack ads, the wave of the future that had gained legitimacy in the prior decade.[85] Although Bailey incorporated the negative campaign to cut "Carter down to size," he acknowledged that engaging in the strategy would be "the most politically sensitive area that we will face in the campaign." "This is the first year in history that political advertising has been paid for by the people. The very worst thing that we could do would be to use that money for advertising that was misleading, or designed solely to undercut the opponent. We feel, however, that Carter is vulnerable to an honest, straightforward challenge on his positions."[86] Bailey recognized that he was incorporating a risky strategy, but it was a risk he and the Ford campaign, trailing Carter by seemingly insurmountable odds, were willing to take.[87] Incorporating Rafshoon's popular cinema-vérité technique, the end result was a series of anti-Carter, man-on-the-street ads featuring Georgians "underscor[ing] the doubts that most voters often voice[d] about Jimmy Carter."[88] "I'm from Atlanta, Georgia," one man told viewers. "My choice for president is Mr. Ford. Two months ago, I would've voted for Jimmy Carter. The more I know about Jimmy Carter, the less I think I'll vote for him." Bailey hoped the moderately negative spots might provoke Carter's campaign to engage in a comparable tactic, which would damage the Georgian's image as a good and decent candidate by exposing him as an unscrupulous politician and a mean southerner.[89] But Carter's advisors were too shrewd to respond to the bait and instead continuously encouraged Carter to allow Mondale to counter any political attacks on the trail.

Carter's imagecraft team, by contrast, disseminated a steady series of advertisements throughout the general election campaign, but with news that Ford had gained significant ground "among those groups that are most likely to vote," they allocated $2.5 million, the remainder of their advertising budget, to develop a new series of spots designed to generate a presidential persona.[90] After suffering internal criticism over Carter's declining appeal, Rafshoon sought assistance from political advertising expert Tony Schwartz, who had gained national recognition in the mid-1960s for Johnson's "daisy ad."[91] Rafshoon approached political advertising with a filmmaker's eye, looking to manufacture a simulacrum of the authentic candidate for voters, but Schwartz hoped to package voters for the candidate with simplistic advertisements featuring the next president of the United States in suit and tie speaking directly to the American people.[92] Schwartz endeavored to enhance the authentic, antiestablishment themes serving as the Carter campaign's foundation by repositioning the former Georgia governor as Roosevelt's heir.

Although Carter's staff encouraged Schwartz to avoid attack advertisements, he gained approval to offer one retort.[93] In "Reality," the candidate, donning presidential attire and speaking directly into the camera, addressed America's lived reality:

> When I look around, this is what I see—Eight million people, every one of them out of work. Every trip to the supermarket—a shock. Cities collapsing, suburbs

scared, hospitals closing, teachers fired, crime growing. Police departments—cut. Fire departments—cut. Daycare centers—shut. Welfare skyrocketing, energy in foreign hands.

That's our reality. It won't disappear because the Republicans say it's not there. But that doesn't mean we can't face it and work together, and change it. Americans have had to do it before, and we'll do it again. It's a long, tough job. It's time we got started.[94]

Rafshoon secured peak daytime and primetime network slots for the campaign's final month, and Schwartz's series of five-minute and sixty-second spots appeared alongside popular television programming, such as ABC's *General Hospital, Monday Night Football,* and *Happy Days.*[95]

As they had throughout the campaign, frontline reporters deconstructed spots designed to sell the next president to potential voters, and veterans quickly recognized the shift in how both candidates were packaged and underscored the role reversals to readers. *New York Times* media critic Joseph Lelyveld, who had introduced Rafshoon to Schwartz in the spring, appreciated the change earlier than most of his colleagues, and as he wrote, the new series of spots represented a transformation in philosophy and style.[96] Nonetheless, *Baltimore Sun* headline composers described Carter's makeover most succinctly ("Ties in, jeans out.") before Washington bureau chief Jim Mann articulated the transition in imagecraft strategy to readers. As Mann reported, Carter ditched his farmer's attire and southern backdrop for a suit and production studio to deliver a presidential image.[97]

Consensus-minded frontline reporters, however, did not limit scrutiny of showbiz politics to advertising spots. They also increasingly inspected various roles and functions of campaign imagecraft apparatuses. *Los Angeles Times* political reporter Bill Boyarsky, for instance, described the "little-known breed of political worker, advance men and women, people who are acutely aware of a fundamental rule of politics: not much happens that is spontaneous."[98] Boyarsky acknowledged the instrumental role advance staff had played in presidential campaigns since midcentury before dissecting the performances of Carter's advance staff at recent events in Scranton and New Orleans.[99] On the eve of the election, newspaper readers gained even greater insights into how Carter's staff staged campaign pseudo-events when UPI distributed the Knight News Service story deconstructing Carter's entire 111-page advance manual.[100]

★ ★ ★

Frontline reporters situated at mainstream outlets, yearning to avoid accusations of bias, pursued audiences with a detached brand of horse race analysis, but as the candidates entered the "homestretch," they embraced a more critical mode to voice final thoughts on the 1976 race. Despite diverse backgrounds, the consensus-minded pack settled on a general reproach of the "barren and petty" system of showbiz politics that echoed media criticism uttered since midcentury.[101] *New York Times* veteran political reporter R. W. Apple Jr., for instance, rebuked both candidates for colluding with campaign staffs to slickly "sell themselves as men worthy of trust" and engaging in underhanded attacks. But he did not overlook the pack's complicity, censuring them for their part in contributing to the emerging cultural malaise over trivial campaign coverage. "It is not possible to say whether the news media or the candidates themselves have had the most to do with the creation and perpetuation of these controversies, but both have certainly contributed, the candidates reaching for headlines and television time, the reporters seeking to enliven a pallid campaign."[102]

Pundits, such as Tory-leaning columnist George Will, echoed the consensus-minded pack's condemnation of the "grotesque campaign process" involved in the new age of showbiz politics. Within the system, staffs "moved heaven and earth to get forty seconds of television film" of their media pseudo-events, and reporters tried "to satisfy the public's sad superstition that the conduct of personal affairs can be televised and thereby made somehow accessible to all."[103] The bicentennial campaign devolved into the "most trivialized campaign in several generations," he contended, and all parties were to blame for the lack of commitment to the public interest and the loss of "a community of shared values."[104]

Will and his like-minded colleagues grappling with the "disease of American politics" echoed critiques cultural commentators had voiced since midcentury.[105] Critics only diverged in the shrillness of attacks against opposition forces. In formulating their assault, they collectively constructed a golden age of American politics, an environment free from artifice with candidates committed to the public interest debating about substantive issues affecting various interest groups, and they bemoaned in unison the loss of a sacred community with shared political values. In reality, this idyllic political milieu never existed. Post-1968 reforms stripped substantial power from traditional political elite and allowed more individuals to have a voice in the party nomination and electoral processes, but in the end, many individuals remained undecided and disillusioned based on their exposure to reformed showbiz politics.

The political cynicism and apathy many Americans experienced manifested themselves in data collected by polling experts, in subsequent news reports, and in letters to the editor of U.S. newspapers. The *New York Times* published new findings released by the Committee for the Study of the American Electorate, which revealed that "for the first time in 50 years, a majority of eligible voters may not cast ballots," and pundits speculated over whether apathy would be "the landslide winner in the election."[106] CBS News correspondent Roger Mudd indicated that this might be the case in his retrospective campaign summary and suggested that the new permutation of showbiz politics was the central cause.[107] Letters to the editor supported his claims: individuals, such as J. Schwartz of Newton, Massachusetts, were disenchanted by the political "sales campaign" and bemoaned the rise of a post-truth culture.[108]

To combat malaise, Carter unquestioningly turned to showbiz politics, enlisting the razzle-dazzle of sports celebrities, such as New England Patriots wide receiver Randy Vataha, to encourage citizens to engage in their civic duties. "We feel that no one can afford to neglect his obligation as a citizen," Vataha said. "We urge everyone to vote for a better future for our country." Vataha's name appeared aside those of fifty-three prominent athletes, including Grand Slam champion Arthur Ashe and home run king Henry "Hank" Aaron, on the list of the Committee of Professional Athletes for Carter-Mondale, distributed by Carter's staff to trail reporters.[109] In the final analysis, however, not even the home run king himself could inspire civic engagement in the bicentennial campaign.

★ ★ ★

Amid widespread apathy on election eve, newspaper publishers grappled with decisions over whether to continue the longstanding partisan tradition of candidate endorsements.[110] After more than a decade of attacks of bias, *Los Angeles Times* publisher Otis Chandler, concerned with the "credibility factor," ceased the practice, while *New York Times* publisher Arthur Ochs "Punch" Sulzberger continued with reservations.[111] However, one prominent national newspaper revived the tradition in Watergate's aftermath. The *Washington Post* staff explained its decision to readers: "A reasonable and respectable case can be made for the election of Gerald Ford. . . . A marginally stronger case can be made for the election of Jimmy Carter, if you believe the immediate and long-term future will require something else. We are inclined to the second of these propositions. . . . If this doesn't strike you as much of an endorsement, well, that's fine. It isn't meant to be. Not being in the business of manufacturing or marketing candidates, we offer no warranties."[112] Contrary to the "liberal establishment media" attack, newspaper publishers continued to offer Republican candidates their overwhelming support.[113] UPI reported that publishers were backing Ford (albeit rather unenthusiastically) by a margin of three to one.[114] And though Carter landed the tepid backing of several circulation leaders, including the *Times* and the *Post,* he struggled to gain widespread support, especially from southern newspaper publishers.[115]

When reporters scoured the latest neutral data to deliver sporting contest-inspired speculation on the presidential race's outcome, the polling data suggested that Carter was hemorrhaging support. The AP reported the latest results of the Harris Poll, which revealed that Carter retained a one-point lead, but acknowledged that the data "clearly indicate[d] a contest too close to call and an election outcome that could go either way."[116] As the newswire indicated, the presidential election would be decided by close contests in the ten largest states, including California, New York, Pennsylvania, Ohio, Illinois, and Michigan.

These close contests in mind, both candidates delivered final campaign performances. Ford traveled to Detroit to rally voters in Michigan with his "back home speech," and Carter journeyed to the West Coast in hopes of solidifying support in California.[117] But they both encountered last-minute crises that threatened to undermine support with key constituencies upon their arrival. Ford hoped to persuade undecided voters to join the Republican bandwagon with his "peace and prosperity" campaign in the election's closing days, but key indicators released by the Commerce Department sparked news of another downturn, lending credence to Carter's attacks of Ford's record on the economy.[118] But amid headlines that threatened to undermine support among African American and liberal voters, Carter could not capitalize on the national economic recovery's pause.

When news emerged that deacons from Carter's home church refused to admit Reverend Clennon King and three fellow African Americans to a regular worship service, consensus-minded campaign reporters collectively offered a final probe into Carter's faith and his commitment to social justice. "To some extent, 110 years after the nation's Civil War," *Chicago Tribune* Press Service correspondent Eleanor Randolph explained, "Jimmy Carter was trying to convince this country that a man from the South could be its President. But now, on the eve of the election, when every vote matters, his religion and his roots once again had become the most emotional issue in his campaign."[119]

Behind the scenes, consensus-minded campaign reporters never stopped scrutinizing Carter's character, and his roots, religion, and record on race were central to their probe of the most well-known, little-known New South son. Inspecting Carter's roots and his record on race required extensive investigative reporting, but an examination of his faith necessitated far less gumshoe effort. Trail reporters instead only had to arrive promptly at the site of their regular Sunday assignment—Plains Baptist Church, as they did two Sundays before the November 2 presidential election.

While sitting in pews during worship service, several frontline reporters noted Reverend Bruce Edwards's declaration condemning the creation of a "color line" in worship, and at an informal press session after the service, consensus-minded watchdogs once again collectively probed Carter at length concerning his faith. In response, Carter discussed his Bible-reading and prayer habits and even teased worldly wise reporters about their presence in his Sunday school class. Newshounds, however, soon turned to queries over Edwards's comments. When asked why the church was still segregated, Carter indicated that the church was integrated until 1880, "when blacks broke away by choice," and he presumed the church was now open to all.[120]

When Carter's assertion proved false, consensus-minded frontline reporters, biased toward chic character examinations and sensational campaign controversies, recognized a major story and initiated their final collective probe into Carter's religion, roots, and record on race. Carter reached out to advisor Andrew Young, who suggested that Carter should condemn the deacons' actions and reiterate his consistent opposition to the rule. Although many critics and some supporters suggested Carter should leave the church if King were not admitted, the candidate listened to Young's advice and, when probed about the matter at a press conference, promised "to stay with the church to try to change the attitude which I abhor."[121] Concurrently, Carter's press staff released statements of support from family and key African American supporters and suggested to reporters that King's actions might have been politically motivated.[122]

Invested in the system of reformed showbiz politics, both candidates reserved significant financial resources for a last-ditch media barrage, and now both hoped that culminating efforts—two half-hour television specials broadcast across all three major networks—might overshadow any bad press. However, inspired by the campaign canon, consensus-minded frontline reporters, suspicious of Hollywood-inspired appeals, remained committed to fashionable deconstructions of showbiz tactics.[123] "A presidential campaign probably dominated as never before by television came to an end appropriately last night with Republican nominee Gerald Ford and Democratic nominee Jimmy Carter making 11th-hour, saturation-coverage TV appeals to voters," one reporter told his audience.[124] Before reviewing the final political performances, consensus-minded reporters noted that the specials were accompanied by a steep price tag, approximately $100,000, one both campaigns did not hesitate to invest.[125]

Embracing the journalistic craze over transparent analysis, *Washington Post* veteran political reporter Jules Witcover incisively deconstructed the showbiz tactics behind each special. Making visible obscured backstage decisions, he acknowledged appeals from Ford's celebrity endorsers, NBC sports announcer Joe Garagiola Sr. and Broadway performer Pearl Bailey, before focusing attention on candidate wardrobe transformations: eliciting Carter's everyman appeal, Ford appeared in casual short sleeves and a vest; meanwhile, evoking a presidential image, the folksy former Georgia governor dressed in his Sunday finest and situated himself behind his desk to answer queries posed by average citizens filmed in the streets, on the farm, and in their homes in an "untarnished and undirected and unrehearsed" format he hoped to continue once in the White House.[126] Although Witcover noted showbiz elements in both specials, he expressed the most concern over Carter's Q&A session, which he believed possessed the strongest overtones of Nixon's permanent campaign.[127] In actuality, both candidates modeled their campaigns based on those of recent predecessors, implementing reformed showbiz techniques and evolving media relations tactics honed by presidential imagecraft teams since midcentury.[128]

★ ★ ★

Amid this mediascape, Carter ended his four-year quest for the White House in much the same way he started—a whirlwind campaign tour. However, he no longer shook hands with farmers in Iowa; instead he was the focal point of media pseudo-events staged for the multitudes.[129] But Carter's staff still implemented elements of the grassroots media campaign that contributed to his nomination. For instance, the Peanut Brigade embarked on a nine-day, seven-state bus caravan, and Carter fielded questions from average Americans in his reincarnation of Roosevelt's "Fireside Chats." Nevertheless, these imagecraft acts were mere simulacra of Carter's early grassroots media campaign—performances antagonistic campaign watchdogs were eager to deconstruct and label as evidence that the peanut farmer-nuclear physicist remained an enigma.[130]

Aboard *Peanut One*, tensions among Carter, his staff, and traveling reporters were palpable in the campaign's closing moments. Wielding transparency as a weapon, *Chicago Tribune* Press Service correspondent Bill Neikirk offered fly-on-the-wall analysis: "Jimmy Carter's campaign jet bumped and bounced through a driving Georgia thunderstorm . . . [during] an impromptu 2 a.m. press conference. . . . No single scene better symbolizes Carter's relations with the press in general and individual reporters in particular this election year. For despite his attempts to befriend them, their relationship has been as stormy as the weather was that morning a few days ago."[131]

On their final flight, campaign reporters, following longstanding tradition, offered the candidate a spontaneous tribute, but Carter sat in relative isolation, struggling to make small talk with the political power brokers that he believed were most responsible for his decline in public opinion polls. Instead of offering final thoughts on his meteoric rise, he brushed past celebrity kingmakers with whom he once sought to cull rapport before sequestering himself in his first-class compartment for the flight's duration.[132] The political underdog had negotiated the new rules of American politics to great effect, but despite his campaign's best efforts, he had yet to master one of the most important facets of the permanent campaign—media relations.

Conclusion

The President versus the News Media—Who'll Win?

On the eve of the 1976 election, *Village Voice* staff writer Ken Auletta considered "how Carter play[ed] the press[, and] who'll win" for *More: The Media
Magazine,* a glossy spinoff of the journalism review that sought to reform
mainstream media mired in a credibility crisis.[1] Inspired by introspective
insider accounts of the 1972 campaign, Auletta's exposé revealed the push-
pull dynamics involved in campaign communication under the new rules
of American politics. Auletta presciently deconstructed calculated moves
devised by political actors at the center of the action. "The three principal
actors—candidate, public, and press—are each seeking to manipulate the
other," he wrote. "The candidate carefully picks his spots hoping to maxi-
mize the media impact—the sense of crowds surging and pressing in upon
him," while the public performs for the cameras and reporters jockey to
gather images on deadline.[2] Echoing social historian Daniel Boorstin's argument that American politics was comprised of constructed pseudo-events—
theorized as the hyperreal in postmodern theorist Jean Baudrillard's *Simulacra and Simulation* (1981)—Auletta's incisive analysis suggested that
the meticulous media strategies and practices of Carter's imagecraft team
blurred the private self and the political persona into simulacra and ushered
in the age of the hyperreal in showbiz presidential politics.[3]

As Auletta keenly dissected, Carter's advisors constructed his campaign
around the midcentury bipartisan mentality that became political reality
in the mid-1970s—a well-organized imagecraft apparatus could become *the*
central source of political authority.[4] To that end, the former Georgia governor and his advisors, in reaction to credibility crises that developed in the
1950s and 1960s, consulted public opinion polls and political strategists to

construct a second-order image involving the transfiguration of a simple peanut farmer from Plains into America's moral reformer and political savior, who could heal national wounds inflicted by Vietnam and Watergate by offering the country a government as good as its people.[5] But in reaction to the political milieu, the cynical campaign pack, distrustful of the politician who "with a straight face . . . promises never to lie," greeted Carter with constant scrutiny on the trail. "They are always on guard, watchful of his every move," Auletta wrote. "[Only Carter's] absurd claim gives the press their potential advantage in the chess game. So they spend a fair amount of time searching for evidence Carter is lying—or at least fudging."[6]

Auletta's introspective campaign account supplemented fashionable campaign canon-inspired acts of deconstruction by industry colleagues, such as *Newsweek*'s Peter Goldman and Eleanor Clift, who observed that Carter was like an actor in search of a new leading role, auditioning as: "Gentle Jimmy preaching love and compassion and the Tough Jimmy attacking Gerald Ford as brainwashed; the Democratic Jimmy embracing party tradition and the Independent Jimmy keeping his distance from it. . . . The search has stretched his smile thin in public, reduced him to passages of glowering silence offstage—and only lately returned him full circle to the evangelical Winning Jimmy persona that got him nominated."[7] In the end, his performance as "twice-born" Winning Jimmy, the Democratic party's savior, who promised to unite the nation with a message of love and healing, resonated with the necessary majority of American voters and propelled him to a narrow victory over Ford.

As *More*'s election-eve account suggested, covering Carter's campaign proved as challenging as "playing chess with Bobby Fischer," but in staging the former Georgia governor's miraculous rise, Carter's advisors revealed themselves to be masterful media strategists, prompting frontline reporters to hail the peanut farmer from Plains as a media genius after his narrow victory. And though elite reporters and establishment party regulars tested their media strategy in the marathon campaign, through the media presidency Carter and his staff sought to formalize their permanent campaign to develop a ruling mandate in the White House.[8] But the question remained, in a political landscape pitting the president against news media, who would win the next round, or as the journalism review's name suggested, might a new page be turned?

★ ★ ★

"Governor, congratulations on your victory," ABC News correspondent Sam Donaldson said, extending his hand to commend Carter on his meteoric rise. "What did you say?" Carter responded. "He hadn't heard me right, but he was ready for a fight," Donaldson recalled. "He had just won the presidency, but instead of having that great glow, he was frustrated." Carter was irritated that network news anchors had taken an inordinate amount of time to confirm his victory before announcing it to the American public, and he was aggravated that since August he had watched as what many in the news industry declared was an insurmountable lead nearly slipped away.[9] Instead of witnessing the landslide many believed would serve as his governing mandate, Americans were spectators to "The Carter Tailspin," as a *Wall Street Journal* desk editor framed the collapsing campaign.[10]

Consensus-minded national reporting indicated that conduct aboard *Peanut One* contributed to the tailspin. "As the huge engines roared into reverse, causing a radical deceleration, several reporters unleashed a rolling salvo of empty beer cans down the narrow aisle, cheering lustily as several of the missiles penetrated the private quarters of the Democratic Presidential candidate," *New York Times* rookie trail reporter Jim Wooten offered as evidence of the anger that campaign reporters felt toward the next president. "'Take that, Carter!' challenged an irreverent voice from the rear."[11] Carter and his staff shared equal disdain toward elite reporters at establishment news media, an antipathy that, combined with Carter's rigid adherence to schedules, prompted him to encourage his pilot to take off without members of the traveling press in the wee hours following his historic victory. Only warnings from press aides prevented the president-elect from stranding the group that collectively proved to be the most important architects of Carter's image in the coming years.[12]

In the short term, Carter's aggressions toward reporters did not contribute to adverse media coverage. CBS News correspondent Ed Bradley, for instance, offered telegenic images of a father carrying his dozing daughter off *Peanut One,* a loving mother's embrace, and a small-town celebration of the regional hero's triumphant return. "Any way you looked at it, it was a long night," Bradley introduced his broadcast package with powerful words and footage woven together to accompany his tightly scripted standup delivered from Main Street. "If ever there was a small town boy who grew up, made good and never forgot the home folks, it was Jimmy Carter, and if ever there was a mother proud of her son, it had to be Miss Lillian. . . . Carter was home again in this almost make-believe town." Bradley pivoted to film from Carter's resonant victory speech: "It's been twenty-two months, and I didn't get choked up until . . . until I turned the corner and saw you standing there. I had the best organization . . . the best family . . . the best home community . . . the best supporters in my home state . . . that any candidate ever had, and the only reason we were close last night was because the candidate wasn't quite as good as a campaigner, but I'll make up for that when I am president."[13] The presidential aspirant particularly had struggled with his personal campaign with elite news reporters. Despite their mutual loathing, celebrity frontline reporters temporarily offered Carter a truce akin to the one they had afforded Nixon nearly a decade prior, and Bradley's news package circulated alongside an onslaught of triumphant narratives flooding the airwaves, news wires, and headlines in the coming days.[14] Even so, Carter's media relations during his tailspin affirmed the pack's assessment of the peanut farmer from Plains as a single-minded, calculated, ruthless, or just plain mean politician and contributed to a troubled first term in office that marred Carter's permanent campaign.[15]

★ ★ ★

Broder and his colleagues voiced concern over biases in bicentennial campaign reporting, but despite warnings from veterans, an adversarial mentality was on the rise as pundits at partisan news media outlets privileged ideological purity over political pragmatism and as chic, antiestablishment newshounds at mainstream media outlets sought out political corruption in the aftermath of Vietnam and Watergate.[16] Reflexive reporters acknowledged the emergence of an adversarial mentality on the trail manifesting itself in Watergate-inspired watchdog interrogations of Carter's central campaign promise—to "never tell a lie"—and now investigative-minded reporters, harboring ambitions of being heralded as the next Woodward or Bernstein, sought any evidence of presidential scandal.[17]

In "L'affaire Lance" they uncovered a scandal that doomed Carter's media presidency. Lance-gate originated from Carter's campaign to bring longtime friend and advisor Bert Lance into the White House as the director of the Office of Management and Budget. During Lance's Senate confirmation hearings, news swirled that the Justice Department had investigated the OMB designee the year prior for possible violations of election laws in his 1974 gubernatorial campaign; furthermore, frontline watchdogs uncovered allegations that Lance and his family took advantage of his bank's "permissive policy on overdrafts."[18] Despite initial questions raised by press coverage, the Senate Governmental Affairs Committee confirmed Lance after a light round of questioning and a promise that he would divest himself from any stock held in National Bank of Georgia.

After Lance requested an extension in the summer of 1977, watchdog reporters resumed their investigations. Heeding advice to "follow the money," the investigative mantra made famous in the recent blockbuster *All the President's Men,* they subsequently uncovered a "pattern of corner-cutting and dubious banking practices" ranging from persistent overdrafts to questionable "correspondent" banking relationships that resulted in "sweetheart arrangements" in the form of personal interest-free loans and improper collateral.[19] Reports of new allegations prompted another round of investigations from the Senate Governmental Affairs Committee, the Comptroller of the Currency, the Justice Department, and the Internal Revenue Service. When the Comptroller of the Currency thereafter found the OMB director guilty of fifty violations of regulations and unsound banking practices but deemed he was "innocent of any prosecutable offense," Carter, in haste, "reaffirmed his faith" in Lance.[20] But Carter offered his pronouncement of virtue too soon, and after persistent negative coverage and calls from the Senate for Lance's resignation, Carter felt pressure to cut ties with his longtime advisor.

During Lance-gate, Carter's "Watergate-propelled" presidency directly clashed with a Watergate-obsessed adversarial news media.[21] Editors plastered new allegations of past misdeeds in the headlines of every major U.S. newspaper and newsmagazine, and network crews stationed themselves outside of Lance's Georgetown home ready to break the story they hoped might rival the Watergate break-in scandal.[22] The most damaging coverage for the moral reform president, hailed as a media genius for his campaign to restore ethics in government, included allegations that he enjoyed favorable loans and travel arrangements during the 1976 campaign and speculation that he was an ineffective communicator who mishandled the incident.

The Lance affair ultimately represented a major turning point in Carter's media presidency, a moment in which the image that contributed directly to his election unraveled; in the aftermath, newshounds removed their muzzles and Carter became embittered by coverage and disillusioned by his relationship with frontline reporters. The incident not only tarnished Carter's image as an effective leader, it also contributed to a steep decline in his public approval ratings, which thereafter hovered around 40 percent, down from its peak at around 70 percent shortly after his inauguration. (It eventually plummeted even further.)[23]

Despite plans for an image makeover orchestrated by incoming White House Communications Director Gerald Rafshoon, mediated images of an administration in "disarray" lingered throughout the remainder of Carter's presidency.[24] Carter and his imagecraft apparatus attempted to outmaneuver watchdog reporters through showbiz-inspired controlled media and news management techniques, but when reporters, cynical of hyperreal showbiz politics, learned of these latest developments, they balked at the specter of Nixon's long shadow over Carter's White House. They collectively recoiled at the institution of a White House Actuality Service, and they mocked the Carter administration's imagecraft through satire, sketching "the secretary of symbolism" in Rafshoon's form.[25]

As an adversarial mentality permeated this milieu, attack dogs pounced on a string of self-inflicted "political embarrassments" plaguing Carter's presidency in September 1979, most notably "rapid-fire Cabinet dismissals" in the wake of his "crisis of confidence" speech and allegations that incoming Chief of Staff Hamilton Jordan had snorted cocaine while visiting New York City's infamous Studio 54 disco club the prior April.[26] The subsequent climate prompted some U.S. citizens to ask if Carter was not "part of the 'crisis.'"[27]

In the ensuing months, Carter and his closest advisors faced crises at every turn, from public relations snafus, such as his encounter with a "killer rabbit," and domestic challenges, such as the energy shortage and economic downturn, to international threats, such as the Iran Hostage Crisis. The Carter administration attempted to "beat back" these attacks while navigating its 1980 reelection campaign.[28] But efforts proved largely fruitless, as a series of domestic threats and international crises vanquished the beleaguered president. In the final analysis, however, Carter's efforts to win a second term were thwarted by more than the unfortunate series of events that unfolded in his last year in office; his permanent campaign suffered from a third-order collapse in communication, and future political actors gleaned important insights from miscalculations in Carter's communiqués with news media.

★ ★ ★

Just five days after Carter's unofficial launch of his 1980 reelection campaign aboard the *Delta Queen* on the Mississippi River, he was forced to address his most recent self-inflicted "presidential embarrassment"—the "killer rabbit incident"—before a group of Tampa newspaper editors on the eve of his Labor Day vacation in Plains. It was a "robust-looking rabbit who was swimming without any difficulty," Carter told reporters. "I had a paddle in the boat, and when the rabbit got close enough to the boat for me to recognize it. . . . I just splashed water toward him, and he finally veered his course."[29] The press conference marked the first time the president had publicly addressed the "killer rabbit incident" since the AP broke the story.[30] Carter believed he had settled journalistic queries into the embarrassing matter by addressing it at the press conference, but the nation's consensus-minded adversarial newshounds were not so quick to let the bunny go.

The *Post* provided the most memorable coverage of the killer rabbit incident with its page-one headline, "Bunny Goes Bugs—Rabbit Attacks President," which accompanied the AP story and an unforgettable William Coulter "Paws" cartoon, a parody inspired by Steven Spielberg's 1975 summer blockbuster *Jaws*. But the *Post* was not the only major U.S. newspaper to carry the AP account on its front page.[31] Likewise, network producers featured "breaking news" of the "banzai bunny" attack prominently on evening newscasts.[32]

Germond and Jules Witcover aptly summarized Carter's predicament in their syndicated column "Politics Today." "The story . . . is, no doubt about it, funny," the increasingly prominent analysts observed. "The newspapers and the cartoonists are having a field day with it, and that is inevitable. . . . But it is particularly unfortunate for the story to have surfaced about this beleaguered President: It serves him up for the one ingredient in politics with which few officeholders can effectively deal—ridicule." They concluded "the image of a rabbit swimming torpedo-like through the water with mayhem in his pink eyes toward the hapless canoeist, and the canoeist thrashing at him with his paddle, is too close a parody of how many people see Carter in his job."[33] "The story wasn't very important, except that it took on a life of its own," Jagoda recalled of the incident, which taught him an important political lesson: "If you live by symbolism, you can die by symbolism."[34] In the final analysis, the picture of Carter flailing haplessly at the hands of a killer rabbit afforded, in the eyes of many consensus-minded, adversarial frontline reporters, the perfect metaphor for Carter's presidency, and the image lingered in the American imagination.

Carter's advisors hoped to win reelection in 1980 on an updated version of the evangelical "Winning Jimmy" persona, presenting the nation with the political savior who brought healing to the nation, the candidate of "peace and prosperity."[35] However, regular reports of domestic concerns over unemployment and inflation and breaking coverage of *America Held Hostage: The Iranian Crisis,* which ensued after the seizure of more than sixty American citizens by Iranian revolutionaries in November 1979, thwarted that plan. Consequently, Carter's advisors searched for new themes that might resonate with the last vestige of a consensus-minded American public.[36] When, amid increasingly fragmented, partisan audiences, the Carter campaign struggled to reach its fracturing coalition, Carter's advisors engaged in an emerging best practice in political campaigning.[37] They opted to "go negative" against Republican frontrunner Ronald Reagan by portraying him as an extremist who might create conflict at home and spark nuclear war abroad.[38] It was a fateful mistake.

The president and his advisors failed to consider unintended negative effects to Carter's persona. When candidate Carter slipped into the role of "Tough Jimmy" during the general election campaign, reporters underscored material reinforcing their confirmation bias toward the Georgian as a product of the mean South.[39] Chic, antiestablishment watchdogs deconstructed Carter's image, transparently acknowledging attempts to "go negative" against Reagan, the new anti-Washington outsider, and exposed the public to the image of a frail, crotchety politician. "Just as surely as the werewolf grows long fangs and facial hair on a full moon, the darker side of President Carter emerges in election years," *Boston Globe* veteran campaign reporter Curtis Wilkie wrote.[40]

Based on advice from his campaign manager and public relations specialist Michael Deaver, Reagan also focused attention on "Gentle Jimmy's" change in demeanor.[41] During the 1980 presidential debate on October 28, the savvy political actor masterfully delivered his well-rehearsed zinger. "There you go again," Reagan retorted in response to Carter's attack of his record of opposition to Medicare, thereby accentuating the contradiction in Carter's political persona and the emerging hostility of "Mean Jimmy."[42]

Reagan's staff juxtaposed Carter's image as a cranky, impotent leader with the one that they had surreptitiously constructed for Reagan by borrowing from the tableau of the American west. They had crafted a rugged cowboy, a Washington outsider who envisioned a plan to make America great again and who was optimistic about the nation's future.[43] In the age of the hyperreal, Deaver borrowed from a number of iconic elements that had contributed to Carter's winning formula four years prior to project, in the words of Baudrillard, a fourth-order image of the "Great Communicator."[44] He constructed Reagan as a confident, antiestablishment figure determined to change the course of the national narrative, and the former actor willingly played the role of America's political maverick, deftly jabbing at the president along the trail. "Recession is when your neighbor loses his job. Depression is when you lose yours. And recovery is when Jimmy Carter loses his," Reagan often told crowds at rallies, the modern-day stump, pointing out broken promises and other sins of the moral reform president.[45]

On the night of his presidential debate with Carter, Reagan flawlessly delivered lines from his campaign's primary script: "Are you better off than you were four years ago? . . . Is there more or less unemployment in the country than there was four years ago? Is America as respected throughout the world as it was?"[46] For voters, who struggled to answer these questions in the affirmative, he presented himself as the only solution.[47] Reagan's message resonated with American voters, and with his debate performance he delivered his own "October Surprise" to the neck-and-neck 1980 presidential campaign: an unexpected outcome manifesting itself in an electoral landslide the following Tuesday.[48]

★ ★ ★

During the 1980 election cycle, political actors behaved consistently based on training and experience. Campaign advisors plotted their next move based on the new rules of primary showbiz politics. Consequently, they invested in big-name media consultants to poll constituents of special interest coalition groups to uncover promising themes for paid and unpaid media; they coordinated with skilled advance teams to stage every last detail of campaign pseudo-events designed to provide compelling images for local and national reporters, and they enlisted the services of opposition research teams to plan attacks and counterassaults against their enemies, including celebrity frontline reporters, the national agenda-setters whom they accused of biased, horse race reporting.[49]

Despite moments of reflexive thought and self-criticism, celebrity frontline reporters employed at mainstream media outlets continued to embrace their enhanced roles: they mediated key moments in the election cycle—the (in)visible primaries, the caucuses and primaries, the party conventions, the general election kickoffs, the presidential debates, and election-eve events—and they speculated on these decisive battles and analyzed every move of political frontrunners. In deciding *what* to cover and *how* to cover it, elite reporters remained prominent political gatekeepers and news agenda-setters.[50] These key kingmakers in presidential politics transformed into commanding political actors, and they extended their political influence when they took on roles as moderators and panelists in presidential debates and pundits after prominent political contests.[51] By further injecting themselves into presidential campaigns in such visible manners, however, chic, adversarial watchdogs ultimately lent credence to claims of bias and further undermined the most important facet of their brand—their credibility.[52]

Under these conditions, the modern bias of campaign news toward the drama of conflicts and controversies and the cultural shorthand of stereotypes, gaffes, and zingers defined campaign reportage in the 1980 election cycle. Reagan's campaign managed to limit the damage inflicted from these journalistic inclinations through his controlled news media access, his effective issue-of-the-day strategy, and his opposition attack plan.[53] He also serendipitously benefitted from three enduring crises of the 1970s—the crisis of confidence in American politics and media; the domestic economic crisis; and the geopolitical crisis, which culminated in the Iran Hostage Crisis.[54]

Carter's moderate approach to these political crises, the key to his success in the bicentennial campaign, left him "caught in the middle" throughout his term in office and saddled by popular reporters with the image of being a weak, incompetent incumbent. In the 1980 general election's closing weeks, Carter and his advisors witnessed the complete collapse of their permanent campaign.[55] Once again turning to cultural shorthand, campaign newshounds regularly referred to candidate Carter as mean, and in the aftermath of the presidential debate the consensus-minded pack emphasized the most newsworthy gaffe (Carter's assertion that his daughter Amy offered him advice on nuclear arms proliferation) and zinger (Reagan's infamous "There you go again" quip).[56]

Although Reagan's advisors strategically fretted to consensus-minded campaign reporters over an "October Surprise" (the potential for positive coverage and a subsequent public opinion bump that successful last-minute negotiations for the hostages' release might bring the Carter administration), Reagan's campaign proved the ultimate victor when on the Sunday prior to the election Carter interrupted regular network NFL coverage to tell the American public of new terms for the release of fifty-two U.S. hostages.[57] Robert Kaiser, a campaign reporter at the adversarial, antiestablishment *Washington Post* branded Carter's remarks as an ill-timed, ill-conceived, roll-of-the-dice decision to circumvent elite reporters by sharing promising news of the potential hostage release directly with the American public.[58]

But Carter failed to harness the mainstream national narrative to his advantage, and instead, on election eve, network correspondents focused on the one-year anniversary of the Iran Hostage Crisis. As Kaiser observed, industry leader CBS offered "the longest and most vivid" account: "Correspondent Charles Osgood reviewed the agonies of the past year with accompanying film clips of the worst moments: blindfolded American diplomats in Tehran, a burnt-out American helicopter in the desert, Richard Queen's emotional arrival home, and many more. Osgood recalled Carter's political maneuvering around the hostage crisis, and implicitly also recalled for 25 or 30 million viewers the administration's failure to cope effectively with this national embarrassment."[59] As Kaiser suggested, anniversary specials bombarded American audiences with footage of "the worst moments" of the Iran Hostage Crisis, reinforcing pervasive images from the last year of Carter's first term and the national news narrative of a failed presidency.

In the wake of the 1980 election, reporters—producers of the first draft of history—scorned the man they once hailed as a media genius and labeled Carter's administration as a failure. Carter himself pointed to narrative collapse, amid a storyline more persuasively performed by the former Hollywood B-film actor, as the primary source of his defeat: "As far as I am concerned, the impression didn't change until after I was confronted by Ronald Reagan, until after the 1980 election. He was looked upon as a master communicator, and compared to him, I was inadequate."[60]

Many consensus-minded frontline reporters agreed. "[Carter] *was* a great communicator in one sense," broadcast correspondent Judy Woodruff said.[61] "He had a message that resonated in the aftermath of Watergate and Vietnam." Elite reporters at mainstream media outlets subsequently praised Carter's administration for its open press access and in-tune press secretary, but amid an adversarial milieu surfacing after presidential and journalistic credibility crises, many reporters bristled at his Nixon-inspired media presidency, transparently deconstructing the administration's efforts to go public; its overexposed, staged qualities; its leaks and disjointed message; and its antagonistic relationships with members of the news media.[62]

Reagan, by contrast, was known as the master of the medium, an affable father figure who enjoyed the company of reporters. As historian David Greenberg aptly put it, "Reagan was less an innovator than an apotheosis [of showbiz techniques]."[63] Longtime CBS News correspondent and author of *The Acting President* Bob Schieffer offered an anecdote indicative of Reagan's mastery of communication: "I once watched Reagan step off the helicopter on the South Lawn. He looked to his right then he looked to his left, and he waved. I looked around, and there was nobody there, but [Reagan] never took a bad picture. It was all part of his persona. He once told me that the most important tool in his toolkit was his ability to communicate. . . . He said that he came to understand that everything that a president does—the way he walks, his posture, his attitude—is all part of communicating that 'I am the president.'"[64]

Longtime AP reporter Walter Mears asserted that if a killer rabbit attacked Reagan, the amicable president would have spun a funny little yarn for his friends in the news media about his strength in fending off "some nut rabbit"; instead, combative reporters, frustrated by the humorless president's contentious media relations, deployed the funny little episode to fit a broader image about Carter's "ineffectual" leadership.[65] The killer rabbit incident, like the *Playboy* gaffe, "played into the meme of the moment," as Woodruff aptly put it, and signaled the ascendancy of the adversarial mode.[66] "After Watergate, despite the most noble of journalistic intentions, a gotcha mentality developed amongst younger reporters who dreamed of becoming the next [Bob] Woodward and [Carl] Bernstein," Witcover concurred.

Political actors and scholars often attributed Carter's one-term presidency to a series of unfortunate events, but it was news *images* of these internal and external crises that came to define the Carter administration.[67] Chic, frontline reporters, key national gatekeepers and agenda-setters, (re)-

presented Carter's presidency to the American public based on adversarial perceptions of the U.S. media, politics, and the peanut farmer from Plains, and many members of the American public, internalizing the news media's cultural shorthand, voted against the weak, incompetent leader that they deemed was responsible for failing to solve the nation's crises.

Reagan's advisors certainly recognized this phenomenon. From their vantage point, an adversarial news media had driven the last four presidents from office, and after encountering firsthand the impact of the news media's unpredictable treatment of the Iran Hostage Crisis, they determined that they would not be defined by liberal establishment media coverage of crises. "Their intention from the start was to keep the press from calling the shots: No longer would reporters be the arbiters of what constitutes a crisis, nor be the judges of a President's responsibility," wrote *New York Times* senior White House correspondent Steven Weisman as Reagan's reelection campaign entered its final days in October 1984.[68] Reagan's advisors realized that political communication had evolved into, as Auletta's perceptive reporting in *(More)* suggested, a chess match by the mid-1970s, and they sought to keep the media in check by perfecting the art of controlled media access, which included limiting exposure to unrehearsed televised news conferences, maximizing stage-managed photo-ops with limited opportunities for questions from reporters, and instituting the administration's Nixon-inspired unified line of the day.[69]

This series of moves left probing reporters temporarily vanquished, "relegated to the role of a passive spectator" of the "Great Communicator," while many Americans, who already shared negative perceptions of the news media, expressed little concern over restricted press access and "loss of information to the public."[70] Although some elite reporters situated at mainstream media outlets ultimately challenged Reagan, "in a climate more sympathetic to the needs of the President than to the needs of the press," the president simply dismissed confrontational members of the liberal establishment media and persisted, and the public remained silent.[71]

Though both presidents experienced an adversarial press, as Witcover and Woodruff acknowledged, Reagan learned lessons from Carter's White House follies.[72] Reagan's media handlers limited access to the press and strictly controlled political communication; as a result, Reagan's White House spoke the message of the day with a unified voice, offering a model that future politicians emulated.[73] If Carter's campaign and presidency revealed the importance of media relations in presidential showbiz politics, the Reagan Revolution revealed what the full mastery of presidential image might mean. "Reagan, I think, set the tone," Woodruff said. "Everybody after Reagan has seen how successful they were at focusing on image and presentation and . . . frankly controlling access."[74]

The development of an intricate system of political handlers further contributed to the emerging divide among politicians and journalists and magnified adversarial impulses, Witcover asserted, but as the Cold War era of passive, consensus-minded journalism fractured amid the emergence of niche media outlets and credibility crises in American politics and journalism in the 1960s and 1970s, "a real adversarial relationship developed."[75] In a presidential mediascape dominated by controlled access, relationships among reporters and politicians became more distant, more remote, more adversarial. As Auletta and Weisman predicted, in subsequent years other prominent American presidential actors relied on basic strategies of game theory learned from this pivotal decade in national politics and journalism, and an adversarial mentality permeated the scene, contributing to lingering crises of confidence and legitimacy in U.S. presidential politics and the news media that continue to undermine American democracy.[76]

Epilogue

From "Lust in My Heart" to "Grab 'em by the Pussy"

"You know, I'm automatically attracted to beautiful [women]," reality television star Donald Trump confessed to *Access Hollywood* personality Billy Bush as he fumbled for a Tic Tac on a tour bus on the studio lot nearby the *Days of Our Lives* soap opera set in 2005. "I just start kissing them. It's like a magnet. Just kiss. I don't even wait. And when you're a star, they let you do it. You can do anything. Grab 'em by the pussy. You can do anything."[1] *Access Hollywood*'s live microphone caught private admissions of two public figures, but the tape remained buried in the NBC Universal archives until an anonymous source shared the tip with *Washington Post* campaign reporter David Fahrenthold in October 2016. The veteran political journalist "didn't hesitate."[2] He recognized he was in a race with NBC News to break the biggest story of the 2016 presidential campaign.

Allegations of Trump's sexual misconduct caused unrivaled shock waves on the trail. In the immediate hours following the breaking campaign controversy, frontline reporters and partisan pundits interpreted what the "October Surprise" meant for the Republican nominee's chances on election day. "This is the end," they said, echoing in unison the sentiment one GOP source confided to MSNBC campaign correspondent Katy Tur.[3] But members of the political establishment and media elite were mistaken. News scandals did not signal the end of Trump's antiestablishment campaign; instead, they portended the demise of establishment opponent Hillary Clinton and the commencement of the Trump administration.

★ ★ ★

Forty years after the miraculous rise of a peanut farmer from Plains, cultural observers of the 2016 U.S. election cycle witnessed a resurgence of presidential dark horses, such as Republicans Ben Carson, Carly Fiorina, and Donald Trump and Democratic socialist Bernie Sanders, who railed against the establishment from an overcrowded field and exploited favorable tendencies in the news media to gain free advertising and national exposure during the (in)visible primaries.[4] Carter introduced the nation to the marathon campaign, and by the 2016 race, contenders toiled for grassroots appeal, fundraising dollars, political endorsements, and national media attention more than a year prior to the first caucus or primary. With the rules established in the mid-1970s now ingrained as the common-sense logic of presidential politics, candidates sought "pure gold" that accompanied free media exposure and recognized that wins in early contests served as "psychological springboards" to their party's nomination in a landscape biased toward the news media's presidential horse race.[5] Much as they had forty years prior, elite reporters predicted that eventual nominees would arise from the Washington establishment, but one antiestablishment candidate practicing a long-perfected brand of hyperreal showbiz politics thrived in a contentious primary season battle, surviving media scrutiny and party resistance by attacking the establishment.[6]

Amid a divisive, hyper-partisan cultural climate provoked by lingering crises of confidence and legitimacy in American presidential politics and news media, Trump rose to power harnessing the well-tested tools of reformed showbiz politics and the medium of the moment to "go public" with his "authentic," antiestablishment image.[7] Trump's persona as the "blue-collar billionaire" and his politics of rage—his fear-mongering populist and authoritarian strongman messages delivered in his campaign autobiographies, his reality television show, his tweets, his political rallies, and his Facebook ads—resonated with his base of mostly white male, rural, and working-class voters, who felt left behind by the American establishment.[8]

During the (in)visible primaries, despite lagging endorsements, campaign funding, and poll numbers, Trump and his advisors recognized that audiences, fragmented by the advent of cable and online news, increasingly consumed partisan tirades and sensational scandals in ideological echo chambers, and they harnessed grassroots social media to gain vast amounts of free news coverage by exploiting profit-driven news values with a novel campaign fueled by drama-filled conflict and bizarre controversies surrounding Trump's politics of rage.[9] Like his victorious predecessors, Trump harnessed a grassroots media campaign and news coverage biased toward the presidential horse race to win key early contests and then capitalized on momentum to generate a psychological advantage and a bandwagon effect that could withstand establishment resistance and media scrutiny and carry him to his party's nomination.[10] And much as they had forty years prior, the establishment news media became a "dependable, if unwitting ally" in the rise of a political outsider.[11]

Legacy reporters resented claims that they contributed to Trump's rise. Invested in their decades-old mission of vetting presidential character, they recommitted themselves to scrutinizing deviant messages from the controversial presumptive Republican nominee. But Trump survived additional scrutiny and campaign controversies during his late primary and general election campaigns by attacking his adversaries, establishment politicians, and the "liberal" media, and with mistrust in establishment news media at an all-time high, especially among conservatives, he not only survived but thrived in spite of (or perhaps even because of) controversies, such as the "pussy thing."[12] As *Rolling Stone* trail reporter Matt Taibbi wrote referencing Crouse's seminal work in the campaign canon: "[Trump] ran against the Bus . . . and it worked. . . . We not only couldn't draw blood against Trump, we actually helped him every time we tried and failed to knock him out."[13]

Elite reporters from legacy media outlets still committed to detached analysis responded with what media historian David Mindich referred to as a "Murrow moment" of slanted, righteous indignation.[14] But with each editorial rebuke of his latest controversy, Trump further denounced his two prevailing establishment enemies—the Clintons and the biased news media[15]—and his conservative, alt-right followers, who long distrusted the "liberal establishment media," coalesced behind the candidate, who "was ultimately more of a product of a polarized political environment and an increasingly hard-edged media climate than a producer of it."[16]

Trump ultimately benefited from shifting terrain in the hybrid media campaign.[17] Despite any disaffection toward establishment news media, Carter and his successors were expected to cull rapport with elite reporters, key architects of their presidential images.[18] And, this in mind, they begrudgingly offered reporters on the bus human interest crumbs, only cautiously critiquing campaign journalism with acknowledged risk to their political fortunes, but Trump defied this common-sense political logic and "ran against the Bus."[19] Trump and his advisors understood that during their lifetimes political reporters had lost credibility with many Americans by publicly injecting themselves into the system as political actors, and they circumvented any remaining authority of establishment reporters to vet political actors through calculated attacks on social media.[20]

Trump's sudden, improbable rise signaled for some cultural observers an unexpected end to the world of U.S. politics as we know it, a disruption of the "matrix that used to tie politics, media, technology, and the citizenry in fairly predictable ways."[21] But as most incisive analyses of the 2016 U.S. presidential campaign suggested, Trump's campaign bore the indelible imprint of crises of confidence and legitimacy in showbiz politics and adversarial journalism rooted in the last half of the twentieth century, and his administration's Reagan-inspired shock-and-awe media barrage masked a moment of disjunction in presidential politics not encountered since the Carter administration.[22] Amid this milieu, historian and media critic Eric Alterman recently warned that we have moved closer to the world that distinguished twentieth-century commentator Walter Lippmann foretold in his seminal *Liberty and the News* (1920): "Men who have lost their grip upon the relevant facts of their environment are the inevitable victims of agitation and propaganda. The quack, the charlatan, the jingo . . . can flourish only where the audience is deprived of independent access to information."[23] And, though it remains to be seen whether long-formed ruptures in American politics and culture can be bridged, we should recognize that without restoration of historical thinking we are prone to be complicit victims in the rise of an authoritarian regime.[24] However, in times that "try [our] souls," we might find solace in the faith of ABC News chief Watergate correspondent Sam Donaldson in the resolve of the American people.[25] "Sometimes, I look into the future and say how is the system going to survive," Donaldson admitted. "And then I have to believe it will . . . because I think that Winston Churchill was right when he said, 'Americans will always do the right thing, after they have tried everything else.'"[26]

NOTE ON SOURCES

In researching and writing this history of Jimmy Carter's rise and the marathon campaign to control the mainstream news narrative, I consulted a variety of sources for documentation, including primary source materials, such as manuscripts and archives, media texts, and memory texts, and secondary source materials, such as books, articles, and reference literature.

Primary source research involved analysis of white papers, strategic memoranda, letters, telex messages, handwritten notes, message logs, clipping files, and interview transcripts, among other texts, located in the files of campaign operatives and reporters housed at the Jimmy Carter Presidential Library and Museum and the Stuart A. Rose Manuscript, Archives, and Rare Book Library at Emory University in Atlanta, Georgia; the Gerald R. Ford Presidential Library and Museum in Grand Rapids, Michigan; the Minnesota Historical Society in Minneapolis; the Alabama Department of Archives and History in Montgomery; the Harry Ransom Center at the University of Texas at Austin; the Country Music Hall of Fame and Museum in Nashville, Tennessee; and the Modern Political Archives at the University of Tennessee in Knoxville. In all, I inspected more than ten thousand documents culled from approximately four hundred archival boxes. As materials in these collections indicated, *Wall Street Journal* managing editor Fred Taylor was not exaggerating when he acknowledged layers of campaign reportage, and though this study delved into cursory analysis of the negotiation of political communication in alternative news sources, such as the black press, the underground press, and conservative media, and through alternative modes, such as advocacy journalism and literary reportage, this book concentrates on interaction with frontline reporters practicing detached analysis at mainstream, mass-distributed news outlets.

Though millions of Americans increasingly relied on television as their primary news source by the mid-1970s, as the dilemma of ink rub-off suggested, many individuals still habitually thumbed through at least one newspaper each day and regularly pored over their favorite newsweekly. Consequently, I examined approximately fifteen thousand newspaper articles published in the top six circulating national newspapers between December 1974 and November 1980, as identified through the *Ayers Directory* and available for access through ProQuest Historical Newspapers, an online full-text searchable database; approximately one thousand newspaper articles published in select regional and local newspapers, such as the *Atlanta Constitution* and the *Baltimore Sun,* between December 1974 and November 1980, as identified and accessed through ProQuest Historical Newspapers and clipping files housed at JCPL and MARBL; approximately 250 news and feature stories published in the top three circulating newsmagazines and popular magazines between May 1971 and November 1980, as identified through the *Ayers Directory* and the Readers' Guide Retrospective Index and available for access through ProQuest Historical Periodicals and microfilm; and more than one hundred hours of campaign news and entertainment programming broadcast over the Big Three networks (CBS, NBC, and ABC), the Public Broadcasting System, and Manhattan Cable, as identified and accessed through the Paley Center for Media in New York; the Vanderbilt Television News Archive in Nashville, Tennessee; the Walter J. Brown Media Archives and Peabody Awards Collection, the Richard B. Russell Library for Political Research and Studies, and the Hargrett Rare Book and Manuscript Library in Athens, Georgia; and even YouTube. Research in select chapters also involved analysis of Burrelle's Clipping Service files, broadcast specials, cable clips from Image Union's *The Five Day Bicycle Race,* select episodes of *Saturday Night Live,* and popular films from the mid-1970s, such as *Jaws* (1975), *Rocky* (1976), and *Network* (1976).

As media historians and journalism studies scholars, such as John Nerone, Michael Buozis, Brian Creech, and Matt Carlson suggest, I read these media texts as narratives that offered insights into the objects and subjects under study, and when possible, engaged in a consideration of industry practices and norms, including the production and consumption processes. In that vein, I also meticulously scrutinized analysis offered by leading reporters and ombudsmen in the industry trade press and their trail narratives, inspired by key texts in the campaign canon, such as Theodore

White's *The Making of the President* series, Timothy Crouse's *Boys on the Bus,* and Hunter S. Thompson's *Fear and Loathing on the Campaign Trail '72.* Trail journalism and campaign biographies from R. W. Apple Jr., David Broder, Jimmy Carter, Sam Donaldson, Elizabeth Drew, Martin Schram, Kandy Stroud, Jules Witcover, Judy Woodruff, and many others offered the chronological and narrative framework for this book, while seminal texts from media sociologists, such as Gaye Tuchman and Michael Schudson; political scientists, such as James David Barber, Betty Glad, Thomas Patterson, and Nelson Polsby; and mass communication scholars, such as James Carey, Steven Chafee, Maxwell McCombs, and Donald Shaw, offered insight into the range of heuristic frameworks applied to make sense of the historical phenomena under investigation. While these primary sources offered the main chronological, narrative, and contextual framework for this study, 130 memory texts—oral histories and long-form interviews collected by researchers, including myself, over a period of forty years—offered important personal and social context for these sources.

As Carter reminded me, biographies and histories of the bicentennial campaign line his bookshelves, and these materials, written by journalists, campaign operatives, political scientists, biographers, and historians, offered key insights about Carter's background and the chronology of his rise in the bicentennial campaign. My perspective also was enriched by insightful existing histories on this era—in particular, Kathryn Brownell's *Showbiz Politics: Hollywood in American Political Life*; Jefferson Cowie's *Stayin' Alive: The 1970s and the Last Days of the Working Class*; David Greenberg's *The Republic of Spin: An Inside History of the American Presidency*; Nicole Hemmer's *Messengers of the Right: Conservative Media and the Transformation of American Politics*; Kevin Kruse and Julian Zelizer's *Fault Lines: A History of the United States since 1974*; Kevin Lerner's *Provoking the Press: (More) Magazine and the Crisis of Confidence in American Journalism*; Charles Ponce de Leon's *That's the Way It Is: A History of Television News in America*; Matthew Pressman, *On Press: The Liberal Values That Shaped the News*; and Bruce Schulman and Julian Zelizer's *Media Nation: The Political History of News in Modern America.*

NOTES

ABBREVIATIONS

ADAH	Alabama Department of Archives and History
BRDP	Betty Rainwater Donated Papers
BRSF	Betty Rainwater Subject Files
CDO-HJCSF	Campaign Director's Office-Hamilton Jordan's Correspondence/Subject File
CFP-CF	Carter Family Papers-1976 Campaign Files
CLSFNC	Cooke Lutkefedder's Subject Files as National Coordinator of the 51.3% Committee
CMCC	Carter-Mondale Campaign Committee
DC-FSCMPM	Democratic Convention-Field Staff Correspondence through Memorandums-Paul Hemmann, 5/76–10/76
FPCF	1976 Florida Primary Campaign Files
GCWC	George C. Wallace Collection
GRFPL	The Gerald R. Ford Presidential Library, Ann Arbor, Michigan
HRBML	Hargrett Rare Book and Manuscript Library, the University of Georgia Libraries, Athens, Ga.
IO-NS	Issues Office-Noel Sterrett
IO-SE	Issues Office-Stuart Eizenstat
JCFP	Jimmy Carter Family Papers
JCPL	Jimmy Carter Presidential Library, Atlanta, Ga.
JCPPP	Jimmy Carter Papers/Pre-Presidential
JGSF	Jim Gammill's Subject Files
JPP-SF	Jody Powell Papers, Subject Files
JWP-JWSF	James Wall Papers, James Wall's Subject Files
MARBL	Stuart A. Rose Manuscript, Archives, and Rare Book Library, Emory University, Atlanta, Ga.
MHSM	Minnesota Historical Society in Minneapolis
MCPA-POHP-CPP	Miller Center of Public Affairs; The Miller Center of Public Affairs Presidential Oral History Program, Carter Presidency Project

NCC-RH   National Campaign Coordinator-Rick Hutcheson
LP-PO-SF   Linda Peek, Press Office, Subject Files
PAC   Peabody Awards Collection
PAE   Peabody Award Entries
PC   1976 Presidential Campaign
PPJC   Presidential Papers of Jimmy Carter
PWP   Phillip Wise Papers
ROGPOHC   Reflections on Georgia Politics Oral History Collection
RBRLOHDC   Richard B. Russell Library Oral History Documentary Collection
RBRLPRS   Richard B. Russell Library for Political Research and Studies, University of Georgia Libraries, Athens, Ga.
RCCEJC   Records of the 1976 Campaign Committee to Elect Jimmy Carter
RSC   Records of Susan Clough, Personal Secretary to the President
RWHPO   Records of the White House Press Office
SCCTF   Susan Clough's 1975–1976 Campaign Trip Files
VTNAC   Vanderbilt Television News Archive Collection
WFMP   Walter F. Mondale Papers
WJBMAPAC   Walter J. Brown Media Archives and Peabody Awards Collection, University of Georgia, Athens, Ga.

PREFACE

The title of this preface refers to the apathy that ensued when the promise of primary politics surrendered to the excesses of showbiz politics; it alludes to Gil Scott-Heron's critique of the countercultural motto "turn on, tune in, and drop out," crafted by media theorist Marshall McLuhan and made famous by Timothy Leary in the mid-1960s. In "The Revolution Will Not Be Televised" (1970), Heron intoned you will not be able "to plug in, turn on, and drop out" of the revolution. Timothy Leary, *Flashbacks: A Personal and Cultural History of an Era* (New York: G. P. Putnam's Sons, 1983), 253.

1. Chevy Chase, "Weekend Update," *Saturday Night Live,* season two, episode 6, NBC, October 30, 1976, http://snltranscripts.jt.org/76/76fupdate.phtml; William Horner and Heather Carver, *Saturday Night Live and the 1976 Presidential Election: A New Voice Enters Campaign Politics* (New York: McFarland, 2018), 125. *Saturday Night Live* was referred to as *Saturday Night* from 1975 to 1977.

2. Lou Harris, "Carter Clings to One-Point Lead," *Boston Globe,* November 2, 1976, 12; AP, "Down to Wire, Neck and Neck," *Hartford Courant,* November 2, 1976, 1B. The Gallup Poll indicated a one-point advantage for Ford, his first lead during the general election campaign, prompting one reporter to tell Kandy Stroud she might have to change the title of her forthcoming book to "How Jimmy LOST." Kandy Stroud, *How Jimmy Won: The Victory Campaign from Plains to the White House* (New York: Morrow, 1977), 402.

3. Jules Witcover, *Marathon, 1972–1976: The Pursuit of the Presidency* (New York: Viking, 643; AP, "Presidential Candidate Jimmy Carter Emerged from Voting Booth in Plains, Ga., on

November 2, 1976," https://www.wsj.com/articles/SB10001424052970204076204578078692647559714.

4. As quoted in Joshua Meyrowitz, *No Sense of Place: The Impact of Electronic Media on Social Behavior* (New York: Oxford Univ. Press, 1986), 299; Kathryn Brownell, *Showbiz Politics: Hollywood in American Political Life* (Chapel Hill: Univ. of North Carolina Press, 2014), 213; David Greenberg, *The Republic of Spin: An Inside History of the American Presidency* (New York: Norton, 2016), 317–95; Daniel Boorstin, *The Image: A Guide to Pseudo-Events in America* (Random House, 2012), 3–45; Alvin Sanoff, "Remark: The Pack Is Back on the Campaign Trail," *The Quill,* February 1976, 28–29; Joe McGinnis, *The Selling of the President* (New York: Penguin Books, 1968); Theodore White, *Theodore White at Large: The Best of His Magazine Writing* (New York: Pantheon, 1992), 459–76.

5. Chase, "Weekend Update," http://snltranscripts.jt.org/76/76fupdate.phtml.

6. Michael Connor, "It's Election Day: Vote the Network of Your Choice," *Wall Street Journal,* November 2, 1976, 1.

7. Ibid. In 1976, circulation was 1,406,192. *Ayer Directory of Publications* (Philadelphia, IMS Press, 1976), 1229. Connor engaged in horse race journalism, a favorite reportorial campaign mode, by embracing the sports metaphor; nonetheless, he was apt—election night was the "first big made-for-television news story," and by the mid-1970s it was a media event attracting viewership comparable to popular sporting events. Thomas Littlewood, *Calling Elections: The History of Horse-Race Journalism* (Notre Dame, Ind.: Univ. of Notre Dame Press, 1998), 132, 2–5, 108–9. Broadcast returns compelled newspapers to shift focus to previews and analyses. Historian Erik Barnouw noted that election day broadcasts "forever doomed the newspaper 'election specials.'" Erik Barnouw, *The Golden Web: A History of Broadcasting in the United States, vol. 2, 1933 to 1953* (New York: Oxford Univ. Press, 1968), 18.

8. Connor, "It's Election Day," 1; James M. Perry, "Us and Them This Time," *The Quill,* November 1976, 16–18; Ken Auletta, "Covering Carter Is Like Playing Chess with Bobby Fischer," *More: The Media Magazine* 6.10 (November 1976): 12–22.

9. As Americans demanded more autonomy in the presidential nomination process through party reforms and the implementation of primaries, the power of party bosses and machines dwindled throughout the twentieth century amid the rise of interest group and mass mediated politics. Kathleen Kendall, *Communication in the Presidential Primaries: Candidates and the Media, 1912–2000* (Westport, Conn.: Praeger, 2000), 6, 38; Bruce Schulman, "Farewell to 'Smoke-Filled Rooms': Parties, Interests, Public Relations, and the Election of 1924," in *America at the Ballot Box: Elections and Political History,* ed. Gareth Davies and Julian Zelizer (Philadelphia: Univ. of Pennsylvania Press, 2015), 139–52. Leaders of new special interest factions, such as women's rights groups and the Religious Right, understood this, and mobilized media messages for political influence. Nicole Hemmer, *Messengers of the Right: Conservative Media and the Transformation of American Politics* (Philadelphia: Univ. of Pennsylvania Press, 2016). Dissatisfaction with the divisive 1968 Democratic National Convention and the nomination of Hubert Humphrey, who eschewed primaries and courted party elites, prompted "the greatest systematic change in presidential nominating procedures in all of American history" in the form of additional reforms promising a more inclusive, transparent process. As quoted in Byron Shafer, *Quiet Revolution: Struggle for the Democratic Party and the Shaping of Post-Reform Politics* (New York: Russell Sage Foundation, 1984), 28. The McGovern-Fraser

Commission (1969–72) produced significant reforms, including the requirement that state parties develop written rules to govern the delegate selection process to increase transparency; the abolishment of ex-officio delegates and the limitation of state party-appointed delegates to 10 percent so as to decrease the role of political bosses; and the abolishment of the winner-take-all unit in favor of proportional representation so as to increase inclusivity. The Mikulski Commission (1972–73) upheld earlier reforms, eliminated the delegate quota system in favor of affirmative action, and instituted more complex rules for the caucus delegate selection process. These reforms resulted in candidate-bound delegates and contributed to a dramatic rise in state primaries from sixteen in 1968 to twenty-nine in 1976. James Davis, *U.S. Presidential Primaries and the Caucus-Convention System: A Sourcebook* (Westport, Conn.: Greenwood, 1997), 1–44; Nelson Polsby, "The News Media as an Alternative to Party in the Presidential Selection Process," in *Political Parties in the Eighties,* ed. Robert Goldwin (Washington, D.C.: The American Enterprise Institute for Public Policy Research, 1980), 50–66; Nelson Polsby, *Consequences of Party Reform* (New York: Oxford Univ. Press, 1983), 1–88; Marty Cohen, David Karol, Hans Noel, John Zaller, *The Party Decides: Presidential Nominations Before and After Reform* (Chicago: Univ. of Chicago Press, 2008), 1–5.

10. FECA regulated campaign financing by requiring disclosure of candidate contributions, setting strict limitations on individual and organizational contributions, and establishing public financing for presidential elections. Representing the culmination of Progressive-era reforms, FECA temporarily ended the era of unlimited campaign financing, capping the amount candidates could spend to secure nomination at $10 million, with an additional $2 million for fundraising, less than any victorious candidate had spent since 1952. To limit the influence of wealthy donors, the law restricted the amount an individual could give to a candidate in any one race to $1,000; to limit the influence of a candidate's personal wealth, the law limited the amount a candidate's family could contribute to their own campaign to $50,000. The act also erected a system of matching federal funds; to be eligible, a candidate needed to raise $5,000 in each of twenty states drawing on individual contributions limited to $250. FECA Amendments of (January 30) 1976 upheld public financing of presidential campaigns, but, citing restrictions to individual First Amendment liberties, eliminated spending limits for candidate family contributions and individual contributions uncoordinated with one candidate. Bruce Freed, "Political Money and Campaign Finance Reform, 1971–1976," in *Parties in an Anti-Party Age,* ed. Jeff Fishel (Bloomington: Indiana Univ. Press, 1978), 241–55. As a complete unknown outsider, Carter especially benefited from FECA. He only retained $42,000 in December 1975, and public funds allowed him to continue campaigning before key early contests in Iowa and New Hampshire. Andrew Busch, *Outsiders and Openness in the Presidential Nominating System* (Pittsburgh, Pa.: Univ. of Pittsburgh Press, 1997), 141; Michael Malbin, ed., *The Election after Reform: Money, Politics, and the Bipartisan Campaign Reform Act* (New York: Rowman and Littlefield, 2006), 242. Through paid advertisements and free news exposure, mass media offered candidates the capability to share ideas directly with Americans for a relatively small price tag. But with the onslaught of candidates inspired by new rules, frontline reporters in the age of space limitations further succumbed to horse race journalism, speculating on winners and losers. David Paletz, "Candidates and the Media in the 1976 Election," in *Parties in an Anti-Party Age,* 256; Arthur Hadley, *The Invisible Primary* (Englewood Cliffs, N.J.: Prentice-Hall, 1976), 7, 1 3, 99; Peter Kindsvatter, "Who Runs Presidential Campaigns," *Freedom of Information Center*

Reporter 417 (Columbia: University of Missouri School of Journalism, 1980), 1–8; Kendall, *Communication in the Presidential Primaries,* 8–9; Davis, *U.S. Presidential Primaries and the Caucus-Convention System,* 134–45. Elite *Washington Post* journalist David Broder observed that the frontline campaign pack consisted of political reporters from national news organizations, including "the three news magazines, the two news wire services, the three radio-television networks, and the *New York Times,* the *Washington Post,* the Washington *Evening Star,* the *Los Angeles Times,* the *Christian Science Monitor,* the *Baltimore Sun,* the Knight newspapers, the Field papers, the Gannett, Newhouse, Scripps-Howard, and Hearst chains . . . plus a few syndicated columnists who cover politics along with other subjects." As quoted in William Keech and Donald Matthews, "The Presidential Nominating Process," in *Parties in an Anti-Party Age,* 206; Timothy Crouse, *Boys on the Bus* (New York: Random House, 1973); James Perry, *Us and Them: How the Press Covered the 1972 Election* (New York: Clarkson Potter, 1973), 3–15.

11. As quoted in Kendall, *Communication in the Presidential Primaries,* 37.

12. Horner and Carver, *Saturday Night Live and the 1976 Presidential Election*; Littlewood, *Calling Elections*; Kindsvatter, "Who Runs Presidential Campaigns," 1–8.

13. Connor, "It's Election Day," 1.

14. Mike Conway, *The Origins of Television News in America: The Visualizers of CBS in the 1940s* (New York: Peter Lang, 2009), 275–76. ABC News had trailed industry leaders since the inception of its news division in 1948, but in 1976 even CBS felt pressure. For CBS News president Richard Salant, election night represented a crusade to retain its reputation of excellence in news. Charles Ponce de Leon, *That's the Way It Is: A History of Television News in America* (Chicago: Univ. of Chicago Press, 2015), 123–64.

15. Connor, "It's Election Day," 1.

16. After a botched call by two networks in Wisconsin's Democratic primary, news divisions were "feeling the pressure" to adhere to news values more than ever as they supplemented actual results from precincts supplied by the News Election Service, a consortium of news organizations, with reports from key precincts selected by private political consultants. Ibid.; Witcover, *Marathon,* 5.

17. Brownell, *Showbiz Politics,* 129–232.

18. Polsby, "The News Media as an Alternative to Party in the Presidential Selection Process," 50–66; Polsby, *Consequences of Party Reform,* 1–88. Public opinion founders George Gallup and Elmo Roper served as election night experts for the networks in 1948. Conway, *The Origins of Television News in America,* 275. Sheehan and Lord hoped to rejuvenate the ABC News team, anchored by veteran Harry Reasoner—referred to by one journalist as the "comfortable old shoe of broadcasting," and Walters became television's highest-paid journalist by signing the million-dollar contract. As quoted in Witcover, *Marathon,* 5; Ponce de Leon, *That's the Way It Is,* 43, 141–44. Backlash to Walters's arrival represented anxieties associated with the sexist, patriarchal newsroom culture, as well as a pervasive concern since the infancy of television news: the presence of celebrities might result in the ascendancy of infotainment. Kristin Heflin, "The Future Will Be Televised: Newspaper Industry Voices and the Rise of Television News," *American Journalism* 27.2 (2010): 87–110. For instance, *Washington Post* ombudsman Charles Seib wrote: "We might as well face it: the line between the news business and show business has been erased forever. It was a mighty thin line at best so not much has been lost." As quoted in Douglass Daniel, *Harry Reasoner: A Life in the News* (Austin: Univ. of Texas Press,

2009), 163. Many critics expressed frustration over the trend to package newscasts based on market research that dictated everything from A-Block selection to personalities hired as anchors and correspondents. Ron Powers, *The Newscasters* (New York: St. Martin's Press, 1977).

19. Brownell, *Showbiz Politics*, 3; Brian Balogh, "From Corn to Caviar: The Evolution of Presidential Election Communications, 1960–2000," in *America at the Ballot Box: Elections and Political History*, ed. Gareth Davies and Julian E. Zelizer (Philadelphia: Univ. of Pennsylvania Press, 2015); Kathryn McGarr, "'We're All in This Thing Together': Cold War Consensus in the Exclusive Social World of Washington Reporters," in *Media Nation: The Political History of News in Modern America*, ed. Bruce Schulman and Julian Zelizer, (Philadelphia: Univ. of Pennsylvania Press, 2017), 77–95; Polsby, *Consequences of Party Reform*, 142–46; Larry J. Sabato, "Open Season: How the News Media Cover Presidential Campaigns in the Age of Attack Journalism," in *Under the Watchful Eye*, ed. Matthew McCubbins (Washington D.C.: Congressional Quarterly Press), 127–52.

20. As quoted by William F. Buckley Jr. in Scott Porch, "The Book That Changed Campaigns Forever," *Politico*, April 22, 2015, https://www.politico.com/magazine/story/2015/04/teddy-white-political-journalism-117090_full.html; "Election Night 1976 ABC News Coverage," https://www.youtube.com/watch?v=kevKSmE-xdY.

21. "Election Night 1976 ABC News Coverage," https://www.youtube.com/watch?v=kevKSmE-xdY.

22. Kindsvatter, "Who Runs Presidential Campaigns," 1–8; Eric Page, "Theodore H. White, Award-Winning Chronicler of U.S. Politics, Dies at 71," *New York Times,* May 17, 1986, 14; Porch, "The Book That Changed Campaigns Forever," https://www.politico.com/magazine/story/2015/04/teddy-white-political-journalism-117090_full.html; Erving Goffman, *The Presentation of Self in Everyday Life* (New York: Penguin Books, 1990), 70.

23. Brownell, *Showbiz Politics*, 5.

24. Lily Geismer, *Don't Blame Us: Suburban Liberals and the Transformation of the Democratic Party* (Princeton, N.J.: Princeton Univ. Press, 2014); Jonathan Bell and Timothy Stanley, *Making Sense of American Liberalism* (Urbana Champaign: Univ. of Illinois Press, 2012).

25. Harris established his own polling firm in 1956, eschewing the public service focus of Gallup to offer politicians advice on how to shape campaigns around issues important to constituents. Harris gained national fame for his role in John Kennedy's 1960 presidential campaign, prompting a "data arms race," and politicians at every level armed themselves with private pollsters and consultants in the years ahead. As quoted in Balogh, "From Corn to Caviar," 252. Networks soon looked to pollsters, such as Harris, to select key precincts to determine projections, to predict and interpret incoming returns, and to offer analysis on supplemental exit polls, providing insight into the influence of factors, such as geography, race, gender, education, income, and religion. Zach Cohen, "Lou Harris Pollster for Presidents and Other Officeholders, Dies at 95," *New York Times,* December 19, 2016, https://www.washingtonpost.com/politics/lou-harris-pollster-for-presidents-and-others-officeholders-dies-at-95/2016/12/19/e7f49c2a-c626-11e6-bf4b-2c064d32a4bf_story.html?utm_term=.7acab26fe359; Susan Ohmer, *George Gallup in Hollywood* (New York: Columbia Univ. Press, 2006), 1–77. Developed by legendary pollsters Walter Mitofsky and George Fine, exit polling debuted as a feature of CBS News coverage in the late 1960s; it was a staple of broadcast new's primary and election night coverage by 1976, the year Mitofsky designed the CBS/*New York Times* polling operation.

Adam Clymer, "Warren J. Mitofsky, 71, Innovator Who Devised Exit Polls, Dies," *New York Times,* September 4, 2006, https://www.nytimes.com/2006/09/04/obituaries/04mitofsky .html?_r=2&oref=slogin. Scholars and cultural observers debated the influence of early exit polls on voter turnout in 1976. "Election Night 1976 ABC News Coverage," https://www.youtube .com/watch?v=kevKSmE-xdY.

26. "Election Night 1976 ABC News Coverage," https://www.youtube.com/watch?v=kev KSmE-xdY. Based on Sheehan's new celebrity strategy, Smith transitioned from his role as coanchor to commentator. Stanley Cloud and Lynne Olson, *The Murrow Boys: Pioneers on the Front Lines of Broadcast Journalism* (New York: Houghton Mifflin, 1996), 347. More than 36 million Americans—or slightly more than half the television viewing audience—watched portions of the 1976 election night coverage. "Election Night Coverage: Historical Ratings, 1960– 2004," *Nielsen,* http://www.nielsen.com/us/en/insights/news/2008/election-night-coverage-historical-ratings-1960-2004.html. Despite ABC's best efforts, only 18 percent of America's primetime audience tuned into *Political Spirit of '76.* The majority of households—30 percent of the Nielsen share—instead turned to trusted CBS News anchor Walter Cronkite. Witcover, *Marathon,* 5.

27. Brownell, *Showbiz Politics,* 7; Hadley, *The Invisible Primary,* 90, 150, 256–57; Curtis Wilkie, "Carter: Strong on the Road, but Weak at Home," *Boston Globe,* January 25, 1976, 1; Jules Witcover, "Carter Stumps on Birthday to Overcome Apathy," *Washington Post,* October 2, 1976, A3; AP, "Voter Apathy Target," October 27, 1976, Athletes, Box 404: AFL-CIO through First Person Articles, JCPPP, PC, LP-PO-SF, JCPL; Harry Kelly, "Will Apathy Be a Landslide Winner in Election," *Chicago Tribune,* November 2, 1976, 1; Perry, "Us and Them This Time," 16–18. In 1976, voter turnout declined to its second lowest level in modern history when only 53 percent of eligible voters—approximately 81.5 million Americans—cast ballots. Arthur H. Miller, "The Majority Party Reunited?" in *Parties in an Anti-Party Age,* 140. Low turnout in the 1976 election marked a steady decline defining the period from 1960 to 2000. "Voter Turnout in Presidential Elections: 1828–2012," The American Presidency Project, http://www.presidency .ucsb.edu/data/turnout.php; Thomas Patterson, "The Vanishing Voter: Why Are Voting Booths So Empty?" *National Civic Review* 91.4 (2002): 367–78.

28. By the mid-1970s, the nation reached the height of the network television age, the moment in which the technological medium reached a 97 percent saturation rate. The majority of American households actually owned more than one set. Moreover, the average adult watched more than three hours of television each day, and 65 percent of Americans said television was their main source of news. Thus, for millions of Americans, to wait and see in 1976 involved a simple flip of a switch on the color set of their choice. James Davis, *National Conventions in an Age of Party Reform* (Westport, Conn.: Greenwood Press, 1983), 193; Heflin, "The Future Will Be Televised," 87–110; Harris, "Carter Clings to One-Point Lead," 12; "Election Night 1976 ABC News Coverage," https://www.youtube.com/watch?v=kevKSmE-xdY.

29. Littlewood, *Calling Elections,* 156–65.

30. Witcover, *Marathon,* 10–12.

31. As quoted in Witcover, *Marathon,* 12. Several minutes earlier, Carter's national finance chairman, Frank Moore, holding the receiver with Finch's call in his hand, said: "Let me be the first to congratulate you, Mr. President." Carter replied: "Not yet, Frank. Let's wait until Cronkite says it." Frank Moore, ROGPOHC, ROGP 162, RBRLPRS.

32. As Schulman notes, a decade earlier most Americans considered the South to be the "land of moonshine and fiddle music, racism and possum stew—a place they passed through as quickly as possible on the way to Florida." Television shows such as *The Andy Griffith Show* (1961–1968) and *The Beverly Hillbillies* (1962–1971) and films such as *Deliverance* (1972) otherized the South; nonetheless, by the mid-1970s, the New South witnessed a revival in American popular culture, manifesting itself in the celebration of country music, cowboy boots, and pickup trucks. Bands such as Lynyrd Skynyrd, the Allman Brothers Band, and the Charlie Daniels Band produced national hits such as "Free Bird," "Sweet Home Alabama," "Midnight Rider," and "The South's Gonna Do It Again" in the early 1970s. Bruce Schulman, *The Seventies: The Great Shift in American Culture, Society, and Politics* (New York: Da Capo, 2001), xiii, 102–17; David Jansson, "Internal Orientalism in America: W. J. Cash's *The Mind of the South* and the Spatial Construction of American National Identity," *Political Geography* 22 (2003): 293–316; Melton A. McLaurin, "Songs of the South: The Changing Image of the South in Country Music," in *You Wrote My Life: Lyrical Themes in Country Music,* ed. Melton A. McLaurin and Richard A. Peterson (New York: Taylor and Francis, 1992), 25–26; Gary Orren, "Candidate Style and Voter Alignment," in *Emerging Coalitions in American Politics,* ed. Seymour Martin Lipset (San Francisco: Institute for Contemporary Studies, 1978), 173–76; Thomas Sugrue and John Skrentny, "The White Ethnic Strategy," in *Rightward Bound: Making America Conservative in the 1970s,* ed. Bruce Schulman and Julian Zelizer (Cambridge, Mass.: Harvard Univ. Press, 2008), 171–92; Steven Patrick Miller, *The Age of Evangelicalism: America's Born Again Years* (New York: Oxford Univ. Press, 2014), 40–49.

33. David Broder, "Mr. Carter When He's Out Front," *Washington Post,* March 23, 1977, A11; Lewis Wolfson, "The President and the Press: The First Report Card," *The Quill,* October 1977, 12–14; Michael Schudson, *The Power of News* (Cambridge, Mass.: Harvard Univ. Press, 1982), 120. Evidence suggests Carter's margin of victory would have increased with voter turnout. Sixty percent of nonvoters preferred him over Ford. Miller, "The Majority Party Reunited?" 140.

34. As quoted in Schudson, *The Power of News,* 120; Meyrowitz, *No Sense of Place,* 320.

35. Polsby, "The News Media as an Alternative to Party in the Presidential Selection Process," 55; Thomas Patterson, *The Mass Media Election: How Americans Choose Their President* (Westport, Conn: Praeger, 1976), 3–8; James David Barber, *Race for the Presidency: The Media and the Nominating Process* (Englewood Cliffs, N.J.: Prentice Hall, 1978), 3–25; Balogh, "From Corn to Caviar," 238–64. At first glance, it appeared as if Carter claimed victory by cobbling together the remnants of the New Deal Coalition, the bread-winner liberalism of blue-collar workers, minorities, and the "Solid South," but on closer inspection it became apparent Carter tapped into a "winning coalition of something old, something borrowed, and something new. . . . Carter recaptured the alliance, at least temporarily, of blacks and working-class whites. He also revived the status cleavage between white-collar and blue-collar voters which had been a hallmark of the New Deal. . . . Carter could only 'borrow' the support of some groups who had been in the vanguard of those ideological struggles [of the 1960s]. His support among the most liberal and most conservative segments of the party—the New Politics left and the conservative South—came on 'borrowed time.' . . . The Carter coalition also added some new elements to the traditional Democratic victory formula . . . Carter won strong support from such un-Democratic groups as Northern, white Protestants and rural voters. He enticed many weakly committed Republicans. . . . The instability of this coalition is unmistakable." Orren,

"Candidate Style and Voter Alignment," 173–76; Shafer, *Quiet Revolution,* 530–39. Carter's moderate coalition of special interest factions attracted majorities of individuals identifying as liberal across both parties, recently enfranchised African Americans, the working class, southerners, evangelical Christians, women, and recently enfranchised young voters. Carter attracted disparate factions around moral, thematic issues, such as Watergate and family values. Miller, "The Majority Party Reunited?" 136–38; Samuel Popkin, *The Reasoning Voter: Communication and Persuasion in Presidential Campaigns* (Chicago: Univ. of Chicago Press, 1991), 166; Robert Self, *All in the Family: The Realignment of American Democracy since the 1960s* (New York: Hill and Wang, 2012), 248–75, 309–66.

36. "Election Night 1976 ABC News Coverage," https://www.youtube.com/watch?v=kevKS mE-xdY.

37. Carter was elected by 27 percent of the U.S. voting population. Thomas Raber, *Election Night* (New York: Lerner Publications, 1988), 57. Sam Donaldson, interview with the author, January 17, 2017; Curtis Wilkie, "What, indeed, about Jody Powell," *The Quill,* January 1977, 12–15; Wolfson, "The President and the Press," 12–14; Mark Rozell, "President Carter and the Press: Perspectives from White House Communication Advisors," *Political Science Quarterly* 105.3 (autumn 1990): 419–34.

38. Donaldson, interview with the author, January 17, 2017; Greenberg, *The Republic of Spin,* 397–407.

39. Auletta, "Covering Carter Is Like Playing Chess with Bobby Fischer," 12–22, "Clippings and Publications," Box 3: Interviews JC through Office Structure, Barry Jagoda Donated Papers, JCPL.

40. Ibid.; Sabato, "Open Season," 127–52; Self, *All in the Family,* 309–66; J. Brooks Flippen, *Jimmy Carter, The Politics of Family, and the Rise of the Religious Right* (Athens: Univ. of Georgia Press, 2011).

INTRODUCTION

1. Cover, *Time,* January 3, 1977; Douglas Martin, "Bernard Green Dies at 91, Founded Newsstand Chain," *New York Times,* March 1, 2002, https://www.nytimes.com/2002/03/01/nyregion /bernard-green-dies-at-91-founded-newsstand-chain.html; Rodger Lyle Brown, *Party out of Bounds: The B-52s, R.E.M., and the Kids Who Rocked Athens, Georgia* (Athens: Univ. of Georgia Press, 2016), 39, 65; Bill Durrence, "Nudists and Nudity: More than 1,500 People Ran in Mass Streak," *Atlanta Constitution,* March 1974, http://digitalcollections.library.gsu.edu/cdm/ref /collection/ajc/id/7252.

2. As quoted in "Man of the Year: 'I'm Jimmy Carter, and . . .'" *Time,* January 3, 1977, 10.

3. Ibid.; Crouse, *Boys on the Bus,* 99–128.

4. Schulman, *The Seventies*; Jefferson Cowie, *Stayin' Alive: The 1970s and the Last Days of the Working Class* (New York: New Press, 2010); Kevin Kruse and Julian Zelizer, *Fault Lines: A History of the United States Since 1974* (New York: Norton, 2019); Kevin Lerner, *Provoking the Press: (More) Magazine and the Crisis of Confidence in American Journalism* (Columbia: Univ. of Missouri Press, 2019); Raymond Williams, *The Long Revolution* (New York: Chatto and Windus, 1961), 146; Paul Pierson, "Increasing Returns, Path Dependence, and the Study of Politics," *American Political Science Review* 94.2 (2000): 251–67; Paul Pierson, *Politics in*

Time: History, Institutions, and Social Analysis (Princeton, N.J.: Princeton Univ. Press, 2014), 17–54; David Ryfe, *Journalism and the Public* (Cambridge: Polity Press, 2017), 32–33.

5. United Press International, "Time Names Carter Its Man of '76," *Boston Globe,* December 27, 1976, 8; Carolyn Kitch, "'Useful Memory' in Time, Inc., Magazines," *Journalism Studies* 7.1 (2006): 94–110.

6. Joe Klein, "The White House Whiz Kids," *Rolling Stone,* May 19, 1977, https://www .rollingstone.com/politics/politics-news/hamilton-jordan-and-jody-powell-the-white-house-whiz-kids-64641/; Brownell, *Showbiz Politics,* 1–11; Stroud, *How Jimmy Won,* 185; Hamilton Jordan to Jimmy Carter, November 4, 1972, PC, CDO, CD-HJ, Box 199, JCPL, http:// presidentiallibraries.c-span.org/Content/Carter/CarterStrategy.pdf; Gerald Rafshoon, interview with the author, August 12, 2014; "Carter: I Look Forward to the Job," *Time,* January 3, 1977, 23–25; Cowie, *Stayin' Alive,* 176–77.

7. Cover, *Time,* January 3, 1977.

8. Zachary Lechner, *The South of the Mind: American Imaginings of White Southernness, 1960–1980* (Athens: Univ. of Georgia Press, 2018), 135–61.

9. McGinnis, *The Selling of the President*; Hoyt Purvis, *The Presidency and the Press* (Austin: The University of Texas, 1976).

10. "Man of the Year,'" 10; Matthew Pressman, *On Press: The Liberal Values That Shaped the News* (Cambridge, Mass.: Harvard Univ. Press, 2018).

11. During the campaign, Carter's press staff contracted with Burrelle's Clipping Service, one of the nation's oldest news monitoring agencies, and Rainwater incorporated reprints of all clips in weekly, in-house news summaries, such as *What the Press Had to Say,* and favorable clips into public relations materials, such as *Carter News.* Though the small press staff produced internal and external publicity materials by incorporating repurposed clips, one transition advisor believed they failed to effectively harness materials to trace Carter's past comments on the record. Undated memorandum, Mark Cohen to Jody, Betty, Rex, "The Clips from the Burrell's Clipping Service," N.D., Memorandums, Box 346: Media Schedules [7] through Presidential Debates, JCPPP, PC, Press Office-BRSP, JCPL; BRPOSF, Boxes 317–401, CMCC, Press Office, JCPPP, PC, JCPL. Carter's staff eventually flipped through the *White House News Summary,* courtesy of White House Media Liaison Patricia Bauer. Patricia E. Bauer's News Summary Files, Boxes 3–11, Donated Collections, JCPL; Greg King's News Summary Files, Boxes 13–36, WHPOC, JCPL; Janet McMahon's Files, Boxes 1–108, WHPOC, JCPL; Richard Popp, "Information, Industrialization, and the Business of Press Clippings, 1880–1925," *Journal of American History* 101.2 (2014): 427–53.

12. "Man of the Year," 10.

13. Ibid.; Art Buchwald, "The Carter Syndrome," *Hartford Courant,* January 4, 1977, 4.

14. "Man of the Year," 10; UPI, "Time Names Carter Its Man of '76," 8.

15. "Man of the Year," 10. Before 1976, success in the presidential nomination and election processes required support from party leaders. Martin Wattenberg, "Participants in the Nominating Process: The Role of the Parties," in *Before Nomination: Our Primary Problems,* ed. George Grassmuck (Washington, D.C.: American Enterprise Institute for Public Policy Research, 1985), 47–59. After Kennedy's 1960 campaign and McGovern's 1972 campaign revealed popular support in presidential primaries might serve as the central vehicle to claim the nomination, Carter illustrated that the process could breed the begrudged unity necessary

to *win* the general election in a postreform landscape. Davis, *U.S. Presidential Primaries and the Caucus-Convention System,* 62–63. Keech and Matthews, "The Presidential Nominating Process," 213; Brownell, *Showbiz Politics,* 183.

16. Recognizing the unfortunate trend for political historians to relegate "the mass media to supporting roles" in their narratives, this volume offers an intervention into modern political history and takes its methodological cue from media studies scholar Matt Carlson, who argues for representational and relational studies of journalistic authority that consider norms, such as professionalism, texts and textual authority, and industry criticism. Schulman and Zelizer, *Media Nation,* 3; Matt Carlson, *Journalistic Authority: Legitimating News in the Digital Era* (New York: Columbia Univ. Press, 2017).

17. Brownell, *Showbiz Politics*; Balogh, "From Corn to Caviar," 238–64.

18. Early global leaders recognized this as cultural truth, revealing the scope of their power through images embedded in engravings, coins, and portraits. Martin Jay, *Downcast Eyes: The Denigration of Vision in Twentieth-Century French Thought* (Oakland: Univ. of California Press, 1993), 83. After post-1968 reforms, campaign consultants interested in securing the nomination through party caucuses and primaries relied on the prevailing logic of "new politics," candidate-centered, showbiz-inspired campaigns designed to appeal to individual constituents and special interest groups. Though political scientist Martin Wattenberg dates the rise of candidate-centered politics to the 1980s, recent historians locate roots of the national phenomenon in the midcentury pursuit of consensus politics and the integration of Hollywood and Madison Avenue showbiz techniques that emphasized that images become reality. Martin Wattenberg, *The Rise of Candidate-Centered Politics: Presidential Politics of the 1980's* (Cambridge, Mass.: Harvard Univ. Press, 1991); Brownell, *Showbiz Politics,* 1–11, 129–88, 213; Balogh, "From Corn to Caviar," 238–64. Rafshoon, interview with the author, August 12, 2014; Greenberg, *The Republic of Spin,* 317–95; Boorstin, *The Image,* 3–45; McGinnis, *The Selling of the President*; Gene Wycoff, *The Image Candidates: American Politics in the Age of Television* (New York: Macmillan, 1968); James Perry Moorehead, *The New Politics: The Expanding Technology of Manipulation* (New York: Potter Publishing, 1968); Melvin Bloom, *Public Relations and Presidential Campaigns: A Crisis in Democracy* (New York: Crowell Publishers, 1973); White, *Theodore White at Large,* 459–76.

19. Brownell, *Showbiz Politics*; Kevin Sullivan and Mary Jordan, "The Un-Celebrity President," *Washington Post,* August 17, 2018, https://www.washingtonpost.com/news/national/wp/2018/08/17/feature/the-un-celebrity-president-jimmy-carter-shuns-riches-lives-modestly-in-his-georgia-hometown/?utm_term=.5d79c2637f38.

20. Stephen Ponder, *Managing the Press: Origins of the Media Presidency, 1897–1933* (New York: Palgrave, 1998), xvi; Susan Douglas, "Presidents and the Media," in *Recapturing the Oval Office: New Historical Approaches to the American Presidency,* ed. Brian Balogh and Bruce Schulman (Ithaca: Cornell Univ. Press, 2015), 152–71.

21. As media studies scholar Josh Lauer observes, the fallacy of perfect reconstruction was well-illustrated by Argentine fabulist Jorge Luis Borges, who often recounted the story of an ancient cartographer who spent his entire life consumed by the futile quest to draw a precise map of his empire that perfectly corresponded to the dimensions of the empire itself. Josh Lauer, "Introduction: Communication and History," in *Explorations in Communication and History,* ed. Barbie Zelizer (New York: Routledge, 2008), 15–16.

22. Michael Schudson, *Watergate in American Memory: How We Remember, Forget, and Reconstruct the Past* (New York: Basic Books, 1993), 70–75; Kruse and Zelizer, *Fault Lines*. As critical theorist Michel Foucault reminded his audiences: "each society has its regime of truth, its general politics of truth: that is the types of discourse which it accepts and makes function as true; the mechanisms and instances which enable one to distinguish true and false statements, the means by which each is sanctioned, the techniques and procedures accorded value in the acquisition of truth, the status of those who are charged with saying what counts as true." As quoted in Noam Chomsky and Michel Foucault, *The Chomsky-Foucault Debate: On Human Nature* (New York: New Press, 2006), 170. By probing these institutional regimes, this manuscript hopes to offer a new politics of truth with tools to exert agency and stage critical interventions in the political sphere. Williams, *The Long Revolution,* 146.

1. INTRODUCING JIMMY WHO

1. Rafshoon, interview with the author, August 12, 2014.

2. Ibid., Brownell, *Showbiz Politics*; David Blake, *Liking Ike: Eisenhower, Advertising, and the Rise of Celebrity Politics* (New York: Oxford Univ. Press, 2016), 181.

3. Rafshoon, interview with the author, August 12, 2014; Norman Mailer, "Superman Comes to the Supermarket," *Esquire* (November 1960), https://www.esquire.com/news-politics /a3858/superman-supermarket/; Boorstin, *The Image*; John E. Miller, "The Making of Theodore H. White's 'The Making of the President, 1960,'" *Presidential Studies Quarterly* 29.2 (June 1999): 389–406; Joyce Hoffmann, *Theodore H. White and Journalism as Illusion* (Columbia: Univ. of Missouri Press, 1995), 107–45; P. J. O'Connell, *Robert Drew and the Development of Cinema Verite in America* (Carbondale: Southern Illinois. Univ. Press, 2010), 62–196.

4. As quoted in Stanly Godbold, *Jimmy and Rosalynn Carter: The Georgia Years, 1924–1974* (New York: Oxford Univ. Press, 2010), 141, 129–43.

5. Gerald Rafshoon, oral history interview, April 8, 1983, by Joseph Devaney et. al, MCPA-POHP-CPP, http://web1.millercenter.org/poh/transcripts/ohp_1983_0408_rafshoon.pdf; Julian Zelizer, *Jimmy Carter: The American Presidents Series: The 39th President, 1977–1981* (New York: Times Books, 2010), 21–23, 30; Peter Bourne, *Jimmy Carter: A Comprehensive Biography from Plains to Post-Presidency* (New York: Scribner, 1997), 157–59; Schudson, *Watergate in American Memory,* 70.

6. Roland Barthes, *Mythologies* (New York: Hill and Lang, 2013), 15–19, 89–92, 181–84, 215–74.

7. Brownell, *Showbiz Politics*.

8. Goffman, *The Presentation of Self in Everyday Life*; Charles Ponce de Leon, *Self-Exposure: Human-Interest Journalism and the Emergence of Celebrity in America, 1890–1940* (Chapel Hill: Univ. of North Carolina Press, 2002).

9. Boorstin, *The Image,* 27, 218.

10. Ibid., 24–30; Will Irwin, *The American Newspaper: A Series First Appearing in Collier's, January–July 1911* (Ames: Iowa State Univ. Press, 1969); Walter Lippmann, *Liberty and the News* (New York: Harcort, Brace and Howe, 1920), 4–5; Walter Lippmann, *Public Opinion* (New York: Norton, 1922), 98, 125–43; Silas Bent, *Ballyhoo: The Voice of the Press* (New York: Boni and Liveright, 1927); George Seldes, *You Can't Print That: The Truth Behind the News,*

1918–1928 (New York: Payson and Clarke, 1929); Walter Benjamin, *The Work of Art in the Age of Mechanical Reproduction* (New York: CreateSpace, 1936/2016); Theodor Adorno and Max Horkheimer, *Dialectic of Enlightenment* (New York: Verso, 1947/1997), 120–68.

11. Boorstin, *The Image,* 24–30; Harold Innis, *The Bias of Communication* (Toronto: Univ. of Toronto Press, 1951/1999); Marshall McLuhan, *The Gutenberg Galaxy: The Making of Typographic Man* (Toronto: Univ. of Toronto Press, 1962); Warren Sussman, *Culture as History* (New York: Pantheon Books, 1973), 252–311; Michael Schudson, *Discovering the News: A Social History of American Newspapers* (New York: Basic Books, 1978), 12–160; Richard Ohmann, *Selling Culture: Magazines, Markets, and Class at the Turn of the Twentieth Century* (New York: Verso, 1996); Kevin Barnhurst and John Nerone, *The Form of News: A History* (New York: Guilford Press, 2001), 68–140; Ponce de Leon, *Self-Exposure,* 1–76; Paul Starr, *The Creation of the Media: Political Origins of Modern Communications* (New York: Basic Books, 2004); Benedict Anderson, *Imagined Communities: Reflections on the Origins and Spread of Nationalism* (New York: Verso, 2006), 6; David Paul Nord, "The Victorian City and the Urban Newspaper," in *Making News: The Political Economy of Journalism in Britain and America from the Glorious Revolution to the Internet,* ed. Richard John and Jonathan Silberstein-Loeb (New York: Oxford Univ. Press, 2015), 55–89. This book sought to advance James Carey's call for a new brand of journalism history that offers insight into transformations in the "idea of a report" and to avoid functionalist explanations and Whiggish narratives by offering radical cultural context to explain how strategic political communication and news media practices of the mid-1970s emerged. Tim Vos, "Functionalist Explanations in Media Histories: A Historiographical Essay," *American Journalism* 35.4 (2019): 490–503; James Carey, "The Problem of Journalism History," in *The American Journalism History Reader,* ed. Bonnie Brennen and Hanno Hardt (New York: Routledge, 2011), 22–27; Lori Amber Roessner, Rick Popp, Brian Creech, and Fred Blevins, "A Measure of Theory?: Considering the Role of Theory in Media History," *American Journalism* 30.2 (2013): 260–78.

12. Boorstin, *The Image,* xvi, 26; Bent, *Ballyhoo*; Marion Tuttle Marzolf, *Civilizing Voices: American Press Criticism 1880–1950* (New York: Longman, 1991); Hazel Dicken-Garcia, *Journalistic Standards in Nineteenth-Century America* (Madison: Univ. of Wisconsin Press, 1989); David Mindich, *Just the Facts: How "Objectivity" Came to Define American Journalism* (New York: New York Univ. Press, 1998); W. Joseph Campbell, *The Year That Defined American Journalism: 1897 and the Clash of Paradigms* (New York: Routledge, 2006); Brian Creech and Amber Roessner, "Declaring the Value of Truth," *Journalism Practice* 13.3 (2018): 263–79.

13. Since the nation's founding, political leaders recognized the power of news media to shape public sentiment by "broad casting" their messages and images, and they engaged in spinning facts through the vibrant partisan press and later, as the partisan press eroded, by establishing rapport and entering into symbiotic relationships with accommodating publishers, editors, and reporters. Barnhurst and Nerone, *The Form of News,* 10; David Copeland, *Colonial American Newspapers: Character and Content* (Newark: Univ. of Delaware Press, 1997); David Nord, "Teleology and the News: The Religious Roots of American Journalism." *Journal of American History* 77.1 (1990): 9–38; Jeffrey Paisley, *The Tyranny of Printers: Newspaper Politics in the Early American Republic* (Charlottesville: Univ. of Virginia Press, 2002); James F. Hamilton, *Democratic Communications: Formations, Projects, Possibilities* (New York: Lexington Books, 2008); Scott Cutlip, *Public Relations History: From the 17th to the 20th Century: The Antecedents* (New York: Routledge, 2013). Savvy political advisors came to "believe that

likenesses broad cast, are excellent means of electioneering." As quoted in Kiku Adatto, *Picture Perfect: The Art and Artifice of Public Image Making* (New York: Basic Books, 2003), 4. Nonetheless, the halls of Congress remained the center of action for Washington correspondents until the late nineteenth century, when, recognizing the reach and influence of stories that circulated through newswires and mass-distribution newspapers and magazines, William McKinley and his advisors extended their sophisticated strategic communication campaign to the White House by formalizing the relationship between the president and Washington press. Ponder, *Managing the Press,* 152–71.

14. As quoted in Creech and Roessner, "Declaring the Value of Truth," 271; George Edwards III, *The Public Presidency: The Pursuit of Popular Support* (New York: St. Martin's Press, 1983); Greenberg, *Republic of Spin,* 6.

15. During Roosevelt's administration, he and his aides courted the press by providing a press office and daily briefings, but they denied access to reporters who offered adverse coverage, practices public relations agents, such as George Fredrick Parker and Ivy Ledbetter Lee, quickly translated to presidential campaigns and administrations. Lewis Gould, *The Modern American Presidency* (Lawrence: Univ. Press of Kansas, 2003); Greenberg, *Republic of Spin,* 13–77; Scott Cutlip, *The Unseen Power: Public Relations—A History* (New York: Routledge, 2013), 20–37; Campbell, *The Year That Defined American Journalism.*

16. Roosevelt's immediate successors Woodrow Wilson and Calvin Coolidge introduced news-making publicity techniques, such as regular press conferences for the White House press corps; deployed elaborate propaganda campaigns, such as George Creel's Committee on Public Information; and engaged in showbiz politics by entreating Hollywood royalty, such as Louis Mayer, to tout virtuous qualities they sought to project. Elmer Cornwell Jr., *Presidential Leadership of Public Opinion* (Bloomington: Indiana Univ. Press, 1965); Brownell, *Showbiz Politics*; Douglas, "Presidents and the Media," 152–71. After extensive national propaganda campaigns during World War I, presidential actors encountered disillusionment from the Washington press and the general public over slick campaigns in what media critic Silas Bent referred to as "the Age of Ballyhoo." Bent, *Ballyhoo*; Hemmer, "From 'Faith in Facts' to 'Fair and Balanced,'" 128. For instance, after publicity genius Herbert Hoover's 1928 campaign, elite reporters, still committed to the objective mode, but increasingly engaging in interpretative analysis, critiqued his "extraordinary feat" of "selling himself" as a hero through new media technologies, such as radio and newsreels, and resolved to serve as watchdogs against presidential propaganda. As quoted in Greenberg, *Republic of Spin,* 176; Brownell, *Showbiz Politics,* 36–38; Tim Vos and Christopher Matthews, "A History of the Watchdog Metaphor in Journalism," Conference Proceeding, Association for Education in Journalism and Mass Communication, 2013. Within this climate, media critic Walter Lippmann, in his seminal work *Public Opinion* (1921), considered how propaganda and censorship operated to form faulty pictures of reality inside the heads of the American public and encouraged reporters to offer reliable pictures. Walter Lippmann, *Public Opinion* (Washington, D.C.: Filiquarian Publishing, 2007), 35–77. Other critics rejected objectivity altogether. Seldes, *You Can't Print That,* 9; Martin Buber, *I and Thou* (New York: Scribner, 1958). Moreover, still attuned to the rise of showbiz politics, presidential actors increasingly recognized that amid lingering suspicion over propaganda, elite journalists were inclined to critique their messages. Franklin Roosevelt initiated the practice of "going public," as political scientist Samuel Kernell described it, to

sidestep these influential intermediaries and the bias of conservative media owners during the interwar period. He did so through the mass medium with the greatest sustained reach, a practice his successors emulated with various degrees of success. Brownell, *Showbiz Politics,* 39–52; David Greenberg, "The Ominous Clang: Fears of Propaganda from World War I to World War II," in *Media Nation,* 50–63; Pickard, *America's Battle for Media Democracy,* 45–52; Michelle Hilmes, *Radio Voices: American Broadcasting, 1922–52* (Minneapolis: Univ. of Minnesota Press, 1997), 218; Lawrence and Cornelia Levine, *The People and the President: America's Conversation with FDR* (New York: Beacon, 2002); Samuel Kernell, *Going Public: New Strategies of Presidential Leadership* (Washington, D.C.: CQ Press, 1986).

17. As quoted in Ray Frazer, "The Origin of the Term 'Image,'" *ELH* 27.2 (June 1960):149. In *Keywords,* cultural theorist and historian Raymond Williams explained how competing notions of "physical likeness" and phantom mental ideas bound up in the term's earliest usage became muddled with perceived reputation after the emergence of professional public relations and advertising and the ascendancy of visual media. Raymond Williams, *Keywords: A Vocabulary of Culture and Society,* (New York: Routledge, 1976/2011), 130; Boorstin, *The Image,* 32–48; Greenberg, *Republic of Spin,* 276. Prescient news workers, such as prominent editor Silas Bent, recognized the cultural currency of the image: "The old forms are breaking up and new ideas are coming in." As quoted in Barbie Zelizer, "Words against Images," in *Newsworkers: Toward a History of the Rank and File,* ed. Hanno Hardt and Bonnie Brennen (Minneapolis: Univ. of Minnesota Press, 1995), 142.

18. Postman, *Amusing Ourselves to Death,* 129.

19. Ibid., 74; Pamphlet, "Senator Investigates," Estes Kefauver Papers, MPA, https://digital .lib.utk.edu/collections/islandora/object/ekcd%3A633; Charles Fontenay, *Estes Kefauver: A Biography* (Knoxville: Univ. of Tennessee Press, 1991), 195; David Halberstam, *The Fifties* (New York: Villiard, 1993), 277–85; Jamie Bumpus, "Dawning Revelation: An Examination of Developments That Culminated in Estes Kefauver's Emergence as Political TV Star" (master's thesis, University of Tennessee, 2014), 13.

20. Theodore White as quoted in Fontenay, *Estes Kefauver,* 194; Theodore White, *America in Search of Itself: The Making of the President, 1956–1980* (New York: Harper and Row, 1982), 77–78.

21. Fontenay, *Estes Kefauver,* 164–208.

22. Senator John Kennedy, "Television as I See It: A Force That Has Changed the Political Scene," *TV Guide,* November 14–20, 1959.

23. Ibid.; Conway, *The Origins of Television News in America,* 231–55; Jim Baughman, *The Republic of Mass Culture: Journalism, Filmmaking, and Broadcasting in America Since 1941* (Baltimore: Johns Hopkins Univ. Press, 2006), 30–91; as quoted in Brownell, *Showbiz Politics,* 150; 146–75.

24. Blake, *Liking Ike,* 68; Brownell, *Showbiz Politics,* 169–70.

25. Brownell, *Showbiz Politics,* 170; Pam Parry, *Eisenhower: The Public Relations President* (New York: Lexington, 2014), 54.

26. Brownell, *Showbiz Politics,* 146–75; Greenberg, *Republic of Spin,* 276–85; Blake, *Liking Ike,* 16–102.

27. Blake, *Liking Ike,* 70.

28. Brownell, *Showbiz Politics,* 175–250; Blake, *Liking Ike,* 126; Douglas, "Presidents and the Media," 152–71.

29. Parry, *Eisenhower.*

30. Ibid.; Brownell, *Showbiz Politics,* 146–75; Blake, *Liking Ike,* 12, 71; Greenberg, *Republic of Spin,* 286–316; Craig Allen, *Eisenhower and the Mass Media* (Chapel Hill: Univ. of North Carolina Press, 1993); Hemmer, *Messengers of the Right,* xiv, 48; Gregg Herken, *The Georgetown Set: Friends and Rivals in Cold War Washington* (New York: Vintage, 2014); Innis, *The Bias of Communication.*

31. As quoted in Kent Anderson, *Television Fraud: The History and Implications of the Quiz Show Scandals* (New York: ABC-CLIO, 1978), 129; Patrick Brantlinger, *Bread and Circuses: Theories of Mass Culture as Social Decay* (New York: Cornell Univ. Press, 2016); Boorstin, *The Image,* 33–34; Thomas Doherty, *Cold War, Cool Medium: Television, McCarthyism, and American Culture* (New York: Columbia Univ. Press, 2005); Halberstam, *The Fifties,* 367–68, 960–61; McGarr, "We're All in This Thing Together," 77–95; Crouse, *Boys on the Bus,* 46–48.

32. John E. Miller, "The Making of Theodore H. White's 'The Making of the President,'" *Presidential Studies Quarterly* 29.2 (1999): 389–406; Hoffmann, *Theodore H. White and Journalism as Illusion,* 107–45.

33. As quoted in Greenberg, *Republic of Spin,* 320.

34. Theodore White, *The Making of the President, 1960* (New York: Harper Collins, 1961/2009), 35–81; Greenberg, *Republic of Spin,* 319–26.

35. As quoted in Mark White, *Kennedy: A Cultural History of An American Icon* (New York: Bloomsbury, 2013), 14.

36. Henry Cordes, "John F. Kennedy: Young Candidate's Charisma Endures in Omaha Photo," *Omaha World-Herald,* November 17, 2013, https://www.omaha.com/news/john-f-kennedy-young-candidate-s-charisma-endures-in-omaha/article_b8686992-bdf6-5a21-85a5-601168daa711.html.

37. Ibid., Margaret Loke, "Jacques Lowe, 71, Who Etched Kennedys' Camelot on Film," *New York Times,* May 14, 2001, https://www.nytimes.com/2001/05/14/arts/jacques-lowe-71-who-etched-kennedys-camelot-on-film.html.

38. Crouse, *Boys on the Bus,* 44; Greenberg, *Republic of Spin,* 319–26; Blake, *Liking Ike,* 214–15; Gary Donaldson, *The First Modern Campaign: Kennedy, Nixon and the Election of 1960* (New York: Rowman and Littlefield, 2007), 142; White, *The Making of the President, 1960,* 81–113; O'Connell, *Robert Drew and the Development of Cinema Verite in America,* 62–74; Robert Drew, *Primary,* DVD, Docudrama, 1960.

39. White, *The Making of the President, 1960,* 82.

40. Ibid., 85–96; Drew, *Primary*; Boorstin, *Image,* 24.

41. As quoted in White, *The Making of the President, 1960,* 94, 95–96; Barthes, *Mythologies,* 181–84; Brownell, *Showbiz Politics,* 175–83.

42. Mailer, "Superman Comes to the Supermarket," https://www.esquire.com/news-politics/a3858/superman-supermarket/; White, *The Making of the President, 1960,* 145–46; Boorstin, *The Image,* 39–41; Greenberg, *Republic of Spin,* 322–23; Blake, *Liking Ike,* 217–22.

43. Greenberg, *Republic of Spin,* 319–54; White, *The Making of the President, 1960,* 164–65; Herken, *The Georgetown Set,* 298–302; Mailer, "Superman Comes to the Supermarket," https://www.esquire.com/news-politics/a3858/superman-supermarket/; Brownell, *Showbiz Politics,* 183.

44. Brownell, *Showbiz Politics,* 185–86; Blake, *Liking Ike,* 222–31; Robert Mann, *Daisy Petals and Mushroom Clouds: LBJ, Barry Goldwater, and the Ad that Changed American Politics* (Baton Rouge: Louisiana State Univ. Press, 2011), 104–5.

45. Kathleen Hall Jamieson, *Packaging the Presidency: A History and Criticism of Presidential Campaign Advertising* (London: Oxford Univ. Press, 1996), 12.

46. Mann, *Daisy Petals and Mushroom Clouds,* 104–5; Brownell, *Showbiz Politics,* 185–86; Blake, *Liking Ike,* 222–31.

47. Boorstin, *The Image,* 41, 54–57; Brownell, *Showbiz Politics,* 186–87; Greenberg, *Republic of Spin,* 334–39.

48. Victor Pickard, *America's Battle for Media Democracy: The Triumph of Corporate Libertarianism and the Future of Media Reform* (New York: Cambridge Univ. Press, 2015), 111–15; Alan Schroeder, *Presidential Debates: Fifty Years of High-Risk TV* (New York: Columbia Univ. Press, 2008), 1–10; Newton Minow and Craig LaMay, *Inside the Presidential Debates: Their Improbable Past and Promising Future* (Chicago: Univ. of Chicago Press, 2008), 1.

49. Douglas, "Presidents and the Media," 162.

50. Greenberg, Republic of Spin, 334–46.

51. Ibid., 335; as quoted in White, *The Making of the President, 1960,* 260; Boorstin, *The Image,* 54–55.

52. Boorstin, *The Image,* 57.

53. Marshall McLuhan, *Understanding Media: The Extensions of Man* (New York: Mentor, 1964), 9.

54. Boorstin, *The Image,* 48–57; Douglas, "Presidents and the Media," 162; Brownell, *Showbiz Politics,* 186–87.

55. Greenberg, *Republic of Spin,* 340–54; Herken, *The Georgetown Set,* 298–327; Hemmer, *Messengers of the Right,* 107–9; Hemmer, "From 'Faith in Facts' to 'Fair and Balanced,'" 126–30; Pickard, *America's Battle for Media Democracy,* 116–22.

56. Greenberg, *Republic of Spin,* 340–54; Hemmer, *Messengers of the Right,* 107–9.

57. As quoted in Greenberg, *Republic of Spin,* 353.

58. Hoffmann, *Theodore H. White and Journalism as Illusion,* 145–76; Greenberg, *Republic of Spin,* 354–64; Rick Perlstein, *Nixonland: The Rise of a President and the Fracturing of America* (New York: Simon and Shuster, 2010); Rick Perlstein, *The Invisible Bridge: The Fall of Nixon and the Rise of Reagan* (New York: Simon and Shuster, 2015); Laura Kalman, *Right Star Rising: A New Politics, 1974–1980* (New York: Norton, 2010).

59. Godbold, *Jimmy and Rosalynn Carter,* 109–29; Tim Boyd, *Georgia Democrats, the Civil Rights Movement, and the Shaping of the New South* (Gainesville: Univ. of Florida, 2012).

60. Greenberg, *Republic of Spin,* 364–83; Mann, *Daisy Petals and Mushroom Clouds*; Rick Perlstein, *Before the Storm: Barry Goldwater and the Unmaking of the American Consensus* (New York: Nation Books, 2001); Pickard, *America's Battle for Media Democracy*; Hemmer, *Messengers of the Right*; Pressman, *On Press.*

61. Greenberg, *Republic of Spin,* 374–83; Randall Bennett Woods, *J. William Fulbright, Vietnam, and the Search for a Cold War Foreign Policy* (Cambridge, UK: Cambridge Univ. Press, 1998), 137; William W. Prochnau, *Once Upon a Distant War: David Halberstam, Neil Sheehan, Peter Arnett—Young War Correspondents and Their Early Vietnam Battles* (New York: Random House, 1995).

62. Greenberg, *Republic of Spin,* 374–83; Perlstein, *Nixonland,* 227–28; Amber Roessner and Lindsey Bier, "Pardon Me, Mr. Carter: Amnesty and Unfinished Business of Vietnam in Jimmy Carter's 1976 Campaign," *Journalism History* 43.2 (2017): 86–92; Michael Cohen, *American Maelstrom: The 1968 Election and the Politics of Division* (New York: Oxford Univ. Press, 2016); Allen Matusow, *The Unraveling of America: A History of Liberalism* (Athens: Univ. of Georgia Press, 1984); Calvin MacKenzie and Robert Weisbrot, *The Liberal Hour: Washington and the Politics of Change in the 1960s* (New York: Penguin, 2008); Kim Phillips-Fein and Julian Zelizer, *What's Good for Business: Business and American Politics since World War II* (New York: Oxford Univ. Press, 2012).

63. Erik Barnouw, *The Image Empire: A History of Broadcasting in the United States, vol. 3, From 1953* (New York: Oxford Univ. Press, 1970), 281.

64. Greenberg, *Republic of Spin,* 374–83; Doherty, *Cold War, Cool Medium,* 161–84; Jon Marshall, *Watergate's Legacy and the Press: Investigative Impulse* (Chicago: Northwester Univ. Press, 2011), 39–66; Daniel Hallin, *The Uncensored War: The Media and Vietnam* (Berkeley: Univ. of California Press, 1986), 159–211; Clarence Wyatt, *Paper Soldiers: The American Press and the Vietnam War* (New York: Norton, 1993), 183–88; James Landers, *The Weekly War: Newsmagazines and Vietnam* (Columbia: Univ. of Missouri Press, 2004); Joseph Campbell, *Getting It Wrong: Ten of the Greatest Misreported Stories in American Journalism* (Oakland: Univ. of California Press, 2010), 85–101; as quoted in Don Oberdorfer, *Tet!: The Turning Point in the Vietnam War* (Baltimore: Johns Hopkins Univ. Press, 2001), 251.

65. As quoted in Campbell, *Getting It Wrong,* 85.

66. Greenberg, *Republic of Spin,* 384; Perlstein, *Nixonland,* 227–32.

67. Perlstein, *Nixonland,* 227–53.

68. Greenberg, *Republic of Spin,* 388–89.

69. Feldstein, *Poisoning the Press,* 76–77; John Anthony Maltese, *Spin Control: The White House Office of Communications and the Management of Presidential News* (Chapel Hill: Univ. of North Carolina Press, 1992), 55–57; David Greenberg, *Nixon's Shadow: The History of an Image* (New York: Norton, 2004), 46–53, 122–24.

70. Lippmann as quoted in Greenberg, *Republic of Spin,* 390; Greenberg, *Nixon's Shadow,* 125; Nixon as quoted in Feldstein, *Poisoning the Press,* 85, and Perlstein, *Nixonland,* 232; Hoffmann, *Theodore H. White and Journalism as an Illusion,* 107–45.

71. Perlstein, *Nixonland,* 232–53.

72. As quoted in Tim Crouse, *Boys on the Bus,* 52. After skyrocketing to the top of the national best-seller list, White's first volume remained in the coveted spot for a year and earned the Pulitzer Prize for general nonfiction in 1962.

73. Greenberg, *Republic of Spin,* 389; Greenberg, *Nixon's Shadow,* 124–27.

74. As quoted in Greenberg, *Republic of Spin,* 389, 388–92; Pressman, *On Press.*

75. Perlstein, *Nixonland,* 232–53; Cohen, *American Maelstrom,* 219–43; Michael Flamm, *Law and Order: Street Crime, Civil Unrest, and the Crisis of Liberalism in the 1960s* (New York: Columbia Univ. Press, 2007), 165–67.

76. Cohen, *American Maelstrom,* 222.

77. Perlstein, *Nixonland,* 608; Greenberg, *Republic of Spin,* 388; Ponce de Leon, *That's the Way It Is,* 41–84; Doherty, *Cold War, Cool Medium.*

78. McLuhan, *The Gutenberg Galaxy*; Gitlin, *The Sixties,* 230–33; Ponce de Leon, *That's the Way It Is,* 84; Schulman and Zelizer, *Media Nation,* 96–114, 136, Mathew Pressman, "Remaking the News: The Transformation of American Journalism, 1960–1980" (Ph.D. diss., Boston University, 2016), 6.

79. Heather Osborne-Thomson, "Tracing the 'Fake' Candidate in American Television Comedy," *Satire TV: Politics and Comedy in the Post-Network Era,* ed. Jonathan Gray, Jeffrey P. Jones, and Ethan Thompson (New York: New York Univ. Press, 2009), 71.

80. Perlstein, *Nixonland,* 272–327; Flamm, *Law and Order,* 154–61; Cohen, *American Maelstrom,* 261–87.

81. Perlstein, *Nixonland,* 272–327; Frank Kusch, *Battleground Chicago: The Police and the 1968 Democratic National Convention* (Chicago: Univ. of Chicago Press, 2008), "Archival Video: Protests Turn Violent at the 1968 Democratic National Convention," https://abcnews.go.com /Politics/video/archival-video-protests-turn-violent-1968-democratic-national-37639406.

82. Aniko Bodroghkozy, *Groove Tube: Sixties Television and the Youth Rebellion* (Durham, N.C.: Duke Univ. Press, 2001), 108; Theodore White, *The Making of a President, 1968* (New York: HarperCollins, 2009), 29–48; as quoted in Todd Gitlin, *The Sixties,* 335, 319–40; Perlstein, *Nixonland,* 334–37; Charles McDowell Jr., "Carnival of Excess: TV at the Conventions," *Atlantic Monthly,* July 1968, http://www.theatlantic.com/magazine/archive/1968/07/carnival -of-excess/303478/.

83. Flamm, *Law and Order,* 165–67; Perlstein, *Nixonland,* 232–53.

84. As quoted in Greenberg, *Republic of Spin,* 397. Despite his decisive electoral college victory, Nixon only carried the popular vote by 500,000 ballots. Greenberg, *Republic of Spin,* 388–90; Greenberg, *Nixon's Shadow,* 80–81.

85. Greenberg, *Republic of Spin,* 388; Maltese, *Spin Control,* 41–130.

86. Nixon engaged in fewer than forty formal exchanges with reporters. Maltese, *Spin Control,* 40–44; Greenberg, *Nixon's Shadow,* 128; Greenberg, *Republic of Spin,* 397–402; Perlstein, *Nixonland,* 360–68.

87. Daniel Ellsberg, *A Memoir of Vietnam and the Pentagon Papers* (New York: Penguin, 2003), 260; Edward Herman and Noam Chomsky, *Manufacturing Consent* (New York: Pantheon, 1988), 271.

88. Greenberg, *Nixon's Shadow,* 128; Henry Kissinger, "Leaks, Leaks, Leaks," *New York Times,* July 22, 1973, 195.

89. Campbell, *The Year That Defined American Journalism*; Creech and Roessner, "Declaring the Value of Truth"; Marshall, *Watergate's Legacy and the Press,* 60; Christopher Cimaglio, "'A Tiny and Closed Fraternity of Privileged Men': The Nixon-Agnew Anti-Media Campaign and the Liberal Roots of the U.S. Conservative 'Liberal Media' Critique," *International Journal of Communication* 10 (2016): 1–19; Pressman, *On Press,* 6–87. When progressive reporters, such as CBS *See It Now* anchor Edward Murrow, responded to critiques by countering objective newscasts with previously silenced sources during the McCarthy hearings and the civil rights movement, and later shunning commercial forces, conservative critics condemned the news industry with even greater vehemence. Ponce de Leon, *That's the Way It Is,* 41–84; Doherty, *Cold War, Cool Medium.*

90. As quoted in Greenberg, *Nixon's Shadow,* 128.

91. As quoted in Greenberg, *Nixon's Shadow,* 146, 78–141; Pressman, *On Press,* 67.

92. Kenneth Morris, *Jimmy Carter: American Moralist* (Athens: Univ. of Georgia Press, 1996), 29; Bourne, *Jimmy Carter,* 195; Godbold, *Jimmy and Rosalynn Carter,* 125–26.

93. As quoted in Godbold, *Jimmy and Rosalynn Carter,* 254, 125–26.

94. As quoted in ibid., 154, 165, 156, 143–84; Zelizer, *Jimmy Carter,* 21–23, 30.

95. As quoted in Godbold, *Jimmy and Rosalynn Carter,* 154; Bourne, *Jimmy Carter,* 180–99; Betty Glad, *Jimmy Carter: In Search of the Great White House* (New York: Norton, 1980), 124–25; Boyd, *Georgia Democrats;* Greenberg, *Nixon's Shadow,* 128–41; Feldstein, *Poisoning the Press,* 153.

96. Godbold, *Jimmy and Rosalynn Carter,* 149–51.

97. Ibid., 149–52, 160; "1968 Plains," Carter, Jimmy: Campaign Stuff, Charles M. Rafshoon Papers, MARBL. Rafshoon's images were included in pamphlets designed for the 1970 gubernatorial campaign. Jimmy Carter, File 1, Box 1: Wood and Associates Political Advertising Collection, RBRLPRS.

98. As quoted in Harry Murphy, "Carter Wooing Rednecks, Whitenecks, Blacknecks," *Atlanta Constitution,* July 28, 1970, 25; Morris, *Jimmy Carter,* 178; Godbold, *Jimmy and Rosalynn Carter,* 154–70.

99. As quoted in Godbold, *Jimmy and Rosalynn Carter,* 165, 163; Bourne, *Jimmy Carter,* 189; Morris, *Jimmy Carter,* 81. Through this "Hi Neighbor" blitz, the forerunner of the Peanut Brigade, approximately two hundred Sumter County surrogates vouched for Carter, but he and his family engaged in their share of handshaking, estimating they gripped 600,000 hands at the approximately eighteen hundred stump speeches delivered while taking Carter's message directly to the people.

100. As quoted in Glad, *Jimmy Carter,* 127; Godbold, *Jimmy and Rosalynn Carter,* 160; *Atlanta Constitution,* November 8, 1970, 2A, clipping in President Ford Committee for Reelection File, Box H27, GRFPL.

101. As quoted in Godbold, *Jimmy and Rosalynn Carter,* 160–62. The counterpoint to this spot revealed Carter harvesting peanuts, as a voiceover acknowledged: "Jimmy Carter knows what it's like to work for a living. He still puts in twelve hours a day in his shirt sleeves on the farm. . . . No wonder Jimmy Carter has a special understanding of the problems facing everyone who works for a living. . . . Isn't it time someone spoke up for you?" As quoted in Bourne, *Jimmy Carter,* 189; Glad, *Jimmy Carter,* 130–31.

102. As quoted in Godbold, *Jimmy and Rosalynn Carter,* 164.

103. Ibid., 166–67; as quoted in Bourne, *Jimmy Carter,* 189.

104. Godbold, *Jimmy and Rosalynn Carter,* 161–69; Morris, *Jimmy Carter,* 178–86.

105. As quoted in Godbold, *Jimmy and Rosalynn Carter,* 170, 171–84. After being accused of donning overalls to win over the working man, Sanders critiqued Carter's advertising tactics: "The last time Carter worked in the fields in the hot August sun was when his slick advertising agency took the pictures you see on television every day." As quoted in Bourne, *Jimmy Carter,* 196; Reg Murphy, ROGPOHC, ROGP 104, RBRLPRS.

106. As quoted in Godbold, *Jimmy and Rosalynn Carter,* 180, 188.

107. As quoted in ibid., 188.

108. Ibid., 188; Irving Janis, "Groupthink," *Psychology Today* 5.6 (1971), 84; Zelizer, *Jimmy Carter,* 24–26; Bill Shipp, ROGPOHC, ROGP 004, RBRLPRSR.

109. Cover, "Dixie Whistles a Different Tune," *Time,* May 31, 1971; "New Day a'Coming in the South," *Time,* May 31, 1971, 17; Kathy Roberts Forde, "Ida B. Wells-Barnett and the 'Racist Cover-Up,'" in *Political Pioneer of the Press: Ida B. Wells-Barnett and Her Transnational Crusade for Social Justice,* ed. Lori Amber Roessner and Jodi Rightler-McDaniels (New York: Rowman and Littlefield, 2018), 175–85.

110. "New Day a'Coming in the South," *Time,* May 31, 1971, 17; James Barber, *The Pulse of Politics* (New York: Norton, 1980), 190; Bert Lance, ROGPOHC, ROGP 011, RBRLPRS.

111. As quoted in Morris, *Jimmy Carter,* 189; Godbold, *Jimmy and Rosalynn Carter,* 212; Bourne, *Jimmy Carter,* 251; Glad, *Jimmy Carter,* 152; Jody Powell to Reg Murphy, March 9, 1973, Correspondence—F-J [1], Box 12: Correspondence A-E [3]—Correspondence—K-O [2], JPP-SF, JCPL; '76 Campaign, Rebuttal to News Article, Box 3: News Releases and Schedules, 1/75–2/75 through Magazine [1], BRDB, JCPL; Rex Granum, interview with the author, August 14, 2013.

112. After Carter's failed gubernatorial bid, Kirbo suggested that Carter campaign for president. Such whispers prompted advisor Peter Bourne to ask Carter bluntly about his presidential aspirations in July 1971. Godbold, *Jimmy and Rosalynn Carter,* 194–95, 268; Morris, *Jimmy Carter,* 191; Chip Carter, ROGPOHC, ROGP 036, RBRPRS.

2. POST-REFORM BLUEPRINT FOR THE MARATHON CAMPAIGN

1. Bill Shipp, "Governor Bitten by National Bug," *Atlanta Constitution,* April 22, 1971; Godbold, *Jimmy and Rosalynn Carter,* 238.

2. Perlstein, *Nixonland,* 608–9; Marshall, *Watergate's Legacy and the Press,* 62–64.

3. Thompson, *Fear and Loathing on the Campaign Trail '72,* 191–99; Godbold, *Jimmy and Rosalynn Carter,* 238–49.

4. UPI, "Georgia Governor Endorses Jackson," *Chicago Tribune,* July 12, 1972, B8; Douglas Kneeland, "McGovern Said to Narrow Choice for Running Mate," *New York Times,* July 12, 1972, 1; David Paletz and Martha Elson, "Television Coverage of Political Conventions: Now You See It, Now You Don't," *Political Science Quarterly* 91.1 (1976): 122.

5. Godbold, *Jimmy and Rosalynn Carter,* 248; Bill Anderson, "It's McGovern," *Chicago Tribune,* July 13, 1972, 1.

6. Morris, *Jimmy Carter,* 191–97; Bourne, *Jimmy Carter,* 223–31. "As we were walking away [from the convention], I remember Hamilton [Jordan] says, 'We are never going to go hat in hand to some asshole to see about being on the ticket or getting the job.' And, he said, 'Ed Muskie, George McGovern, Ted Kennedy, Scoop Jackson and Terry Sanford—if all these people could run for president, Jimmy could.' And I remember, he said, 'Yes, if all these assholes around him could run a campaign, we could certainly do that.'" Rafshoon, interview with the author, August 12, 2014.

7. Perry, *Us and Them,* 207–70; Crouse, *Boys on the Bus,* 179–347; Thompson, *Fear and Loathing on the Campaign Trail '72,* 304–15.

8. Mayor John Lindsay, dubbed the "charisma candidate" by elite, frontline reporters, as quoted in Kendall, *Communication in the Presidential Primaries,* 37, 165; Perry, *Us and Them,* 52–54.

9. Kendall, *Communication in the Presidential Primaries,* 22, 161–72; Crouse, *Boys on the Bus,* 37.

10. Perry, *Us and Them,* 81–103.

11. Ibid.; Perlstein, *Nixonland,* 628–29.

12. As quoted in Perry, *Us and Them,* 106.

13. Janis, "Groupthink," 84; Crouse, *Boys on the Bus,* 18–26; 68–129.

14. As quoted in Perry, *Us and Them,* 3; as quoted in Crouse, *Boys on the Bus,* 48.

15. As quoted in Crouse, *Boys on the Bus,* 50.

16. As quoted in ibid., 51.

17. Thompson, *Fear and Loathing on the Campaign Trail '72;* Perry, *Us and Them,* 167; Crouse, *Boys on the Bus,* 169.

18. As quoted in Crouse, *Boys on the Bus,* 63; as ABC News correspondent Ted Koppel explained: "All of the sudden everybody said, 'Oh I get it. They're trying to sell candidates the way they sell soap. From that moment on, we had emerged from the Garden of Eden. We were never able to see candidates or campaigns quite the same way again." As quoted in Greenberg, *Republic of Spin,* 390.

19. McGinnis, *The Selling of the President,* https://books.google.com/books/about/The_Selling_of_the_President.html?id=578AEL8WMAIC; Crouse, *Boys on the Bus,* 49; Perry, *Us and Them,* 9. After the dawn of the twentieth century, newsmakers imagined American audiences craving inside dope about the private lives of the famous, and amid credibility crises in American politics and journalism in the 'Me' Decade, news producers offered American audiences obsessed with authenticity insight into a key question: Were national celebrities really who they claimed to be? Charles Ponce de Leon, *Self Exposure: Human Interest Journalism and the Emergence of Celebrity in America* (Chapel Hill: Univ. of North Carolina Press, 2003). The new quest for authenticity emerged in the writings of radical feminists and members of the New Left in the 1960s and gained widespread cultural currency in the 1970s, manifesting itself in the celebrity reporting of Barbara Walters and the rise of *People Magazine* (1974). The trend was further magnified in the aftermath of Nixon's resignation. Tom Wolfe, "The 'Me' Decade and the Third Great Awakening," *New York Magazine,* August 23, 1976, 27–48; Christopher Lasch, *The Culture of Narcissism: American Life in an Age of Diminishing Expectations* (New York: Norton, 1979); Seifert, *The Politics of Authenticity in Presidential Campaigns, 1976–2008,* 15–35.

20. Perlstein, *Nixonland,* 632–34; Perry, *Us and Them,* 104–18; Thompson, *Fear and Loathing on the Campaign Trail '72,* 80–117.

21. As quoted in Perry, *Us and Them,* 127; Kendall, *Communication in the Presidential Primaries,* 22.

22. Kendall, *Communication in the Presidential Primaries,* 23, 74, 168.

23. Perry, *Us and Them,* 154–67; Crouse, *Boys on the Bus,* 154–55; Marshall, *Watergate's Legacy and the Press,* 73–83.

24. Marshall, *Watergate's Legacy and the Press,* 80; Perry, *Us and Them,* 161.

25. Arlen J. Large, "Fear of the 'Kidlash' Factor," *Wall Street Journal,* July 10, 1972, 1.

26. Paletz and Elson, "Television Coverage of Political Conventions," 122; Thompson, *Fear and Loathing on the Campaign Trail '72,* 257–74; Perry, *Us and Them,* 171; Crouse, *Boys on the Bus,* 164.

27. Godbold, *Jimmy and Rosalynn Carter,* 248; Bourne, *Jimmy Carter,* 233–35.

28. As quoted in Zelizer, *Jimmy Carter*, 28; Witcover, *Marathon*, 107–8; Stroud, *How Jimmy Won*, 23–26; Glad, *Jimmy Carter*, 484.

29. Godbold, *Jimmy and Rosalynn Carter*, 238–59.

30. As quoted in Crouse, *Boys on the Bus*, 328, 326, 333; Thompson, *Fear and Loathing on the Campaign Trail '72*, 304–15; Perry, *Us and Them*, 183–206; Perlstein, *Nixonland*, 699–703.

31. Perlstein, *Nixonland*, 703.

32. Ibid., 703–46; Marshall, *Watergate's Legacy and the Press*, 83–94.

33. Peter Bourne, Charles Kirbo, and Don Carter also contributed valuable insights. Bourne, *Jimmy Carter*, 236; Chip Carter, ROGPOHC, ROGP 036, RBRLPRS; Hamilton Jordan to Jimmy Carter, November 4, 1972, PC, CDO CD-HJ, Box 199, JCPL. Carter's advisor and national finance chairman Frank Moore observed that the memorandum provided key instructions for "a moderate Democrat from the South with a good record on Civil Rights" to reach the White House. Frank Moore, ROGPOHC, ROGP 162, RBRLPRS. Stroud called the memorandum Carter's "magna carta," and Carter acknowledged that Jordan's memo was a "timeless user's guide for anyone with political aspirations." As quoted in Stroud, *How Jimmy Won*, 185; Godbold, *Jimmy and Rosalynn Carter*, 255.

34. Hamilton Jordan to Jimmy Carter, November 4, 1972, Section A, PC, CDO, CD-HJ, Box 199, JCPL; Schulman, *The Seventies*, 42–52.

35. Brownell, *Showbiz Politics*; Barber, *Race for the Presidency*, 3–25.

36. Hamilton Jordan to Jimmy Carter, November 4, 1972, PC, CDO CD-HJ, Box 199, JCPL.

37. Ibid.

38. Ibid.; Barber, *Race for the Presidency*, 26–54.

39. Witcover, *Marathon*, 113; Shogan, *Bad News*, 69–70; Crouse, *Boys on the Bus*, 85–98.

40. Despite his understanding of the importance of broadcast news, Jordan's list of elite reporters lacked any broadcast contacts. Moreover, twenty-two spaces remained blank, evidence of the campaign's limited knowledge of elite national reporters. Hamilton Jordan to Jimmy Carter, November 4, 1972, PC, CDO CD-HJ, Box 199, JCPL.

41. Schulman and Zelizer, *Media Nation*, 89.

42. Hamilton Jordan to Jimmy Carter, November 4, 1972, PC, CDO CD-HJ, Box 199, JCPL.

43. Bourne suggested several of these tactics in his initial memorandum. Stroud, *How Jimmy Won*, 23–26.

44. Sam Donaldson, interview with the author, January 17, 2017; Schulman and Zelizer, *Media Nation*.

45. Peter Bourne to Jimmy Carter, August 1, 1974, Memoranda, 1974, Box 211, JCPPP, PC, National Campaign Coordinator—Rick Hutcheson, Memoranda, 1974 through Memoranda, General Election, JCPL.

46. Schulman, *The Seventies*, xiii, 102–17; Sandbrook, *Mad As Hell*, 121–38; Cowie, *Stayin' Alive*, 167–209; 262.

47. Hamilton Jordan to Jimmy Carter, November 4, 1972, PC, CDO CD-HJ, Box 199, JCPL.

48. Ibid.; Martin Schram, *Running for President* (New York: Pocket Books, 1978), 57; Zelizer, *Jimmy Carter*, 33; Patterson, *The Mass Media Election*, 43–49; Barber, *Race for the Presidency*, 10–11.

49. Christopher Lydon, "Gov. Carter Sees Hoax in U.S. Aid," *New York Times*, February 10, 1973, 29.

50. As quoted in Bourne, *Jimmy Carter,* 238; Witcover, *Marathon,* 116–18.

51. Godbold, *Jimmy and Rosalynn Carter,* 272–74; Bourne, *Jimmy Carter,* 243–47. Jay Beck, Hamilton Jordan's close friend and a Carter presidential staff member, described the role as the campaign's Trojan horse. Jay Beck, ROGPOHC, ROGP 157, RBRLPRS; Frank Moore, ROGPOHC, ROGP 162, RBRLPRS. From this post, Carter and Jordan interacted with elite reporters, such as Robert Shogan. Correspondence from the Media, District of Columbia [1]; Box 319: Correspondence from the Media, Colorado through Correspondence from the Media, Georgia [2]; JCPPP, 1PC, PO-BR, JCPL.

52. Gerald Rafshoon to Jimmy Carter, April 24, 1973, File: Correspondence, Rafshoon, Gerald, Box 4: Correspondence, Northside Drive Baptist Church through Democratic National Committee Publication and Information, 1974, CFP, Governor Carter's Personal Working Files, 1970–1974, JCPL. Despite urging from Rafshoon, Carter was slow to repudiate Nixon; in early 1973, Carter warned Democrats not to emphasize Watergate in an "overly partisan manner." As quoted in Glad, *Jimmy Carter,* 214.

53. Hamilton Jordan to Governor, Personal and Confidential, April 20, 1973, Correspondence, Jordan, Hamilton [2], Box 3: Correspondence, Jordan, Hamilton [1] through Correspondence, Nix, Jack P., CFP, Governor Carter's Personal Working Files, 1970–1974. In the fall of 1973, Kirbo encouraged Carter to subtly address the scandal without issuing an official public rebuke on the Nixon administration: "I think at your convenience over the next several months you need to put together a speech . . . which addresses itself to Watergate without ever mentioning Watergate." The memo offered sample language Carter might incorporate: "America wants to be proud of our government at home and abroad. . . . The President may make mistakes and admit them but should not be lacking in honor or courage." "This particular thought can be developed to shaft Kennedy [still reeling from the drowning death of Mary Jo Kopechne at Chappaquiddick] without getting in the mud," Kirbo offered parenthetically. Charles Kirbo to Jimmy Carter, September 26, 1973, File: Memorandums [1], Box 30: Invitations through Memorandum from Pat Caddell, JPP, JCPL. In a handwritten note, Carter replied to Powell that he already had pursued that course, but he could construct more formal remarks for a scandal-focused speech.

54. Godbold, *Jimmy and Rosalynn Carter,* 253–54.

55. Glad, *Jimmy Carter,* 214; Victor Lasky, *Jimmy Carter: The Man and the Myth* (New York: Richard Marek Publishers, 1979), 193.

56. In October 1973, the *Washington Post* reported on Carter's critique of Nixon's revenue-sharing plans, but they erroneously identified him as "Governor Jimmy Collins." Glad, *Jimmy Carter,* 216.

57. Jimmy Carter, "What's My Line," CBS, https://www.youtube.com/watch?v=4jJYqcoaUAI.

58. Godbold, *Jimmy and Rosalynn Carter,* 257; Lasky, *Jimmy Carter,* 127; James David Barber, "Tone-Deaf in the Oval Office," *Saturday Review,* January 12, 1974, 10–14, File: National Politics: General [3], Box 85, CFP—Governor Carter's Press Office Files, National Politics General [1] through News Conferences, 1/72–3/72, JCPL.

59. Stroud, *How Jimmy Won,* 185.

60. As quoted in Lasky, *Jimmy Carter,* 127.

61. Glad, *Jimmy Carter,* 221–23.

62. Carter's campaign may not have cured the national malaise that Thompson predicted, but it inspired the gonzo journalist. Thompson, *Fear and Loathing on the Campaign Trail '72,* 63; Hunter S. Thompson, *Fear and Loathing at Rolling Stone: The Essential Writings of Hunter S. Thompson,* (New York: Simon and Schuster, 2011), 373.

63. Jimmy Carter, Law Day Address, Address by Jimmy Carter at University of Georgia's Law Day in Honor of Dean Rusk, Athens, Ga., May 4, 1974, http://www.americanrhetoric.com /speeches/jimmycarterlawday1974.htm. References to theologian Reinhold Niebuhr and folk musician Bob Dylan were offered on numerous occasions throughout Carter's campaign, appealing to the educated elite on one hand and the liberal youth on the other. Gitlin, *The Sixties,* 200–203.

64. Thompson, *Fear and Loathing at Rolling Stone,* 373.

65. Clipping List, Watergate, File: Watergate, Watergate, Box 8, CFP—Governor Carter's Personal Working Files, 1970–74, Trips-Georgia Dept. of Industry and Trade-New York City, 11/27/74 through Watergate, JCPL; "NBC's Meet the Press," Meet the Press Transcript, 6/74, Box 83, CFP—Governor Carter's Press Office Files, Medical Issues through News Clippings, 1975, JCPL; Bourne, *Jimmy Carter,* 249; Crouse, *Boys on the Bus,* 99–128.

66. As quoted in Godbold, *Jimmy and Rosalynn Carter,* 278–79. During the midterm campaign's closing weeks, Carter confided that he planned on running for president while at an editorial board meeting with Shannon's *Times* colleagues. Bourne, *Jimmy Carter,* 250.

67. Hamilton Jordan to Jimmy Carter, August 4, 1974, Peter Bourne File, Box 1, JCPPP, PC, JCPL. In the fall of 1974, news that probable Democratic frontrunners Ted Kennedy and Walter Mondale had decided to sit out the 1976 presidential race prompted Carter and his staff to subtly adjust their plan. Most notably, the development prompted an accelerated announcement timetable designed to edge out any new competitors. Andrew Downer Crain, *The Ford Presidency, a History* (New York: McFarland, 2009), 5–74; Kalman, *Right Star Rising,* 24–43; Witcover, *Marathon,* 132–38; Morris, *Jimmy Carter,* 153; Godbold, *Jimmy and Rosalynn Carter,* 274.

68. Shogan, *Bad News,* 75.

69. As quoted in Bourne, *Jimmy Carter,* 256; Schulman and Zelizer, *Media Nation,* 77–96. By contrast, after capturing national exposure, Carter's imagecraft apparatus sought to eschew Washington and exploit the small-town, rural image of Plains. Drew, *American Journal,* 145; Crouse, *Boys on the Bus,* 20–26; 99–128.

70. Joe Mitchell to Jimmy Carter, November 19, 1974, File: Political Strategy [3], Box 40: Memorandums-Political Strategy [3] through Network News Transcripts, 10/4/76–10/10/76, JCPL.

71. Jack Burris to Jimmy Carter, September 19, 1974, File: '76 Campaign, Box 1, JCPPP, Eizenstat, PC, JCPL.

72. Ibid.

73. Ibid.

74. Jack Burris to Jimmy Carter, October 25, 1974, File: '76 Campaign, Box 1, JCPPP, Eizenstat, PC, JCPL.

75. Jimmy Carter, November 21, 1974, File: RG 1-1-145, JC, Box 13, JCPPP, PC, JCPL; Stuart Eizenstat to Jimmy Carter, November 25, 1974, File: '76 Campaign, Box 1, JCPPP, Eizenstat, PC, JCPL; Stuart Eizenstat to Jimmy Carter, December 1, 1974, File: '76 Campaign, Box 1, JCPPP, Eizenstat, PC, JCPL.

76. Jimmy Carter, Address by Jimmy Carter Announcing His Candidacy for the 1976 Democratic Presidential Nomination to the National Press Club, Washington, D.C., December 12, 1974, http://www.4president.org/speeches/carter1976announcement.htm; Bourne, *Jimmy Carter,* 254–58; Glad, *Jimmy Carter,* 225–26. U.S. Representative Morris Udall of Arizona announced his candidacy on November 28. In advance of his announcement, Carter crafted a letter to select friends and supporters throughout the nation, including Atlanta-based sportswriter Furman Bisher. "Before the official announcement is made on December 12," he wrote, "I would like you to know that I intend to seek the Democratic nomination and election as President of the United States in 1976. . . . I would not enter this formidable race if I did not believe that I can win; but neither would I run for President without a deep conviction that I can make an essential contribution to the United States government and the people that it serves." Jimmy Carter to Furman Bisher, December 4, 1974, File: Media Correspondence, Box 336: Magnetic Cards through Media Mailing Lists, JCPPP, PC, PO-BRSF, JCPL.

77. Jimmy Carter, Address by Jimmy Carter Announcing His Candidacy for the 1976 Democratic Presidential Nomination to the National Press Club, Washington, D.C., December 12, 1974, http://www.4president.org/speeches/carter1976announcement.htm.

78. Ibid.

79. Though Carter's campaign achieved a political coup d'état in advance of his announcement, when one of the nation's most influential journalists, Godfrey Sperling Jr., introduced Carter at one of his infamous dinners, most elite reporters wrote off his campaign. As quoted in Bourne, *Jimmy Carter,* 258. Wayne King, "Georgia's Gov. Carter Enters Democratic Race for President," *New York Times,* December 13, 1974, 1; David Broder, "Georgia Governor Declares '76 Bid," *Washington Post,* December 13, 1974, A1.

80. Reg Murphy, "Jimmy Carter's Running for WHAT?" *Atlanta Constitution,* July 10, 1974; "Off and Running," *Atlanta Constitution,* December 13, 1974, File, Media Publications [7], Box 343, JCPPP, PC, PO-BRSF, Media Publications [7] through Medial Publications [13], JCPL; Glad, *Jimmy Carter,* 225; Reg Murphy, ROGPOH, ROGP 104, RBRLPRS.

81. "Who Is Jimmy Carter," *Baltimore Sun,* December 15, 1975, K4.

82. Carl Leubsdorf, interview with the author, August 10, 2013.

3. ROCKIN', DOWN-HOME, GRASSROOTS MEDIA CAMPAIGN AND THE (IN)VISIBLE PRIMARIES

1. Crouse, *Boys on the Bus,* 75; R. W. Apple Jr., "Carter Appears to Hold a Solid Lead in Iowa as the Campaign's First Test Approaches," *New York Times,* October 27, 1975, 17.

2. Crouse, *Boys on the Bus,* 75; Apple, "Carter Appears . . . ," 17; Hugh Winebrenner and Dennis J. Goldford, *The Iowa Precinct Caucuses: The Making of a Media Event,* 3rd ed. (Iowa City: Univ. of Iowa Press, 2010), 60, 78.

3. Apple, "Carter Appears . . . ," 17. After Kennedy announced that he would not run for president in September 1974, fifteen Democrats announced their candidacies during the (in)visible primaries. Idaho's Senator Frank Church and California governor Jerry Brown entered the race in 1976.

4. Zelizer, *Jimmy Carter,* 35; Winebrenner and Goldford, *The Iowa Precinct Caucuses,* 60; John Skipper, *The Iowa Caucuses: The First Tests of Presidential Aspiration, 1972–2008* (New York: McFarland, 2010), 42–43.

5. As quoted in Zelizer, *Jimmy Carter,* 35; as quoted in *More: The Media Magazine* and cited in Todd S. Purdam, "R. W. Apple, a Times Journalist in Full, Dies at 71," *New York Times,* October 5, 2006, https://www.nytimes.com/2006/10/05/nyregion/05applecnd.html; Crouse, *Boys on the Bus,* 60.

6. Apple, "Carter Appears . . . ," 17; Witcover, *Marathon,* 200–202.

7. Apple, "Carter Appears . . . ," 17.

8. ". . . and picked it up. It was on the front page of every major newspaper the next day." As quoted in Crouse, *Boys on the Bus,* 85; Janis, "Groupthink," 84; McGarr, "We're All in This Thing Together," 86.

9. Apple, "Carter Appears . . . ," 17; Witcover, *Marathon,* 3–117; Hadley, *Invisible Primary.*

10. Jordan to Carter, November 4, 1972, PC, CDO-HJCSF, JCPL; White, *The Making of the President, 1960*; Crouse, *Boys on the Bus*; James David Barber, *The Presidential Character: Predicting Performance in the White House* (New York: Taylor and Francis, 1972/2017).

11. Lechner, *The South of the Mind,* 135–60.

12. On December 15, Carter appeared on NBC's *Meet the Press,* but he was not invited onto CBS's *Face the Nation.* Despite his imagecraft apparatus's attempts, he only received to-ken newspaper coverage, and his national name recognition remained low. "Meet the Press," NBC, December 15, 1974, http://www.nbcnews.com/video/nightly-news/45848277; AP, "Geor-gia's Gov. Carter Jumps into '76 Presidential Race," *Los Angeles Times,* December 12, 1974, 2; Wayne King, "Georgia's Gov. Carter Enters Democratic Race for President," *New York Times,* December 13, 1974, 1; David Broder, "Georgia Governor Declares '76 Bid," *Washington Post,* December 13, 1974, A1. "The resounding reaction from the national news media was to ask 'Jimmy who?' and then to disregard the incident as one man's folly," NBC News correspondent Judy Woodruff recalled. "But I knew Jimmy Carter from covering him during his one-term governorship of Georgia, while I was reporting on the statehouse for WAGA-TV. I took him very seriously." As quoted in Judy Woodruff with Kathleen Maxa, *"This Is Judy Woodruff at the White House"* (Reading, Mass.: Addison-Wesley, 1982), 95; Woodruff, interview with the author, March 31, 2017. Carter's staff sought to exploit Woodruff. In a handwritten letter to Carter, Powell wrote that Woodruff had "become a believer and is anxious to make sure she gets to cover you for NBC. We have set up a regular schedule for getting campaign info to her. I think she is going places with the network and sees your campaign as a big help for her ambitions." JLP to JC, "RE: SGC," N.D., Memorandums [1], Box 30: Invitations through Memorandum from Pat Caddell, JPP-SF, JCPL.

13. "Washington, D.C., 1/15–16/75," Box 25, SCCTF, RSC, JCPL; Bourne, *Jimmy Carter,* 260.

14. Cover, "Dixie Whistles a Different Tune," *Time,* May 31, 1971; Jordan to Carter, Novem-ber 4, 1972, PC, CDO-HJCSF, Box 199, JCPL.

15. "When Jimmy goes anywhere, he does editorial board meetings . . . ," Powell said. "We do that as a standard part of the schedule. That's to meet as many papers as there are." As quoted in James David Barber, ed., *The Race for the Presidency: The Media and the Nominating Process* (Englewood Cliffs, N.J.: Prentice Hall, 1978), 37.

16. White, *The Making of the President, 1960,* 92.

17. "Louisiana, Texas, New Mexico, and California, 1/20–25/75," Box 25, SCCTF, RSC, JCPL; Bourne, *Jimmy Carter,* 261–62; Maxwell McCombs and Donald Shaw, "The Agenda-Setting Function of the Mass Media," *Public Opinion Quarterly* 36.2 (1972): 176–87; Kurt Lewin, "Frontiers in Group Dynamics: Concept, Method, and Reality in Social Science; Social Equilibra and Social Change," *Human Relations* 1.5 (1947): 145.

18. Glad, *Jimmy Carter,* 229; Witcover, interview with the author, January 18, 2017.

19. Tom Wicker, "McGovern with Tears," *New York Times,* November 5, 1972, 36; Thompson, *Fear and Loathing on the Campaign Trail,* 76–77.

20. "Kentucky and Washington, D.C., 1/27–28/75," Box 25, SCCTF, RSC, JCPL; "Phoenix, Arizona, 2/3–4/75," Box 25, SCCTF, RSC, JCPL; "Dayton Beach, Florida, 2/14–15/75," Box 25, SCCTF, RSC, JCPL; "Palm Beach, California, 2/1–2/75," Box 25, SCCTF, RSC, JCPL; "Tampa, Florida and St. Petersburg, Florida, 2/20–21/75," Box 25, SCCTF, RSC, JCPL; "Columbia, South Carolina, 2/6/75," Box 25, SCCTF, RSC, JCPL; "Wisconsin, 2/7–8/75," Box 25, SCCTF, RSC, JCPL; "New Jersey, and New York, 2/10/75," Box 25, SCCTF, RSC, JCPL. While campaigning in Florida in early 1975, Carter and his surrogates learned valuable lessons about grassroots campaigning, which Rosalynn outlined: "Head for the large radio and television antennas; Stay in people's homes. You saved money, learned about people's real concerns, established close ties and loyalty. . . ." Rosalynn spent seventy-five days in Florida prior to March 1976. As quoted in Bourne, *Jimmy Carter,* 264.

21. Carter's early February trip to New York did not yield instant national exposure, but it did afford him an opportunity to speak with *People Magazine*'s editorial board. "New Jersey, and New York, 2/10/75," Box 25, SCCTF, RSC, JCPL.

22. "New Hampshire, 2/11–13/75," Box 25, SCCTF, RSC, JCPL.

23. "Iowa, 2/26–27/75," Box 26, SCCTF, RSC, JCPL.

24. Carter, interview with the author, October 17, 2014.

25. As quoted in Skipper, *The Iowa Caucuses,* 44.

26. Carter, interview with the author, October 17, 2014.

27. As quoted in Winebrenner and Goldford, *The Iowa Precinct Caucuses,* 60; Zelizer, *Jimmy Carter,* 34; Witcover, *Marathon,* 194–95.

28. As quoted in Barber, *Race for the Presidency,* 37; Witcover, *Marathon,* 195.

29. As cited in Glad, *Jimmy Carter,* 233.

30. Unpaid volunteers willing to canvas for Carter and to advocate strengths of the populist, antiestablishment candidate in key primary states, such as New Hampshire and Florida, comprised Carter's caravan, as Jordan labeled them. Campaign volunteer Dorothy "Dot" Padgett organized the surrogate campaign initiative modeled after the "Hi Neighbor Day" program initiated by Carter's 1970 gubernatorial supporters in Sumter County. The downhome Peanut Brigade, as reporters dubbed them, knocked on doors, shook hands, chatted about Carter's virtues, distributed press kits and other literature, and attracted a tremendous volume of good press on campaign blitzes. Newspaper Clippings, Norm Chamberland, "Carter Campaign Wagon Rolls through Woonsocket," *Call and Reporter,* September 30, 1975, Media Publications [10], Box 343, JCPPP, Press Office-BRSF, Media Publications [7] through Media Publications [13], JCPL; Chip Carter, ROGPOHC, ROGP 036, RBRLPRS; Godbold, *Jimmy and*

Rosalynn Carter, 171; Dorothy Padgett, *Jimmy Carter: Elected President with Pocket Change and Peanuts* (Macon, Ga.: Mercer Univ. Press, 2016).

31. Carter, Jimmy: Campaign Stuff, Charles M. Rafshoon Papers, MARBL.

32. Jordan wrote in August 1974: "No serious candidate will have the luxury of picking and choosing among the early primaries. To propose such a strategy would cost that candidate votes and increase the possibility of being lost in the crowd. . . . The crowded field enhances the possibility of several inconclusive primaries. . . . Such a muddled picture will not continue long, as the press will begin to make 'winners' of some and 'losers' of others. The intense press coverage which naturally focuses on the early primaries plus the decent time intervals which separate the March and mid-April primaries dictates a serious effort in all the first five primaries." As quoted in Witcover, *Marathon,* 134–36. Carter's trip marked his only appearance in Iowa until June; he was not often in New Hampshire during this period either—though he did spend several more days in the area with two additional trips to New Hampshire before May. Itineraries, Boxes 25–31, SCCTF, RSC, JCPL; Jordan to Carter, November 4, 1972, PC, CDO-HJCSF, Box 199, JCPL; Zelizer, *Jimmy Carter,* 33.

33. An early trip to New Mexico prompted the *Roswell Record* (with a circulation of ten thousand) to publish a house editorial about Carter's five-day journey, acknowledging the enthusiasm with which the former governor hit the campaign trail and the "contradiction in terms" the peanut farmer-physicist represented, an appeal upon which Jordan initially sought to capitalize. Reporters continued to consider the paradoxical elements of his persona. "Peanuts, Physics," *Roswell Record,* January 21, 1975, Media Publications [10], Box 343, JCPPP, Press Office-BRSF, Media Publications [7] through Media Publications [13], JCPL.

34. Burrelle's clipping service indicated the *Milwaukee Journal*'s circulation was 350,005. Leon Hughes, "Carter Confident After State Visit," *Milwaukee Journal,* February 9, 1975, Media Publications [10], Box 343, JCPPP, Press Office-BRSP, Media Publications [7] through Media Publications [13], JCPL.

35. "Carter was brilliant," Auth continued. "Watergate had changed things, and I think he was wise enough to know the time was right for someone exactly like himself—a non-Washington, Southern politician." Tony Auth, interview with the author, March 14, 2012.

36. Barber, *Race for the Presidency,* 32.

37. Kathryn McGarr, *The Whole Damn Deal: Robert Strauss and the Art of Politics* (New York: Public Affairs, 2011), 175–76. Witcover, *Marathon,* 3–200; Hadley, *Invisible Primary.*

38. Witcover, *Marathon,* 145–55; Brownell, *Showbiz Politics,* 1–12; 129–88; Eric Louw, *The Media and Political Process* (New York: Sage, 2010), 87; Maltese, *Spin Control,* 15–74.

39. Jimmy Carter Workshop, February 14–16, 1975, Jimmy Carter Workshop, 2/14–16/75, Box 2: Griffith Agency, 1975–1976 through [Schedule-Florida Primary, 1975–1976] [1], PWP, JCPL; Lasky, *Jimmy Carter,* 127.

40. Knox to Jimmy Carter, Hamilton Jordan, "Targeting," May 7, 1975, Memoranda, March–June 1975, Box 211: Memoranda, 1974 through Memoranda, General Election [2], JCPPP, PC, NCC-RH, JCPL. Rafshoon shared Jordan's sentiment, suggesting Carter was known to reporters, his opponents, and the public primarily as an attractive outsider who might offer "others a run for their money," and encouraged the campaign to hire pollster Patrick Caddell to assist in refining the governor's image to strike a "responsive chord" with the public. Jerry

Rafshoon to Jimmy Carter, "Issue, Research, and the public perception of Jimmy Carter," March 26, 1975, Memorandums [2], Box 30: Invitations through Memorandum from Pat Caddell, JPP-SF, JCPL. Impressed with Carter's visceral understanding of the national scene, the prodigy of new politics offered the campaign findings from Cambridge Research Group's 1974 study of political attitudes of two thousand Americans, which revealed many citizens shared deep desires for restoration of national values and nonideological political transformation, and Caddell believed Carter was the candidate best positioned to capitalize on his findings. Bourne, *Jimmy Carter,* 265; Sidney Blumenthal, *The Permanent Campaign* (New York: Simon and Schuster, 1982), 50–55.

41. Ken Auletta, *Hard Feelings: Reporting on the Pols, the Press, the People and the City* (New York: Random House, 1976), 346.

42. 1972 Campaign Manual, Preparation-1972 Campaign Manual, Box 8: Preparation—[Campaign Manual, 1972] through Wisconsin Primary, 1974–1976, PWP, JCPL; Jody Powell and Betty Rainwater to JCPC Field Persons, "Standardizing Contact with News Media," Administrative, Box 1: Administrative through Ethics, BRDP, JCPL; Campaign Media Planning and Execution, Box 2: Executive Department Records—Records During Carter's Gubernatorial Term through Natural Resources Management in Georgia, BRDP, JCPL; File: Good Clips—Betty's File [News Releases] 1975, Box 2: Executive Department Records—Records During Carter's Gubernatorial Term through Natural Resources Management in Georgia, BRDP, JCPL; Dennis W. Johnson, *Democracy for Hire: A History of American Political Consulting* (New York: Oxford Univ. Press, 2016), 222.

43. Burrelle's delivered all Carter clips, complete with newspaper name and circulation figures, to Carter's Atlanta headquarters. Listing, "Favorable Press: Suitable for Reprint," July 7, 1975, Media Publications [10], Box 343, JCPPP, PC Press Office-BRSF, Media Publications [7] through Media Publications [13], JCPL, Good Clips—Betty's File [News Releases] 1975, Box 2: Executive Department Records—Records During Carter's Gubernatorial Term through Natural Resources Management in Georgia, BRDP, JCPL; *Carter News,* February 1975, 1(3), File, Media Publications [10], Box 343, JCPPP, PC, Press Office-BRSF, Media Publications [7] through Media Publications [13], JCPL; File: Carter, Jimmy 1975–1976, Collected Materials [2 of 2], Box 9: Newsweek, Inc., Newsweek Atlanta Bureau Records, MSS 629, MARBL; Carter—Policies, Issues, Platforms (1 of 4), Box7: New York Times Research Materials, Series II: Carter, RBRLPRS.

44. Hutcheson considered the logic of the anomalous approach involved in campaigning in seventeen key states; basic organizing strategies, including communication logistics; and key leaders to contact to bolster Carter's appeal. Rick Hutcheson to Hamilton Jordan, May 1975, Memoranda, March–June 1975, Box 211: Memoranda, 1974 through Memoranda, General Election [2], JCPPP, PC, NCC-RH, JCPL. Unlike Wallace, who employed New Right direct-mail guru Richard Viguerie, Carter relied on a limited direct-mail campaign in the (in)visible primary, primary, and general election campaigns. Kalman, *Right Star Rising,* 170.

45. Erving Goffman, *Framing Analysis: An Essay on the Organization of Experience* (Cambridge, Mass.: Harvard Univ. Press, 1974).

46. As quoted in "Tim Kraft on the History of the Iowa Caucuses," CSPAN, November 7, 2015, https://www.c-span.org/video/?400279-2/tim-kraft-history-iowa-caucuses; "Nebraska, Kansas, Iowa, and California, 6/6–10/75," Box 28, SCCTF, RSC, JCPL; Zelizer, *Jimmy Carter,* 34. By December 1975, Carter's campaign employed three full-time field staff members—Kraft, Chris Brown,

and Phil Wise—operating in the three key states of Iowa, New Hampshire, and Florida. Bourne, *Jimmy Carter,* 261; Witcover, *Marathon,* 197–98. Apple acknowledged that, in lieu of appointing a campaign chair, Kraft shrewdly organized the "Iowa Carter for President Steering Committee," which was comprised of twenty individuals throughout the state, including key party leaders, who represented a wide variety of ideological perspectives. As one Iowan quipped to Apple, they were so diverse they could never be compelled to meet "because they would all shout at each other." Apple, "Carter Appears . . . ," 17; Winebrenner and Goldford, *The Iowa Precinct Caucuses,* 60.

47. Stroud, *How Jimmy Won,* 185.

48. Hamilton Jordan to Jimmy Carter, June 1975, Memorandum-Hamilton Jordan to Jimmy Carter, 6/75, Box 199: DC-FSCMPM, 5/76–10/76, PC, CDO-HJCSF, JCPL.

49. Witcover, *Marathon,* 30, 219; Freed, "Political Money and Campaign Finance Reform, 1971–1976," 241–55.

50. Busch, *Outsiders and Openness in the Presidential Nominating System,* 141.

51. Jordan to Carter, June 1975, Memorandum-Hamilton Jordan to Jimmy Carter, 6/75, Box 199: DC-FSCMPM, 5/76–10/76, PC, CDO-HJCSF, JCPL.

52. Brownell, *Showbiz Politics,* 169.

53. Ibid., 129–225; Rick Hutcheson to Hamilton Jordan, "My Reaction to the Cambridge Poll," May 27, 1975, Memoranda, March–June 1975, Box 211: Memoranda, 1974 through Memoranda, General Election [2], JCPPP, PC, NCC-RH, JCPL.

54. Inspired by the 1972 campaign, Carter's staff culled materials related to newly enfranchised young voters, such as Characteristics of America's Youth (1974), an informational booklet published by the U.S. Census Bureau. Characteristics of America's Youth, 1974, Cambridge Survey Research-Characteristics of American Youth, Box 37: Cabinet-Miscellaneous through Cambridge Survey Research-Gallup Poll and the Kettering Foundation-Spring 1976, Rafshoon, PPJC, JCPL. Inspired by Nixon's southern strategy, Carter and his imagecraft apparatus tapped into southern culture's appeal. Cowie, *Stayin' Alive,* 178–89; Schulman, *The Seventies,* 102–17; Lechner, *The South of the Mind,* 135–60. Art Harris, "Candidate Jimmy Carter: Rock's Good Ol' Boy," *Rolling Stone,* December 4, 1975, Media Publications [8], Box 343, JCPPP, Press Office-BRSF, Media Publications [7] through Media Publications [13], JCPL; Press Release, "Allman Bros.," October 20, 1975, [Carter/Mondale Press Releases, 10/20/75–9/29/76], Box 1: Andrus, Cecil through [Carter/Mondale Press Releases, 10/20/75–9/29/76], PPJC, JCPL.

55. Littlewood, *Calling Elections.*

56. Hamilton Jordan to Jimmy Carter, August 4, 1974, Peter Bourne File, Box 1, JCPPP, PC, JCPL; as quoted in Witcover, *Marathon,* 135.

57. Jayne Brumley, "Florida Primary Seen As Crucial Test for Carter," *Florida Times-Union and Journal,* July 13, 1975, A-8, Media Publications [8], Box 343, JCPPP, PC, Press Office-BRSF, Media Publications [7] through Media Publications [13], JCPL.

58. Hamilton Jordan to Jimmy Carter, June 1975, Memorandum-Hamilton Jordan to Jimmy Carter, 6/75, Box 199: DC-FSCMPM, 5/76–10/76, PC, CCDO-HJCSF, JCPL.

59. Robert Shogan, *Bad News: Where the Press Goes Wrong in the Making of the President* (Chicago: Ivan Dee, 2001), 72.

60. Though Carter's campaign activities attracted a groundswell of local and regional press, he complained about lagging coverage from elite reporters in the Peach State and D.C. Glad, *Jimmy Carter,* 235.

61. As quoted in Shogan, *Bad News,* 72.

62. National coverage remained elusive; Carter's trip to Washington, D.C., in July did not elicit coverage in the *Post* or the *Star.* "Tallahassee, Florida, Washington, D.C., 7/7–10/75," Box 29, SCCTF, RSC, JCPL.

63. "Missouri, Illinois, Wisconsin, Minnesota, 7/12–16/75," Box 29, SCCTF, RSC, JSPL; Pat Washburn, *The African-American Newspaper: Voice of Freedom* (Chicago: Northwestern Univ. Press, 2006), 197–207.

64. At Rafshoon's behest, Charles Kirbo struck up a conversation with Broder at a governor's conference in Austin, Texas, in 1974. But much to Broder's amusement, Kirbo mistakenly referred to him as Dean throughout the course of the meal. Rafshoon, interview with the author, August 12, 2014.

65. Hamilton Jordan to Jimmy Carter, N.D., Memorandum-Political Strategy [2], Box 39: Issues Task Force-Members List and Resumes through Memorandums-Political Strategy [2], CFP-PC, JCPL.

66. Stroud, *How Jimmy Won,* 185.

67. Jody Powell to Jimmy Breslin, July 24, 1975, Correspondence from the Media, District of Columbia [1]; Box 319: Correspondence from the Media, Colorado through Correspondence from the Media, Georgia [2]; JCPPP, PC, Press Office-BRSF, JCPL.

68. Barber, *Race for the Presidency,* 37–38.

69. Newspaper Clippings, Jayne Brumley, "Florida Primary Seen As Crucial Test for Carter," *Florida Times-Union and Journal,* July 13, 1975, A-8, Media Publications [8], Box 343, JCPPP, PC, Press Office-BRSF, Media Publications [7] through Media Publications [13], JCPL.

70. Godbold, *Jimmy and Rosalynn Carter,* 260–75.

71. Campaign finance reform capped individual donations at $1,000, limiting Carter's ability to accept a $50,000 check from country music star Johnny Cash. Carter's staff recognized that accepting federal matching funds imposed financial constraints on advertising budgets, and they subsequently relied on campaign pseudo-events to harness relatively free exposure from news coverage. Carter's press staff followed its release of Carter's statement with a letter to supporters and potential contributors. Zelizer, *Jimmy Carter,* 33; Glad, *Jimmy Carter,* 233–34; Bourne, *Jimmy Carter,* 270–73; interview with Peter Conlon, Alex Cooley, and Tom Beard, RBRLOHDC, RBRLPRS. In advance of this news, Carter traveled to New York for an interview with the *Daily News* and recorded sessions with CBS Radio News and local stations. "New York, Washington, D.C., Maryland, 8/12–15/75," Box 29, SCCTF, RSC, JCPL.

72. Jimmy Carter, "Why I Am Running," *New York Times,* September 5, 1975, Media Publications [8], Box 343, JCPPP, PC, Press Office-BRSF, Media Publications [7] through Media Publications [13], JCPL. Rainwater assisted the candidate in drafting the op-ed piece. File: Interviews; Box 2: Executive Department Records—Records During Carter's Gubernatorial Term through Natural Resources Management in Georgia, BRDP, JCPL.

73. Glad, *Jimmy Carter,* 235.

74. Ibid.; Winebrenner and Goldford, *The Iowa Precinct Caucuses,* 60. Carter finished first with 9.9 percent of the straw poll's 5,762 voters.

75. Winebrenner and Goldford, *The Iowa Precinct Caucuses,* 67–68.

76. "In truth, my only real interest was getting a news story that no one else had. The paper published the results for all comers, and everyone involved in national politics has been

hooked on straw polls ever since," Flansburg wrote. James Flansburg, "Iowa's GOP Poll, It's Straw, All Right," *Washington Post,* August 8, 1999, B1.

77. As quoted in Witcover, *Marathon,* 201.

78. As quoted in "Iowa Caucus History: Jimmy Carter Connects with Iowans in 1976," Iowa Public Television, https://www.youtube.com/watch?v=2N7gJDbxvIs. Due to limited budgets, only four national print reporters and three broadcast correspondents attended, but others trained their eyes on Iowa. The bicentennial campaign was not a major broadcast story until the 1976 primary season. Donaldson, interview with the author, January 17, 2017.

79. Jules Witcover as quoted in Winebrenner and Goldford, *The Iowa Precinct Caucuses,* 62.

80. Press Release, October 9, 1975, News Release-10/75–12/75, Box 42: News Releases, 10/75–12/75 through News Summaries, 9/6/76–3/13/76, CFP-CF, JCPL.

81. Zelizer, *Jimmy Carter,* 35; Witcover, *Marathon,* 200.

82. Winebrenner and Goldford, *The Iowa Precinct Caucuses,* 60–68.

83. Ibid., 62; James Flansburg, "Carter Tops Democratic Straw Poll," *Des Moines Register,* October 27, 1976, 1A.

84. Apple, "Carter Appears . . . ," 17. *New York Times* editor Abe Rosenthal nearly pulled Apple's story after expressing objections due to its speculative nature, but Apple convinced him that the story was accurate. Elizabeth Drew, *American Journal: The Events of 1976* (New York: Vintage, 1978), 6.

85. As quoted in "Iowa Caucus History: Jimmy Carter Connects with Iowans in 1976," Iowa Public Television, https://www.youtube.com/watch?v=2N7gJDbxvIs; Apple, "Carter Appears . . . ," 17; Leubsdorf, interview with the author, August 10, 2013.

86. Apple, "Carter Appears . . . ," 17.

87. Crouse, *Boys on the Bus,* 85. "Political reporters . . . are interested in who is going to win," Apple acknowledged. "It's true that I understood how the system worked better than most of the reporters that were here. . . . It is also true that a lot of them came and looked at my lede." As quoted in "Iowa Caucus History: Jimmy Carter Connects with Iowans in 1976," Iowa Public Television, https://www.youtube.com/watch?v=2N7gJDbxvIs.

88. Drew, *American Journal,* 6; Witcover, *Marathon,* 202.

89. Elite reporters from *Time, Newsweek,* and the *Washington Post* confirmed they decided to pay more attention to Iowa because of Apple's analysis. Cited in Winebrenner and Goldford, *The Iowa Precinct Caucuses,* 68; Barber, *Race for the Presidency,* 39.

90. Jordan to Carter, November 4, 1972, PC, CDO-HJCSF, JCPL; Stroud, *How Jimmy Won,* 185; Crouse, *Boys on the Bus,* 25–30.

91. "Favorable Press: Suitable for Reprint," July 7, 1975, Media Publications [10], Box 343, JCPPP, PC, Press Office-BRSF, Media Publications [7] through Media Publications [13], JCPL; "Florida, 10/28–30/75," Box 31, SCCTF, RSC, Personal Secretary to the President, JCPL; "Tucker Band Plays Carter Benefit," *Record World,* November 15, 1975, Magazines [3], Box 334, JCPPP, PC, Press Office-BRSF, Libassi, Peter through Magazines [3], JCPL. Four thousand people attended the sold-out concert. Bourne, *Jimmy Carter,* 273. Jordan's intern Peter Conlon and staff member Tom Beard worked with Walden and music promoter Alex Cooley to organize the concert series. Interview with Peter Conlon, Alex Cooley, and Tom Beard, RBRLOHDC, RBRLPRS.

92. The Macon native managed soul icons, such as Otis Redding, before launching the Southern Rock craze with the release of the Allman Brothers Band's debut studio album in

November 1969. Mark Kemp, *Dixie Lullaby: A Story of Music, Race, and Beginnings in a New South* (Athens: Univ. of Georgia Press, 2007), xvii, 19–20. In 1971, Carter convened with Walden and expressed interest in promoting the state's record business. Carter's offer sparked a cordial relationship prompting Capricorn artist meet-and-greets at the governor's mansion in Atlanta and jam sessions in Macon. Newspaper Clippings, Art Harris, "Candidate Jimmy Carter: Rock's Good Ol' Boy," *Rolling Stone,* December 4, 1975, Media Publications [8], Box 343, JCPPP, PC, Press Office-BRSF, Media Publications [7] through Media Publications [13], JCPL.

93. As quoted in Kemp, *Dixie Lullaby,* 273. Marshall Tucker Band front man Doug Gray recalled that the group consented to the concert out of a sense of loyalty to Walden and not a deep political affinity for Carter. Cited in Saby Reyes-Kulkarni, "40 Years Ago: Marshall Tucker Band Play Benefit Show for Jimmy Carter," Ultimate Classic Rock, http://ultimateclassicrock .com/marshall-tucker-band-jimmy-carter/.

94. Art Harris, "Candidate Jimmy Carter: Rock's Good Ol' Boy," *Rolling Stone,* December 4, 1975, Media Publications [8], Box 343, JCPPP, PC, Press Office-BRSF, Media Publications [7] through Media Publications [13], JCPL.

95. Ibid. Carter's campaign earned $30 for each $15 ticket purchased at the sold-out event thanks to federal matching funds.

96. "Tucker Band Plays Carter Benefit," *Record World,* November 15, 1975, Magazines [3], Box 334, JCPPP, PC, Press Office-BRSF, Libassi, Peter through Magazines [3], JCPL.

97. Betty Rainwater to Vicki, November 6, 1975, Correspondence from the Public, New York [2], Box 325: Correspondence from the Public, New York [1] through Correspondence from the Public, New York [2], JCPPP, PC, Press Office-BRSF, JCPL.

98. Hunter S. Thompson to Jimmy, November 24, 1975, Correspondence from the Media, Colorado, Box 319: Correspondence from the Media, Colorado through Correspondence from the Media, Georgia [2], JCPPP, PC, Press Office-BRSF, JCPL.

99. Charles H. Kirbo to Jimmy Carter, November 20, 1975, Political Strategy [1] Box 39: Issues Task Force-Members List and Resumes through Memorandums-Political Strategy [2], CFP, CF, JCPL.

100. "Iowa and Kentucky, 11/21–23/75," Box 31, SCCTF, RSC, JCPL; as quoted in "New York, Massachusetts, and Rhode Island, 11/25–26/75," Box 31, SCCTF, RSC, JCPL; "Front-running Dark Horse," *Evening Journal,* November 5, 1975, Media Publications [8], Box 343, JCPPP, PC, Press Office-BRSF, Media Publications [7] through Media Publications [13], JCPL.

101. "New York, Massachusetts, and Rhode Island, 11/25–26/75," Box 31, SCCTF, RSC, JCPL.

102. Clift notified Carter's staff that she or another reporter would travel for a full week with the campaign in late November. Betty Rainwater to Vicki, N.D., Correspondence from the Public, New York [2], Box 325: Correspondence from the Public, New York [1] through Correspondence from the Public, New York [2], JCPP, PC, Press Office-BRSF, JCPL. Cloud telephoned to arrange a meeting for Hugh Sidey, a fourth-generation journalist who wrote about every president since Eisenhower for *Time,* the legacy newsmagazine. Betty Rainwater to Jody Powell, Correspondence from the Media, District of Columbia [2]; Box 319: Correspondence from the Media, Colorado through Correspondence from the Media, Georgia [2]; JCPPP, PC, Press Office-BRSF, JCPL.

103. "New York, Massachusetts, and Rhode Island, 11/25–26/75," Box 31, SCCTF, RSC, JCPL; as quoted in Chris Charlesworth, "Jimmy Carter: Rock 'n' roll President?—A Classic Piece

from the Vaults," *The Guardian,* October 30, 2012, https://www.theguardian.com/music/2012/oct/30/jimmy-carter-president-interview; Kemp, *Dixie Lullaby,* 115. Forsaking his commitment to objectivity, Rivera became the first non-southern celebrity to endorse Carter. Bourne, *Jimmy Carter,* 273.

104. "Allman Bros.," October 20, 1975, [Carter/Mondale Press Releases, 10/20/75–9/29/76], Box 1: Andrus, Cecil through [Carter/Mondale Press Releases, 10/20/75–9/29/76], PPJC, JCPL.

105. As quoted in Jill Vejnoska, "Jimmy Carter Helps Give Gregg Allman an Honorary Degree," *Atlanta Journal-Constitution,* May 17, 2016, http://www.ajc.com/entertainment/music/jimmy-carter-helps-give-gregg-allman-honorary-degree/2QVSkLije0kzHOwY6LwBNL/; Alan Paul, *One Way Out: The Inside History of the Allman Brothers Band* (New York: St. Martin's Press, 2014), 238; Bourne, *Jimmy Carter,* 273. Ten thousand concert-goers paid $8 each for tickets.

106. "CBS' Face the Nation," Clippings, 1974–1976, Box 5: Administrative Manual-Field Offices-Press Instructions, 1975–1976 through Economy, 1974, PWP, JCPL.

107. Hamilton Jordan to Jimmy Carter, June 1975, Memorandum-Hamilton Jordan to Jimmy Carter, 6/75, Box 199: DC-FSCMPM, 5/76–10/76, PC-CDO-HJCSF, JCPL.

108. S. Stephen Selig III to Jimmy Carter Telethon Party Captains and Hosts, Telethon Party, 12/75, Box 49: Speeches—Master File, 10/76–11/76 through Women's Issues, CFP-CF, JCPL.

109. "Frontrunning Dark Horse," *Evening Journal,* November 5, 1975, Media Publications [8], Box 343, JCPPP, PC, Press Office-BRSF, Media Publications [7] through Mediations [13], JCPL.

110. Ibid.

111. "Whistling Dixie," *Newsweek* 86.19 (November 3, 1975), 19.

112. Cover, "Dixie Whistles a Different Tune," *Time,* May 31, 1971.

113. Eleanor Clift, interview with the author, August 14, 2013; Lynn Povich, *The Good Girls Revolt: How the Women of Newsweek Sued Their Bosses and Changed the Workplace* (New York: Public Affairs, 2013), 121–22, 181, 213–14. Clift started working at *Newsweek* as a secretary in the 1960s but was promoted to reporter as the result of the mandate from the 1970 gender discrimination suit filed by forty-six women against her employer. After attending a magazine institute internship, she transitioned to a position as a bylined reporter and exploited her experience in the South to cover the civil rights movement and the emergence of Carter's longshot candidacy. Clift took advantage of friendly associations with Jordan and campaign aide Bebe Smith. Such associations, on occasion, resulted in scoops over her competition. When *Newsweek* published a cover story based on Clift's reporting on key campaign strategy documents, her competitor Stanley Cloud complained about inequitable treatment. Nonetheless, Carter's staff used leaks as a strategic tool to reward friendly reporters. Glad, *Jimmy Carter,* 285.

114. Other characterizations were more benign; in the same piece, *Newsweek* called Carter the "down-home politician," the "voice of a new politics of amazing grace." Tom Mathews and Eleanor Clift, "Suddenly He Is No Longer Jimmy Who?" *Newsweek* 86.22 (December 1, 1975), 37. Georgia Secretary of State Ben Fortson described Carter as "stubborn as a South Georgia land turtle." As quoted in Eleanor Randolph, "Can Ex-Sub Skipper Run Ship of State," *Chicago Tribune,* February 11, 1976, 1. Rex Granum, the *Atlanta Constitution* political reporter who accepted a position with Carter's staff as press director of its Atlanta headquarters in Jan-

uary 1976, recalled the disdain that some Georgia politicians shared for Carter. "You had House Speaker Tom Murphy, who was not a Carter fan. Murphy once said [at a press conference], 'Jimmy Carter lies by the clock.' Well, I didn't know what that meant, and so I said, 'Mr. Speaker, I don't understand that term. What do you mean by 'lies by the clock?' And he said, 'Son, see that clock over there?' It was some government regulation clock. Well, 'Yes, sir,' I said, and he replied, 'You see that second hand, how it moves?' 'Yes, sir,' I said, and he replied, 'Every time it moves, Jimmy Carter lies.'" These anecdotes from hostile state politicians reverberated in national coverage about Carter's campaign. Rex Granum, interview with the author, August 14, 2013; Glad, *Jimmy Carter,* 236.

115. Newspaper Clippings, Art Harris, "Candidate Jimmy Carter: Rock's Good Ol' Boy," *Rolling Stone,* December 4, 1975, Media Publications [8], Box 343, JCPPP, PC, Press Office-BRSF, Media Publications [7] through Media Publications [13], JCPL.

116. Ibid.; Glad, *Jimmy Carter,* 236.

117. Lechner, *The South of the Mind,* 135–60; Jimmy Carter, *Why Not the Best: The First Fifty Years* (Fayetteville: Univ. of Arkansas Press, 1975/1996).

118. Douglas Brinkley, "Introduction," in Carter, *Why Not the Best,* xi–xx; Brownell, *Showbiz Politics.*

119. Lechner, *The South of the Mind,* 135–60; Bourne, *Jimmy Carter,* 265; Drew, *American Journal,* 97.

120. Brinkley, "Introduction," xvii.

121. Erika Seifert, *The Politics of Authenticity in Presidential Campaigns, 1976–2008* (Jefferson, N.C.: McFarland, 2012), 41; Mathews and Clift, "Suddenly He Is No Longer Jimmy Who?" 37.

122. Rafshoon, interview with the author, August 12, 2014.

123. Unsigned to Phil Wise, February 24, 1976, Media Contacts, 1975–1976, Box 3: Schedule-Florida Primary, 1975–1976], [2] through, [Schedule]-Pensacola-Tampa-Miami, 12/1–3/75, PWP, FPCF, JCPL.

124. As quoted in Seifert, *The Politics of Authenticity in Presidential Campaigns,* 41; White, *The Making of the President, 1960,* 85–96. Carter's print advertisements also were effective. File: Advertising, Box 1: Administrative through Evans and Novak, BRDP, JCPL.

125. Joseph Lelyveld, "Cheap TV Time in Iowa Aids Drives by Three Democrats," *New York Times,* January 17, 1976, 25; Rafshoon, interview with the author, August 12, 2014; Gerald Rafshoon, "Washington Classroom with Gerald Rafshoon," C-SPAN, October 7, 2013, https://www.c-span.org/video/?315502-1/washington-classroom-gerald-rafshoon.

126. Carter's national name recognition rate increased from 6.2 percent in December 1974 to 50 percent in November 1975. Mathews and Clift, "Suddenly He Is No Longer Jimmy Who?" 37.

127. Patrick Anderson, "Peanut Farmer for President," *New York Times Magazine,* December 14, 1975, SM4. Jimmy Carter, Anderson wrote, "may or may not become President, but he is certainly one of the more interesting men to seek that office in recent times." Anderson decided to profile Carter after discovering him at a cocktail party at Bourne's Washington home, and he came on board the campaign as Carter's speechwriter in 1976. Rainwater wrote a memo to Carter on October 30 explaining that since the *New York Times Magazine* accepted Anderson's piece, she was "supplying them with photos." "Pat said he was interested to hear about the Iowa success because 'it supports what he said in the piece about your strength in key states.'" Betty Rainwater to Governor, October 30, 1975, Correspondence from the Public,

New York [2], Box 325: Correspondence from the Public, New York [1] through Correspondence from the Public, New York [2], JCPPP, PC, Press Office-BRSF, JCPL. Carter was among the first wave of Democratic candidates that CBS News anchor Walter Cronkite interviewed for his series on the candidates and the issues. Overall Coverage of Campaign '76. The Candidates and the Issues [entry title: CBS News Coverage of Campaign '76], PAC, 76061 NWT 1 of 4, WJBMAPAC; Supporting Materials, File 76061 NWT, Box 99: PAE, HRBML. Rainwater suggested Carter's field staff circulate the broadcast transcript. File: Speeches/Issues, Box 4: BRDP, JCPL, Glad, *Jimmy Carter,* 236.

128. "Peanuts, Physics," *Roswell Record,* January 21, 1975, Media Publications [10], Box 343, JCPPP, PC, Press Office-BRSF, Media Publications [7] through Media Publications [13], JCPL; File: Campaign News Releases and Schedules, 11/75–2/76, Box 3, BRDP, JCPL.

129. Bourne, *Jimmy Carter,* 273.

130. National contenders devoted more than ten times the number of days to the state than had their 1972 predecessors. Carter, for instance, logged his seventeenth day in the state by mid-January, and Udall devoted ten days and $80,000 in limited funds to Iowa in January. Winebrenner and Goldford, *The Iowa Precinct Caucuses,* 60–68; Stroud, *How Jimmy Won,* 238–39.

131. Polsby, "The News Media as an Alternative to Party in the Presidential Selection Process," 55.

132. David Broder, "Political Reporters in Presidential Politics," in *Inside the System,* 3rd ed., ed. Charles Peters and James Fallows (New York: Praeger, 1976), 211–22.

133. Ernest May and Janet Fraser, "The Press in the 1972 Campaign: The Harvard Conference on Campaign Decision-Making," *Neiman Reports* 27.3 (fall 1973): 3–9; James David Barber, *The Pulse of Politics,* 186; Shogan, *Bad News,* 70–71.

134. R. W. Apple Jr., "Carter and Bayh Favored in Iowa," *New York Times,* January 19, 1976, 1.

135. Drew, *American Journal,* 6.

136. As quoted in Schram, *Running for President,* 20.

137. Carter, interview with the author, October 17, 2014.

4. MAN TO BEAT

1. Jeff Prugh, "News 'Hard to Believe': Vote Results Surprise, Elate Carter," *Los Angeles Times,* March 10, 1976, B18; Apple, "Carter Appears," 17; Goffman, *Framing Analysis*; Lasky, *Jimmy Carter,* 129; Carl Leubsdorf, "Wallace Is Still Man to Beat in Florida," *Baltimore Sun,* January 27, 1976, A7.

2. Prugh, "News 'Hard to Believe,'" B18; White, *The Making of the President, 1960,* 111–12; Barber, *Race for the Presidency,* 42; McCombs and Shaw, "The Agenda-Setting Function of the Mass Media," 176–87.

3. Prugh, "News 'Hard to Believe,'" B18; Godbold, *Jimmy and Rosalynn Carter,* 165; Bourne, *Jimmy Carter,* 300.

4. AP, "Mother Carter Gloats over 'Stinker's' Defeat," *Los Angeles Times,* March 10, 1976, A2.

5. Witcover, *Marathon,* 256–59; Crouse, *Boys on the Bus,* 61–62; Niall Palmer, *The New Hampshire Primary and the American Electoral Process* (New York: Westview, 1999), 13–15.

6. Shafer, *Quiet Revolution*; Jordan to Carter, November 4, 1972, PC, CDO-HJCSF, Box 199, JCPL; Witcover, *Marathon,* 134–36.

7. Goffman, *Framing Analysis*; Kamarck, *Primary Politics,* 27.

8. Charles Seib, "Missing the Election Story," *Washington Post,* February 13, 1976, A23.

9. Brownell, *Showbiz Politics,* 129–88.

10. Skipper, *The Iowa Caucuses,* 47–48.

11. Winebrenner and Goldford, *The Iowa Precinct Caucuses,* 67. Approximately 150 national reporters covered the 1976 Iowa precinct caucuses.

12. As quoted in ibid., 67; Boorstin, *The Image,* 3–45. *New York Times* media critic Joseph Lelyveld wrote that Iowa fit "the working definition of a 'media event,' an occasion on which the discussion overwhelms and finally obscures the fragile reality that gives rise to it." Though only approximately 10 percent of Iowans participated in the first stage of precinct caucuses, the news media billed Iowa as an important test and Carter as the winner and emerging frontrunner in the race for the Democratic nomination. Joseph Lelyveld, "Press, TV, and Politics," *New York Times,* January 31, 1976, 17.

13. As quoted in Crouse, *Boys on the Bus,* 37.

14. Winebrenner and Goldford, *The Iowa Precinct Caucuses,* 67; Skipper, *The Iowa Caucuses,* 41–50. Some critics declared that the Iowa caucuses were an overblown media event. Witcover, *Marathon,* 202. As field director Tim Kraft contended, Iowa became the "national media's starting gun." As quoted in "Tim Kraft on the History of the Iowa Caucuses," CSPAN, November 7, 2015, https://www.c-span.org/video/?400279-2/tim-kraft-history-iowa-caucuses.

15. Donaldson, interview with the author, January 17, 2017.

16. "Iowa Caucus/Demo-Republican Results/Carter/Mississippi," *CBS Evening News,* January 20, 1976, VTNAC. NBC *Nightly News* anchor John Chancellor concurred: "Carter was . . . grinning from ear to ear. . . . His victory yesterday was of great symbolic importance. There were those today who were using the word frontrunner to describe Carter." "Jimmy Carter Wins 1976 Iowa Caucus," NBC Nightly News, January 2, 2012, https://www.nbcnews.com/video/jimmy-http://www.nbcnews.com/video/jimmy-carter-wins-1976-iowa-caucus-44462659792.

17. "Iowa Caucus/Demo-Republican Results/Carter/Mississippi," *CBS Evening News,* January 20, 1976, VTNAC.

18. As quoted in Dominick Sandbrook, *Mad as Hell: The Crisis of the 1970s and the Rise of the Populist Right* (New York: Random House, 2012), 148.

19. Stories of victorious underdogs, such as Rocky Balboa, resonated amid despair in American culture. Cowie, *Stayin' Alive,* 328.

20. As quoted in James Baker, *Jimmy Carter: A Southern Baptist in the White House* (Philadelphia: Westminster, 1977), 21.

21. As quoted in Winebrenner and Goldford, *The Iowa Precinct Caucuses,* 70; Stroud, *How Jimmy Won,* 237; Glad, *Jimmy Carter,* 239.

22. Walter Mears, interview with the author, August 18, 2014; Leubsdorf, interview with the author, August 10, 2013; Rafshoon, interview with the author, August 12, 2014; Gerald Rafshoon, "Washington Classroom with Gerald Rafshoon," C-SPAN, October 7, 2013, https://www.c-span.org/video/?315502-1/washington-classroom-gerald-rafshoon; Jay Beck, ROGPOHC, ROGP 157, RBRLPRS; Chip Carter, ROGPOHC, ROGP 036, RBRLPRS.

23. As quoted in Drew, *American Journal,* 65–66.

24. Littlewood, *Calling Elections*; R. W. Apple Jr., "Carter Defeats Bayh by 2–1," *New York Times,* January 20, 1976, 1; Jules Witcover, "Carter Takes Early Lead in Iowa," *Washington Post,* January 20, 1976, A1; UPI, "Carter Takes Strong Lead in Iowa Caucuses," *Boston Globe,* January 20, 1976, 1. On February 2, the big three newsmagazines focused tremendous attention on Carter's campaign, devoting 726 lines to Carter and his Peanut Brigade compared with an average of thirty each for all other contenders, and characterized the peanut farmer from Plains as the winner of the recent Iowa caucuses and the Democratic frontrunner. Glad, *Jimmy Carter,* 241, 289.

25. David Broder, "Trims Due in Political Roster," *Los Angeles Times,* February 29, 1976, D1. Barber, *Race for the Presidency,* 1; Barber, *The Pulse of Politics,* 184–210; Shogan, *Bad News,* 69–71. Though Barber and Broder warned that horse race coverage acted as "psychological springboards" for victors and served to artificially "trim political rosters," Mears, who won the Pulitzer Prize for his 1976 campaign reporting, defended the trope, acknowledging that it was his job to blend issues analysis with coverage that interested readers. Mears, interview with the author, August 18, 2014.

26. Apple, "Carter Defeats Bayh by 2–1," 1.

27. UPI, "Carter Takes Strong Lead in Iowa Caucuses," 1.

28. Barber, *The Pulse of Politics,* 187.

29. Godfrey Sperling, "Iowa's Real Winner," *Christian Science Monitor,* January 26, 1976, 1. *Chicago Tribune* columnist Jim Squires concurred: "The significance attached by some in the media to those state caucuses is only the first example of what must surely be the greatest absurdity of the American political system—a circumstance in which the reporting and media analysis of an event actually becomes more important than the event itself." Jim Squires, "The Importance of Being Analyzed," *Chicago Tribune,* February 1, 1976, A5.

30. Leubsdorf, interview with the author, August 10, 2013.

31. John Kifner, "Carter Campaigns in New Hampshire," *New York Times,* January 21, 1976, 27.

32. Witcover, "Carter Takes Early Lead in Iowa," A1.

33. AP, "Finishing 1st Causes Problems for Carter," *Baltimore Sun,* January 25, 1976, A2.

34. Tom Wicker, "The Press and the Campaign," *New York Times,* January 20, 1976, 29.

35. Thompson, *Fear and Loathing on the Campaign Trail '72,* 225; Tom Wicker, "McGovern with Tears," *New York Times,* November 5, 1972, 36.

36. As quoted in Barber, *The Pulse of Politics,* 191. Carter strategically confided his concerns about the new adversarial brand: "To have this concentrated attention on myself and the other candidates by the press at this early stage is really extraordinary. I think that [it] possibly will make the press more demanding than they should be on final answers on complicated questions." As quoted in Witcover, *Marathon,* 226; Crouse, *Boys on the Bus,* 99–128.

37. Leubsdorf, interview with the author, August 10, 2013. Though elite reporters examined celebrity connections to all campaigns, they focused on the frontrunner, scrutinizing the symbiotic relationship between Carter and Walden. Larry Rohter, "Rock on the Band Wagon," *Washington Post,* January 21, 1976, B1.

38. Joseph Lelyveld, "Press, TV, and Politics," *New York Times,* January 31, 1976, 17. "Fuzzy" images emerged from his complex issues stances. When asked by a reporter from a small, Catholic publication about his stance on abortion on January 1, Carter responded that al-

though he was personally against abortion, he could not support an anti-abortion amendment to the U.S. Constitution. When pressed, Carter responded that he might instead support a national statute restricting abortions. Witcover, *Marathon*, 206–7; Drew, *American Journal*, 20; Laurence H. Tribe, *Abortion: The Clash of Absolutes* (New York: Norton, 1992), 148; John Dillin, "Carter Plan: One Down, and Two More to Go," *Christian Science Monitor*, January 21, 1976, 1.

39. Carl Leubsdorf, "'Nonpolitical Image' May Hurt Carter," *Baltimore Sun*, January 23, 1976, A8.

40. Telex, Newsweek NY to Newsweek ATL, 1-21-76, Carter, Jimmy Correspondence, 1974–1976, Box 9: Newsweek, Inc., Newsweek Atlanta Bureau Records, MSS 629, SRMARBL. David Alpern explained the system: "After the story conference at the beginning of the week, generally Tuesday, writers would send queries out to relevant correspondents saying, 'Here's the general scope or thrust of the story we have in mind. Here's the questions that occurred to us based on what we read in the news and what we have seen in the clips. And you know, we look forward to amplification of those points,' . . . The writers in New York would then keep up with the story in the news, in the papers, on TV, and maybe do some research if it was relevant. . . . Then the files would come in—generally, from more than one reporter because what we tried to do is look at stories not just as an event but in the context of the larger events of the day. . . . It was my job to tuck in any late developments, you know, from the scene and that was the sentence or two that I stitched in. . . . You know, in different stories, there might be files from several different locations. The job of the writer was to stitch them together in a narrative . . . that would give . . . the facts of the matter, the context . . . and maybe a little bit more. It was a system that at its finest . . . with two or three narrative pieces would cover all the developments in a week which would have been covered by dozens of different newspaper articles through the week." David Alpern, interview with the author, August 25, 2014.

41. Renate Holub, *Antonio Gramsci: Beyond Marxism and Postmodernism* (New York: Routledge, 2005), 71; James Martin, *Gramsci's Political Analysis: A Critical Introduction* (New York: Palgrave Macmillan, 1998), 89.

42. "[Carter] is familiar with deadlines, and understands the difference between what will make news in a small town and what will make news on the national level." As quoted in Lasky, *Jimmy Carter*, 127, 141; Godbold, *Jimmy and Rosalynn Carter*, 254.

43. Greg Schneiders, interview with the author, August 25, 2014. Though the *Constitution* did not devote substantive resources to covering Carter's early efforts, Granum "treated the possibility of a Carter presidential run as a serious proposition." Rex Granum, interview with the author, August 14, 2013.

44. Powell did not include broadcast correspondents on his initial list of journalists with whom Carter should develop rapport, but by 1976 broadcast correspondents were "big dogs" on the trail, as Donaldson put it, and Powell understood he needed to hire someone who could capitalize on the medium. Donaldson, interview with the author, January 17, 2017. Powell approached CBS News correspondent Ed Bradley, who suggested that Emmy Award-winning CBS News producer Barry Jagoda, well-known for his space race coverage, might be interested in the opportunity. Barry Jagoda, interview with the author, January 10, 2017.

45. "When he did so well in [a given primary], the question was what would he do the next day," Jagoda explained. But increasingly the consensus-minded campaign pack noticed how

candidates staged events for television. Mears, interview with the author, August 18, 2014; Donaldson, interview with the author, January 17, 2017.

46. As quoted in Barber, *Race for the Presidency,* 43; Crouse, *Boys on the Bus,* 99–128.

47. Jody Powell, Betty Rainwater, and Hamilton Jordan to Key Campaign Members, January 10, 1976, Atlanta Correspondence, 1975–1976, Box 5: Administrative Manuals to Economy, 1974, PWP, JCPL; Barber, *The Pulse of Politics,* 193. Powell likewise offered "Georgia Snow Bunnies," dubbed the Peanut Brigade by national news media, "a word or two on the press." "Although this is a working trip, not a media event, you will probably have some contact with the news media . . . ," he wrote. "The press has a legitimate interest in your reactions to the trip, what sort of response you are getting, why you came, why you are supporting Jimmy etc. . . . The press is interested in a good story. They will want your candid opinions in your own words." Powell reminded volunteers of the old publicity adage "if you don't want to read it, don't say it" before sharing the opposition position (their presence was an indication Carter was "unable to recruit enough New Hampshire volunteers") and a request that they treat national media "with caution but report activities and progress to their hometown newspapers and radio stations." Jody Powell to Georgia Snow Bunnies, January 4, 1976, Correspondence from the Media, New Hampshire, Box 321: Correspondence from the Media, New Hampshire through Correspondence from the Media, Virginia, JCPPP, PC, Press Office-BRSF, JCPL. A February *Newsweek* summed up the Peanut Brigade's value, noting that Carter made "the most dramatic impression in the campaign so far by fielding a force of 98 Georgians to sing his praises door-to-door all over snow-blanketed New Hampshire." As quoted in Winebrenner and Goldford, *The Iowa Precinct Caucuses,* 69. Covered as a novelty by many media outlets, the Peanut Brigade became an effective political tool in Carter's campaign, and future contenders constrained by finance reform emulated the surrogate strategy. Bourne, *Jimmy Carter,* 287–89; Jay Beck, ROGPOHC, ROGP 157, RBRLPRS.

48. Though Broder conceded that Carter restored a message of love to the American "political lexicon," he maintained that the candidate was a "thoroughly tough, opportunist politician who comes into almost any competition with his elbows out." As quoted in David Broder, "Carter's Image," *Charlotte Observer,* January 22, 1976, Clippings-Carter, Jimmy [1], Box 2: Card File on TV Phoners through Clippings-Carter, Jimmy Magazines, RWHPO-Bradley Woodward's Subject Files, PPJC, JCPL. Carter characterized his relationship with Broder as a "failure," indicative of his relationship with many elite reporters, quipping that he "never did admit that I was elected president." Carter, interview with the author, October 17, 2014.

49. Louw, *The Media and Political Process,* 87; Maltese, *Spin Control,* 15–74. Carter's press staff generated rebuttals, alongside relevant position papers, for distribution to offending reporters and for submission as letters to the editor. Jody Powell to Georgia Snow Bunnies, January 4, 1976, Correspondence from the Media, New Hampshire, Box 321: Correspondence from the Media, New Hampshire through Correspondence from the Media, Virginia, JCPPP, PC, Press Office-BRSF, JCPL; Jody Powell to Carter Field Staff and Key People, N.D., Atlanta Correspondence, 1975–1976, Box 5: Administrative Manuals to Economy, 1974, PWP, JCPL; Witcover, *Marathon,* 206–7.

50. Leubsdorf, "'Nonpolitical Image' May Hurt Carter," A8.

51. Lasky, *Jimmy Carter,* 139–40; Peter Goldman and Eleanor Clift, "Carter on the Rise," *Newsweek,* March 8, 1976, 25.

52. "Carter and Murphy were arch enemies," Granum recalled. Granum, interview with the author, August 14, 2013.

53. Reg Murphy, "The New Jimmy Carter," *New Republic*, February 14, 1976, 14–15.

54. Steven Brill, "Jimmy Carter's Pathetic Lies," *Harper's Magazine*, March 1976, 77–88.

55. Ibid.

56. Wilkie, interview with the author, January 16, 2017; Curtis Wilkie, "Carter Camp Braces for a Critical Article," *Boston Globe*, February 1, 1976, 13; Crouse, *Boys on the Bus*, 12–13.

57. Wilkie, "Carter Camp Braces for a Critical Article," 13; Witcover, *Marathon*, 225–26; Glad, *Jimmy Carter*, 291. Rumors of Brill's "hatchet job" circulated among reporters in November, and shortly after Brill's four-hour interview with Carter in mid-December, Powell contacted Lapham to request an advance copy "to prepare ourselves to reply," promising "'on [his] honor' not to distribute it." Mary McGrory, "The Carter Behind the Smile," *Chicago Tribune*, May 12, 1976, A4; Barber, *The Pulse of Politics*, 193; "Media Definitely Covering JC in New Hampshire," Media Schedules [1], Box 345: Media Schedules [1] through Media Schedules [6], JCPP, PC, Press Office-BRSP, JCPL. Powell enlisted Rainwater's assistance to construct the rebuttal. File: Harper's Article/Rebuttal, Box 1: BRDP, JCPL. Powell integrated principles from John Marston's four-step approach, involving research, action, communication, and evaluation. John Marston, *The Nature of Public Relations* (New York: McGraw-Hill, 1963).

58. Jody Powell to Members of the Press, N.D., Media Publications [7], Box 343: Media Publications [7] through Media Publications [13], JCPPP, PC Press Office-BRSF, JCPL, Lasky, *Jimmy Carter*, 139–41.

59. Adam Bernstein, "Jody Powell, 65, Trusted Aide Helped Carter Reach White House," *Washington Post*, September 15, 2009, http://www.washingtonpost.com/wp-dyn/content/article/2009/09/14/AR2009091402738.html; McGrory, "The Carter Behind the Smile," A4; James Wooten, "As Carter Moves into the Limelight, He Becomes Highly Visible and Vulnerable," *New York Times*, February 4, 1976, 15.

60. As quoted in Barber, *The Pulse of Politics*, 193.

61. Charlie Shepard, "Liberals and 'Progressives' Trying to Reconcile Themselves to Jimmy Carter," *Harvard Crimson*, July 16, 1976, http://www.thecrimson.com/article/1976/7/16/pulp-pliberals-and-progressives-trying-to/.

62. James Fallows, "Turning the Other Chic," *Texas Monthly* 4.5 (May 1976): 29–30; Charles Seib, "Missing the Election Story," *Washington Post*, February 13, 1976, A23.

63. Leubsdorf, interview with the author, August 10, 2013.

64. As quoted in Shogan, *Bad News*, 80.

65. Joseph Lelyveld, "News Media Magnify Campaign," *New York Times*, February 23, 1976, 29.

66. Wooten, "As Carter Moves into the Limelight, He Becomes Highly Visible and Vulnerable," 15.

67. Fallows, "Turning the Other Chic," 29–30.

68. Ibid., Curtis Wilkie, "Carter Camp Braces for a Critical Article," *Boston Globe*, February 1, 1976, 13; Barber, *The Pulse of Politics*, 193.

69. Overall Coverage of Campaign '76. Daily Coverage of Carter and Ford [entry title: CBS News Coverage of Campaign '76], PAC, 76061 NWT 3 of 4, WJBMAPAC; Supporting Materials, File 76061 NWT, Box 99: PAE, HRBML.

70. Ibid.

71. Ibid. Maddox continued his assault on Carter's credibility in Manchester, where he indicated plans to run as an independent, third-party candidate. But the CBS Evening News downplayed Maddox's charge, instead accentuating Powell's sensational response—"being called a liar by Lester Maddox is like being called ugly by a frog." As quoted in Bourne, *Jimmy Carter*, 290.

72. Overall Coverage of Campaign '76. Daily Coverage of Carter and Ford [entry title: CBS News Coverage of Campaign '76], PAC, 76061 NWT 3 of 4, WJBMAPAC; Supporting Materials, File 76061 NWT, Box 99: PAE, HRBML. Engaged in a journalistic balancing act, Rabel transitioned into his interview with Carter champion Andrew Young with this voiceover: "[Carter] declared in his inaugural address that the time for racial discrimination was over. He appointed blacks to office, and he hung this portrait of the late Martin Luther King, Jr., a symbolic act that took a degree of courage. . . . but the question is how to reconcile the pro-civil rights Carter with the 'I am basically a redneck Carter.' Which is the real Carter?" Carter and Wallace engaged in friendly correspondence prior to the 1972 DNC. File: '76 Campaign, Rebuttal to News Article, Box 3: BRDP, JCPL.

73. Overall Coverage of Campaign '76. Daily Coverage of Carter and Ford [entry title: CBS News Coverage of Campaign '76], PAC, 76061 NWT 3 of 4, WJBMAPAC; Supporting Materials, File 76061 NWT, Box 99: PAE, HRBML. The same day, Carter told NBC News correspondent Tom Pettit he was "getting tired of critics who say that he stands on both sides of critical issues." "New Hampshire Primary/Thomson/Democrats," NBC Evening News, February 11, 1976, VTNAC.

74. Barber, *The Pulse of Politics*, 191. For instance, in November 1975 Carter convened with Winship's editorial board, but despite Carter's initial overtures and later critiques, the crusading publisher, committed to an adversarial mode in the aftermath of presidential abuses associated with Vietnam and Watergate, exposed the campaign to the same scrutiny other candidates encountered. Wilkie, interview with the author, January 16, 2017; Paul Szep, interview with the author, February 28, 2012. On March 26, Winship confronted Carter for critiquing the *Globe*'s coverage, including Wilkie's trail coverage, Szep's editorial cartoons, and Evans and Novak's columns. Thomas Winship to Honorable Jimmy Carter c/o Jody Powell, 3/26/76, Primaries—JLP's Briefcase Contents, 3/4/76–4/4/76, Box 5: National Governor's Conference, 11/12/76-11/14/76 [CF, O/A 751] through Schedules/Pool Reports, 10/4/76–11/10/76 [CF, O/A 751], Staff Offices, Press, Powell, JCPL. News colleagues, such as Witcover, monitored Carter's stump speeches and his published issues stances. Jules Witcover, "Carter Finds His Words Are Watched," *Washington Post*, January 27, 1976, A4.

75. As expected, Loeb leveled a vicious assault on Carter's campaign, calling Carter an "out and out leftist coated over and disguised with peanut oil," but Carter's campaign was unprepared for the intensity of left-leaning attacks. As quoted in Martin Weil, "William Loeb, 75, Controversial Newspaper Publisher Dies," *Washington Post*, September 14, 1981, https://www .washingtonpost.com/archive/local/1981/09/14/william-loeb-75-controversial-newspaper -publisher-dies/b9a2ef26-67f5-40ed-af49-0da8821fbf5a/?utm_term=.bf30591a8e71; Carl Leubsdorf, "11th-Hour Obstacles Hinder Carter in N.H.," *Baltimore Sun*, February 20, 1976, A2; Glad, *Jimmy Carter*, 239–40. On February 9, for instance, Cockburn critiqued Carter's record, labeling him as a phony liberal based on his 1970 gubernatorial campaign tactics and his memo of support for Wallace. McGrory, "The Carter Behind the Smile," A4.

76. Paul Szep, "Three Versions of Jimmy Carter," *Boston Globe,* February 22, 1976, A6. Conjuring the literary metaphor of Lewis Carroll's *The Adventures of Alice in Wonderland,* Szep sketched John Tenniel's Cheshire Cat smile and Tweedledee and Tweddledum's overgrown bodies onto Carter's figure. Szep first (re)presented Carter on October 26, 1975, as one of "10 little Indians" remaining in the battle for the Democratic nomination, and he delivered the cartoon with his "best wishes" to Carter. Both cartoons also were included in the entry package that yielded Szep's second Pulitzer Prize. File: Questions and Answers/Questionnaires, Box 3: News Releases and Schedules, 1/75–2/75 through Magazine [1], BRDP, JCPL. Szep's cartoons attracted fury from Carter's staff, his supporters, and even Szep's colleagues. On April 16, for instance, *Globe* editor Anne Wyman apologized for Szep's recent "unfunny and unfair" cartoon. "I want to add my voice personally to the *Globe*'s regrets about our editorial page cartoon of April 11," she wrote to Powell, informing him that Szep's "ethnic purity" cartoon prompted eleven letters of rebuke from *Globe* readers and of her intent to publish three alongside a box score in the following Saturday's edition. Anne Wyman to Jimmy Carter, April 16, 1976, Correspondence from the Media, Massachusetts, Box 320: Correspondence from the Media, Hawaii through Correspondence from the Media, Nebraska, JCPPP, PC, Press Office-BRSF, JCPL.

77. Witcover, "Carter Finds His Words Are Watched," A4; Geismer, *Don't Blame Us*; Bell and Stanley, *Making Sense of American Liberalism.*

78. Brownell, *Showbiz Politics*; Drew, *American Journal,* 38–43.

79. Overall Coverage of Campaign '76. Correspondent Roger Mudd Reporting from the Campaign Trail [entry title: CBS News Coverage of Campaign '76], PAC, 76061 NWT 4 of 4, WJBMAPAC; Supporting Materials, File 76061 NWT, Box 99: PAE, HRBML.

80. Ibid. By 1976, advertising was big business. The American Association of Advertisers estimated the average consumer was exposed to sixteen hundred advertisements each day, and spending on television spots reached $5.9 billion. "History: 1970s," *Advertising Age,* September 15, 2003, https://adage.com/article/adage-encyclopedia/history-1970s/98703. Despite exorbitant costs, campaigns with tremendous reach became a necessary evil in the age of campaign finance reform. Rafshoon allocated approximately $215,000 for Carter's Florida broadcast blitz, a substantive portion of available funds, but only a fraction of what some campaigns invested.

81. Brownell, *Showbiz Politics*; Mann, *Daisy Petals and Mushroom Clouds*; Rafshoon, interview with the author, August 12, 2014; Joseph Lelyveld, "Some TV Stations Resist Political Ads of Five Minutes," *New York Times,* January 24, 1976, 38.

82. Wilbur Schramm and Richard F. Carter, "Effectiveness of a Political Telethon," *Public Opinion Quarterly* 23.1 (1959): 121–27; John W. Ellwood and Robert J. Spitzer, "The Democratic National Telethons: Their Successes and Failure," *Journal of Politics* 41.3 (1979): 828–64; Emil Steiner, "Binge-Watching Killed the Idiot Box: The Changing Identities of Viewers and Television in the Experiential Streaming Video Age," Ph.D. diss., Temple University, 2018; Brownell, *Showbiz Politics,* 208. Campaign telethons have existed in presidential politics since the radioathons of the 1940s, but Carter's advisors harnessed the mode as a means of generating primary campaign funds.

83. Hamilton Jordan to Jimmy Carter, June 1975, Memorandum-Hamilton Jordan to Jimmy Carter, 6/75, Box 199: CDO-HJCSF, PC-CDO-HJCSF, JCPL.

84. Bourne, *Jimmy Carter*, 274. Paulsen contributed to Carter's emergent enigmatic image, quipping that sculptors considered adding Carter's image to Mount Rushmore, "but they didn't have room for two faces." As quoted in Schram, *Running for President*, 11.

85. S. Stephen Selig III to Jimmy Carter Telethon Party Captains and Hosts, Telethon Party, 12/75, Box 49: Speeches—Master File, 10/76–11/76 through Women's Issues, CFP, PC, JCPL.

86. Mailer, "Superman Comes to the Supermarket," https://www.esquire.com/news-politics /a3858/superman-supermarket/.

87. S. Stephen Selig III to Jimmy Carter Telethon Party Captains and Hosts, Telethon Party, 12/75, Box 49: Speeches—Master File, 10/76–11/76 through Women's Issues, CFP, PC, JCPL. Television party captains understood that under reform guidelines they could write off up to $500 in expenses associated with hosting events.

88. Despite Carter's posturing, evidence suggested the former governor lacked public support at home. Curtis Wilkie, "Carter: Strong on the Road, but Weak at Home," *Boston Globe*, January 25, 1976, 1. After the *Globe* published the front-page story, Carter—who recognized an upsurge of political enemies and petitioned to delay Georgia's primary while governor—derided Wilkie: "I'm so glad to see you, my friend. . . . I see you've been down in Georgia talking with all my other friends." Wilkie, interview with the author, January 16, 2017. Wilkie's coverage prompted Rainwater to warn the candidate: "As you can see, we have a problem with the Globe." File: Press & Media Issues, Box 3: News Releases and Schedules, 1/75–2/75 through Magazine [1], BRDP, JCPL.

89. Leubsdorf, "Wallace Is Still Man to Beat in Florida," A7; Witcover, *Marathon*, 202.

90. Overall Coverage of Campaign '76. Correspondent Roger Mudd Reporting from the Campaign Trail [entry title: CBS News Coverage of Campaign '76], PAC, 76061 NWT 4 of 4, WJBMAPAC; Supporting Materials, File 76061 NWT, Box 99: PAE, HRBML.

91. 1976 Carter vs. Ford, The Living Room Candidate, Museum of the Moving Image, http:// www.livingroomcandidate.org/commercials/1976. Moreover, as Paul Simon's hit single "50 Ways to Leave Your Lover" faded from the airwaves, listeners heard Jimmy Carter's voice crackle, echoing the primary theme of his 1970 gubernatorial campaign: "My folks have been farmers in Georgia for more than 200 years . . . I think the country needs an understanding of working people, and not an understanding of big shots who have enough money to hire high-powered lobbyists." Unsigned to Phil Wise, February 24, 1976, Media Contacts, 1975–1976, Box 3: Schedule-Florida Primary, 1975–1976], [2] through, [Schedule]-Pensacola-Tampa-Miami, 12/1–3/75, PWP, 1976 Florida Primary Campaign Files, JCPL.

92. Charles Seib, "Missing the Election Story," *Washington Post*, February 13, 1976, A23.

93. Albert Hunt, "That Campaigning in Iowa Adds Up to Just About Zero," *Wall Street Journal*, January 15, 1976, 1.

94. The Social Science Research Council invested more than $1 million to determine "how political elites interacted with media elites to affect the media agenda." Seib, "Missing the Election Story," A23; Shogan, *Bad News*, 71.

95. Lothar Wedekind, "Horserace Handicapped by the Media," *Washington Post*, January 23, 1976, A18

96. Ibid.

97. Crouse, *Boys on the Bus*, 63.

98. Barber, *Race for the Presidency,* 79–110. All candidates said they must finish third or higher to avoid media humiliation. "New Hampshire Primary/Thomson/Democrats," *NBC Evening News,* February 11, 1976, VTNAC. Though many frontline reporters, still operating in "[geographical] zone coverage," acknowledged the crowded field, they offered the frontrunner more attention and scrutiny. Barber, *Race for the Presidency,* 41–42; 64–65; Witcover, *Marathon,* 225, 233. "In the natural rhythms of a campaign, when somebody strikes success, as Governor Carter did at that point, a lot of people shift to him," NBC News correspondent Tom Brokaw said. Tom Brokaw, interview with the author, April 3, 2017. Twenty to twenty-five national reporters covered Carter on a regular basis at this juncture, a relatively small number when compared to modern conditions. Curtis Wilkie, interview with the author, January 16, 2017.

99. Stroud, *How Jimmy Won,* 247; Witcover, *Marathon,* 237.

100. Only approximately 33 percent of those eligible voted in the New Hampshire primary; nonetheless, it was a drastic increase from the 2.5 percent turnout in the Iowa caucuses. Steven Smith and Melanie Springer, eds., *Reforming the Presidential Nomination Process* (New York: Brookings Institution Press, 2009), 46.

101. Schulman, *The Seventies,* 50; Sandbrook, *Mad as Hell,* ix–xiii; Patterson, *The Mass Media Election,* 44.

102. Witcover, *Marathon,* 222–24.

103. Barber, *Race for the Presidency,* 93; Glad, *Jimmy Carter,* 238. Prior to the campaign, network representatives decided to define victory based on vote count alone, and though they agreed to avoid frontrunner labels until a clear leader emerged, they succumbed to competitive, profit-driven news values that privileged immediacy and drama and labeled Carter the clear victor and definitive frontrunner. Supporting Materials, File 76061 NWT, Box 99: PAE, HRBML.

104. As quoted in Glad, *Jimmy Carter,* 63, 22; Lasky, *Jimmy Carter,* 129. While Carter earned fewer than 23,000 votes, a fraction of the 76 million votes cast in the prior election, print reporters echoed this assessment. Curtis Wilkie, "Carter Wins; Ford Leading Close Race," *Boston Globe,* February 25, 1976, 1; Schulman, *The Seventies,* 50; Sandbrook, *Mad as Hell,* ix–xiii. After Carter's victory in New Hampshire, "the money just started falling in," said national finance chairman Frank Moore. Frank Moore, ROGPOHC, ROGP 162, RBRLPRS.

105. Adam Clymer, "Top Coverage Makes Carter's N.H. Win Sweeter," *Baltimore Sun,* February 27, 1976, A5.

106. Jagoda, interview with the author, January 10, 2017. Paul Weaver once told *Fortune* readers: "television news likes a man who can be presented as having genuinely been raised up out of obscurity by the people alone. He emerges as the good guy on the nightly news." As quoted in Lasky, *Jimmy Carter,* 131, 142. Bob Schieffer offered evidence of this phenomenon: "Jimmy Carter came out of nowhere. First, it was 'Jimmy Who,' and then he won that first primary. Jack Germond and Jules Witcover wrote that this—*this*—was a serious campaign, and it was very, *very* different. He was this surprise on the political scene. He just came out of nowhere." Bob Schieffer, interview with the author, August 12, 2014; Lasky, *Jimmy Carter,* 142.

107. As quoted in Barber, *Race for the Presidency,* 41–42; Glad, *Jimmy Carter,* 285.

108. As quoted in Stroud, *How Carter Won,* 255.

109. Woodruff, interview with the author, March 31, 2017. Animosity also increased over trail conditions. Though other candidates plied reporters with creature comforts, Carter's

penny-pinching campaign, while maintaining their breakneck schedule, did not afford such niceties. Stroud, *How Jimmy Won,* 254–55; Glad, *Jimmy Carter,* 243; Witcover, *Marathon,* 226–27, 232; Crouse, *Boys on the Bus*; Thompson, *Fear and Loathing at Rolling Stone,* 357–83.

110. As quoted in Stroud, *How Carter Won,* 254.

111. Ponce de Leon, *Self-Exposure*; Pressman, *On Press,* 143–70.

112. R. W. Apple Jr., "Carter and the Poll," *New York Times,* February 13, 1976, 29; R. W. Apple Jr., "New Political Universe," *New York Times,* March 3, 1976, 1.

113. Other moderate politicians, including Ford, constructed nuanced stances around the emerging hot-button issue. Flippen, *Jimmy Carter, the Politics of Family, and the Rise of the Religious Right,* 65–66, 92; Daniel K. Williams, *God's Own Party: The Making of the Christian Right* (New York: Oxford Univ. Press, 2010), 129–59.

114. James Reston, "Survival of the Slickest," *New York Times,* February 29, 1976, 147; Jon Margolis, "Jimmy Carter's Many Faces," *Chicago Tribune,* March 3, 1976, A4; David Broder, *The Party's Over: The Failure of Politics in America* (New York: Harper and Row, 1972).

115. Goldman and Clift, "Carter on the Rise," 25; Clift, interview with the author, August 14, 2014.

116. Wills, "Carter's Bases All Covered," A15; Robert Turner, "Carter: Evangelical Message," *Boston Globe,* February 28, 1976, 1.

117. Bourne, *Jimmy Carter,* 291–94; Witcover, *Marathon,* 240–52; Leubsdorf, "Wallace Still the Man to Beat in Florida," A7.

118. As quoted in Schram, *Running for President,* 259; David Broder, "Greatest Pressure Is on Carter," *Boston Globe,* March 8, 1976, 17; Carl Leubsdorf, "Carter Discounts Mass., Places Hopes on Fla.," *Baltimore Sun,* March 3, 1976, A6.

119. Memorandum, Hamilton Jordan to Jimmy Carter, November 4, 1972, Section A, PC, CDO, CD-HJ, JCPL. Since June 1975, Florida field manager Phil Wise had engaged in organizing a "credible campaign" capable of challenging "Wallace and proving [Carter] was a different type of Southern politician." Phil Wise, RGPOHC, ROGP 158, RBRLPRS; Chip Carter, RGPOHC, ROGP 036, RBRLPRS; Phil Wise to Key Florida Supporters, December 11, 1975, Activity Report 1976, Box 1: Activity Report, 1976 through Get Out the Vote Program, 1976, PWP, 1976 Florida Primary Campaign Files, JCPL; Boxes 1–4, PWP, 1976 Florida Primary Campaign Files, JCPL; Bourne, *Jimmy Carter,* 287–89.

120. Alan Otten, "Just Plain Jimmy? Carter Finds Projecting an 'Outsider's' Image is Paying Off in Votes," *Wall Street Journal,* February 26, 1976, 1; "Carter Leads Wallace in the South, Poll Indicates," *New York Times,* March 3, 1976, 17.

121. Otten, "Just Plain Jimmy," 1.

122. Cloud, interview with the author, August 11, 2014.

123. Memorandum, Hamilton Jordan to Jimmy Carter, November 4, 1972, Section A, PC, CDO-HJCSF, Box 199, JCPL.

124. Both Chip Carter and his father described Florida as a pivotal test and seminal victory. Carter's efforts required extensive grassroots fundraising, but his victory over Wallace and his status as the decisive, media-anointed frontrunner contributed to a new wave of donations and scrutiny. Carter, interview with the author, October 17, 2014; Chip Carter, ROGPOHC, ROGP 036, RBRLPRS; Bourne, *Jimmy Carter,* 301–2.

125. Witcover, *Marathon,* 219, 233.

126. Kamarck, *Primary Politics,* 27.

127. Otten, "Just Plain Jimmy," 1; Kenneth Reich, "Carter, Jackson Aim at Pennsylvania," *Los Angles Times,* March 11, 1976, B1.

128. Though Carter won over many establishment players, from policy experts, such as Cyrus Vance, to *Washington Post* publisher Katherine Graham, prominent national Democrats, including House Majority Leader Tip O'Neill of Massachusetts and Florida's Governor Reubin Askew, remained lukewarm toward Carter as Democratic opponents mounted a Stop Carter movement. Glad, *Jimmy Carter,* 268–69.

129. Hamilton Jordan to Jimmy Carter, N.D., Memorandum/Analysis-Hamilton Jordan to Jimmy Carter, Post Florida Primary, Box 199: CDO-HJCSF, PC-CDO-HJCSF, JCPL.

5. FRONT-RUNNING DARK HORSE ENCOUNTERS RESISTANCE

1. Carter, interview with the author, October 17, 2014; Hedley Donovan, exit interview, August 14, 1980, by Emily Williams, The White House, JCPL; Henry Grunwald, *One Man's America: A Journalist's Search for the Heart of His Country* (New York: Anchor Books, 1998), 463; Jack Davis, *Jack Davis: Drawing American Pop Culture* (New York: Fantagraphics Books, 2011), 158–59.

2. Godbold, *Jimmy and Rosalynn Carter,* 188; Bourne, *Jimmy Carter,* 201; Cover, "Dixie Whistles a Different Tune," *Time,* May 31, 1971; "New Day a'Coming in the South," *Time,* May 31, 1971, 17; "On to the Showdown in Florida," *Time,* March 8, 1976, 11; Cover, *Time,* March 8, 1976. *Time* coverage represented a prime example of horse race journalism. Littlewood, *Calling Elections,* 151–73.

3. "Jimmy Carter: Not Just Peanuts," *Time,* March 8, 1976, 16, 19.

4. Sanoff, "Remark," 28–29; Anne Wexler et al., "Press Coverage in the Primaries: A Conversation with David Broder," *Democratic Review,* July/August 1976, Democratic Review, Box 4: "Correspondence-Request for Actuality Phone Number through Forms-Talk Show Final Disposition," RWHPO, Media Liaison Office, Bradley Woodward's Subject Files, JCPL; Kindsvatter, "Who Runs Presidential Campaigns," 1–8; "The Men Behind a Frontrunner," *Time,* March 8, 1976, 21.

5. Cover, *Time,* March 8, 1976.

6. Popkin, *The Reasoning Voter,* 131–32; 149–50.

7. *Times* reporter R. W. Apple Jr. first isolated the coalescing Stop Carter movement in the immediate aftermath of the New Hampshire primary. He reported that members of the Washington establishment, "an amorphous but powerful group of lawyers, politicians, lobbyists, and journalists," convened to discuss how to deal with the "Carter problem," but temporarily tabled the topic out of concern that critics condemning an "anti-Carter cabal" might benefit the Washington outsider's campaign. En route to a campaign event in Norfolk, Virginia, Carter brashly asserted: "They can hurt me by propping up someone like [Senator Frank] Church [of Idaho] for a while, or somebody else, but I don't think they can decide who the nominee will be." R. W. Apple Jr., "Carter Target of Liberals after New Hampshire Gain," *New York Times,* February 27, 1976, 1.

8. After being pronounced frontrunner, McGovern encountered intense scrutiny in the 1972 Democratic primaries, but this chapter contends that, in the aftermath of presidential cred-

ibility crises, Carter encountered incisive, adversarial probes. Thompson, *Fear and Loathing on the Campaign Trail '72,* 225.

9. Matthew Pressman, "Objectivity and Its Discontents," in Schulman and Zelizer, *Media Nation,* 96–113. Some members of this generation of journalists were antagonistic toward authority figures as a means to validate their independent professionalism. Reporters, as Polsby explained, are not necessarily "purveyors of radical chic," but they are "chic. . . . That is, news professionals are highly permeable to currents of thought among people like themselves, an increasingly educated and articulate segment of the population." Polsby, *Consequences of Party Reform,* 142–43. Individuals practicing New Journalism brought the art of deconstruction into style, and antiestablishment sentiment was pervasive in American culture; adversarial relationships and attack journalism were the extension of this milieu. Pressman, "Remaking the News," 306–10. All candidates encountered this new brand, but frontrunners—initially Bayh, Udall, Jackson, and Wallace during the (in)visible primaries, then Carter after the New Hampshire and Florida primaries, experienced more intense scrutiny over their background, personality, imagecraft techniques, and issues stances. Sanoff, "Remark," 28–29; Jack Germond and Jules Witcover, "Inside Politics," *National Journal* 18 (1986): 97; Mark Joslyn, *Mass Media and Elections* (Reading, Mass: Addison-Wesley, 1984), 131.

10. Wise, who managed Carter's southern base in the general election, observed that the secrets to his success were his message of hope, his nucleus of early supporters, and the ability of the campaign to "adapt without huge shifts in strategy." Phil Wise, ROGPOHC, ROGP 158, RBRLPRS; Hunter S. Thompson, "Jimmy Carter and the Great Leap of Faith," *Rolling Stone* 214 (June 3, 1976), reprinted in Thompson, *The Great Shark Hunt: Strange Tales from a Strange Time* (New York: Simon and Schuster, 1979), 462–85.

11. Caddell and national finance director Morris Dees served in similar roles in McGovern's 1972 campaign, and many Carter staff members, such as Jordan and Eizenstat, gained insights into post-1968 reforms and the Democratic primaries through extensive reading on the 1972 election and personal experiences with the DNC beyond 1972. Memorandum, Hamilton Jordan to Jimmy Carter, November 4, 1972, Section A, PC, CDO-HJCSF, Box 199, JCPL. After Carter's victory over Wallace in Florida, his status as the media-anointed frontrunner contributed to a new wave of donations. Chip Carter, ROGPOHC, ROGP 036, RBRLPRS; Bourne, *Jimmy Carter,* 301–2.

12. Leubsdorf, interview with the author, August 10, 2013; Thomas Kuhn, *The Structure of Scientific Revolutions* (Chicago: Univ. of Chicago Press, 2012); Kamarck, *Primary Politics,* 27.

13. Hamilton Jordan to Jimmy Carter, N.D., Memorandum/Analysis-Hamilton Jordan to Jimmy Carter, Post Florida Primary, Box 199: DC-FSCMPM, PC, CDO-HJCSF, JCPL.

14. Ibid.; Charles Kirbo to Jimmy Carter, March 26, 1976, Political Strategy [1], Box 39: Issues Task Force-Members List and Resumes through Memorandums-Political Strategy [2], CFP, PC, JCPL. For instance, in light of Carter's "progress in developing some depth to [his] 'national image,'" Jordan recommended continued use of survey work conducted by Caddell, which was particularly "effective in pinpointing problem areas and opportunities," and ten-day advertising blitzes prior to respective election days concentrated in states with primaries and supplemented with "special media for blacks and certain ethnic groups." Prominent advisor Charles Kirbo concurred with these recommendations. Jordan also discussed strategies for withstanding backlash associated with Carter's recent victories over Wallace and last-ditch efforts of the southern son, but warned Carter to "treat Wallace with quiet respect." Wallace

often criticized Carter in advance of the North Carolina primaries, but Wallace's staff urged him to adopt a similar strategy after his loss. "Do not discuss Carter," his campaign manager Charles Snider advised, "Leave this to the other candidates who apparently have decided on a direct attack in this respect. Questions posed to you of this nature should be thrown back as you have already stated your position in reference to his inconsistencies." Drew, *American Journal,* 122–27; Witcover, *Marathon,* 253–73. George C. Wallace Collection, LPR124, Box 43, Folder 1, ADAH.

15. Polsby, *Consequences of Party Reform,* 144; Matthews, "Winnowing," 71–74; Schram, *Running for President,* 57; Patterson, *The Mass Media Election,* 43–49; Barber, *Race for the Presidency,* 10–11; Kamarck, *Primary Politics,* 27.

16. Perry, *Us and Them,* 155, 162; Crouse, *Boys on the Bus,* 303–4; Thompson, *Fear and Loathing on the Campaign Trail '72,* 225; Kendall, *Communication in the Presidential Primaries,* 22–23; Pressman, "Remaking the News," 307–10; Philip Seib, *Campaigns and Conscience: The Ethics of Political Journalism* (Westport, Conn.: Greenwood, 1994), 47.

17. Mary Brennan, *Turning Right in the Sixties: Conservative Capture of the GOP* (Chapel Hill: Univ. of North Carolina Press, 1995), 121; Kendall, *Communication in the Presidential Primaries,* 168.

18. Crouse, *Boys on the Bus,* 36; Perry, *Us and Them,* 162; Barber, *The Pulse of Politics,* 198.

19. Hadley, *Invisible Primary*; Witcover, *Marathon.*

20. Polsby, *Consequences of Party Reform,* 76; Popkin, *The Reasoning Voter,* 115–48; Cohen et al., *The Party Decides,* 157–86; Arthur Paulson, *Donald Trump and the Prospect for American Democracy: An Unprecedented President in the Age of Polarization* (New York: Lexington Books, 2018), 52–55.

21. Sean Toolan, "Carter Booed for Rejecting Amnesty for Draft Dodgers," *Chicago Tribune,* March 11, 1976, 5; Drew, *American Journal,* 85–101.

22. John Gorman to the Jimmy Carter Campaign, "Re: The Results of Illinois Polling," March 8, 1976, Carter Campaign Organization, 9/75–6/76, Box 1: Asia Pacific Unit, 9/76–11/76 through Carter Campaign, 1976-Scrapbook [1], JWP-JWSF, JCPL; Balogh, "From Corn to Caviar," 238–64.

23. Toolan, "Carter Booed for Rejecting Amnesty for Draft Dodgers," 5; Drew, *American Journal,* 85–101; Zelizer, *Jimmy Carter,* 40.

24. McGovern and his aides were "bitterly critical" over issue-devoid, horse race coverage in the primaries and of biased, one-sided coverage of McGovern's mistakes in the general election. Tom Wicker, "McGovern with Tears," *New York Times,* November 5, 1972, 36. Following the historic cue of their print colleagues, broadcast news producers exploited horse race tropes to deliver incoming primary results and, in turn, perpetuated the form. As the number of primaries escalated dramatically in the 1970s, computerized polling allowed journalists, shielding themselves from claims of bias, to objectively report standings in primary races. Littlewood, *Calling Elections.*

25. Kindsvatter, "Who Runs Presidential Campaigns," 1–8; Bicker, "Network TV News and the 1976 Primaries," in *Race for the Presidency,* 94–96; Barber, *The Pulse of Politics,* 184–210; Polsby, *Consequences of Party Reform,* 142–43; Pressman, "Objectivity and Its Discontents," 96–113; Pressman, "Remaking the News," 306–10.

26. Sanoff, "Remark," 28–29; Donald Matthews, "The News Media and the 1976 Presidential Nominations," in *Race for the Presidency,* 57–61.

27. "Harris Survey, Amnesty with Price Wins Favor," N.D., Amnesty [1] and Amnesty [2], JCPPP, PC, IO-NS, Clippings-Domestic Issues, Science, Technology, and the Arts through Amnesty, JCPL; Bill Strauss to Peter Bourne, "Our Discussion About What a Good Position on Amnesty Might Be," February 17, 1976, Amnesty [2], JCPPP, PC, IO-NS, Clippings-Domestic Issues, Science, Technology, and the Arts through Amnesty, JCPL; Roessner and Bier, "Pardon Me, Mr. Carter," 86–96.

28. Balogh, "From Corn to Caviar," 238–64. Carter's staff was "measuring overnight the effect of a political development or issue in a given state" and tailoring his strategies based on incoming results. Hamilton Jordan to Jimmy Carter, N.D., Memorandum/Analysis-Hamilton Jordan to Jimmy Carter, Post Florida Primary, Box 199: DC-FSCMPM, PC, CDO-HJCSF, JCPL; Eizenstat, interview with the author, September 28, 2015; File: Questions and Answers/Questionnaires, Box 3: News Releases and Schedules, 1/75–2/75 through Magazine [1], BRDP, JCPL; Charles Kirbo to Jimmy Carter, March 26, 1976, Political Strategy [1] Box 39: Issues Task Force-Members List and Resumes through Memorandums-Political Strategy [2], CFP, PC, JCPL.

29. Though polling data indicated Carter showed "astonishing strengths" by standing "squarely in the middle of the ideological spectrum," Apple warned that his "ability to reconcile seemingly contradictory viewpoints" might wane as the campaign progressed. R. W. Apple Jr., "Carter and the Poll," *New York Times,* February 13, 1976, 29. Overall Coverage of Campaign '76. Daily Coverage of Carter and Ford [entry title: CBS News Coverage of Campaign '76], PAC, 76061 NWT 3 of 4, WJBMAPAC; Supporting Materials, File 76061 NWT, Box 99: PAE, HRBML; "New Hampshire Primary/Thomson/Democrats," NBC, 1976-02-11. Conservative columnists Rowland Evans and Robert Novak aptly suggested Carter's "ideologically nondescript posture" was constructed as a "moderate middle course to unite the country." Rowland Evans and Robert Novak, "Carter's Campaign: The McGovern Factor," *Washington Post,* March 16, 1976, A19.

30. "Jimmy Carter: The Candidate on the Issues," *Washington Post,* March 21, 1976, B1. CBS News anchor Walter Cronkite concentrated on candidate issues stances with his series, "The Candidates and the Issues." The Candidates and the Issues [entry title: CBS News Coverage of Campaign '76], PAC 76061 NWT 1 of 4, WJBMAPAC; Supporting Materials, File 76061 NWT, Box 99: PAE, HRBML.

31. In late March, press aide Betty Rainwater culled clippings to produce the latest "What the Press Had To Say" bulletin for dissemination to the former Georgia governor and his staff. On the cover, as an indicator of lingering criticisms, Rainwater included an editorial cartoon from Ben Sargent of the *Austin American-Statesman,* who sketched Carter as Alice in Wonderland and offered the following quotation: "You should say what you mean," the March Hare went on. "I do," Alice hastily replied, "at least—at least, I mean what I say—that's the same thing you know." Based on these reports, Carter and his advisors discerned coverage, but they also gleaned strategic insights about how reporters contested images they supplied, how to combat journalistic probes, and how to renegotiate Carter's image. "What the Press Had to Say: Jimmy Carter and the Issues," News Summaries 3/76, Box 89: Meyer, Henry through News Summaries 5/76, JCPPP, PC, IO-NS, JCPL; Anne Wexler et al., "Press Coverage in the Primaries: A Conversation with David Broder," *Democratic Review,* July/August 1976, *Democratic Re-*

view, Box 4: "Correspondence-Request for Actuality Phone Number through Forms-Talk Show Final Disposition," RWHPO, Media Liaison Office, Bradley Woodward's Subject Files, JCPL.

32. Carter claimed his "most impressive" victory to date with 48 percent of the vote, but he failed to deliver landslides; thus, only Shriver exited the race after the Illinois primary (Bayh, Pennsylvania Governor Milton Shapp, U.S. Senator Lloyd Bentsen, and former North Carolina Governor Terry Sanford exited the race prior to the Illinois primary). Bill Boyarsky, "Ford, Carter Sweep Primaries in Illinois," *Los Angeles Times,* March 17, 1976, B1; Jim Squires, "A Big Bouquet for Carter," *Chicago Tribune,* March 17, 1976, 17; Reich, "Carter, Jackson Aim at Pennsylvania," B1. Journalists were accustomed to such posturing. Thompson, *Fear and Loathing on the Campaign Trail '72,* 144–45.

33. Overall Coverage of Campaign '76. Correspondent Roger Mudd Reporting from the Trail [entry title: CBS News Coverage of Campaign '76], PAC, 76061 NWT 4 of 4, WJBMAPAC; Supporting Materials, File 76061 NWT, Box 99: PAE, HRBML; The Candidates and the Issues [entry title: CBS News Coverage of Campaign '76], PAC 76061 NWT 1 of 4, WJBMAPAC; Supporting Materials, File 76061 NWT, Box 99: PAE, HRBML.

34. David Broder, "Trims Due in Political Roster," *Los Angeles Times,* February 29, 1976, D1.

35. Barber, *Race for the Presidency,* 71; Drew, *American Journal,* 85–101.

36. Crouse, *Boys on the Bus,* 36; McGinnis, *The Selling of the President,* https://books .google.com/books/about/The_Selling_of_the_President.html?id=578AEL8WMAIC; Anne Wexler et al., "Press Coverage in the Primaries: A Conversation with David Broder," *Democratic Review,* July/August 1976, *Democratic Review,* Box 4: "Correspondence-Request for Actuality Phone Number through Forms-Talk Show Final Disposition," RWHPO, Media Liaison Office, Bradley Woodward's Subject Files, JCPL; Sanoff, "Remark," 28–29.

37. Brownell, *Showbiz Politics,* 129–232; Greenberg, *Republic of Spin,* 317–95; Greenberg, *Nixon's Shadow,* 126–71; Matthews, "The News Media and the 1976 Presidential Nominations," 59.

38. Sanoff, "Remark," 28–29; Anne Wexler et al., "Press Coverage in the Primaries: A Conversation with David Broder," *Democratic Review,* July/August 1976, *Democratic Review,* Box 4: "Correspondence-Request for Actuality Phone Number through Forms-Talk Show Final Disposition," RWHPO, Media Liaison Office, Bradley Woodward's Subject Files, JCPL.

39. Steven Brill, "Jimmy Carter's Pathetic Lies," *Harper's Magazine,* March 1976, 77–88. Prior to this era, journalists only focused on personal lives when behaviors interfered with governing ability, but in the 1976 campaign, pack leaders recognized that this norm was shifting. In June, for instance, the *New York Magazine* reported on the *Washington Post*'s deliberation over whether to run news of Mo Udall's "extracurricular activities." "Udall Hanky-Panky Won't See the Light Unless Washington 'Post' Says Go," *New York Magazine,* June 7, 1976, 67; Matthews, "The News Media and the 1976 Presidential Nominations," 67.

40. Vann Woodward, "W. J. Cash Reconsidered," *New York Review of Books,* December 4, 1969, http://www.nybooks.com/articles/1969/12/04/wj-cash-reconsidered/; Gene Roberts and Hank Klibanoff, *The Race Beat: The Press, the Civil Rights Struggle, and the Awakening of a Nation* (New York: Knopf, 2006).

41. Barber, *Pulse of Politics,* 199–200.

42. Forde, "Ida B. Wells-Barnett and the 'Racist Cover-Up,'" 175–85.

43. As quoted in, Schram, *Running for President,* 93; Glad, *Jimmy Carter,* 330–40; Peter Goldman and Eleanor Clift, "Carter on the Rise," *Newsweek,* March 8, 1976, 25. *Los Angeles*

Times correspondent Robert Shogan and newsmagazine staff writers reported on Carter's faith during the (in)visible primaries, but his religious beliefs remained a footnote in coverage until daily reporters concentrated their attention on scrutinizing the frontrunner's message and his background. Barber, *Pulse of Politics,* 200–203.

44. Axel Schafer, ed., *American Evangelicals and the 1960s* (Madison: Univ. of Wisconsin Press, 2013), 20; Randall Balmer, *Mine Eyes Have Seen the Glory: A Journey into the Evangelical Subculture in America* (New York: Oxford Univ. Press, 2014), 173.

45. Cited in Orren, "Candidate Style and Voter Alignment in 1976," 127–34; Steven Patrick Miller, *Age of Evangelicalism: America's Born-Again Years* (New York: Oxford Univ. Press, 2014), 32–36; David R. Swartz, *Moral Minority: The Evangelical Left in an Age of Conservatism* (Philadelphia: Univ. of Pennsylvania Press, 2012), 213–19. Carter considered faith to be a personal matter, and even though he acknowledged that it was a relevant campaign issue, he struggled to talk to trail reporters about the topic. Nonetheless, even the most skeptical campaign reporters agreed that Carter's deeply held religious beliefs were genuine. Bourne, *Jimmy Carter,* 307–8; Wilkie, interview with the author, January 16, 2017.

46. Carter's advisors continuously encouraged the candidate to avoid discussions of his Christian faith. In the spring of 1975, Powell told Carter that one recent article might have been a great clip if the candidate discussed "'religious' principles rather than Christianity." File: Press and Media Issues, Box 3: News Releases and Schedules, 1/75–2/75 through Magazine [1], BRDP, JCPL.

47. Peter Goldman and Eleanor Clift, "Carter on the Rise," *Newsweek,* March 8, 1976, 25; Joseph Kraft, "Is U.S. Ready for Carter," *Baltimore Sun,* March 18, 1976, A19; Richard Reeves, "The Secret of Jimmy Carter," *Boston Globe,* March 21, 1976, A1.

48. Reeves, "The Secret of Jimmy Carter," A1.

49. Ibid. As political columnist Garry Wills noted: "Nothing embarrasses most journalists like talk of God. They do not know how to pursue such a subject or [evaluate a] candidate's sincerity." Garry Wills, "Carter's Bases All Covered," *Baltimore Sun,* February 25, 1976, A15.

50. Jules Witcover, "'Profound' Event," *Washington Post,* March 21, 1976, 1; Barber, *The Pulse of Politics,* 200–202.

51. As quoted in Barber, *The Pulse of Politics,* 201.

52. Carter, interview with the author, October 17, 2014.

53. Wes Pippert, interview with the author, September 5, 2014. Pippert believed reporting on the matter lacked nuance, and he sought to offer more thoughtful coverage of Carter's faith. Pippert's efforts culminated in the release of *The Spiritual Journey of Jimmy Carter: In His Own Words* (New York: Macmillan, 1978).

54. Miller, *Age of Evangelicalism,* 32–114; Flippen, *Jimmy Carter, the Politics of Family, and the Rise of the Religious Right.*

55. Nancy Ammerman, "North American Protestant Fundamentalism," in *Media, Culture, and the Religious Right,* ed. Linda Kintz and Julia Lesage (Duluth: Univ. of Minnesota Press, 1998), 96; Miller, *The Age of Evangelicalism,* 42; R. W. Apple Jr., "Breakthrough for Carter," *New York Times,* April 28, 1976, 85; Susan Fraker and Eleanor Clift, "Carter and the God Issue," *Newsweek,* April 5, 1976, 19; George Will, "The Spirit That Moves Jimmy," *Washington Post,* April 1, 1976, A15.

56. Will, "The Spirit That Moves Jimmy," A15.

57. Balogh, "From Corn to Caviar," 238–64; David Broder, "Jimmy Carter: Promising or Pretending," *Los Angeles Times,* March 31, 1976, D5.

58. Broder, "Jimmy Carter," D5.

59. Matthews, "The News Media and the 1976 Presidential Nominations," 68–69.

60. Purvis, *The Presidency and the Press.*

61. Hemmer, *Messengers of the Right,* 32; Pressman, "Remaking the News," 68–147.

62. David Broder, *Behind the Front Page: A Candid Look at How the News Is Made* (New York: Simon and Schuster, 1987), 249.

63. "There's a Growing Circle," *Boston Globe,* May 16, 1976, A3. Despite unfavorable odds, less than ten days after his arrival in Wisconsin, Wise opened offices throughout the state, called more than 100,000 voters, and initiated a grassroots blitz with help from Iowa, Illinois, Florida, and Georgia volunteers.

64. Bicker, "Network TV News and the 1976 Presidential Primaries," 86; Bill Carter, "The Wisconsin TV Boo-Boo," *Baltimore Sun,* April 8, 1976, B1.

65. Drew, *American Journal,* 152; Stroud, *How Jimmy Won,* 282–84; Witcover, *Marathon,* 284–85; Carl Leubsdorf, "Wisconsin Race Tight," *Baltimore Sun,* April 7, 1976, A1; Leubsdorf, interview with the author, August 10, 2013.

66. Chris Foran, "When Jimmy Carter 'Lost' the Wisconsin Primary," *Milwaukee Journal Sentinel,* March 22, 1976, http://archive.jsonline.com/greensheet/when-jimmy-carter-lost -the-wisconsin-primary-1976-b99687539z1-373144611.html.

67. Bourne, *Jimmy Carter,* 310–11; Witcover, *Marathon,* 286.

68. Orren, "Candidate Style and Voter Alignment in 1976," 127–34; Thomas Segrue and John Skrentny, "The White Ethnic Strategy," in *Rightward Bound: Making America Conservative in the 1970s,* ed. Bruce Schulman and Julian Zelizer (Cambridge, Mass.: Harvard Univ. Press, 2008), 171–92; Richard Moss, *Creating the New Right Ethnic in 1970s America: The Intersection of Anger* (New York: Roman and Littlefield, 2017), 184–88.

69. "What Jimmy Carter Said About 'Ethnic Purity,'" *Boston Globe,* April 8, 1976, 23; Barber, *Race for the Presidency,* 69–70; Barber, *The Pulse of Politics,* 194–99.

70. "Campaign 1976/Carter/Integration," CBS, 1976-04-07, VTNAC.

71. Ibid.; Glad, *Jimmy Carter,* 293–95.

72. Stroud, *How Jimmy Won,* 276–79; Bourne, *Jimmy Carter,* 312. Schneiders recognized Carter's mistake. He told Powell: "Jody, wee Jimmy stuck his foot in his mouth." As quoted in Barber, *The Pulse of Politics,* 195. Convinced that the "ethnic purity" remarks were a major campaign issue, trail reporters hounded Rainwater for additional Carter comments. Nonetheless, most staff thought that the controversy would not last. Albert Hunt, "Jimmy Carter's Advisers," *Wall Street Journal,* May 25, 1976, 20; Glad, *Jimmy Carter,* 294. Broadcast correspondents, journalists, columnists, and letter-to-the-editor writers offered nearly three hundred accounts and observations about Carter's "ethnic purity" gaffe from April 7–27.

73. "Carter on Ethnic Purity," *Boston Globe,* April 8, 1976, 32.

74. Christopher Lydon, "Carter Defends All-White Areas," *New York Times,* April 7, 1976, 1; Joel Weisman, "Carter Supports 'Ethnic Purity' of Neighborhoods," *Washington Post,* April 7, 1976, A9; Martin Nolan, "Democratic Standings the Day After," *Boston Globe,* April 8, 1976, 18.

75. Jack Nelson, "Vital Support Imperiled," *Los Angeles Times,* April 10, 1976, 1; Bourne, *Jimmy Carter,* 313.

76. Lydon, "Carter Defends All-White Areas," 1. Glad offered insight into Carter's heated interaction with Lydon. "If you are trying to make something out of nothing, I resent that effort," the tense, angry candidate told the elite reporter. Carter sought to make amends with Lydon, but the watchdog reporter pressed him once again. As quoted in Glad, *Jimmy Carter,* 294.

77. As quoted in "People Are Talking About," *Jet,* May 13, 1976, 45; "Black Caucus Hits Carter for 'Ethnic Purity' Views," *Jet,* April 29, 1976, 12–13; "Americans Can't Deal with 'Ethnicity,'" *Jet,* May 6, 1976, 5.

78. R. W. Apple Jr., "Jackson, Carter and Udall Turn to Pennsylvania," *New York Times,* April 8, 1976, 1. Carter received extensive correspondence in reaction to his comments. Vernon Jordan, the executive director of the Urban League, told the former Georgia governor he was "deeply disturbed" by his "inflammatory language." Young and Martin Luther King Sr. privately insisted that he recant his comments. File: April Correspondence; Box 221: Campaign Strategy for Elderly Vote through Daily Reports; JCPPP, PC, Minority Affairs Director Andy Chisholm, JCPL.

79. Samuel Popkin, *The Candidate: What It Takes to Win—and Hold—the White House* (New York: Oxford Univ. Press, 2012), 250; Bourne, *Jimmy Carter,* 313.

80. File: Ethnic Purity; Box 8: Convention Planning [File 1] through [Stationary], Gerald Rafshoon Papers, JCPL; "A List of Charges and Responses Relating to the Carter Candidacy During the 1976 Primary Campaign (March–June)," Ford Themes; Box 83: Ford Themes through Hardware [2], Jimmy Carter Papers-Pre Presidential, PC IO-NS, JCPL; File: Black Affairs, Box 1: Administrative through Ethics, BRDP, JCPL; Christopher Lydon, "Carter Issues an Apology," *New York Times,* April 9, 1976, 1. Carter's statement read: "I think most of the problem has been caused by my ill-chosen agreement to use the words ethnic purity. I think that was a very serious mistake on my part. I think it should have been the words ethnic character or ethnic heritage. . . ." As quoted in Bourne, *Jimmy Carter,* 313.

81. "Campaign 1976/ Carter/Ethnic Issue," NBC, 1976-04-08, VTNAC; "Campaign 1976/ Carter/ Ethnic Issue/Ford," NBC, 1976-04-08, VTNAC.

82. Overall Coverage of Campaign '76. Daily Coverage of Carter and Ford [entry title: CBS News Coverage of Campaign '76], PAC, 76061 NWT 3 of 4, WJBMAPAC; Supporting Materials, File 76061 NWT, Box 99: PAE, HRBML; "Campaign 1976/ Carter/Ethnic Issue/Ford/Hubert Humphrey," CBS, 1976-04-08, VTNAC.

83. "Jimmy Carter Doing Damage Control for 'Ethnic Purity' Remarks," NBC Today Show, New York: NBC Universal, 4/9/1976, https://archives.nbclearn.com/portal/site/k-12/flatview ?cuecard=33592.

84. "Campaign 1976/ Carter/Udall/Jackson/Ford/Hubert Humphrey," ABC, 1976-04-08, VTNAC; Barber, *The Pulse of Politics,* 195.

85. "Commentary (Carter)," ABC, 1976-04-08, VTNAC. Smith was not alone. Local television reporters, content to serve as eye witnesses, also missed an opportunity to offer in-depth reporting. The evening prior, ABC's Chicago-based veteran political editor Hugh Hill had the opportunity to ask Carter a question; he lobbed a softball: "At this point, Governor, after you've won in Wisconsin, is there anybody who can beat you?" As quoted in Powers, *The Newscasters,* 72.

86. Witcover, *Marathon,* 305. "[Carter said] I understand there is the need and the desire for ethnic purity, and I said to him at this news conference, 'Well, so did Adolf Hitler, Governor.' 'I mean, when you use the words, ethnic purity, you are referring to Nazism.' Well, I think

that shook him up. Of course he didn't mean it . . . in that way," Donaldson said in a moment of reflexivity. Donaldson, interview with the author, January 17, 2017.

87. Drew, *American Journal,* 154. This mind-set still persists among some journalist. "I don't think that was a gaffe," Cloud said. "I think he intended to do that. . . . I remember my boss Murray Gart calling me, and he said, 'Well, what do you think of this?' . . . I said, 'Well, I think he is doing it on purpose.'" Cloud, interview with the author, August 12, 2014.

88. As quoted in Barter, *The Pulse of Politics,* 197.

89. Ibid., 196–97; Barber, *Race for the Presidency,* 43. Issues specialist Milt Gwirtzman suggested that "an issues person" travel with Carter at all times to better prepare him. "Whether or not such an arrangement could have prevented the language use in the housing incident, it can I believe prevent similar things from happening again." Milt Gwirtzman to Hamilton, April 11, 1976, Memos to Press Staff, Box 2: Executive Department—Records during Carter's Gubernatorial Term through Natural Resources Management in Georgia, 1975, BRDP, JCPL.

90. Jules Witcover, "Black Backers Forgive Carter's 'Slip of Tongue,'" *Boston Globe,* April 14, 1976, 1; Drew, *American Journal,* 154.

91. As quoted in Glad, *Jimmy Carter,* 295; Barber, *Race for the Presidency,* 49–50, 70. Barber contended that gaffe stories had a plot of their own by 1976: "The extraction of the slip. The shocked reactions of opponents and friends. The candidate's inadequate explanations. The demand for an apology. The candidate's repentance. The forgiveness of the offended. The press's own judicious absolution." As quoted in Barber, *The Pulse of Politics,* 198.

92. Drew, *American Journal,* 96–97.

93. As quoted in ibid., 90; Blumenthal, *The Permanent Campaign,* 48.

94. As quoted in Blumenthal, *The Permanent Campaign,* 36–37.

95. Drew, *American Journal,* 166.

96. Ibid. "[Rafshoon] simply changed the tag line on the spots," Caddell said. "We were polling every day so we could monitor those kinds of problems and see in a tactical way that they had been addressed." As quoted in Blumenthal, *The Permanent Campaign,* 36–37; Caddell's recommendations resulted in staff asking Eizenstat to serve in a full-time capacity and to build a stronger issues staff, and in the hiring of a full-time speechwriter, first Robert Shrum and later Patrick Anderson. Bourne, *Jimmy Carter,* 318.

97. Kernell, *Going Public,* 1.

98. Rafshoon, interview with the author, August 12, 2014.

99. 1976 Carter vs. Ford, The Living Room Candidate, Museum of the Moving Image, http://www.livingroomcandidate.org/commercials/1976.

100. Rafshoon, interview with the author, August 12, 2014.

101. *Baltimore Sun* reporter Carl Leubsdorf, for instance, deconstructed Carter's new advertising campaign. Carl Leubsdorf, "Carter Uses TV Spots to Focus on Fuzzy Image," *Baltimore Sun,* April 21, 1976, A1.

102. McGinnis, *The Selling of the President.*

103. Carter, interview with the author, October 17, 2014.

104. Overall Coverage of Campaign '76. Daily Coverage of Carter and Ford [entry title: CBS News Coverage of Campaign '76], PAC, 76061 NWT 3 of 4, WJBMAPAC; Supporting Materials, File 76061 NWT, Box 99: PAE, HRBML.

105. The veteran replaced Judy Woodruff in March. "That was tough for me because I really wanted to stay with Carter," Woodruff recalled. "He was clearly the rising star, yet I knew that as a green network reporter with fewer years of experience than any of my colleagues at NBC—I knew that the odds were that somebody was going to bigfoot me." Woodruff, interview with the author, March 31, 2017; "Campaign 1976/ Pennsylvania Primary/Carter/Jackson," NBC, 1976-04-21, VTNAC; Woodruff, *This Is Judy Woodruff at the White House,"* 96.

106. As quoted in Drew, *American Journal,* 158.

107. Sanford Ungar, "How Jimmy Carter Does It," *Atlantic Monthly,* July 1976, http://www .theatlantic.com/magazine/archive/1976/07/how-jimmy-carter-does-it/307258/.

108. Ibid.; Overall Coverage of Campaign '76. CBS News Poll; Coverage of the Issues and Candidates [entry title: CBS News Coverage of Campaign '76], PAC, 76061 NWT 2 of 4, WJBMAPAC; Supporting Materials, File 76061 NWT, Box 99: PAE, HRBML. Carter attributed his victory to the secret of his campaign, "the candidate-voter intimate personal relationship." As quoted in Drew, *American Journal,* 165.

109. Mary McGrory, "Ex-Carter Aide Brands Him a Liar," *Boston Globe,* May 9, 1976, A7. Schneiders sensed Shrum might not be a good fit from the start: "When Bob Shrum arrived on the campaign, I remember saying that I didn't think that Governor Carter would say some of this stuff [in his speech before a group of coal miners in Pennsylvania], but he told me that this was what the audience wanted to hear. . . . [The next morning] Carter starts reading through the speech as we were driving to the event, and he got his pen out and started crossing stuff out and saying, 'No, I'm not going to say that.'" Schneiders, interview with the author, August 25, 2014. After Shrum's comments to national reporters about his abrupt exit from Carter's campaign, staff fielded requests from national media for Carter's reaction, but on the heels of the ethnic purity gaffe, the incident did not elicit significant coverage. As Witcover explained, "though the Shrum affair did not hurt Carter that much, it was precisely the kind of incident that might have, for it challenged the core element of his candidacy—his own credibility." As quoted in Witcover, *Marathon,* 326. File: Shrum's Letter to Carter: Box 4: Rebuttal to News Article by Steven Brill "Jimmy Carter's Pathetic Lies"—New York Magazine [2] through Women—Committee of the 51.3 Percent, BRDP, JCPL; Dick Rohter [on behalf of Sam Donaldson] to Jody Powell, May 5, 1976, Correspondence from the Media, New York [2]; Box 321: Correspondence from the Media, New Hampshire through Correspondence from the Media, Virginia; JCPPP, PC, Press Office-Betty Rainwater, JCPL; Glad, *Jimmy Carter,* 295–96; Drew, *American Journal,* 173–74; Bourne, *Jimmy Carter,* 318–19.

110. "On the night of the Pennsylvania victory the big-shot treatment suddenly began," wrote reporter Kandy Stroud. "In the early days when Carter was hungry for media coverage it was easy to get 'five minutes' in the candidate's suite, even the night of the primary. . . . [Now we] found ourselves tailing Carter down the carpet like puppy dogs hoping for a crumb, before he gave the big bones to the networks." As quoted in Stroud, *How Jimmy Won,* 290. In advance of the June 8 primaries, Carter recorded major losses in Rhode Island, Oregon, Nevada, Montana, Maryland, and Idaho, spurring Donaldson to assert at a press conference in the Los Angeles airport: "When it comes unraveled, it really comes unraveled. . . . It's been my theory all along that the simple Carter plan, the magical, mystical, trust-in-me thing wasn't enough. The more people saw of Carter the less they saw was there." At the press conference,

Stroud asked Carter whether his fate might mimic that of Kefauver. As quoted in Stroud, *How Jimmy Won,* 304.

111. Carter eventually won twenty-one of thirty-two primaries or caucuses, and slowly, in the days leading up to the mid-July DNC in New York, ABC movement members fell into line and lent support to the peanut farmer from Plains. Stroud, *How Jimmy Won,* 300–10; Witcover, *Marathon,* 327–54.

112. See, for example, Stanley, "Going Beyond the New Deal," 71.

113. Drew, *American Journal,* 252–55; Blumenthal, *The Permanent Campaign,* 48.

114. As quoted in Barber, *Race for the Presidency,* 46–47. Brown, who defeated Carter in New Jersey and California, criticized this news coverage.

115. Overall Coverage of Campaign '76. Daily Coverage of Carter and Ford [entry title: CBS News Coverage of Campaign '76], PAC, 76061 NWT 3 of 4, WJBMAPAC; Supporting Materials, File 76061 NWT, Box 99: PAE, HRBML.

116. By the Pennsylvania primary, many news organizations had assigned a permanent reporter to cover the candidate for the campaign's duration, which resulted in commitment to institutional coverage with its inherent biases. Atherton, "The Media Politics of Presidential Campaigns," in Barber, *Race for the Presidency,* 33–36. As Glad noted, Crouse documented this symbiotic relationship in his *Boys on the Bus* (1973), but the symbiotic relationship took on a new character in 1976 as young journalists, many of whom were southern born or bred, such as Wilkie, Wooten, Randolph, Clift, Woodruff, and Donaldson, among others, sought to unseat the journalistic establishment and launch their careers. *New York Times* reporter Richard Reeves aptly described the phenomenon: "Jimmy Carter, it turned out, was my candidate. . . . He was, as I thought about it, the candidate of a frustrated generation of American political reporters. My generation . . . had seen our business defined by a generation that came along with John Kennedy—the Hugh Sideys and Joe Krafts. . . . Then we found someone they didn't know—an outsider." As quoted in Glad, *Jimmy Carter,* 399–400. Journalists interviewed affirmed this perspective. Donaldson, interview with the author, January 17, 2017, and Wilkie, interview with the author, January 16, 2017.

117. Matthews, "Winnowing," 55–78; Patterson, *The Mass Media Election,* 38; Popkin, *The Reasoning Voter,* 135; Seib, *Campaigns and Conscience,* 41–58; Davis, *U.S. Presidential Primaries and the Caucus-Convention System,* 88–100; Cohen et al., *The Party Decides,* 168–69, 194–95.

118. Cover, *Rolling Stone,* June 3, 1976.

119. Thompson, "Jimmy Carter and the Great Leap of Faith," reprinted in *The Great Shark Hunt,* 485. Little did readers know a perceived snub on a marathon day in Illinois jeopardized the favorable portrait. An ailing Carter only allowed Thompson half his promised time, and the "irrepressible High Priest of Gonzo Journalism grabbed the first available flight back from Chicago . . . with blood in his eye." As quoted in Witcover, *Marathon,* 262.

120. Sally Quinn, "Rolling Stone 'Bash' Outrages Carter Bunch," *Boston Globe,* July 14, 1976, 31.

121. Jody Powell, *The Other Side of the Story* (New York: Morrow, 1984), 108.

122. As quoted in Glad, *Jimmy Carter,* 298–99.

123. Drew, *American Journal,* 97.

6. PARTY REDEEMER CHOREOGRAPHS MADE-FOR-TELEVISION "LOVE-IN"

1. Martin Nolan, "Enter the Faith Healers," *Boston Globe,* July 16, 1976, 1. Pool cameras stationed throughout the venue supplied live feeds to all three networks. Minicams that could capture script deviations were not in use until 1980. Charles H. Fant, "Televising Presidential Conventions, 1952–1980," *Journal of Communication* 30 (1980): 133.

2. "1976 Jimmy Carter Democratic Convention Acceptance Speech," Kansas State Politics, https://www.youtube.com/watch?v=KepvUaukvqw.

3. Bruce Evenson, "John Chancellor," in *Encyclopedia of American Journalism,* ed. Stephen L. Vaughn (New York: Routledge, 2007), 90–91; Davis, *National Conventions in an Age of Party Reform,* 189–90; Brownell, *Showbiz Politics,* 129–58; Kruse, "Why Don't You Just Get an Actor?" 167–83; Four networks—the Big Three plus DuMont—offered limited live coverage to approximately 1 million viewers in the nation's largest urban hubs in 1948. Conway, *The Origins of Television News in America,* 235–36.

4. McGarr, *The Whole Damn Deal,* 173–97.

5. Conway, *The Origins of Television News in America,* 248–50; Davis, *National Conventions in an Age of Party Reform,* 205–6; Paletz and Elson, "Television Coverage of Political Conventions," 109–31; Crouse, *Boys on the Bus,* 160–86; Thompson, *Fear and Loathing on the Campaign Trail '72,* 328–36; Brownell, *Showbiz Politics,* 168, 188–224; Sandy Maisel and Mark Brewer, *Parties and Elections in America: The Electoral Process* (New York: Rowman and Littlefield, 2009), 367.

6. Kindsvatter, "Who Runs Presidential Campaigns," 1–8; Conway, *The Origins of Television News in America,* 248; Boorstin, *The Image,* 3–45; Sander Vanocur, "Screening the Carter Love-In: Television, the Media and the Carter Love-In," *Washington Post,* July 18, 1976, 133; Alon Reininger, "The Love-In: Carter's Appeal and Strength Produce Unity," *New York Times,* July 18, 1976, 112.

7. All parties understood that McGovern became the first candidate since the inception of public opinion polling to lose ground after the nomination, and, with this in mind, they exploited the networks' tendency to coalesce around an inspirational candidate with a unified message. Paletz and Elson, "Television Coverage of Political Conventions," 121, 128.

8. Greenberg, *Nixon's Shadow,* 98; McGarr, *The Whole Damn Deal,* 174. Paletz and Elson, "Television Coverage of Political Conventions," 130. After watching positive crowd response to Walter Mondale's unscripted entrance, Carter's imagecraft apparatus suggested that he weave his way through the crowd much as he had in one of his campaign commercials. Glad, *Jimmy Carter,* 279; Drew, *American Journal,* 284–317.

9. Carter's antiestablishment act was symbolic. He sought the support of party insiders late in the primary season to secure the nomination, and he depended on their support to win the general election and a potential second term. Cohen et al., *The Party Decides,* 197.

10. The first indication of this transition occurred at the 1924 RNC when incumbent Calvin Coolidge apprehended the power of the convention as a mass-mediated showcase to reach beyond the "smoke-filled room" to special interest groups. Schulman, "Farewell to 'Smoke-Filled Rooms,'" 139–52; David Greenberg, *Calvin Coolidge* (New York: Times Books, 2007), 61–66; Greenberg, "The Ominous Clang," 59.

11. Byron E. Shafer, *Bifurcated Politics: Evolution and Reform in the National Party Convention* (London: Harvard Univ. Press, 1988), 1–76, 226–90.

12. Conway, *The Origins of Television News in America,* 248.

13. Ibid., 231–33; Kindsvatter, "Who Runs Presidential Campaigns," 1–8.

14. Conway, *The Origins of Television News in America,* 248. Critics lamented "lords of kitsch" who exploited "needs of the masses in order to make a profit and/or to maintain their class rule" and condemned politicians wielding "the evil eye" for turning presidential politics into "staged nonsense." As quoted in ibid., 164, 166, 169; Dwight MacDonald, "A Theory of 'Popular Culture,'" *Politics* 1.1 (1944): 20–22. They simultaneously grumbled over the rise of showbiz influences in American politics and infotainment in American journalism.

15. As quoted in Conway, *The Origins of Television News in America,* 235.

16. Allen, *Eisenhower and the Mass Media;* Brownell, *Showbiz Politics;* Greenberg, *Republic of Spin,* 350–402; Schulman and Zelizer, eds., *Media Nation,* 77–113.

17. Fant, "Televising Presidential Conventions, 1952–1980," 130–39; Davis, *National Conventions in an Age of Party Reform,* 190, 202.

18. Fant, "Televising Presidential Conventions, 1952–1980," 131. In 1964, they also observed the juxtaposition of the Alabama and Mississippi delegate walkouts and the boardwalk civil rights demonstrations in Atlantic City. Herbert Waltzer, "In the Magic Lantern: Television Coverage of the 1964 National Conventions," *Public Opinion Quarterly* 30.1 (1966): 33–53.

19. Charles McDowell, "Carnival of Excess: TV at the Conventions," *Atlantic Monthly,* July 1968, http://www.theatlantic.com/magazine/archive/1968/07/carnival-of-excess/303478/; Bodroghkozy, *Groove Tube,* 108; Gitlin, *The Sixties,* 319–340; Perlstein, *Nixonland,* 334–37.

20. As quoted in Joan Didion, *Slouching Towards Bethlehem* (New York: Macmillan, 1991), 84.

21. Brownell, *Showbiz Politics;* Thompson, *Fear and Loathing on the Campaign Trail '72,* 329; Paletz and Elson, "Television Coverage of Political Conventions," 129; Fant, "Televising Presidential Conventions, 1952–1980," 132.

22. Fant, "Televising Presidential Conventions, 1952–1980," 130.

23. Judith Trent and Robert Freedenberg, *Political Campaign Communication: Principles and Practices,* 5th ed. (Lanham, Md.: Rowman and Littlefield, 2004), 55–57.

24. Hamilton Jordan to Jimmy Carter, "Democratic National Convention," May 1976, Memorandum-Hamilton Jordan to Jimmy Carter, General Election, Box 39: Issues Task Force-Members List and Resumes through Memorandums-Political Strategy [2], CFP-CF, JCPL.

25. Ibid.; Joseph Lelyveld, "On TV, the Jimmy Carter Show Followed the Script," *New York Times,* July 17, 1976, 7.

26. David E. Rosenbaum, "Democrats Adopt a Platform Aimed at Uniting Party," *New York Times,* June 16, 1976, 1.

27. Eizenstat, interview with the author, September 28, 2015. Carter previously promised evaders a "blanket pardon," but Brown, a leading antiwar activist, suggested an amendment offering pardons to both evaders and deserters. To avoid the divisiveness that the controversial measure might spark, Eizenstat urged Brown to revise the amendment to include a provision for "case-by-case pardons for deserters." Davis, *National Conventions in an Age of Party Reform,* 116; Roessner and Bier, "Pardon Me, Mr. Carter," 86–96.

28. Stanley, "Going Beyond the New Deal," 71; "Jimmy Carter's Presentation to the Platform Committee of the Democratic Party," "Democratic National Committee, 1/75–10/76," Box 11: Defense, 9/76–10/76 through Economics, 1/75–2/75, JCPPP, PC, IO-SE, JCPL.

29. "Alabama, Georgia, New York, Texas, Indiana, 6/12–19/76," Box 33: Florida, North Carolina, Illinois, California, 3/7–12/76 through California, Michigan, 10/26/76–11/1/76, Susan Clough's 1975–1976 Campaign Trip Files, RSC, JCPL; Memoranda, Campaign Staff General Election, 6/76, Box 199: DC-FSCMPM, CDO-HJCSF, RCCEJC, JCPL; Carl Leubsdorf, "Staffers Map Strategy as Carter Fishes Off Georgia," *Baltimore Sun,* June 17, 1976, A6.

30. Notes through Notes in '72 Convention Press Operation, 6/10/76, Democratic National Convention (DNC)/New York, Box 229: Advisory Opinion through DNC—Campaign Consultation Program Material, JCPPP, PC, Finance and Convention Planning, JGSF, JCPL. They also informally chatted about how to overcome media images of an arrogant staff. During the convention, Carter resided on the twenty-first floor of the Americana Hotel, one *Godfather* filming location.

31. Glad, *Jimmy Carter,* 274–75; Drew, *American Journal,* 284–317; File: Democratic National Convention (DNC)/New York, Box 229: Advisory Opinion through DNC—Campaign Consultation Program Material, JCPPP, PC, Finance and Convention Planning, JGSF, JCPL. The simulacra instead functioned as a volunteer recruitment center. Baudrillard, *Simulacra and Simulation,* 123–24.

32. Promotional Materials, "DNC-Press Kit," Box 230: DNC-Car Rental through DNC-Staff Information, JGSF, RCCEJC, JCPL; File: "Democratic Convention—Carter Family Packet," Box 36: "Defense, 9/74–12/74 through Foreign Policy Defense-Correspondence/Recommendations/ Analysis [1]," CFP-CF, JCPL.

33. Tom Conway to Local Carter Campaign Headquarters, "Memorandum of Explanation," "Correspondence, 3/13/74–8/31/76," Box 3: "[Correspondence, 3/13/74–8/31/76] through [Credit Card & Social Security Numbers—Traveling Party]," Staff Offices, Press, Granum, PPJC, JCPL; Printing Operation, Democratic National Convention (DNC)/New York, Box 229: Advisory Opinion through DNC—Campaign Consultation Program Material, JCPPP, PC, Finance and Convention Planning, JGSF, JCPL; File: DNC-Convention News, Box 230: DNC-Car Rental through DNC-Staff Information, JCPPP, PC, Finance and Convention Planning, JGSF, JCPL.

34. Drew, *American Journal,* 286; Witcover, *Marathon,* 359–66.

35. Polling feedback from average Americans elicited what one would expect; individuals with high name recognition polled favorably. White, *The Making of the President, 1960,* 164–65; Glad, *Jimmy Carter,* 271; Charles Mohr, "Carter Confers on Running Mate," *New York Times,* July 3, 1976, 14; AP, "Carter, Muskie Meet Today," *Boston Globe,* July 5, 1976, 20; Jack Nelson, "Mondale and Muskie Believed Top Choices," *Los Angeles Times,* July 12, 1976, B1. Carter also consulted influential journalists for advice during the vetting process and explained his choice of Mondale in an hour-long, off-the-record DNC meeting. Auletta, "Covering Carter Is Like Playing Chess with Bobby Fischer," 12–22; Wilkie, "What, indeed, about Jody Powell," 12–15.

36. Inspired by a biopic on Kennedy featured during the 1964 DNC, Nixon's imagecraft apparatus produced the first promotional biography at the 1972 RNC. Fant, "Televising Presidential Conventions, 1952–1980," 132; Sander Vanocur, "Tuning in on Carter's 'Vision,'" *Wash-*

ington Post, July 14, 1976, E9; "Film to Trace Carter Candidacy from Its Start to Its Triumph," *New York Times,* July 15, 1976, 24.

37. Walter Naedale, "Roger F. Goodwin, 69; Filmed Campaign Ads," *Philadelphia Inquirer,* June 2, 2010; Rafshoon, interview with the author, August 12, 2014; Curtis Wilkie, "It'll Be Carter's Debut," *Boston Globe,* June 28, 1976, 9; Vanocur, "Tuning in on Carter's 'Vision,'" E9; Lelyveld, "On TV, the Jimmy Carter Show Followed the Script," 7; Transcript, Gerald Rafshoon, oral history interview, April 8, 1983, by Joseph Devaney et al., MCPA-POHP-CPP, http://web1 .millercenter.org/poh/transcripts/ohp_1983_0408_rafshoon.pdf; Rod Goodwin and Gerald Rafshoon, "Jimmy Who?" July 16, 1976, https://www.c-span.org/video/?409401-1/jimmy; 1976 Carter vs. Ford, The Living Room Candidate, Museum of the Moving Image, http://www.living roomcandidate.org/commercials/1976.

38. "Film to Trace Carter Candidacy from Its Start to Its Triumph," 24; Christopher Lydon, "Dimmycrats to See a Film on Mr. Dooley," *New York Times,* July 5, 1976, 22.

39. Opposition toward Carter was pro forma; even delegate divisions were relatively tame. Interest group conflicts were Carter's only real challenge to harmonious images. Shafer, *Bifurcated Politics,* 177–79. Political crises shifted to message crises after the post-1968 reforms. Sam Garrett, "Evolution of Convention Crises," in *Rewiring Politics: Presidential Nominating Conventions in the Media Age,* ed. Costas Panagopoulos (Baton Rouge: Louisiana State Univ. Press, 2007), 122; Eileen Shanaham, "Democratic Women to Discuss Party Role with Carter in an Attempt to Avoid a Convention Fight," *New York Times,* July 8, 1976, 17; Women's Meeting with Carter at the Convention, 7/11/76, Box 300: Talent Bank Forms through Work Schedule-Issues for Women, CLSFNC, RCCEJC, JCPL; William Claiborne, "News Agencies Cut Democratic Convention Coverage," *Washington Post,* June 24, 1976, A6. Carter and his staff mitigated developments such as these by building relationships with key interest group leaders and instituting a two-way communication model to allow relevant political actors to voice concerns. Public relations theorist James Grunig conceptualized two-way strategies in his 1984 public relations model. James Grunig and Todd Hunt, *Managing Public Relations* (New York: Cengage Learning, 1984).

40. Women's rights leaders were disillusioned by the drop in representation of women from 38 percent in 1972 to 34 percent in 1976. Shanaham, "Democratic Women to Discuss Party Role with Carter in an Attempt to Avoid a Convention Fight," 17; Women's Meeting with Carter at the Convention, 7/11/76, Box 300: Talent Bank Forms through Work Schedule-Issues for Women, CLSFNC, RCCEJC, JCPL. The rendezvous prevented a floor fight and resulted in a compromise that stopped short of requiring a fifty-fifty split but encouraged steps toward ensuring equity. Simeon Booker, "Carter Squashes Rumor, Wins Black Dems' Votes," *Jet Magazine,* July 29, 1976, 10–12.

41. As quoted in Glad, *Jimmy Carter,* 274. With assistance from Rainwater, Carter established the Committee of 51.3 Percent for the constituency, but many prominent women's rights activists became disillusioned with the candidate when they learned of the marginalization of women on his staff and when they witnessed his failure to appoint a significant number of women in his administration. File: Women—Committee of the 51.3 Percent, Box 4: Rebuttal to News Article by Steven Brill "Jimmy Carter's Pathetic Lies"—New York Magazine [2] through Women—Committee of the 51.3 Percent, BRDP, JCPL; Bourne, *Jimmy Carter,* 345; Carolyn Heilbrun, *The Education of a Woman: The Life of Gloria Steinem* (New York: Dial,

1995), 312–13; Lisa Young, *Feminists and Party Politics* (New York: Univ. of British Columbia Press, 2000), 95–97.

42. Purvis, *The Presidency and the Press*; Anne Wexler et al., "Press Coverage in the Primaries: A Conversation with David Broder," *Democratic Review,* July/August 1976, *Democratic Review,* Box 4: "Correspondence-Request for Actuality Phone Number through Forms-Talk Show Final Disposition," RWHPO, Media Liaison Office, Bradley Woodward's Subject Files, JCPL; Sanoff, "Remark," 28–29.

43. Anne Wexler et al., "Press Coverage in the Primaries: A Conversation with David Broder," *Democratic Review,* July/August 1976, *Democratic Review,* Box 4: "Correspondence-Request for Actuality Phone Number through Forms-Talk Show Final Disposition," RWHPO, Media Liaison Office, Bradley Woodward's Subject Files, JCPL.

44. Ibid.; Pressman, "Objectivity and Its Discontents," 96–113. Broder articulated one critique of objectivity gaining traction among political reporters, such as Brit Hume, a muckraking reporter who learned his craft from "Washington-Merry-Go-Round" columnist Jack Anderson before transitioning to a career as a broadcast correspondent for ABC News and later a conservative political pundit with Fox News. "[Trail journalists] report what one candidate said, then they go and report what the other candidate said with equal credibility. They never get around to finding out if the guy is telling the truth." As quoted in Crouse, *Boys on the Bus,* 305. Hume recommended that journalists instead embrace investigative reporting on campaign fundraising.

45. Phil Stanford, "'The Most Remarkable Piece of Fiction' Jimmy Carter Ever Read," *Columbia Journalism Review* 15.2 (1976): 13–18. File: Magazines [2], Box 334: Libassi, Peter through Magazines [3], JCPPP, PC Press Office—BRSF, JCPL. Stanford also contended that Powell's lengthy rebuttal was more damaging than Brill's journalism, an assertion with which some Carter staff agreed. Eizenstat sent a memorandum to Carter and his closest advisors in the immediate aftermath of Brill's story, encouraging Powell to avoid "over-react[ing] . . . with virulent rebuttal[s]" in the future. Doing so gave negative stories more publicity, lent credence to problematic claims, and gave the campaign a negative image, he claimed. Memorandum, Stuart Eizenstat to Jimmy Carter, Hamilton Jordan, Jody Powell, and Steve Starke, "Reaction to Criticism," February 10, 1976; Harper's Article/Rebuttal, Box 2: Executive Department—Records During Carter's Gubernatorial Term through Natural Resources Management in Georgia, 1975, BRDP, JCPL.

46. Claiborne, "News Agencies Cut Democratic Convention Coverage," *Washington Post,* June 24, 1976, A6.

47. Ibid.

48. Davis, *National Conventions in an Age of Party Reform,* 191.

49. Polsby, *Consequences of Party Reform,* 143.

50. Nolan, "Big Apple Takes on a Special Shine," 29.

51. James Naughton, "This Time, Democrats Dress Up," *New York Times,* July 14, 1976, 16.

52. David Broder, "Four Years Later, The Wounds Have Been Healed," *Washington Post,* July 11, 1976, 1. In March 1974, Broder asserted that the greatest dilemma facing Democrats was a "candidate problem." David Broder, "The Democrats' Dilemma," *Atlantic Monthly,* "Democratic National Committee (DNC), 1974," Box 11: Defense, 9/76–10/76 through Economics, 1/75–2/75, JCPPP, PC, IO-SE, PPJC, JCPL.

53. "A Blessed Bore," *Wall Street Journal,* July 12, 1976, 10; Hamilton Jordan to Jimmy Carter, "Democratic National Convention," May 1976, Memorandum-Hamilton Jordan to Jimmy Carter, General Election, Box 39: Issues Task Force-Members List and Resumes through Memorandums-Political Strategy [2], CFP-CF, JCPL.

54. Boorstin, *The Image,* 3–45.

55. Brownell, *Showbiz Politics,* 129–58; Vanocur, "Screening the Carter Love-In," 133.

56. Bruce McCabe, "Last Hope of Suspense Fading for Networks," *Boston Globe,* July 15, 1976, 75.

57. Ibid.; Albert Hunt, "Bob Strauss: Carpenter of Consensus," *Wall Street Journal,* July 16, 1976, 6; Myra MacPherson, "A Time of Volleyball and Candidates," *Washington Post,* July 17, 1976, A6; Reininger, "The Love-In: Carter's Appeal and Strength Produce Unity," 112.

58. James Wooten, "Carter Hears Sermon by Black Pastor, Then Hears 'Dixie' Played at 21 Club," *New York Times,* July 12, 1976, 61; Curtis Wilkie, "Carter Hailed in New York City," *Boston Globe,* July 12, 1976; 29; McGarr, "'We're All in This Thing Together,'" 77–95.

59. Wilkie, for instance, wrote that Carter "seemed perfectly at home" in Manhattan. Wilkie, "Carter Hailed in New York City," 29. Elements of regional bias crept into some accounts, which depicted Carter as a country hick visiting the city. Jon Margolis, "To the Big Apple, Carter's Just Peanuts," *Chicago Tribune,* July 11, 1976, 1; Charlotte Curtis, "5,000 Picnic," *New York Times,* July 12, 1976, 61; Marlene Cimons, "'Miss Lillian' Tackles the Big Apple," *Los Angeles Times,* July 14, 1976, G1; Jude Wanniski, "A Peanut in a Poke," *Wall Street Journal,* July 16, 1976, 16. In March, Powell penned a handwritten note to Carter reprimanding him for his belief that "prejudice against the South was legitimate." He warned Carter that regional bias would come to bother him. Jody Powell to Governor, N.D., Primaries—JLP's Briefcase Contents, 3/4/76–4/4/76, Box 5: National Governor's Conference, 11/12/76–11/14/76 [CF, O/A 751] through Schedules/Pool Reports, 10/4/76–11/10/76 [CF, O/A 751], Staff Offices, Press, Powell, JCPL.

60. Kindsvatter, "Who Runs Presidential Campaigns," 1–8; Dan Schill, *Stagecraft and Statecraft: Advance and Media Events in Political Communication* (New York: Rowman and Littlefield, 2009), 89.

61. Polsby, *Consequences of Party Reform,* 142; Gay Talese, *The Kingdom and the Power: Behind the Scenes at* The New York Times*: The Institution that Influences the World* (Cleveland: World Publishing, 1969), 208; Pressman, "Objectivity and Its Discontents," 96–113; Pressman, *Remaking the News,* 68–146.

62. Jody Powell, Betty Rainwater, and Hamilton Jordan to Key Campaign Members, January 10, 1976, Atlanta Correspondence, 1975–1976, Box 5: Administrative Manuals to Economy, 1974, PWP, JCPL.

63. George Skelton, "Trappings of the White House," *Los Angeles Times,* July 12, 1976, B1. Skelton observed that the open campaign morphed into an "unwieldy affair with many of the trappings of a White House operation." Pack frustrations intensified during the convention due to Powell's absences. Wilkie, "What, indeed, about Jody Powell," 12–15.

64. Tracking down Carter for an interview evolved into something of a challenge. Griff to Jody, "JC Media Time," "Memos—Interview Schedules, 6/29/76–9/1/76," Box 4: [Dole, Sen. Robert—Voting Record] through [Memos—Interview Schedules, 6/29/76–9/1/76], Staff Offices Press Granum, PPJC, JCPL.

65. The presumptive nominee now controlled the "rules of engagement" and exercised the power to freeze out unpromising sources. Auletta, "Covering Carter Is Like Playing Chess with Bobby Fischer," 12–22; Kindsvatter, "Who Runs Presidential Campaigns," 1–8; Schill, *Stagecraft and Statecraft,* 89.

66. Hunter S. Thompson to Jimmy [Carter], June 29, 1976, Correspondence from the Media, Colorado, Box 319: Correspondence from the Media, Colorado through Correspondence from the Media, Georgia [2], JCPPP, PC, Press Office-Betty Rainwater, Subject Files, JCPL. In truth, Thompson did not plan on going to the convention until the week prior. He was bitter with *Rolling Stone* publisher Jann Wenner for the cover line to his centerfold piece—"An endorsement, with fear and loathing"—and a dispute over payment for his expenses. Nonetheless, when he realized he was "deep in another money-hole," he went on assignment. As quoted in Hunter S. Thompson, *Fear and Loathing in America: The Brutal Odyssey of an Outlaw Journalist* (New York: Simon and Schuster, 2000), 987, 966–67. Thompson contended that the idea for another annual conversation came upon reflection on Carter's rise: "[Carter's] reality has changed so drastically since I met him that the most amazing thing about the change is that it now seems entirely logical." Ibid., 987; William McKeen, *Outlaw Journalist: The Life and Times of Hunter S. Thompson* (New York: Norton, 2009), 244–45.

67. As quoted in Thompson, *Fear and Loathing in America,* 706.

68. Ibid., 987–88; Norman Sims, *True Stories: A Century of Literary Journalism* (Evanston, Ill.: Northwestern Univ. Press).

69. Sanoff, "Remark," 28–29.

70. Drew, *American Journal,* 290. The buzzword shifted to "love-in," which also was not a completely accurate descriptor. As Drew recognized, frames served to exaggerate and distort the event's nature. Polsby, *Consequences of Party Reform,* 143–46. Paletz and Elson, "Television Coverage of Political Conventions," 120.

71. Schieffer, interview with the author, August 12, 2014.

72. "A Blessed Bore," 10; Robert L. Healy, "Democrats Battle Boredom," *Boston Globe,* July 9, 1976, 19; Marilynn Preston, "TV-Radio: Exciting Truth about 'Boring' Dem Convention," *Chicago Tribune,* July 15, 1976, B6, B1; David Broder, "Don't Yawn: A Real Drama Is Beginning," *Los Angeles Times,* July 12, 1976, D5.

73. Broder, "Four Years Later," 1; Davis, *National Conventions in an Age of Party Reform,* 206–7.

74. Healy, "Democrats Battle Boredom," 19; Lelyveld, "The Medium's the Thing at the National Convention," 55. Yielding to advertiser expectations and engaging in ratings wars contributed to the battle for entertainment personalities and renewed critique of celebrity-entertainment forces in television news. After fulfilling her duties at NBC, Walters considered these trends from afar. Powers, *The Newscasters,* 163–82.

75. Broder, "Don't Yawn," D5.

76. Ibid.

77. One of the primary debates concerned whether networks should provide gavel-to-gavel or abridged coverage: CBS and NBC offered live, gavel-to-gavel coverage, and ABC featured abridged reporting. Paletz and Elson, "Television Coverage of Political Conventions," 110. Approximately 17.5 million viewers tuned into the 1976 DNC, earning a Nielsen rating of 25.2 and marking one of the highest audiences to date. Nonetheless, the unified affair could not com-

pete with the contentious RNC, which attracted nearly 22 million viewers several weeks later. "Historical TV Ratings Democratic Conventions," Nielsen Newswire, 08/27/2008, http://www .nielsen.com/us/en/insights/news/2008/historical-tv-ratings-democratic-conventions-1960 -2004.html; "Historical TV Ratings Republican Conventions," Nielsen Newswire, 08/27/2008, http://www.nielsen.com/us/en/insights/news/2008/historical-tv-ratings-republican-con ventions.html.

78. Lydon, "Dimmycrats to See a Film on Mr. Dooley," 22; Jack Nelson, "Democrats Hear Call for Morality," *Los Angeles Times,* July 13, 1976, B1.

79. Joseph Lelyveld, "The Convention on TV: Mixed Impressions," *New York Times,* July 14, 1976, 19; "Barbara Jordan Keynote Address to 1976 Democratic National Convention," Educational Video Group, https://www.youtube.com/watch?v=sKfFJc37jjQ.

80. Journalists in the gallery and living room audiences tuned out. In some cases, they flipped to local cable channels broadcasting *Casablanca* or the *Five Day Bicycle Race,* Image Union's live black-and-white coverage featuring authentic images of the convention—raw, unfiltered footage of Yippie protests and uncut interviews with delegates, party leaders, and prominent journalists. Nelson, "Democrats Hear Call for Morality," B1. Critics also debated whether cameras should focus solely on the podium or on extraneous events. Paletz and Elson, "Television Coverage of Political Conventions," 110–11; Davis, *National Conventions in an Age of Party Reform,* 205–6. John O'Connor, "TV: 'Media Clutter' Mars Coverage of the Convention," *New York Times,* July 14, 1976, 52; "Five Day Bicycle Race," Media Burn: Independent Video Archive, http://mediaburn.org/video/five-day-bicycle-race-5/; Healy, "Democrats Battle Boredom," 19; Preston, "TV-Radio: Exciting Truth about 'Boring' Dem Convention," B6. On Wednesday, the *Children's Express* beat competitors when, based on eight-year-old Amy's leak, they reported Mondale would be Carter's running mate. Glad, *Jimmy Carter,* 278.

81. Goffman, *Framing Analysis*; "Barbara Jordan Keynote Address to 1976 Democratic National Convention," Educational Video Group, https://www.youtube.com/watch?v=sKfFJc37jjQ. Consensus-minded analysis confirmed that Jordan's keynote provided the one moment of excitement the night prior and speculated that the only remaining drama involved Carter's expected running mate announcement. As evidence of the contrast from years past, newspapers offered readers an image of a delegate yawning early in the opening session. Harry Kelly and Jon Margolis, "United Dems Are 'Hell Bent on Victory,'" *Chicago Tribune,* July 13, 1976, 1; R. W. Apple Jr., "Party Is United," *New York Times,* July 13, 1976, 1; "A Moving Plea," *Christian Science Monitor,* July 14, 1976, 32.

82. Lou Cannon and David Broder, "Democrats Convene, Stress Unity," *Washington Post,* July 13, 1976, A1; Sander Vanocur, "The Restless Camera," *Washington Post,* July 16, 1976, B1; Glad, *Jimmy Carter,* 275; Apple, "Party Is United," 1.

83. Jack Nelson, "Party Chieftains Hail Carter," *Los Angeles Times,* July 14, 1976, 1.

84. With television's rise in the 1950s, *New York Times* decision-makers, understanding they could not match broadcasting speed in covering spot news, transitioned to a more analytical, interpretive mode. Talese, *The Kingdom and the Power,* 208, 479. Other newspapers with national circulations adapted in an analogous manner. Pressman, *Remaking the News,* 37–67. Scholars in the 1960s acknowledged the distancing effect of the press as compared to television's intensifying effect. Henry Fairlie, "The Unreal World of Television News," in *Sight, Sound, and Society,* ed. David Manning White and Richard Averson (Boston: Beacon, 1968), 127–35.

85. Polsby, *Consequences of Party Reform,* 142–43; Pressman, "Objectivity and Its Discontents," 96–113; Pressman, *Remaking the News,* 306–10.

86. R. W. Apple Jr., "Humphrey Hailed," *New York Times,* July 14, 1976, 1.

87. Bruce McCabe, "Baseball Giving Politics a Stiff Fight," *Boston Globe,* July 14, 1976, 9.

88. Hadley, *The Invisible Primary,* 90; Wilkie, "Carter: Strong on the Road, but Weak at Home," 1.

89. David Weaver et al., *Media Agenda-Setting in a Presidential Election: Issues, Images, and Interests* (New York: Praeger, 1981), 15, 28, 39; Orren, "Candidate Style and Voter Alignment," 173–76.

90. David Nyhan, "It's Official Now . . . Carter Nominated," *Boston Globe,* July 15, 1976, 1.

91. McCabe, "Last Hope of Suspense Fading for Networks," 75; Marlene Cimons, "Rosalynn Carter's Ringside View," *Los Angeles Times,* July 16, 1976, F1; as quoted in Glad, *Jimmy Carter,* 277.

92. McCabe, "Last Hope of Suspense Fading for Networks," 75.

93. R. W. Apple Jr., "A Quick Victory," *New York Times,* July 15, 1976, 1.

94. Harry Kelly, "Carter Wins Big on First Ballot," *Chicago Tribune,* July 15, 1976, 1.

95. McCabe, "Last Hope of Suspense Fading for Networks," 75.

96. Bruce McCabe, "Carter Answered the Only Question for the 10 a.m. Viewers," *Boston Globe,* July 16, 1976, 2.

97. Naedale, "Roger F. Goodwin, 69; Filmed Campaign Ads"; Rafshoon, interview with the author, August 12, 2014; Wilkie, "It'll Be Carter's Debut," 9; Vanocur, "Tuning in on Carter's 'Vision,'" E9; Lelyveld, "On TV, the Jimmy Carter Show Followed the Script," 7; Transcript, Gerald Rafshoon, oral history interview, April 8, 1983, by Joseph Devaney et al., MCPA-POHP-CPP, http://web1.millercenter.org/poh/transcripts/ohp_1983_0408_rafshoon.pdf; Rod Goodwin and Gerald Rafshoon, "Jimmy Who?" July 16, 1976, https://www.c-span.org/video/?409401-1 /jimmy.

98. "Film to Trace Carter Candidacy from Its Start to Its Triumph," 24.

99. Ibid. Nearly forty years later, several political reporters who covered Carter's campaign recalled the efficacy of the cinema-vérité documentary. "The campaign film they made for the convention was very effective," Olson remembered. Cloud agreed: "It was brilliant. Portraying him as a farmer-nuclear physicist, and the message . . . 'I want to be as good as the American people.' It was a direct refutation of Nixon and Watergate. The country was poised for that at that time. That's what the voters wanted to hear." Lynne Olson, interview with the author, August 11, 2014; Cloud, interview with the author, August 11, 2014.

100. Fant, "Televising Presidential Conventions, 1952–1980," 134.

101. In the days prior to the convention, Carter and his staff reviewed drafts of his acceptance speech. Before speechwriter Patrick Anderson drafted the first line, Carter advised: "I want to say my campaign started with nothing, and formed an alliance with the people, and I don't fear being president as long as I can keep my alliance with the people." As the convention commenced, Anderson and Eizenstat offered final comments, suggestions to delete a reference to the "economic and power elite," which indicated belief in a "conspiratorial group," and to "deal directly" with Ford's pardon of Nixon, among others. Carter insisted a line inspired by philosopher Reinhold Niebuhr remain and the word "explicitly" be removed from the text. "I want to use words that people down in Plains can understand," he told advisors. Two days later, Carter convened with Anderson, Rafshoon, Caddell, and Powell to fine-tune the speech.

Nevertheless, until the final moments, Carter tinkered with text, penciling in a new opening referencing his campaign's roots—"My name is Jimmy Carter, and I'm running for president." He added the witty line based on advice from Rafshoon's friend Jack Kaplan. As quoted in Bourne, *Jimmy Carter,* 335; Stuart Eizenstat to Jimmy Carter, "Final Comments on Acceptance Speech," July 11, 1976, "Acceptance Speech, 7/76," Box 1: Abortion, 9/76 through Armenian National Committee, 8/76, JCPPP, PC, IO-SE, JCPL; File: "Democratic Nominee Acceptance Speech, 1976," Box 67: Gubernatorial Speeches, 1974 through Transcript of Speech, Hot Springs, Arkansas, 9/17/76, JCFP, Jimmy Carter's Speech File, JCPL; "1976 Jimmy Carter Democratic Convention Acceptance Speech," https://www.youtube.com/watch?v=KepvUaukvqw; "Carter Acceptance Speech," CSPAN, July 15, 1976, https://www.c-span.org/video/?3435-1/carter-1976-acceptance-speech.

102. File: Acceptance Speech, 7/76, Box 1: Abortion 9/76 through Armenian National Committee, 8/76, Stuart Eizenstat's Subject Files, CMCC, RCCEJC, JCPL; Nyhan, "Sees 'New Mood' in US," 1; Speech, Jimmy Carter, "Our Nation's Past and Future: Address Accepting the Presidential Nomination at the Democratic National Convention in New York City," July 15, 1976, online, by Gerhard Peters and John T. Wooley, *The American Presidency Project,* https://www.presidency.ucsb.edu/documents/our-nations-past-and-future-address-accepting-the-presidential-nomination-the-democratic.

103. Bourne, *Jimmy Carter,* 336; Witcover, *Marathon,* 368–370; McGarr, *The Whole Damn Deal,* 174.

104. Orren, "Candidate Style and Voter Alignment," 173–76; Shafer, *Quiet Revolution,* 534–35; Steven Miller, "The Persistence of Antiliberalism: Evangelicals and the Race Problem," in *American Evangelicals and the 1960s,* ed. Axel Schafer (Madison: Univ. of Wisconsin Press, 2013), 82–83.

105. McCabe, "Last Hope of Suspense Fading for Networks," 75; Nyhan, "Sees 'New Mood' in US," 1.

106. "Text of Carter's Acceptance Speech," *Boston Globe,* July 16, 1976, 12; "Carter's Text: 'A New Mood in America,'" *Los Angeles Times,* July 16, 1976, 21; "Carter Vows to Lead U.S. to Greatness," *Hartford Courant,* July 16, 1976, 1; "Transcript of Carter Address," *New York Times,* July 16, 1976, 10.

107. Carl Leubsdorf, "Minnesotan Called Symbol of Unification," *Baltimore Sun,* July 16, 1976, A1.

108. Ibid.; "Carter: 1976 Will See Government Returned to the People," *Chicago Tribune,* July 16, 1976, 6; Jack Nelson, "Nation's Best Is Still Ahead," *New York Times,* July 16, 1976, B1.

109. Tom Mathews, Joseph Cumming, Andrew Jaffe, Stephan Lesher, Elaine Shannon, and Deborah Beers, "The Southern Mystique," *Newsweek,* July 19, 1976, 30–33.

110. "The Convention: Onward to November," *Time,* July 26, 1976, 8.

111. Crouse, *Boys on the Bus,* 15; Albert Hunt, "Bob Strauss: Carpenter of Consensus," *Wall Street Journal,* July 16, 1976, 6; MacPherson, "A Time of Volleyball and Candidates," A6; Vanocur, "Screening the Carter Love-In," 133; Reininger, "The Love-In," 112.

112. Nolan, "Enter the Faith Healers," 1; Peter Goldman, Eleanor Clift, Hal Bruno, and James Doyle, "The Jimmycrats," *Newsweek,* July 26, 1976, 16; "The Convention: Onward to November," 8–15.

113. "The Convention: Onward to November," 8–15.

114. Kindsvatter, "Who Runs Presidential Campaigns," 1–8; Fant, "Televising Presidential Conventions, 1952–1980," 130; Davis, *U.S. Presidential Primaries and the Caucus-Convention System,* 134. Networks and parties existed in a state of "cordial concurrence." Larry Davis Smith and Dan Nimmo, *Cordial Concurrence: Orchestrating National Party Conventions in the Telepolitical Age* (New York: Praegar, 1991).

115. Arnold Rose, *The Power Structure: Political Process in American Society* (New York: Oxford Univ. Press, 1967), 398.

116. Polsby, *Consequences of Party Reform,* 69.

117. Davis, *National Conventions in an Age of Party Reform,* 212–13. Although interest in the convention declined throughout the week, one 1976 study revealed that conventions boosted voter engagement and influenced behavior among undecided voters. Trent and Freedenberg, *Political Campaign Communication,* 52.

118. Francis Clinest, "Lower the Bunting and Pay the Bills," *New York Times,* July 17, 1976, 19; Kenneth Reich, "Carter Returns Home," *Los Angeles Times,* July 17, 1976, A3.

119. "Democrats: 'I Don't Think I'll Ever Be Tentative,'" *Time,* July 19, 1976, 23; "Where Carter Comes From," *Newsweek,* May 3, 1976, 18; Jansson, "Internal Orientalism in America: W. J. Cash's *The Mind of the South* and the Spatial Construction of American National Identity," 293–316.

120. Perry, "Us and Them This Time," 16–18.

121. Kindsvatter, "Who Runs Presidential Campaigns," 1–8; Polsby, *Consequences of Party Reform,* 142–43; Pressman, *Remaking the News,* 306–10.

122. Carter, interview with the author, October 17, 2014.

7. THE BATTLE TO CONTROL THE NEW SOUTH NOMINEE'S NARRATIVE

1. As quoted in Stroud, *How Jimmy Won,* 329–30. Leubsdorf's sketch shared qualities with a recent *Rolling Stone* cover, but he borrowed the tagline of Southern Baptist Convention president Bailey Smith. Cover, *Rolling Stone,* June 3, 1976; David Swartz, *Moral Minority: The Evangelical Left in an Age of Conservatism* (Philadelphia: Univ. of Pennsylvania Press, 2012), 216–17.

2. As quoted in Stroud, *How Jimmy Won,* 330; Kalman, *Right Star Rising,* 183.

3. As quoted in, Schram, *Running for President,* 93.

4. Brokaw, interview with the author, April 3, 2017.

5. Mears, interview with the author, August 18, 2014; Crouse, *Boys on the Bus,* 20–26; Perry, *Us and Them,* 168–69.

6. Davis, *U.S. Presidential Primaries and the Caucus-Convention System,* 224; Corwin Smidt et al., *The Disappearing God Gap?: Religion in the 2008 Presidential Election* (New York: Oxford Univ. Press, 2010), 107.

7. Crouse, *Boys on the Bus,* 339–55; Thompson, *Fear and Loathing on the Campaign Trail '72,* 304–70.

8. Carter, Jimmy: Campaign Stuff, Charles M. Rafshoon Papers, MARBL; 1976 Carter vs. Ford, The Living Room Candidate, Museum of the Moving Image, http://www.livingroomcandidate .org/commercials/1976.

9. Carter, *Why Not the Best,* xx, 162; Lechner, *The South of the Mind,* 135–60; Seifert, *The Politics of Authenticity in Presidential Campaigns,* 22.

10. Bourne, *Jimmy Carter,* 256.

11. Memorandum, Hamilton Jordan to Jimmy Carter, "Democratic National Convention," May 1976, File: Memorandum-Hamilton Jordan to Jimmy Carter, General Election, Box 39: Issues Task Force-Members List and Resumes through Memorandums-Political Strategy [2], CFP-PC, JCPL.

12. Ibid.

13. Ibid.

14. Witcover, *Marathon,* 313–16; Carl Leubsdorf, "Fund Limit Puts Carter in Pinch," *Baltimore Sun,* July 25, 1976, A4.

15. Curtis Wilkie, "Americus—the Booming Host City of Pilgrims Bound for Plains," *Boston Globe,* July 23, 1976, 1; "Bar-B-Que Villa vs. the 21," *Baltimore Sun,* July 23, 1976, A9; Curtis Wilkie, "The Good Ole Boys Meet at Billy's Place," *Boston Globe,* July 11, 1976, 29; Jeff Prugh, "Teaches Sunday School Class," *Los Angeles Times,* July 19, 1976, B6; "Carter Pitches for the Press," *Baltimore Sun,* July 24, 1976, A7; Carl Leubsdorf, "Carter's Cousin Hugh Is Plains' No. 1 Citizen," *Baltimore Sun,* July 4, 1976, A5; Carl Leubsdorf, "Plains Tour Includes Carter Tree," *Baltimore Sun,* July 24, 1976, A7; Carl Leubsdorf, "As Carter Explains: Inflation Sours Plains Lemonade," *Baltimore Sun,* July 10, 1976, A9; Mary McGrory, "Campaign Is Mainly in Plains," *Chicago Tribune,* August 2, 1976, A4; Helen Dewar, "Scholars Flocking to Counsel Carter at 'Walden South,'" *Washington Post,* August 17, 1976, A2; Olson, interview with the author, August 11, 2014; Cloud, interview with the author, August 11, 2014. Schieffer described the Plains backdrop and "characters" he encountered as a CBS White House correspondent covering Carter's transition period in the late fall of 1976. Bob Schieffer, *This Just In: What I Couldn't Tell You on TV* (New York: Berkley Books, 2003), 248–49; Schieffer, interview with the author, August 12, 2014.

16. Douglas Kneeland, "Pride and Nostalgia Glow in Carter's Town," *New York Times,* July 28, 1976, 9; Witcover, *Marathon,* 513–16.

17. Charles Seib, "The 'Pap' from Plains," *Washington Post,* August 20, 1976, A27.

18. Glad, *Jimmy Carter,* 374. The team name was a reference to Edith Efron's *New York Times* bestselling book *Newstwisters,* which offered evidence of the liberal bias of network news. Schulman and Zelizer, *Media Nation,* 138–39.

19. Kneeland, "Pride and Nostalgia Glow in Carter's Town," 9.

20. Wilkie, "Americus—the Booming Host City of Pilgrims Bound for Plains," 1; "Bar-B-Que Villa vs. the 21," A9; Wilkie, "The Good Ole Boys Meet at Billy's Place," 29; Prugh, "Teaches Sunday School Class," B6; "Carter Pitches for the Press," A7; Leubsdorf, "Carter's Cousin Hugh Is Plains' № 1 Citizen," A5; Leubsdorf, "Plains Tour Includes Carter Tree," A7; Leubsdorf, "As Carter Explains: Inflation Sours Plains Lemonade," A9; McGrory, "Campaign Is Mainly in Plains," A4; Olson, interview with the author, August 11, 2014; Cloud, interview with the author, August 11, 2014.

21. As quoted in Glad, *Jimmy Carter,* 376.

22. As quoted in ibid., 372; Witcover, *Marathon,* 313–16.

23. Carter, interview with the author, October 17, 2014.

24. As quoted in Glad, *Jimmy Carter,* 376; Pippert, interview with the author, September 5, 2014.

25. James Wooten, "Carter Aides Doubt Change in Campaign Strategy," *New York Times,* July 18, 1976, 24; Kenneth Reich, "Down-Home Image Aids Carter," *Los Angeles Times,* August 1, 1976, G3.

26. Reich, "Down-Home Image Aids Carter," G3.

27. Ibid.

28. *Chicago Tribune* columnist Jim Squires critiqued this trend, which prompted journalists bent on justifying their own existences "to report the most intimate—and often inane—details about the lives of famous people." Jim Squires, "News of Carter's Cat Kills Curiosity," *Chicago Tribune,* July 25, 1976, A6.

29. Theodore H. White to Jody Powell, June 29, 1976, Correspondence from the Public, New York [2], Box 325: Correspondence from the Public, New York [1] through Correspondence from the Public, New York [4], JCPPP, PC, Press Office-BRSF, JCPL.

30. Ibid.; Crouse, *Boys on the Bus,* 37. White was not the only journalist collecting material for a tell-all campaign biography. On July 26, *Newsday* reporter Martin Schram contacted Rainwater to notify Carter and his staff that his series of columns would be published as a forthcoming campaign biography with Simon and Schuster's Pocket Books Division. In the letter, Schram asked Rainwater and the press staff to correct any statements of error found in his columns and requested additional anecdotes that he might incorporate into the volume. Martin Schram to Betty Rainwater, July 26, 1976, Correspondence from the Media, Washington [1], Box 322: Correspondence from the Media, Washington [1] through Correspondence from the Public, California [3], JCPPP, PC, Press Office-BRSF, JCPL.

31. As quoted in Eric Page, "Theodore H. White, Chronicler of U.S. Politics, Is Dead at 71," *New York Times,* May 16, 1986, http://www.nytimes.com/1986/05/16/obituaries/theodore-white-chronicler-of-us-politics-is-dead-at-71.html?pagewanted=all.

32. Theodore H. White to Jody Powell, June 29, 1976, Correspondence from the Public, New York [2], Box 325: Correspondence from the Public, New York [1] through Correspondence from the Public, New York [4], JCPPP, PC, Press Office-BRSF, JCPL.

33. Carter, interview with the author, October 17, 2014.

34. As quoted in Elliott Abrams, "In Search of History," *Commentary Magazine,* November 1, 1978, https://www.commentarymagazine.com/articles/in-search-of-history-by-theodore-h-white/.

35. Theodore H. White to Jody Powell, June 29, 1976, Correspondence from the Public, New York [2], Box 325: Correspondence from the Public, New York [1] through Correspondence from the Public, New York [4], JCPPP, PC, Press Office-BRSF, JCPL; Crouse, *Boys on the Bus,* 37; Scott Porch, "The Book That Changed Campaigns Forever," *Politico,* April 22, 2015, https://www.politico.com/magazine/story/2015/04/teddy-white-political-journalism-117090_full.html.

36. As quoted in Elliott Abrams, "In Search of History," *Commentary Magazine,* November 1, 1978, https://www.commentarymagazine.com/articles/in-search-of-history-by-theodore-h-white/.

37. As quoted in Zelizer, *Jimmy Carter,* 38.

38. As quoted in Witcover, *Marathon,* 513. "There were people who tended to look down their nose at this whole southern culture that we were living in," Wilkie contended. "There was this one reporter, who showed up and bought himself a pair of overalls and a straw hat and put a piece of hay in his mouth. It was disgusting, condescending. He was a New York

reporter, and I won't name him. But . . . it was disgusting." Wilkie, interview with the author, January 16, 2017.

39. Vann Woodward, "W. J. Cash Reconsidered," http://www.nybooks.com/articles/1969 /12/04/wj-cash-reconsidered/; Roberts and Klibanoff, *The Race Beat*; Jansson, "Internal Orientalism in America," 293–316.

40. "The Candidate: How Southern Is He?" *Time,* September 27, 1976, 46–47.

41. Curtis Wilkie, "For Blacks in Carter's Hometown, the Tracks Are Still There," *Boston Globe,* July 25, 1976, 1.

42. Carl Leubsdorf, "Contradictory Traits: Rural South Shaped Carter's Flexibility," *Baltimore Sun,* July 18, 1976, 1.

43. Peter Goldman, Eleanor Clift, Hal Bruno, and James Doyle, "The Jimmycrats," *Newsweek,* July 26, 1976, 16.

44. Wilkie, interview with the author, January 16, 2017.

45. UPI, "Black Man's House Near Carter's Razed," *New York Times,* July 30, 1976, 6.

46. Wilkie, interview with the author, January 16, 2017.

47. Ibid.; UPI, "Black Man's House Near Carter's Razed," 6.

48. Kenneth Reich, "Among the Media: Carter Press Chief Polite but Peppery," *Los Angeles Times,* August 8, 1976, D1.

49. Ibid.

50. The National Press Club did not accept female members until 1971. Schulman and Zelizer, *Media Nation,* 77–96. Western Union Mailgram, Ellen Wadley to Jody Powell and Barbara Blum, 08/10/76, File: Correspondence from the Media, Washington [1], Box 322: Correspondence from the Media, Washington [1] through Correspondence from the Public, California [3], JCPPP, PC, Press Office-BRSF, JCPL; Doreen Mattingly, *A Feminist in the White House: Midge Constanza, the Carter Years, and America's Culture Wars* (New York: Oxford Univ. Press, 2016), 78–79; Bourne, *Jimmy Carter,* 241, 315, 345.

51. Helen Dewar, "Plains Sunday School Class Admits Women Journalists," *Washington Post,* August 16, 1976, 13; "2 Women Cover Men's Class at Carter Church," *Los Angeles Times,* August 16, 1976, B13.

52. Powell was concerned that the episode might contribute to a media firestorm surrounding the campaign's sexist comments about women and its patriarchal treatment of its female staff and journalists. Western Union Mailgram, Ellen Wadley to Jody Powell and Barbara Blum, 08/10/76, Correspondence from the Media, Washington [1], Box 322: Correspondence from the Media, Washington [1] through Correspondence from the Public, California [3], JCPPP, PC, Press Office-BRSF, JCPL; Mattingly, *A Feminist in the White House,* 78–79; Bourne, *Jimmy Carter,* 241, 315, 345.

53. Helen Dewar, "And Then You Can Always Go Over and Listen to the Weevils," *Washington Post,* August 6, 1976, A2.

54. Eleanor Randolph, "Can 'Bionic Peanut' Become a Regular Guy," *Chicago Tribune,* August 8, 1976, 22.

55. David Broder, *Democratic Review,* July/August 1976, Democratic Review, Box 4: "Correspondence-Request for Actuality Phone Number through Forms-Talk Show Final Disposition," RWHPO, Media Liaison Office, Bradley Woodward's Subject Files, JCPL; Randolph, "Can 'Bionic Peanut' Become a Regular Guy," 22; Eleanor Randolph, "Covering Carter's

Camp-aign," *Chicago Tribune,* August 19, 1976, B1; Reich, "Down-Home Image Aids Carter," G3; Dewar, "And Then You Can Always Go Over and Listen to the Weevils," A2; Adam Clymer, "Letters from Plains: Beer, TV Allowed at Camp Carter," *Baltimore Sun,* August 1, 1976, A6.

56. Jeff Prugh, "Winning Pitcher," *Los Angeles Times,* July 25, 1976, 1. "He certainly took it more seriously than [his brother] Billy or many of the journalists [who would often take a sip of beer between pitches]," Wilkie asserted, recalling his infamous collision with Carter: "The first batter hit a pop foul out to me. I'm standing there ready to catch it, and I hear Carter tromping over toward me. And, he damned near knocked me down, and he caught the ball himself. I still have in my office an AP picture of he and I colliding. I said something like, 'Damn governor. Now I know what Scoop Jackson felt like.' And, Carter just quickly responded, 'Ahh . . . just another run-in with the *Boston Globe.*'" Wilkie also recounted another incident from the diamond that spoke to Carter's relentless nature. "I remember one time he declared he was going to be the umpire, and he called Jody [Powell] out at first base, and Jody looked over at the rest of us and says, 'He is a mean little son of a bitch, isn't he?' And, Jimmy Carter did not like that at all. He gave Jody this piercing glare that he was so good at, and I think Jody knew he better not refer to his boss even flippantly as a son of a bitch again." Wilkie, interview with the author, January 16, 2017; Drew, *American Journal,* 349; Witcover, *Marathon,* 523.

57. Clymer, "Letters from Plains: Beer, TV Allowed at Camp Carter," A6; Randolph, "Covering Carter's Camp-aign," B1; Reich, "Down-Home Image Aids Carter," G3.

58. Bill Neikirk, "Democratic Convention: The Candidate—An Enigma Wrapped Up in a Grin," *Chicago Tribune,* July 15, 1976, 10; Barber, *Race for the Presidency,* 111–46; Barber, *The Pulse of Politics,* 205; Alan Elms, *Uncovering Lives: The Uneasy Alliance of Biography and Psychology* (New York: Oxford Univ. Press, 1997), 187–205.

59. Norman Mailer, "The Search for Jimmy Carter," *New York Times Magazine,* September 26, 1976, 15.

60. Ibid., 90.

61. Ibid., 70; Peter Goldman and Eleanor Clift, "Carter on the Rise," *Newsweek,* March 8, 1976, 25; Ernest Freeberg, *The Age of Edison: Electric Light and the Invention of Modern America* (New York: Penguin, 2013).

62. Lauren Budorick, "Work of the Week: Jimmy Carter II," February 20, 2013, Nasher Museum of Art at Duke University, retrieved at https://alnwadi.com/andy-warhol-jimmy-carter/andy-warhol-jimmy-carter-work-of-the-week-jimmy-carter-ii-andy-warhol-the-nasher/.

63. Photograph, Andy Warhol, "Jimmy Carter, 1976," Polaroid Polacolor Type 108, The Andy Warhol Museum, Pittsburgh; Andy Warhol and Bob Colacello, *Andy Warhol's Exposures* (New York: Grosset and Dunlap, 1976), 93–96; Mark Lawrence Rosenthal, *Regarding Warhol: Sixty Artists, Fifty Years* (New York: Metropolitan Museum of Art, 2002), 262; Carter Ratcliff, *Andy Warhol* (New York: Abbeville Press, 1983), 74; Helen Dewar, "Capricorn Picnic: Chicken, Rock and Carter," *Washington Post,* August 20, 1976, B4. Carter's imagecraft apparatus encouraged Carter to forgo the event, asserting that the drug-fueled environment might tarnish his presidential image, but Carter insisted on attending the picnic before he left town for a rare pre–Labor Day campaign tour, a four-day "non-political" campaign trip to the West Coast and Midwest. Stroud, *How Jimmy Won,* 333–36; Glad, *Jimmy Carter,* 375.

64. Neikirk, "Democratic Convention: The Candidate—An Enigma Wrapped Up in a Grin," 10; Christopher Bonanos, *The Instant: The Story of Polaroid,* (New York: Chronicle Books,

2012), 92. Carter claimed the absence of his signature smile reflected the financial struggles dogging his campaign and contributing to a prolonged hiatus in Plains, but it also was indicative of his feelings toward the "establishment media." *Public Papers of the Presidents of the United States, Jimmy Carter, 1977, Book 1: January 20 to June 24, 1977* (Washington, D.C., Government Printing Office, 1978), 1117–18; Curtis Wilkie, "Summer of '76 Is Over in Plains," *Boston Globe,* September 7, 1976, 12; Randolph, "Can 'Bionic Peanut' Become a Regular Guy?" 22.

65. Andy Warhol, "Jimmy Carter 150," Revolver Gallery, http://revolverwarholgallery.com /portfolio/jimmy-carter-150/. In an "inventive" drawing he retained for his personal collection, Warhol considered the more enigmatic elements of Jimmy Carter's political persona. Drawing, Andy Warhol, "Jimmy Carter," Graphite Paper, National Portrait Gallery, Smithsonian, http:// npg.si.edu/object/npg_NPG.2005.53.

66. Cover, *New York Times Magazine,* September 26, 1976; Mailer, "The Search for Jimmy Carter," 90. Some Carter enthusiasts set aside the magazine as a keepsake; others purchased one of the two hundred prints of Jimmy Carter I and Jimmy Carter I FSII.150 offered as a limited-edition series by the DNC as a mechanism to attract the youth vote and to raise funds for Carter's campaign. The screenprints, which represented Warhol's recent foray into experimentation with the incorporation of both photography and printmaking to emulate painting, were based on the same Polaroids collected in Plains, albeit with crudely altered facial features. Drawings, Andy Warhol, "Jimmy Carter, 1976," Graphite on J. Green Paper, The Andy Warhol Museum, Pittsburgh; Screen Prints, Andy Warhol, "Jimmy Carter I, 1976," Screenprint on Strathmore Bristol Paper, The Andy Warhol Museum, Pittsburgh; Warhol, "Jimmy Carter 150," Revolver Gallery, http://revolverwarholgallery.com/portfolio/jimmy-carter-150/; *Public Papers of the Presidents of the United States, Jimmy Carter, 1977, Book 1: January 20 to June 24, 1977* (Washington, D.C., Government Printing Office), 1117–18.

67. Wilkie, "Summer of '76 Is Over in Plains," 12; Olson, interview with the author, August 11, 2014.

68. Olson, interview with the author, August 11, 2014.

69. Jim Gannon, "Who Is Jimmy Carter," *Boston Globe,* July 18, 1976, A6; Harold Melanson, "Illustration for the Globe," *Boston Globe,* July 18, 1976, A6.

70. Cover, *New York Times Magazine,* September 26, 1976.

71. Memorandum, Hamilton Jordan to Jimmy Carter, "Democratic National Convention," May 1976, File: Memorandum-Hamilton Jordan to Jimmy Carter, General Election, Box 39: Issues Task Force-Members List and Resumes through Memorandums-Political Strategy [2], CFP-PC, JCPL.

72. David Broder, "The Computer-Driven Candidate," *Washington Post,* September 12, 1976, 35.

73. Schmidt et al., *The Disappearing God Gap,* 107.

8. LUSTING IN MY HEART FOR JACK KENNEDY AND BOB WOODWARD

1. Eleanor Randolph, "Carter Campaign Gets a Cutting Start," *Chicago Tribune,* September 6, 1976, 2.

2. Ibid.; Blumenthal, *The Permanent Campaign,* 37–38.

3. Stanley, "Going Beyond the New Deal," 71; Giesmer, *Don't Blame Us,* 256, 238–41.

4. Jack Germond and Jules Witcover, "Ridicule: Cruelest of All," *Boston Globe,* September 3, 1979, 35; Robert Scheer, "Playboy Interview: Jimmy Carter," *Playboy,* November 1976, 63–86.

5. Baudrillard, *Simulacra and Simulation,* 123–24.

6. Horner and Carver, *Saturday Night Live and the 1976 Presidential Election*; Crouse, *Boys on the Bus,* 339–55; Thompson, *Fear and Loathing on the Campaign Trail '72,* 304–70; James Naughton, "The 1972 Campaign," *New York Times,* September 3, 1972, 22.

7. Witcover, *Marathon,* 530–38; Memorandum, Robert Teeter to Richard Cheney, "National Poll," December 24, 1975, "Teeter, Robert—Memoranda and Polling Data (3)"; Box 4: Foster Chanock Files, GRFPL; Crain, *The Ford Presidency,* 272; Johnson, *Democracy for Hire,* 223.

8. As political consultant Stu Spencer explained: "Mr. President, as a campaigner, you're no fucking good." As quoted in Crain, *The Ford Presidency,* 272.

9. Ibid.; "Campaign Strategy for President Ford, 1976," Presidential Campaign—Campaign Strategy Program (1), Box 1: Dorothy Dowton Files, GRFPL.

10. As quoted in Blumenthal, *Permanent Campaign,* 38.

11. Hamilton Jordan to Jimmy Carter and Walter Mondale, July 1976, Memorandum/ Analysis-Hamilton Jordan to Jimmy Carter, 7/76, Box 199: DC-FSCMPM, PC-CDO-HJCSF, JCPL; Bourne, *Jimmy Carter,* 342; Witcover, *Marathon,* 518–19.

12. Hamilton Jordan to Jimmy Carter and Walter Mondale, July 1976, Memorandum/ Analysis-Hamilton Jordan to Jimmy Carter, 7/76, Box 199: DC-FSCMPM, PC-CDO-HJCSF, JCPL.

13. As quoted in Drew, *American Journal,* 347, 348–49; Glad, *Jimmy Carter,* 375; Witcover, *Marathon,* 523.

14. Stroud, *How Jimmy Won,* 333–36. In an August memo, Jordan offered an uncharacteristic rebuke: "I thought the tone of your remarks last week in New Hampshire were highly partisan and unpresidential. I feel that you should re-examine the manner in which you publicly discuss Ford's relationship with Richard Nixon. The American people perceive Gerald Ford as being an honest, well-intentioned man who inherited a job bigger than he can handle. They see many of the same attractive personal qualities in you, but have made the tentative judgment that you are more capable of leading the country than Ford. I do not worry in the weeks and months ahead that we can clearly demonstrate that you are a better-qualified person to lead the country and manage the government. I do worry that our campaign rhetoric might undermine the favorable personal image that you have with the American voters." Jordan encouraged Carter to cease personal attacks of Ford and eliminate the term "Nixon-Ford Administration" from his lingo. Carter ignored the recommendation. As quoted in Witcover, *Marathon,* 524.

15. Scheer, "Playboy Interview: Jimmy Carter," 63–86.

16. Jules Witcover, "Carter Race Will Follow Early Plans," *Washington Post,* September 7, 1976, A1.

17. Brownell, *Showbiz Politics,* 1–11.

18. Both Carter and Ford accepted federal financing and budgeted approximately half of their $21.8 million Treasury disbursement for advertising. James M. Naughton, "The 1972 Campaign," *New York Times,* September 3, 1972, 22; Hamilton Jordan to Jimmy Carter, "Democratic National Convention," May 1976, Memorandum-Hamilton Jordan to Jimmy Carter, General Election, Box 39: Issues Task Force-Members List and Resumes through Memorandums-Political Strategy [2], CFP-CF, JCPL; Crain, *The Ford Presidency,* 272–74.

19. Exploiting the power of organized labor, Truman and his successors launched general election campaigns with rousing Labor Day rallies in Detroit's Cadillac Square, but on the eve of the 1968 general election campaign pro-union Democrat Hubert Humphrey could not rely on enough public support from UAW members to stage a successful kickoff rally from Detroit. Aware of fractured union leadership and growing resentment from the working class, McGovern bypassed Detroit to launch his campaign with union rallies in Ohio and California, and Nixon's strategists joked he should consider visiting "Cadillac Square on Labor Day." James M. Naughton, "The 1972 Campaign," *New York Times,* September 3, 1972, 22; Cowie, *Stayin' Alive,* 159–60; David Farber, ed., *The Sixties: From Memory to History* (Chapel Hill: Univ. of North Carolina Press, 2012), 307. Campaign reporters biased toward image deconstruction failed to note echoes of Wallace's trip to the Daytona 500 in 1972. Thompson, *Fear and Loathing on the Campaign Trail '72,* 116. Ford's staff countered Carter's Labor Day kickoff with a Rose Garden appearance and an assault by campaign surrogate Bob Dole. They staged Ford's general election kickoff for September 15 at the University of Michigan's Chrysler Arena, where he attacked Carter's primary campaign theme, contending that "trust must be earned." Crain, *The Ford Presidency,* 273.

20. Hamilton Jordan to Jimmy Carter, "Democratic National Convention," May 1976, Memorandum-Hamilton Jordan to Jimmy Carter, General Election, Box 39: Issues Task Force-Members List and Resumes through Memorandums-Political Strategy [2], CFP-CF, JCPL.

21. Ibid.; Witcover, *Marathon,* 520.

22. Curtis Wilkie, "Carter Fires Opening Gun," *Boston Globe,* September 7, 1976, 1.

23. David Broder, "Carter Pledges Restoration of 'Strength, Hope,'" *Washington Post,* September 7, 1976, A1.

24. Ibid.

25. Wilkie, "Carter Fires Opening Gun," 1.

26. Bill Boyarsky, "Carter Says that People Are His Special Interest," *Los Angeles Times,* September 7, 1976, 1; Broder, "Carter Pledges Restoration of 'Strength, Hope,'" A1; R. W. Apple Jr., "Contrasting Campaign Symbols," *New York Times,* September 7, 1976, 1; R. W. Apple Jr., "Warm Springs: A Taste of Thriving Yesteryear," *New York Times,* September 7, 1976, 25; James Wooten, "Carter, Emulating Truman in '48," *New York Times,* September 21, 1976, 26; Charles Mohr, "Carter Opens Drive by Denouncing Ford as Timid President," *New York Times,* September 7, 1976, 1.

27. Mohr, "Carter Opens Drive by Denouncing Ford as Timid President," 1; Wilkie, "Carter Fires Opening Gun," 1; Zelizer, *Jimmy Carter,* 47.

28. Broder, "Carter Pledges Restoration of 'Strength, Hope,'" A1; Bill Boyarsky, "Trip North Reveals Insights into Carter: Incomplete Source," *Los Angeles Times,* September 9, 1976, 1; Pressman, *On Press,* 77–78.

29. Whillmint Boyster, "The Enigmatic Man," *Wall Street Journal,* September 8, 1976, 22.

30. Aldo Beckman, "For Cameras, Ford Delivers Rose Garden," *Chicago Tribune,* September 8, 1976, 2; Zelizer, *Jimmy Carter,* 46.

31. *Washington Post* and *Chicago Tribune* reporters acknowledged that Ford was engaging in a presidential strategy, a "well-orchestrated plan to match Jimmy Carter minute for minute on the evening network news shows." Edward Walsh, "President Displays Strategy," *Washington Post,* September 8, 1976, A1; Beckman, "For Cameras, Ford Delivers Rose Garden,"

2. Broadcast correspondents also explored the campaign tactic. On September 13, Schieffer acknowledged Ford's strategy in a voiceover: "As part of the strategy suggesting that he's the incumbent, Mr. Ford goes to the Rose Garden almost daily now to sign legislation. Today's ceremony to sign a so-called Sunshine Bill," Schieffer asserted in his lead-in about Ford's enactment of the freedom of information law designed to create greater transparency in government. Overall Coverage of Campaign '76. Daily Coverage of Carter and Ford [entry title: CBS News Coverage of Campaign '76], PAC, 76061 NWT 3 of 4, WJBMAPAC; Supporting Materials, File 76061 NWT, Box 99: PAE, HRBML.

32. Greenberg, *Nixon's Shadow.*

33. Greenberg, *Republic of Spin,* 397–98; Staff Report: "What We Have to Say, 9/20/1976," Staff Reports, Box 275: Nixon Campaign Tracking, 1972 through State Election Monitoring from Notebook [2], JCPPP, PC, Situation Room Administrative Assistant-Bill Simon's Subject Files, JCPL; File: DNC Train, Box 404: AFL-CIO through First Person Articles, JCPPP, PC, LP-PO-SF, JCPL; Wilkie, "Carter Fires Opening Gun," 1; Drew, *American Journal,* 412; Bourne, *Jimmy Carter,* 341. After midcentury, political actors, such as Robert Kennedy, Ed Muskie, and George McGovern, staged whistle-stops as part of their media campaigns. Thompson, *Fear and Loathing on the Campaign Trail '72,* 81.

34. Crain, *The Ford Presidency,* 258–59.

35. Bourne, *Jimmy Carter,* 346; Stroud, *How Jimmy Won,* 349–50; Glad, *Jimmy Carter,* 382–83.

36. As quoted in Patrick Anderson, *Electing Jimmy Carter: The Campaign of 1976* (Baton Rouge, Louisiana State Univ. Press, 1994), 107.

37. Ibid.; Wooten, "Carter, Emulating Truman in '48, 'Whistle-Stops' in Three States," 26; "Campaign 1976/Carter/Train Trip/Playboy Interview," CBS Evening News, September 20, 1976, VTNAC; AP, "Carter Admits to 'Adultery in My Heart': Calls Christ's Standards Almost Impossible," *Los Angeles Times,* September 20, 1976, A2; Witcover, *Marathon,* 562–67.

38. Scheer, "Playboy Interview: Jimmy Carter," 63–86.

39. Ibid.; "He was very defensive about it and so were members of his staff," Wilkie recalled. "I remember just thinking, 'Oh my God, what have we gotten into?'" Wilkie, interview with the author, January 16, 2017; Stroud, *How Jimmy Won,* 352–53.

40. As quoted in Anderson, *Electing Jimmy Carter,* 107.

41. Brokaw reached out to Powell for comment, but he only responded with a quip—"just remind them that this is about Carter not Ham [Jordan] and me." His response indicated to Brokaw that he did not understand the interview's implications. Brokaw, interview with the author, April 3, 2017.

42. Carter resisted the query because of the extensive time commitment. While most trail reporters requested fifteen minutes to an hour with the presidential aspirant, Scheer sought a twelve-hour window to construct his long-form piece. Powell rejected this condition, consenting to five hours in smaller blocks of time and demanding final approval over transcripts before the issue went to print. Stroud, *How Jimmy Won,* 344–46. The interview's origin story lacks a consensus account. Golson contended that Jordan and Powell, impressed with Scheer's interview of Democratic candidate Jerry Brown in the April issue, contacted the magazine to arrange an interview. Barry Golson, *The Playboy Interview* (New York: Playboy Press, 1981), 457–59. Several Carter staff members asserted that they turned down the initial request, but

Powell relented when Scheer and Golson persisted. They contended Caddell, Carter's son Chip, and his new speechwriter Patrick Anderson were interview advocates. Rafshoon, interview with the author, August 12, 2014. "The first person to suggest, as far as I know, the President do the *Playboy* interview was Pat Anderson. . . . Anderson said he was a good, responsible reporter. He convinced Jody that it would be a good thing to do and that *Playboy* would reach a large number of people who did not know Jimmy Carter, young people and liberal people . . . and that would be a good forum for Carter." Schneiders, interview with the author, August 25, 2014; David Alsobrook, exit interview with Greg Schneiders, August 6, 1979, JCPL, https://www.jimmycarterlibrary.gov/assets/documents/oral_histories/exit_interviews/Schneiders.pdf; Josh Sanburn, "Brief History: Playboy," *Time,* January 24, 2011, http://content.time.com/time/magazine/article/0,9171,2042352,00.html. Many reporters also conceded that the *Playboy* interview was a strategic effort to appeal to a broader audience. "I think the *Playboy* interview was calculated. I think they decided that he needed to reach out to a different audience. He was a Sunday school teacher, but he needed to be more than that. And, so he gave that weird interview to *Playboy,*" Mears asserted. Mears, interview with the author, August 18, 2014.

43. Carter, interview with the author, October 17, 2014. "We did the *Playboy* interview to show being a born-again Christian was not a threat to more secular Democrats and young people," Caddell recalled. Transcript, "Jimmy Carter," PBS, American Experience, 2013, https://www.pbs.org/wgbh/americanexperience/films/carter/#transcript; Jagoda, interview with the author, January 10, 2017.

44. As quoted in Robert Scheer, *Playing President: My Close Encounters with Nixon, Carter, Bush I, Reagan, and Clinton—And How They Didn't Prepare Me for George W. Bush* (New York: Akashic, 2006), 60.

45. As quoted in Scheer, "Hullabaloo over Lust Lasts 20 Years," http://articles.latimes.com/1996-12-17/local/me-9919_1_jimmy-carter; Witcover, *Marathon,* 563.

46. As quoted in Scheer, *Playing President,* 59–60.

47. Scheer, "Playboy Interview: Jimmy Carter," 63–86. Carter maintained that the comments were off the record: "It was only when they got to the door, and they were leaving, I didn't even realize that the tape recorder was going still, but it was. They asked me about the, you know, the famous questions. So, then it became a—a very devastating . . . ah . . . report for me, because it made it look as though I—was—you know, lured to many women instead of my wife." Carter, interview with the author, October 17, 2014. Scheer disputed Carter's version: "At the final session, which took place in the living room of Carter's home in Plains, the allotted time was up. A press aide indicated that there were other appointments for which Carter was already late, and the aide opened the front door while niceties were exchanged. As the interviewer and the *Playboy* editor stood at the door, recording equipment in their arms, a final, seemingly casual question was tossed off. Carter then delivered a long, softly spoken monolog [*sic*] that grew in intensity as he made his final points. One of the journalists signaled to Carter that they were still taping, to which Carter nodded his assent." Scheer, "Playboy Interview: Jimmy Carter," 63–86. Twenty years later, Scheer elaborated on the moment: "As Carter began his closing monologue, Golson said to him, as heard clearly on the tape, 'I'm taking mental notes if you don't mind.' At which point I said, waving a large microphone, 'I'm taking real notes,' and Carter laughed and said, 'good,' well before the infamous lust remarks

were uttered." Scheer, "Hullabaloo over Lust Lasts 20 Years," http://articles.latimes.com/1996 -12-17/local/me-9919_1_jimmy-carter.

48. Anderson, *Electing Jimmy Carter,* 108; Bourne, *Jimmy Carter,* 347; Witcover, *Marathon,* 564–67.

49. "Campaign 1976/Carter/Playboy Interview," NBC, September 20, 1976, VTNAC; "Carter/Johnson/Playboy/Comment (Sexual Morality)," CBS, September 23, 1976, VTNAC.

50. As quoted in Mohr, "Carter, on Morals, Talks with Candor," 1.

51. Drew, *American Journal,* 430–31.

52. A search of ProQuest Historical Newspapers, for instance, turned up more than eight hundred news texts featuring Carter's name, alongside *Playboy* and lust, from September 20 until election day; the database isolated 188 texts in the following week alone.

53. Stephen Crimmin, "Theologians Support Carter's Philosophy," *Boston Globe,* September 22, 1976, 17; "The Playboy Adviser," *Boston Globe,* September 22, 1976, 18; UPI, "Interview by Carter Criticized," *Hartford Courant,* September 22, 1976, 8; Myra MacPherson, "Evangelicals Seen Cooling on Carter," *Washington Post,* September 27, 1976, A1; Glad, *Jimmy Carter,* 384; Miller, *The Age of Evangelicalism,* 45. In the aftermath, he encountered a flood of "bad press" in newspapers and magazines. James Reston, "Press, Politics, Power," *New York Times,* October 3, 1976, 157; UPI, "Carter Wrong to Give Playboy Article—Reagan," *Los Angeles Times,* October 1, 1976, B3; Patrick Buchanan, "Carter Is Losing the Race to Himself," *Chicago Tribune,* October 3, 1976, A3; "TV Times Is Offered by a Carter Critic," *New York Times,* October 13, 1976, 23; David Gelman and Ann Lallande, "The Great Playboy Furor," *Newsweek,* October 4, 1976, 70; "The Campaign: When Their Power Failed," *Time,* October 4, 1976, 14–18. He also became a target of ridicule in cartoons and sketch comedy routines. Paul Conrad, "Jimmy Carter," *Los Angeles Times,* September 1976, https://www.latimes.com/local/obituaries/la-me-paul-conrad -20100905-story.html; editorial cartoon, *Toronto Star,* September 28, 1976, File: Playboy, Box 406: Maritime Union through State File: California, JCPPP, PC, LP-PO, JCPL; Williams, *God's Own Party,* 124–29. Although Ford remained the primary target of castigation on *Saturday Night Live,* the cast parodied a Carter campaign commercial, incorporating a "lusty" version of the Beach Boys song "California Girls" on September 24. Saturday Night Live Season Two, Episode One, https://www.nbc.com/saturday-night-live/season-2/episode/1-lily-tomlin-with -james-taylor-65256; Horner and Carver, *Saturday Night Live and the 1976 Presidential Election,* 116–17.

54. Mary McGrory, "Confession in Season," *Boston Globe,* September 22, 1976, 19.

55. Miller, *The Age of Evangelicalism,* 47–48. Encountering allegations of illegal contributions, Ford's staff could not capitalize on the *Playboy* incident as much as they hoped. Crain, *The Ford Presidency,* 274–75.

56. Robert Shogan, "Carter Whistle Stops Through the East," *Los Angeles Times,* September 21, 1976, 1; Zelizer, *Jimmy Carter,* 50.

57. Jody to Gov., Handwritten Notes [4], Box 21: Handwritten Notes [1] through Handwritten Notes [4], JPP-SF, JCPL.

58. As quoted in Bourne, *Jimmy Carter,* 346; Witcover, *Marathon,* 560.

59. As quoted in Kalman, *Right Star Rising,* 174.

60. Mary McGrory, "Carter's Albatross," *Boston Globe,* September 27, 1976, 14.

61. Witcover, *Marathon,* 561.

62. Scheer, "Hullabaloo over Lust Lasts 20 Years," http://articles.latimes.com/1996-12-17 /local/me-9919_1_jimmy-carter; Transcripts, Playboy, Box 417: Agendas and Questionnaires through Telephone Logs, JCPPP, PC, Scott Burnett's Subject Files, JCPL; Jody Telephone Log, Thurs., Sept. 16, Message Logs, Box 31 Message Logs through News Clippings [2], JPP-SF, JCPL; Witcover, *Marathon,* 527, 561–62.

63. "Top 10 Unfortunate Political One-Liners," *Time,* November 17, 2015, http://content .time.com/time/specials/packages/article/0,28804,1859513_1859526_1859518,00.html; Phil Wise, "Media Commentary," September 21, 1976, [Issues—General Election, 1975–1976]: Box 6: Expense Statements—Phil Wise, 1975–1976 through [Media, n.d.], PWP, JCPL; Phil Wise to Landon Butler, "'Letter to the Editors' Campaign," [Issues—General Election, 1975–1976]: Box 6: Expense Statements—Phil Wise, 1975–1976 through [Media, n.d.], PWP, JCPL; Media Clips, File, "1976 Campaign Materials RSC [incl. reaction to Playboy interview]," Box 1: Campaign Materials: Rosalynn's Reaction to Jimmy Carter's Playboy Interview through First Ladies Conference Sponsored by Mrs. Gerald Ford, Mary Finch Hoyt Papers, Donated Historical Material, JCPL; Stroud, *How Jimmy Won,* 356–59.

64. "Rosalynn Carter: He Doesn't Have to Explain," *Chicago Tribune,* September 21, 1976, 14.

65. Chuck Parrish to John Carlin, "Rosalynn Carter's Visit/LBJ," September 23, 1976, "Field Office Information Directories & Memos," Box 272: Daily Political Reports and Reports to Plane, 10/76 through GOP Tracking-State Offices, JCPPP, PC, Situation Room Administrative Assistant-Bill Simon's Subject Files, JCPL; Media Clips, "1976 Campaign Materials RSC [incl. reaction to Playboy interview]," Box 1: Campaign Materials: Rosalynn's Reaction to Jimmy Carter's Playboy Interview through First Ladies Conference Sponsored by Mrs. Gerald Ford, Mary Finch Hoyt Papers, Donated Historical Material, JCPL; Gerald Rafshoon, "Rose," 1976 Democratic Presidential Campaign Committee, Inc., Museum of the Moving Image, The Living Room Candidate: Presidential Campaign Commercials, 1952–2012, http://www.livingroom candidate.org/commercials/1976.

66. Carter, interview with the author, October 17, 2014.

67. "Mrs. Mondale Has No Doubts," *Hartford Courant,* September 23, 1976, 53.

68. UPI, "Jack Carter, 29, Says He's Lusted, Too—In His Heart," *Los Angeles Times,* September 22, 1976, A2.

69. William Benoit, "Image Restoration Discourse and Crisis Communication," *Public Relations Review* 23 (1997): 177–86; Mohr, "Carter, on Morals, Talks with Candor," 1.

70. Image repair and crisis management literature in the coming years indicated the effectiveness of an immediate straightforward apology for image restoration. Grunig and Hunt, *Managing Public Relations,* 1–576; Benoit, "Image Restoration Discourse and Crisis Communication," 177–86.

71. Daily Political Report, September 20, 1976, Daily Political Reports—9/16/76–9/30/76, Box 410: Administration through Daily Political Reports, 9/30/76 [1–3], JCPPP, PC, Tim Kraft, Field Operations Director, Subject Files, JCPL; "The Playboy Adviser," *Boston Globe,* September 22, 1976, 18; Carter's staff monitored coverage of the *Playboy* controversy and supplied colleagues with their analysis. File: "Playboy," Box 406: Maritime Union through State File: California, JCPPP, PC, LP-PO-SF, JCPL; "What the Press Had to Say: Playboy, November 1976,

The Playboy Interview," Playboy Article of Commentary and Correspondence, Box 308: Form Letter-Prot. 1 & Correspondence through Playboy Article of Commentary, JCPPP, PC, Director's Office-Religion Political Affairs Coord., Protestant Desk-David B. Graham, Subject File, JCPL. Carter did not acknowledge any personal responsibility at the outset his self-inflicted wound; instead, he gave a host of other reasons for the evaporation of his lead—a unified Republican Party on the attack, conflicting images of an antiestablishment candidate saddled with the support of the Democratic Party apparatus, and Ford's Rose Garden strategy. Bourne, *Jimmy Carter,* 348–49; Witcover, *Marathon,* 553. Carter later admitted fault: "I can't blame anybody for that article or for the way the press covered it, except myself." As quoted in Witcover, *Marathon,* 570.

72. Overall Coverage of Campaign '76. Daily Coverage of Carter and Ford [entry title: CBS News Coverage of Campaign '76], PAC, 76061 NWT 3 of 4, WJBMAPAC; Supporting Materials, File 76061 NWT, Box 99: PAE, HRBML. Donaldson offered similar perspective. For many, Carter's interview in *Playboy* constituted a mistake in "content and judgment." "Campaign 1976/Carter/Controversies," ABC, September 22, 1976, VTNAC; Drew, *American Journal,* 431. Broadcast reporting not only underscored Carter's gaffe, it also highlighted increasing tension between Carter and the traveling news media.

73. Helen Dewar, "Carter Regrets Implied Insults to LBJ in Playboy," *Washington Post,* September 23, 1976, A5; Robert Shogan, "Carter Rues Johnson Remarks in Texas," *Los Angeles Times,* September 25, 1976, A22; Drew, *American Journal,* 439–41.

74. Carl Leubsdorf, "Carter Sizes Himself Up, Stumbles on Johnson," *Baltimore Sun,* September 25, 1976, A7; Charles Mohr, "Carter, in Texas, Says He's Sorry About His Criticism of Johnson," *New York Times,* September 25, 1976, 1; Bourne, *Jimmy Carter,* 351; Drew, *American Journal,* 444; Witcover, *Marathon,* 581; Stroud, *How Jimmy Won,* 360–72.

75. Scheer, "Hullabaloo over Lust Lasts 20 Years," http://articles.latimes.com/1996-12-17/local/me-9919_1_jimmy-carter.

76. "New York Intelligencer: Campaign Clips," *New York Magazine,* November 15, 1976, 88; Witcover, *Marathon,* 579.

77. Anderson, *Electing Jimmy Carter,* 110–11.

78. As quoted in Schram, *Running for President,* 336.

79. Granum, interview with the author, August 14, 2013.

80. Schram, *Running for President,* 306, 336.

81. John Dillin, "Carter Takes on Newsmen," *Christian Science Monitor,* September 28, 1976, 1.

82. As quoted in Anderson, *Electing Jimmy Carter,* 110–15.

83. Schram, *Running for President,* 342–43.

84. Anderson, *Electing Jimmy Carter,* 116. Donaldson (ABC), Cloud (*Time*), Mears (AP), and Pippert (UPI) did not recall the meeting and noted that Carter and his staff never asked them for advice. Donaldson, interview with the author, January 17, 2017; Cloud, interview with the author, August 11, 2014; Mears, interview with the author, August 18, 2014; Pippert, interview with the author, September 5, 2014.

85. Schram, *Running for President,* 342–43. Witcover declined to attend the impromptu meeting. Witcover, interview with the author, January 18, 2017; Witcover, *Marathon,* 582–83.

86. As quoted in Schram, *Running for President,* 342–43.

87. McGarr, "We're All in This Thing Together," 77–95; Pressman, "Objectivity and Its Discontents," 96–113; Leubsdorf, interview with the author, August 10, 2013; Carl Leubsdorf, "Carter Again Putting Stress on Love, Trust," *Baltimore Sun,* September 27, 1976, A1; Eleanor Randolph, "Aides Think Slip of Lips Sinking Carter's Ship," *Chicago Tribune,* September 27, 1976, 2.

88. Leubsdorf, "Carter Again Putting Stress on Love, Trust," A1.

89. Curtis Wilkie, "Campaign Notebook: Playboy Interview Sidetracks Carter," *Boston Globe,* September 27, 1976, 6.

90. Anderson, *Electing Jimmy Carter,* 116.

91. Perry, "Us and Them This Time," 16–18.

92. Scheer, "Hullabaloo over Lust Lasts 20 Years," http://articles.latimes.com/1996-12-17 /local/me-9919_1_jimmy-carter; Golson, *The Playboy Interview,* 457–59; Granum, interview with the author, August 14, 2013; Rafshoon, interview with the author, August 12, 2014; David Alsobrook, exit interview with Greg Schneiders, August 6, 1979, JCPL, https://www.jimmy carterlibrary.gov/assets/documents/oral_histories/exit_interviews/Schneiders.pdf; Carter, interview with the author, October 17, 2014.

93. Scheer, "Hullabaloo over Lust Lasts 20 Years," http://articles.latimes.com/1996-12-17 /local/me-9919_1_jimmy-carter.

94. Golson, *The Playboy Interview,* 457.

95. Ibid.

96. As quoted in Scheer, "Playboy Interview: Jimmy Carter," 63–86.

97. Brownell, *Showbiz Politics,* 1–11; Greenberg, *Republic of Spin,* 317–95.

98. Robert Scheer, "Jimmy, We Hardly Know Y'All," *Playboy,* November 1976, 98, 186–90.

99. Baudrillard, *Simulacra and Simulation,* 123–24.

100. Hamilton Jordan to Jimmy Carter, "Democratic National Convention," May 1976, Memorandum-Hamilton Jordan to Jimmy Carter, General Election, Box 39: Issues Task Force-Members List and Resumes through Memorandums-Political Strategy [2], CFP-CF, JCPL.

101. Polsby, *Consequences of Party Reform,* 142–43; Crain, *The Ford Presidency,* 272–96.

102. Paul Conrad, "Jimmy Carter," *Los Angeles Times,* September 1976, https://www.la times.com/local/obituaries/la-me-paul-conrad-20100905-story.html.

103. Jill Hackett, "Letters to the Times: Carter's Interview in Playboy Magazine," *Los Angeles Times,* October 3, 1976, E2. Another letter writer, Samira Byron of Arlington, noted that Carter's comments were "refreshing . . . realistic and truthful." Samira Byron, "Letters to the Editor: Reaction to Jimmy Carter's Playboy Interview," *Washington Post,* September 26, 1976, 34.

104. Horner and Carver, *Saturday Night Live and the 1976 Presidential Election.*

105. Carter, interview with the author, October 17, 2014; Zelizer, *Jimmy Carter,* 48–49.

106. John Sides, "The Electoral Effects of Jimmy Carter's Lust," The Monkey Cage, http:// themonkeycage.org/2010/09/the_electoral_effects_of_jimmy/; James Campbell and James Gerrand, *Before the Vote: Forecasting American National Elections* (New York: Sage, 2000), 31.

107. "Top 10 Unfortunate Political One-Liners," http://content.time.com/time/specials /packages/article/0,28804,1859513_1859526_1859518,00.h tml.

108. Schneiders, interview with the author, August 25, 2014.

109. Carter, interview with the author, October 17, 2014.

110. Germond and Witcover, "Ridicule: Cruelest of All," 35.

111. As quoted in Randall Balmer, *Redeemer: The Life of Jimmy Carter* (New York: Basic, 2014), 71.

112. Baudrillard, *Simulacra and Simulation,* 123–24.

9. CONTESTING OPPONENTS, DEBATING THE FUTURE, AND RESISTING MALAISE

1. *Dayton Daily News* published Peters's sketch, and United Features Syndicate distributed it to approximately 250 newspapers, including the *Washington Post.* Peters won a Pulitzer Prize for his political satire in 1981. Mike Peters, "The Trouble Is Not in Your Set," *Washington Post,* October 8, 1976.

2. Ibid. *New York Times* commentator John O'Connor reminded readers: "Suddenly, right there in the middle of Jimmy Carter's sentence, the sound went out . . . and puzzlement momentarily covered the land, which was being force-fed the Presidential debate via live simultaneous transmission on four national hookups. . . . The 'event of the decade,' the confrontation that could possibly decide the next Presidential election, was reduced to the image of two men helplessly waiting on a small stage while anonymous technicians looked for probable causes." John O'Connor, "TV View: Carter Vs. Ford Vs. Television," *New York Times,* October 3, 1976, 87. David Nord described the concepts of *cuing* and *linking* in his taxonomy of newspaper reader response. *Cuing* refers to the religious, political, or ideological reaction triggered by reading a news item. David Nord, "Reading the Newspaper: Strategies and Political Reader Response, Chicago, 1912–1917," *Journal of Communication* 45.3 (1995): 66–94.

3. "What the Press Had To Say," October 10, 1976, Media Publications [1], Box 34: Media Publications [1] through Media Publications [6], JCPPP, PC, Press Office-Betty Rainwater, JCPL; News clip, "Apathy," File, Media Publications [16], Box 344: Media Publications [14] through Media Publications [19], JCPPP, PC, Press Office-Betty Rainwater, Subject Files, JCPL.

4. Scheer, "Playboy Interview: Jimmy Carter," 63–86; Jack Anderson, "Issues Are Lost in Campaign Debris," *Washington Post,* October 3, 1976, 39.

5. Anderson, "Issues Are Lost in Campaign Debris," 39.

6. Brownell, *Showbiz Politics,* 231.

7. Robert Friedenberg, ed., *Rhetorical Studies of National Political Debates, 1960–1992* (New York: ABC-CLIO, 1993), 2–3, 29. Requests for broadcast debates were not novel but were controversial. In May 1948, Republican presidential candidates Harold Stassen and Thomas Dewey debated before a national radio audience. In the aftermath of his 1956 campaign, Adlai Stevenson, lamenting the state of television, recommended transforming "our circus-atmosphere presidential campaign into a great debate conducted in full view of all the people." As quoted in Minow and LaMay, *Inside the Presidential Debates,* 20, 19–27. At his prompting, Congress considered the measure amid loud complaints from the American Civil Liberties Union, which asserted that the amendment should extend free time to *all* legally qualified candidates, and prominent members of the broadcast industry, who contended such a provision impeded their First and Fifth Amendment freedoms by regulating political speech *and* seizing valuable property—airtime.

8. Early commentary by political actors and research suggesting the 1960 presidential debates decided the outcome of the general election exaggerated their significance, but it is not an overstatement to suggest, heaped in myth and enshrined in collective memory, that they transformed the political landscape by cementing emphasis on image and soundbites in modern campaigns. Schroeder, *Presidential Debates,* 1–10; Minnow and LaMay, *Inside the Presidential Debates,* 1.

9. Minnow et al., *Inside the Presidential Debates,* 1–16.

10. Ibid., 2

11. Ibid., 44–49; Sidney Kraus, *Televised Presidential Debates and Public Policy* (New York: Routledge, 2013), 203; Schroeder, *Presidential Debates,* 17. Carter engaged in two of three joint appearances during the primary season.

12. As quoted in John Self, *Presidential Debate Negotiations from 1960 to 1988: Setting the Stage for Prime-Time Clashes* (New York: Lexington Books, 2016), 55–57.

13. As quoted in ibid., 56.

14. Pre-debate negotiations included demands surrounding image projection, indicative of the pronounced influence of reformed showbiz politics. Ibid., 57–60.

15. Schroeder, *Presidential Debates,* 114–20; Jim Squires, "Last of Great Debates Leaves Story Unchanged," *Chicago Tribune,* October 24, 1976, 10.

16. Pressman, *Remaking the News,* 1–100; Schroeder, *Presidential Debates,* 114–20.

17. Schroeder, *Presidential Debates,* 114–20.

18. O'Connor, "TV View: Carter Vs. Ford Vs. Television," 87. Approximately half of all U.S. households tuned into the first debate. Crain, *The Ford Presidency,* 275.

19. Crain, *The Ford Presidency,* 275–76; Schroeder, *Presidential Debates,* 120. Research supported this assessment, suggesting that Ford won the first debate and Carter narrowly claimed victory in the final two performances. According to scholars, neither candidate achieved an optimal politeness strategy. William Dailey et al., *Politeness in Presidential Debates: Shaping Political Face in Campaign Debates from 1960 to 2004* (New York: Rowman and Littlefield, 2008), 56–57.

20. They received hundreds of letters, telegrams, and phone calls regarding Carter's performance from mass communication practitioners and professionals in other areas, such as accountant David Price of Brentwood, Tennessee, who encouraged Carter to deconstruct the "honest John image of President Ford." David Price to Phil Wise, September 25, 1976, [Issues] General Election, 1975–1976 [1], Box 6: Expense Statements-Phil Wise, 1975–1976 through [Media, n.d.], PWP, JCPL.

21. Although Ford was not known as a theatrical president, the logic of showbiz politics permeated his campaign, and he engaged in mock rehearsals involving lights, cameras, makeup, and a Carter stand-in. Schroeder, *Presidential Debates,* 94; Crain, *The Ford Presidency,* 275. Before the first debate, Eizenstat's issues team in cooperation with consultants, such as former Kennedy advisor Theodore Sorenson, provided Carter with one briefing book, divided into six parts, including strategy, Carter themes, Ford themes, potential questions and answers based on the issues, analysis of both platforms, and miscellaneous briefing materials. Harry Kelly, "Ford, Carter Take off Gloves in Round 2," *Chicago Tribune,* October 7, 1976, 1; Box 9: Crime 7/74–12/75 through Debates-Briefing Material for Third Debate [1], JCPPP, PC, IO-SE, JCPL; Box 45: Briefing Book 9/24/76 through Democrat vs. Republican Platform,

JCPPP, 1976 PC, Issues Office-David Rubenstein, JCPL.; Box 79: Debate Issues [1] through Debate Issues [7], JCPPP, PC, IO-NS, JCPL. In addition to preparing comprehensive briefing books and scheduling mock debates, Carter's advisors offered multiple analyses of the first debate, including a question-by-question evaluation of both candidates' performances and a memo insisting that Carter should abstain from showing deference to Ford. The latter was in response to the media critique that Carter "looked like a south Georgia boy who had been asked to debate the president of the United States." As quoted in Crain, *The Ford Presidency,* 276. Box 9: Crime 7/74–12/75 through Debates-Briefing Material for Third Debate [1], JCPPP, PC, IO-SE, JCPL; Box 45: Briefing Book 9/24/76 through Democrat vs. Republican Platform, JCPPP, PC, Issues Office-David Rubenstein, JCPL.

22. DeJohngh Franklin to Jimmy Carter, "Debate Suggestions," September 28, 1976, Debates (Reviewed), 2, Box 45: Briefing Book 9/24/76 through Democrat vs. Republican Platform, JCPPP, PC, Issues Office-David Rubenstein, JCPL.

23. Debate Techniques, Debate Issues [1], Box 79: Debate Issues [1] through Debate Issues [7], JCPPP, PC, IO-NS, JCPL; Debates (Reviewed), 2, Box 45: Briefing Book 9/24/76 through Democrat vs. Republican Platform, JCPPP, PC, Issues Office-David Rubenstein, JCPL.

24. Dailey et al., *Politeness in Presidential Debates,* 54–55.

25. Stroud, *How Jimmy Won,* 373–76; Memorandum, Dick Moe to State and Regional Coordinators, October 7, 1976, [Issues] General Election, 1975–1976 [1], Box 6: Expense Statements-Phil Wise, 1975–1976 through [Media, n.d.], PWP, JCPL.

26. Marshall to Field Desks, "Debate Responses," [Issues] General Election, 1975–1976 [1], Box 6: Expense Statements-Phil Wise, 1975–1976 through [Media, n.d.], PWP, JCPL.

27. Witcover, *Marathon,* 594–95.

28. Belin encouraged Ford to accentuate positive features, including his most important accomplishment (restoring trust and confidence in government) and his underdog status, and to eliminate the negative—the false impression that Ford was not an intelligent leader. Meanwhile, he suggested Ford should emphasize Carter's negative attributes—his fuzzy image, his judgment and stability (as reaffirmed by the *Playboy* gaffe), and his unknown status. David Belin to Gerald Ford, "The Election of President Ford, Basic Strategy Paper No. 12, October 1976," October 1, 1976, PL/Ford (Exec.), 11/18–24/76, Box 14: White House Central Files, Subject Files, GRFPL.

29. Crain, *The Ford Presidency,* 277.

30. As quoted in Schroeder, *Presidential Debates,* 120.

31. Littlewood, *Calling Elections,* 108–9; Friedenberg, *Rhetorical Studies of National Political Debates,* 30–51.

32. Coverage of Debate Two, https://www.c-span.org/video/?33353-1/1976-presidential -candidates-debate.

33. Sidney Kraus, *The Great Debates: Kennedy Vs. Nixon, 1960* (Bloomington: Indiana Univ. Press, 1962), 141, 202, 476; George Skelton, "If Looks Could Decide, Debate Was a Tie," *Los Angeles Times,* October 7, 1976, 1.

34. As quoted in Witcover, *Marathon,* 596.

35. "Partial Text of Ford-Carter Foreign Policy Debate," *Los Angeles Times,* October 7, 1976, 26; Zelizer, *Jimmy Carter,* 51.

36. R. W. Apple Jr., "Carter Seen Ending the Erosion of His Lead by Taking Offensive," *New York Times,* October 8, 1976, 46; Curtis Wilkie, "Carter Turns Combative to Halt Slide," *Boston*

Globe, October 10, 1976, 1; David Nyhan, "Ford Suffers Worst Week of Campaign," *Boston Globe,* October 10, 1976, 1. Historians and cultural critics contended that Ford's Eastern Europe gaffe did not cost him votes, but it did halt his momentum in the general election campaign. Crain, *The Ford Presidency,* 279–80; David Graham, "The Myth of Gerald Ford's Fatal 'Soviet Domination' Gaffe," *The Atlantic,* August 2, 2016, http://www.theatlantic.com/politics/archive /2016/08/the-myth-of-gerald-fords-disastrous-soviet-domination-gaffe/493958/.

37. As quoted in Crain, *The Ford Presidency,* 278.

38. As quoted in Ronald Nessen, *Making the News, Taking the News: From NBC to the Ford White House* (Middletown, Conn.: Weselyan Univ. Press, 2011), 226; Witcover, *Marathon,* 599–600.

39. As quoted in Witcover, *Marathon,* 600–601; "The White House Press Conference," October 6, 1976, "Press Conferences-Campaign Advisers," Box 17: Michael Raoul-Duval Papers, GRFL.

40. Schroeder, *Presidential Debates,* 302; Glad, *Jimmy Carter,* 390–91; Skelton, "If Looks Could Decide, Debate Was a Tie," 1.

41. As quoted in Nessen, *Making the News, Taking the News,* 226.

42. Benoit, "Image Restoration Discourse and Crisis Communication," 177–86; Witcover, *Marathon,* 603–4.

43. Dick Moe to State and Regional Coordinators, October 7, 1976, [Issues] General Election, 1975–1976 [1], Box 6: Expense Statements-Phil Wise, 1975–1976 through [Media, n.d.], PWP, JCPL; Daily Political Reports, October 7, 1976, Daily Political Reports, 10/1/76–10/17/76, Box 411: Daily Political Reports 10/1/76 [4] through Florida Candidates for DNC [1], JCPPP, PC, Tim Craft, Field Operations Director, Subject Files, JCPL.

44. Curtis Wilkie, "Aides Celebrate Carter's 'Home Run,'" *Boston Globe,* October 7, 1976, 20.

45. Glad, *Jimmy Carter,* 391.

46. Press conference of Jim Baker, October 10, 1976, Material Not Released to the Press-Remarks of Administration Officials (2); Box 40: Ron Nessen Files, GRFL.

47. Drew, *American Journal,* 465–66.

48. Crocker Snow Jr., "It's Carter on a Clear-Cut Decision," *Boston Globe,* October 7, 1976, 23; Harry Kelly, "Ford, Carter Take off Gloves in Round 2," *Chicago Tribune,* October 7, 1976, 1.

49. Robert Keatley, "Round Two: Image Is the Goal," *Wall Street Journal,* October 4, 1976, 12; Anthony Lewis, "Carter Turns a Corner," *New York Times,* October 7, 1976, 47; Joseph Lelyveld, "2nd Debate Showed a Change of Character," *New York Times,* October 9, 1976, 8. Although research suggests that coverage changed viewer perceptions about the victor of the second debate, the advantage was short-lived. Some scholars even suggested that Carter's aggressive strategy cost him votes and contributed to his narrow election day victory. Dailey et al., *Politeness in Presidential Debates,* 56–57.

50. The segment was prophetic. Carter was asked a similar question about the wisdom of the *Playboy* interview in the final debate. He was well prepared for the line of inquiry, and his response did much to reassure the American public. Nonetheless, Ford received harsher treatment on *Saturday Night Live.* "Debate '76," SNL, Season 2, Episode 4, https://www.nbc .com/saturday-night-live/video/debate-76/3004161?snl=1; Horner and Carver, *Saturday Night Live and the 1976 Presidential Election,* 117–18.

51. Witcover, *Marathon,* 584–93.

52. "Dole Says Mondale Claim on Watergate Is 'Baseless,'" *Hartford Courant,* October 7, 1976, 37; Gaylord Shaw, "Mondale Calls President's Statement a 'Major Error,'" *Los Angeles Times,* October 8, 1976, A22; R. W. Apple Jr., "Carter Seen Ending His Erosion by Going on the Offensive," *New York Times,* October 8, 1976, 1; Jack Nelson, "Carter Pressing Attack on Ford Relentlessly," *Los Angeles Times,* October 10, 1976, A1; Art Buchwald, "The Rose Garden Problem," *Boston Globe,* October 5, 1976, 27; Mary McGrory, "After a Couple of Stumbles, Carter Is Still on His Feet," *Baltimore Sun,* October 6, 1976, A15; Patt Derian to Phil Wise, "Republican Dirty Trick," October 14, 1976, [Issues] General Election, 1975–1976 [1], Box 6: Expense Statements-Phil Wise, 1975–1976 through [Media, n.d.], PWP, JCPL. Ford's staff took advantage of the *Playboy* gaffe. They approached muckraker Jack Anderson with names of women with whom Carter allegedly engaged in affairs. Bourne, *Jimmy Carter,* 354.

53. On October 9, for instance, one staff member urged Carter to tone down his rhetoric: "You are beginning to press Ford too hard. Beginning to sound strident. I would suggest you leave Ford's problem to the press. . . . This is a widespread consensus." Telenet Message, October 9, 1976, Telenet Messages [5], Box 95: Telenet Messages [5] through Telenet Messages [6], JCPPP, PC, IO-NS SF, JCPL; Rafshoon, interview with the author, August 12, 2014; Jack Nelson, "Carter Softens Rhetoric," *Los Angeles Times,* October 11, 1976, A1. On October 16, Caddell reiterated Jordan's advice with polling data. He acknowledged that the campaign suffered damage from Carter's aggressive personal attacks. Glad, *Jimmy Carter,* 392; Drew, *American Journal,* 487; Witcover, *Marathon,* 605–6. Carter's staff was the first to use e-mail in a presidential campaign. They effectively engaged in emergency internal communication and rallied volunteers through the new medium. Jenna Quitney Anderson, *Imagining the Internet: Personalities, Predictions, Perspectives* (New York: Rowman and Littlefield, 2005), 42.

54. Lou Harris, "Harris Survey: Mondale More Help Than Dole," *Chicago Tribune,* October 7, 1976, B4; Robert Shogan, "Mondale Playing Support Role for All It's Worth," *Los Angeles Times,* October 11, 1976, A12; Warren Brown, "Mondale's Campaigning Marked by Exuberance," *Washington Post,* October 30, 1976, 4; Witcover, *Marathon,* 612–16.

55. Basic Speech, Rough Draft, Speech File, 153.J.4.5B, WFMP, MHSM. Journalists acknowledged this attack strategy and Carter's claim on October 18 that he would not engage in any additional personal attacks. For instance, Peters sketched a cartoon demonstrating the disparity between Carter's promise to "never mention Watergate" and Mondale's attacks by offering a parody of Mondale striking Nixon's famous victory pose. Mike Peters, "We'll Never Mention Watergate," *Dayton Daily News,* Press Clippings, Box 350: Press Clippings through Press Clippings, JCPPP, PC, Press Office-Betty Rainwater, Subject Files, JCPL.

56. Briefing—Tough Questions, 153.J.5.6F, WFMP, MHSM; Transcript, 1976 Vice Presidential Campaign Debate, Vice Presidential Debate Transcript, 1976, 153.J.4.7B, WFMP, MHSM. Ford also engaged in personal attacks in mid-October, claiming Carter "wavers, he wanders, he wiggles, and he waffles." Glad, *Jimmy Carter,* 391; Stroud, *How Jimmy Won,* 377; Memorandum, Bob Mead to Dave Gergen, "Jimmy Carter," July 15, 1976, File, "Carter, Jimmy," Box 14: Michael Raoul-Duval Papers, GRFL.

57. Dole pored over eleven briefing books for several days. Rachelle Paterson, "Both Sides Claim Victory in Debate," *Boston Globe,* October 16, 1976, 4; Sean Toolan, "Before the Bat-

tle: Fritz Hit Tennis Balls, Dole the Books," *Chicago Tribune,* October 16, 1976, N4; Robert Healy, "No Doubt About It—Mondale Was the Winner," *Boston Globe,* October 16, 1976, 1; Basic Speech, Rough Draft, Speech File, 153.J.4.5B, WFMP, MHSM.

58. Brownell, *Showbiz Politics,* 185–86.

59. Box 9: Crime 7/74–12/75 through Debates-Briefing Material for Third Debate [1], JCPPP, PC, IO-SE, JCPL; Box 10: Debates—Briefing Material for the Third Debate [2] through Détente, 7/27/76–8/76, JCPPP, PC, IO-SE, JCPL.

60. "Synopsis of Debate Criticism," Debates-Briefing Material [1], Box 9: Crime 7/74–12/75 through Debates-Briefing Material for Third Debate [1], JCPPP, PC, IO-SE, JCPL.

61. File: Debates—Briefing Material for the Third Debate [1], Box 9: Crime 7/74–12/75 through Debates-Briefing Material for Third Debate [1], JCPPP, PC, IO-SE, JCPL; Debates—Briefing Material for the Third Debate [2], Box 10: Debates—Briefing Material for the Third Debate [2] through Détente, 7/27/76–8/76, JCPPP, PC, IO-SE, JCPL.

62. Playboy, Debates—Briefing Material for the Third Debate [2], Box 10: Debates—Briefing Material for the Third Debate [2] through Détente, 7/27/76–8/76, JCPPP, PC, IO-SE, JCPL. Carter's staff hoped *Los Angeles Times* Washington bureau chief Jack Nelson, a sympathetic panelist, might offer Carter a chance to address the *Playboy* gaffe directly, but *Washington Post* editorial writer Robert Maynard beat Nelson to the punch in the first question posed to Carter: "Governor, by all indications, the voters are so turned off by this election campaign so far that only half intend to vote. One major reason for this apathetic electorate appears to be the low level at which this campaign has been conducted. It has digressed frequently from important issues into allegations of blunder and brainwashing and fixations on lust and *Playboy.* What responsibility do you accept for the low level of this campaign for the nation's highest office?" In his lengthy response about apathy, Carter admitted he had "gone astray" with his *Playboy* interview and promised to find another forum if he should decide to discuss his deeply held Christian beliefs in the future. As quoted in "October 22, 1976 Debate Transcript," *Commission on Presidential Debates,* http://www.debates.org/index.php?page=october-22-1976-debate-transcript.

63. Memorandum, David Gergen to Mike Duval, "The Third Debate," Folder: David Gergen, Box 16: Michael Raoul-Duval Papers, GRFPL.

64. Kraus, *The Great Debates,* 519; Crain, *The Ford Presidency,* 279–80.

65. Adam Clymer, "Stand-Off Called Plus for Carter," *Baltimore Sun,* October 24, 1976, A1; Morton Mintz, "Win or Lose, Debates Viewed as a Worthwhile Exercise," *Washington Post,* October 24, 1976, A14; "Ford Proposes Permanent Debates," *Hartford Courant,* October 26, 1976, 17; Schroeder, *Presidential Debates,* 302.

66. Helen Thomas, "Ford Says He Brought Economic Surge," *Hartford Courant,* October 23, 1976, 1; Curtis Wilkie, "Carter Treads Softly," *Boston Globe,* October 23, 1976, 6; "Polls Show Tie in Final Debate," *Boston Globe,* October 24, 1976, 10; "The Last Debate—Who Won," *Hartford Courant,* October 24, 1976, A1; Robert Healy, "Who Was Hurt?" *Boston Globe,* October 23, 1976, 1; Martin Nolan, "The Last Debate: Cool, Relaxed and Error-Free," *Boston Globe,* October 23, 1976, 1; Stroud, *How Jimmy Won,* 379–82.

67. Joseph Lelyveld, "For Students, Main Difference was in Candidates and Images," *New York Times,* October 24, 1976, 32.

68. As quoted in Shogan, *Bad News,* 71.

69. Kenneth Hacker, *Candidate Images in Presidential Elections* (New York: Praeger, 1995), 111.

70. Judith Trent et al., *Political Campaign Communication: Principles and Practices* (New York: Praeger, 2000), 305–15.

71. Friedenberg, *Rhetorical Studies of National Political Debates,* 40–41.

72. Minnor and LeMay, *Inside the Presidential Debates,* 54; Jim Squires, "Last of Great Debates Leaves Story Unchanged," *Chicago Tribune,* October 24, 1976, 10; Tom Wicker, "Do We Really Need the Debates," *New York Times,* October 24, 1976, 167; Drew, *American Journal,* 488; Lloyd Bitzer and Ted Reuter, *Carter vs. Ford: The Counterfeit Debates of 1976* (Milwaukee: Univ. of Wisconsin Press, 1980). Analysis reflected an extension of political discourse following the 1960 presidential debates. Kraus, *The Great Debates,* 142–50; Brownell, *Showbiz Politics,* 169, 266; Self, *Presidential Debate Negotiation from 1960 to 1988,* 9.

73. Drew, *American Journal,* 436.

74. Tom Wicker, "Do We Really Need the Debates," *New York Times,* October 24, 1976, 167.

75. Jeffery Auer, "The Counterfeit Debates," in Kraus, ed., *The Great Debates,* 142–49.

76. Jack Nelson, "Debate Questions," *Los Angeles Times,* October 25, 1976, B17.

77. Richard O'Mara, "Why So Many People Were Turned Off by the Debates," *Baltimore Sun,* October 31, 1976, K3.

78. Art Buchwald, "Ford, Carter—Sitcom Stillborn," *Los Angeles Times,* October 31, 1976, E3.

79. Chevy Chase and Dan Aykroyd, "Debate '76," *Saturday Night Live,* Season 2, NBC, http://www.nbc.com/saturday-night-live/video/debate-76/3004161?snl=1; Horner and Carver, *Saturday Night Live and the 1976 Presidential Election,* 105–21.

80. Crain, *The Ford Presidency,* 272.

81. David Gergen and Jerry Jones to the President, "The Southern Trip," September 24, 1976, "Political Affairs-Ford (12)," Box 37: Presidential Handwriting File, GRFL; Bourne, *Jimmy Carter,* 354.

82. Crain, *The Ford Presidency,* 272.

83. Gerald Rafshoon, "Washington Classroom with Gerald Rafshoon," C-SPAN, October 7, 2013, https://www.c-span.org/video/?315502-1/washington-classroom-gerald-rafshoon.

84. Sheet Music, Robert Gardner, "I'm Feeling Good About America," https://www.fordlibrarymuseum.gov/library/exhibits/campaign/feeling.asp; Bourne, *Jimmy Carter,* 353; Johnson, *Democracy for Hire,* 223–25. The narrator prompted Americans to consider Ford's steady, dependable leadership: "America is smiling again. And a great many people believe that the leadership of this steady, dependable man can keep America happy and secure. We know we can depend on him to work to keep us strong at home. We know we can depend on him to work to ease tensions among the other nations of the world. We know we can depend on him to make peace his highest priority. Peace with freedom. Is there anything more important than that?" Doug Bailey, "Peace," 1976 Democratic Presidential Campaign Committee, Inc., Museum of the Moving Image, The Living Room Candidate: Presidential Campaign Commercials, 1952–2012, http://www.livingroomcandidate.org/commercials/1976.

85. Mann, *Daisy Petals and Mushroom Clouds;* Blumenthal, *The Permanent Campaign,* 183–201; Johnson, *Democracy for Hire,* 223; Seifert, *The Politics of Authenticity in Presidential Campaigns, 1976–2008,* 36–56; Witcover, *Marathon,* 538–42.

86. Preliminary Media Plan for President Ford Campaign, Bailey, Deardourff and Eyre, Inc., August 21, 1976, Folder: Presidential Campaign-Preliminary Media Plan, Box 1: Dorothy Dowton Files, GRFL.

87. Witcover, *Marathon*, 616–17.

88. "President Gaining in the Polls," President Ford Committee (32), October 19, 1976, "President Ford Committee Newsletters (4)," Box F13: President Ford Committee Records, GRFL.

89. Witcover, *Marathon*, 616–17.

90. "President Gaining in the Polls," President Ford Committee (32), October 19, 1976, "President Ford Committee Newsletters (4)," Box F13: President Ford Committee Records, GRFL; Daily Report, October 18, 1976, Daily Political Reports, 10/18/76–11/1/76, Box 411: Daily Political Reports 10/1/76 [4] through Florida Candidates for DNC [1], JCPPP, PC, Tim Craft, Field Operations Director, Subject Files, JCPL.

91. For Johnson's campaign, Schwartz designed one of the most controversial advertisements in American history. The "daisy ad," featuring a small girl picking flowers followed by a countdown to a nuclear missile launch, triggered fears of nuclear holocaust and contributed to the demise of Republican Barry Goldwater's presidential ambitions. Mann, *Daisy Petals and Mushroom Clouds*; Blumenthal, *The Permanent Campaign*, 119–23; Witcover, *Marathon*, 616–17; Rafshoon, interview with the author, August 12, 2014. Increasingly, dissension existed among establishment figures in the Democratic Party, Carter's campaign staff, his transition staff, and his closest advisors, dubbed by reporters as the "Georgia Mafia." On at least one occasion news of discord went public. Stroud, *How Jimmy Won*, 383–85; Drew, *American Journal*, 471–82; Bourne, *Jimmy Carter*, 342.

92. Schwartz believed Rafshoon "was hopelessly anachronistic in his skills and comprehension of the medium in which he was working." Blumenthal, *The Permanent Campaign*, 120.

93. Rafshoon, interview with the author, August 12, 2014. Carter's campaign engaged in limited negative advertising on a regional basis, emphasizing Ford's Eastern Europe gaffe and the critique of the Ford-Kissinger détente policy. They only broadcast one national negative advertisement, which, capitalizing on Mondale's popularity, featured images of both vice presidential candidates, with the narrator reminding the public that "four of the last six Vice Presidents have wound up being President; who would you like to see a heart beat away from the Presidency?" Glad, *Jimmy Carter*, 393–94; Seifert, *The Politics of Authenticity in Presidential Campaigns*, 36–56; Witcover, *Marathon*, 616.

94. Tony Schwartz, "Reality," 1976 Democratic Presidential Campaign Committee, Inc., Museum of the Moving Image, The Living Room Candidate: Presidential Campaign Commercials, 1952–2012, http://www.livingroomcandidate.org/commercials/1976/reality. Schwartz also designed regional advertisements, stressing southern pride in Dixie's candidate.

95. File: Media Information—By Television Network, 9/76, Box 274: Media Buys-Television and Radio-Colorado-D.C., 9/76–11/76 through National Field Staff Conference—Agenda, 8/76, JCPPP, PC, Situation Room Administrative Assistant-Bill Simon's Subject Files, JCPL.

96. Rafshoon, interview with the author, August 12, 2014; Joseph Lelyveld, "Carter Turns to New York Studio to Tape His Remaining TV Spots," *New York Times*, October 20, 1976, 28. After reports of the move surfaced, Rafshoon allegedly became infuriated that someone else might claim credit for Carter's success, and he lashed out at Schwartz, refusing to pay the ven-

dor and failing to take some of his strategic advice, most importantly his suggestion to have a studio available for the final two weeks of the campaign to generate spots based on any arising developments. Blumenthal, *The Permanent Campaign,* 119–23; Witcover, *Marathon,* 616–17.

97. Jim Mann, "'Presidential' Image Sought; Ties In, Jeans Out in Carter Ads," *Baltimore Sun,* October 27, 1976, A9.

98. Bill Boyarsky, "Advance Men Rally Crowds for Candidates," *Los Angeles Times,* October 30, 1976, A1. Advance staff increasingly were vital to the fortunes of networks, who depended on crowds rallied to pseudo-events for B-roll shots. Boorstin, *The Image,* 3–45; Bourne, *Jimmy Carter,* 345; Witcover, *Marathon,* 522.

99. Carter's staff gleaned insights from the advance manuals of Kennedy, McCarthy, Humphrey, and McGovern and constructed their own manual with advice on how to effectively orchestrate a pseudo-event. Carter, Jimmy and Mondale, Walter Advance Manual, Box 317: Alaska through Contribution Lists, JCPPP, PC, PO-BRSF, JCPL.

100. Glad, *Jimmy Carter,* 395; Drew, *American Journal,* 515–16.

101. R. W. Apple Jr., "Campaign '76: Barren and Petty," *New York Times,* October 20, 1976, 93.

102. Ibid.; Glad, *Jimmy Carter,* 398.

103. George Will, "The Disease of Politics," in George Will, *The Pursuit of Happiness and Other Sobering Thoughts* (New York: Harper and Row, 1978), 190–92.

104. George Will, "Tiresome Little Men Clawing for Lincoln's Chair," *Washington Post,* October 14, 1976, A19; George Will, "Presidency Weakened by Grotesque Campaign Process," *Los Angeles Times,* October 31, 1976, I5.

105. George Will, "The Disease of Politics," 190–92; Brownell, *Showbiz Politics,* 231.

106. Robert Reinhold, "Just Half an Electorate May Vote Nov. 2," *New York Times,* September 26, 1976, E4; Harry Kelly, "Will Apathy Be a Landslide Winner in Election," *Chicago Tribune,* November 2, 1976, 1. Pollsters, the masters of new politics, isolated the source of apathy many months prior: Americans were "more alienated and more cynical than at any point in modern time." Robert Teeter and Stu Spencer to Richard Cheney, November 12, 1975, "11/12/1975 to Dick Cheney—Analysis of Early Research and Strategy Recommendations," Box 63: Robert Teeter Papers, GRFPL 82.

107. Overall Coverage of Campaign '76. Correspondent Roger Mudd Reporting from the Campaign Trail [entry title: CBS News Coverage of Campaign '76], PAC, 76061 NWT 4 of 4, WJBMAPAC; Supporting Materials, File 76061 NWT, Box 99: PAE, HRBML.

108. J. Schwartz, "Sales Campaign Injures Carter," *Boston Globe,* October 4, 1976, 17; Mike Hambly, "Sick of 'Professional Politicians,'" *Boston Globe,* November 1, 1976, 25; Sharon McIntyre, "Letters to the Times," *Los Angeles Times,* October 31, 1976, I4.

109. Aaron served as one of Carter's initial celebrity endorsers in the "Georgian Loves Jimmy Carter" telethon. Associated Press, "Voter Apathy Target," October 27, 1976, Athletes, Box 404: AFL-CIO through First Person Articles, JCPPP, PC, LP-PO, Subject Files, JCPL.

110. Paisley, *The Tyranny of Printers.*

111. Si Sheppard, *The Partisan Press: A History of Media Bias in the United States* (New York: McFarland, 2007) 259–81; Pressman, *On Press,* 69–70.

112. "The Vote for President," *Washington Post,* October 31, 1976, 38; "Washington Post Backs Carter," *Los Angeles Times,* November 1, 1976, B14.

113. Sheppard, *The Partisan Press,* 299–302.

114. Ford received endorsements from 411 out of 661 U.S. daily newspapers, including circulation leaders such as the *Chicago Tribune,* the *Philadelphia Inquirer,* and the *Baltimore Sun.* UPI, "411 of 661 Newspapers Back Ford," *Atlanta Daily World,* October 31, 1976, 6.

115. Some exceptions existed. For instance, on October 24 the *Des Moines Register* offered Carter an enthusiastic endorsement, a clip that quickly found its way into the Carter campaign's *Daily Political Report.* The Daily Political Report, October 25, 1976, Daily Political Reports, 10/18/76–11/1/76, Box 411: Daily Political Reports 10/1/76 [4] through Florida Candidates for DNC [1], JCPPP, PC, Tim Craft, Field Operations Director, Subject Files, JCPL; Daily Political Reporter, October 28, 1976, Telenet Messages [5], Box 95: Telenet Messages [5] through Telenet Messages [6], JCPPP, PC, IO-NS, Subject File, JCPL. Only seven Georgia newspapers endorsed Carter, and the *Atlanta Constitution* reserved their endorsement for election eve. "Atlanta Papers Back Carter," *Boston Globe,* October 28, 1976, 20; Landon Butler to Phil Wise, October 27, 1976, [Issues] General Election, 1975–1976 [1], Box 6: Expense Statements-Phil Wise, 1975–1976 through [Media, n.d.], PWP, JCPL. With polling data and news such as this in mind, Carter's staff scheduled a last-minute southern tour to shore up support below the Mason-Dixon Line. Bourne, *Jimmy Carter,* 354.

116. Lou Harris, "Carter Clings to One-Point Lead," *Boston Globe,* November 2, 1976, 12; AP, "Down to Wire, Neck and Neck," *Hartford Courant,* November 2, 1976, 1B. Gallup indicated Ford held a one-point advantage, his first lead during the general election campaign. Stroud, *How Jimmy Won,* 402.

117. Jack Marsh to the President, "Speech Themes for Michigan," States-Michigan, Box 19: Richard Cheney Files, GRFPL. Ford's speech was meant to stress loyalty to the state and its citizens: "You come to the people of this great state once again to ask for their support for you with their ballots, but unlike previous times when you sought to be their Congressman, you seek the highest office in the land." Ford's effort was a part of "Operation Over the Top," a three-day blitz before election day designed to convince voters to shift to the Ford bandwagon. "Campaign Strategy-Suggestion (3)," Box 13: Michael Raoul Duval Papers, GRFPL.

118. Ibid.; Crain, *The Ford Presidency,* 280–82.

119. Eleanor Randolph, "Carter's Religion an Issue Again," *Chicago Tribune,* November 2, 1976, 1.

120. Press Pool Report, Kandy Stroud et al., October 24, 1976, Pool Reports, Box 308: Form Letter-Prot. 1 & Correspondence through Playboy Article Commentary, JCPPP, PC, Director's Office-Religion Political Affairs Coordinator Protestant Desk, David B. Graham Subject Files, JCPL.

121. Ibid.; Glad, *Jimmy Carter,* 396–98; Witcover, *Marathon,* 632–35; Crain, *The Ford Presidency,* 282.

122. Stroud, *How Jimmy Won,* 402.

123. Godfrey Sperling Jr., "Campaign Cross Fire," *Christian Science Monitor,* October 22, 1976, 1; David Nyhan, "Ford to Start His Media Blitz," *Boston Globe,* October 24, 1976, 1; Robert Murphy and Nancy Pappas, "Politicians Load Up on TV Time," *Hartford Courant,* October 26, 1976, 13; James Reston, "The Television Blitz," *New York Times,* October 27, 1976, 39; Drew, *American Journal,* 526–29.

124. Jules Witcover, "Campaign Finishes with a Saturation Television Appeal," *Washington Post,* November 2, 1976, A4.

125. Ibid. Both candidates allocated the majority of their campaign budgets to advertising. Ford's staff estimated that they devoted between $1.2 and $1.5 million on paid media for the final three days. Carter's campaign saturated media with advertisements throughout the general election campaign season, but nonetheless reserved $2.5 million for the last two weeks. Crain, *The Ford Presidency,* 280–82. Reporters learned of Ford's last-ditch blitz at a press conference with President Ford Committee Deputy Chairman Stu Spencer on October 23. Spencer and Deputy Chairman for Communications for the President Ford Committee William Greener described logistics of the television and radio blitz, but reporters pressed the men for details about finances related to the campaign. Press conference, October 23, 1976, Folder: "Press Conferences-Campaign Advisers," Box 17: Michael Raoul-Duval Papers, GRFPL; Blumenthal, *The Permanent Campaign,* 143–60. Both candidates also allocated funds to radio and print advertisements. Ford's staff, for instance, placed anti-Carter ads on radio stations, such as Chicago's WMAQ, and full-page ads in prominent national newspapers. Several of the advertisements sparked controversy. On October 22, for instance, J. O. Derby contacted Carter's staff by telex to notify them that anti-Carter commercials without clear identification as paid announcements were broadcast on Chicago's WMAQ. In the days leading up to the election, Ford's staff sparked additional controversy by encouraging undecided voters to make their decision based on "last week's *Newsweek* and this month's *Playboy.*" In their last newspaper advertisement, however, they returned to the campaign's central themes—credibility and authenticity. In "One Final Thought," Ford's imagecraft apparatus emphasized "trust must be earned." "It is not enough to say 'trust me.' Trust is not having to guess what a candidate means. Trust is not being all things to all people, but being the same thing to all people. Trust is leveling with the people before the election about what you're going to do after the election. Trust is saying plainly and simply what you mean—and meaning what you say. Trust must be earned." As quoted in Barber, *The Pulse of Politics,* 209–10; Lies (GOP), Box 405: Greece through Lithuanians, JCPPP, PC, LP-PO SF, JCPL.

126. Witcover, "Campaign Finishes with a Saturation Television Appeal," A4. Although Ford did not garner endorsements from celebrities in the same league as Frank Sinatra or Sammy Davis Jr., Garagiola and Bailey campaigned on his behalf in the final two weeks, appearing in eleventh-hour advertisements and specials. Brownell, *Showbiz Politics,* 158–225; Pearl Bailey, 1976 Democratic Presidential Campaign Committee, Inc., Museum of the Moving Image, The Living Room Candidate: Presidential Campaign Commercials, 1952–2012, http://www .livingroomcandidate.org/commercials/1976. Patt Derian recommended the "Fireside Chat" on October 16: "From the very beginning of Jimmy's quest for the nomination and presidency, the nation has seen him on the run. . . . I've been thinking that there ought to be an early 'fireside chat' and that it could be the most important speech of the campaign because it introduces the presidential character." Patt Derian to Jody Powell, October 16, 1976, Telenet Messages [5], Box 95: Telenet Messages [5] through Telenet Messages [6], JCPPP, PC, IO-NS, Subject File, JCPL. Carter's imagecraft apparatus discussed the media message for the last week at length on October 18, 1976. Daily Political Reporter, October 18, 1976, Telenet Messages [5], Box 95: Telenet Messages [5] through Telenet Messages [6], JCPPP, PC, IO-NS, Subject File, JCPL; "Jimmy Carter's People's Program," *Toledo Blade,* February 19, 1977; File: People Program Transition Book, Box 57: People Program Transition Book through Presidential Libraries— Material Re, Rafshoon Papers, JCPPP, JCPL.

127. Witcover bemoaned staged qualities, including Carter's response to a man of Latino decent in Spanish. Witcover, "Campaign Finishes with a Saturation Television Appeal," A4; Glad, *Jimmy Carter,* 394; Kernell, *Going Public,* 1, 92; McGinnis, *The Selling of the President.*

128. Brownell, *Showbiz Politics,* 158–225.

129. Hugh Carter Jr. to Hamilton Jordan and Rick Hutcheson, October 31, 1976, Telenet Messages [5], Box 95: Telenet Messages [5] through Telenet Messages [6], JCPPP, PC, IO-NS, Subject File, JCPL.

130. Homefolks for Carter & Mondale—Peanut Brigade, 9/76–11/76; Box 273: GOP Tracking-Voter Registration-By State Through Media Buys-Television and Radio-Arkansas-Arizona, 9/76–11/76, JCPPP, PC, Situation Room Administrative Assistant-Bill Simon's Subject Files, JCPL; Daily Political Report, October 12, 1976, Telenet Messages [5], Box 95: Telenet Messages [5] through Telenet Messages [6], JCPPP, PC, IO-NS, Subject File, JCPL. Stroud, *How Jimmy Won,* 386–88; 397–98; Glad, *Jimmy Carter,* 395; Drew, *American Journal,* 422–23; 471–86; James Kilpatrick, "The Meaning of Tuesday," *Hartford Courant,* October 28, 1976, 26.

131. Neikirk offered a bulleted list detailing examples of poor media relations, including criticism that Carter directed toward *Boston Globe* editor Thomas Winship for negative primary coverage; complaints directed toward *Time* for its "anti-Carter slant"; impromptu gripe sessions with individual reporters, such as Mohr; and press interventions to combat unfavorable coverage. Bill Neikirk, "A Penchant for Overreacting," *Chicago Tribune,* October 25, 1976, 5.

132. Stroud, *How Jimmy Won,* 399–403.

CONCLUSION

1. Kevin Lerner, "(More) Guided Journalists during the 1970s Media Crisis of Confidence," *Columbia Journalism Review,* May 10, 2018, https://www.cjr.org/the_profile/more-journalism-review.php; Lerner, *Provoking the Press*; Ken Auletta, "How Carter Plays the Press: Who'll Win," *More: The Media Magazine,* October 1976, 12–22, File: "Clippings and Publications," Box 3: Interviews JC through Office Structure, Barry Jagoda Donated Papers, JCPL.

2. Auletta, "How Carter Plays the Press," 22.

3. Boorstin, *The Image,* xvi; Baudrillard, *Simulacra and Simulation,* 2, 47. If Watergate, as Baudrillard indicated, was a case of the hyperreal ("the desert of the real itself") in American politics, then Carter's campaign, as a final chapter of Watergate, in many ways represented the "precision of the simulacra."

4. Brownell, "The Making of the Celebrity President," 180–83.

5. Carter's image and narrative bore the indelible imprint of this sociopolitical landscape. Schudson, *Watergate in American Memory,* 70.

6. Auletta, "How Carter Plays the Press: Who'll Win," 17.

7. Peter Goldman, "Sizing Up Carter: The Question of Character," *Newsweek,* September 13, 1976, 22; Peter Goldman and Eleanor Clift, "Mr. Outside in Stride," *Newsweek,* November 1, 1976, 29.

8. Douglas, "Presidents and the Media," 153.

9. Donaldson, interview with the author, January 17, 2017.

10. "The Carter Tailspin," *Wall Street Journal,* November 1, 1976, 14.

11. James Wooten, *Dasher: The Roots and Rising of Jimmy Carter* (New York: Summit, 1978), 7; Robert Shogan, *Promises to Keep: Carter's First Hundred Days* (New York: Crowell, 1977), 13; Curtis Wilkie, "Carter Plane Antics Soothe Bleary Press," *Boston Globe,* October 30, 1976, 4.

12. Aboard *Peanut One,* Carter grumbled about delays prompted by deadline reporters: "They've had their forty minutes. Let's go." Unbeknownst to Carter, these print reporters, who had scrambled to file stories after negotiating months of grueling trail conditions, were aboard a bus heading in the wrong direction on Interstate 85. Shogan, *Promises to Keep,* 13; Donaldson, interview with the author, January 17, 2017.

13. Overall Coverage of Campaign '76. Daily Coverage of Carter and Ford [entry title: CBS News Coverage of Campaign '76], PAC, 76061 NWT 3 of 4, WJBMAPAC; Supporting Materials, File 76061 NWT, Box 99: PAE, HRBML.

14. Carter's imagecraft team presented the American public with the "People's President" on Inauguration Day, and the pack hailed Carter as a media genius for breaking with tradition to walk with his family among the people down Pennsylvania Avenue after his Inaugural Address of "hope and healing." Glad, *Jimmy Carter,* 409–14. In his lead, front-page story, *Washington Post* staff writer Haynes Johnson offered his interpretative analysis, an act of reserved deconstruction: "Washington was full of symbolism yesterday as Carter came to power. . . . what will undoubtedly be most remembered about Jimmy Carter's inauguration was that long walk from the Capitol to the Executive Mansion. . . . As he walked along, with Amy prancing . . . at his side, he was shattering recent presidential practice and legend—the idea that a President must be remote and removed from the people." Haynes Johnson, "Georgian Ends Long Quest Today," *Washington Post,* January 20, 1977, A1; Crouse, *Boys on the Bus,* 99–128. *Christian Science Monitor* veteran Godfrey Sperling Jr. added that if Carter "keeps up such a pace—[he] seems likely to take our breath away." Godfrey Sperling, "Now U.S. Finds Out," *Christian Science Monitor,* January 21, 1977, 3.

15. Greenberg, *Republic of Spin,* 397–407.

16. Anne Wexler et al., "Press Coverage in the Primaries: A Conversation with David Broder," *Democratic Review,* July/August 1976, *Democratic Review,* Box 4: "Correspondence-Request for Actuality Phone Number through Forms-Talk Show Final Disposition," RWHPO, Media Liaison Office, Bradley Woodward's Subject Files, JCPL. His colleague Jack Germond voiced his concern over "superficial non-sense" in campaign reporting on *The MacNeil/Lehrer Report*'s election special, but he contended that the *Playboy* and Eastern Europe gaffes offered important insights into candidates. "It's done badly and overdone, but it's not illegitimate," he admitted. Nonetheless, leaders in the news media industry needed to reassess campaign journalism, Ford's media advisor Doug Bailey interjected, asserting an age-old critique: substantive issues coverage was lacking. "It's a constantly changing process," Washington correspondent Jim Lehrer admitted, acknowledging the visibly enhanced role of reporters as political kingmakers amid post-1968 reforms. Under the new rules of American politics, frontline reporters were political actors. News organizations now participated in the construction of pseudo-events and enlisted political journalists to vet the character of presidential aspirants and to mediate key contests, including primaries and caucuses, party conventions, and presidential debates. "Everyone's still learning how to do it," Lehrer defended with a mea culpa on behalf of the most influential political power brokers in the bicentennial campaign before transitioning

to the final topic of the evening—the president-elect's governing mandate. In the end, panelists agreed that it remained to be seen whether Carter might develop the mandate he needed to govern the nation, acknowledging that it depended on the balance of votes in Congress. The assessment was apt, but the panel failed to consider the new role of frontline reporters in contributing to that balance. "The MacNeil/Lehrer Report," PBS Special, November 3, 1976, VTNAC. In the aftermath of Senate Watergate Hearings, PBS gained increasing visibility and prestige as a high-quality supplement to network news with its public affairs reporting of national politics. Inspired by NBC's *Meet the Press,* the *MacNeil/Lehrer Report* gained national recognition for its low-key, ideologically inclusive dialogues around major stories. Ponce de Leon, *That's the Way It Is,* 85–121; Pressman, *On Press,* 143–95; Hemmer, *Messengers of the Right,* xvi.

17. Carter and his staff experienced these collective impulses firsthand on the trail, but in the opening days of the administration, they encountered relatively positive coverage from frontline reporters committed to a temporary cease-fire. Auletta, "How Carter Plays the Press: Who'll Win," 17, File: "Clippings and Publications," Box 3: Interviews JC through Office Structure, Barry Jagoda Donated Papers, JCPL; "The MacNeil/Lehrer Report," VTNAC; Feldstein, *Poisoning the Press,* 374. Nonetheless, as the first one hundred days of the Carter administration drew to an end, frontline reporters, leery of Carter's savvy imagecraft strategies and news management techniques and weary of his rapport with the news media, determined to expose symbolic acts for what they were: imagecraft techniques designed to maintain the president's popular appeal; thus, when the Carter White House unveiled their People's Program, which included the live call-in show *Ask President Carter,* or *Dial-A-President,* and a series of televised "Fireside Chats," many reporters decried "cardigan gimmicks" involved in the "selling of the President." Joseph Kraft, "After Carter's First 100 Days," *Boston Globe,* May 1, 1977, H4. "These have been a hundred days of busy activity," wrote columnist James Kilpatrick, capturing the collective mood of newshounds, who had recently gained access to Caddell's ten thousand-word memo on the necessity of the permanent campaign. "Days of symbols, gestures and cardigan gimmicks. In terms of public relations, the record is spectacular. In terms of political accomplishments, the record is not so much." James Kilpatrick, "Carter's 'Presence' Still Looks Absent," *Hartford Courant,* May 3, 1977, 18.

18. Anthony Marro, "Lance-Run Bank Criticized in '74 in Federal Study," *New York Times,* January 16, 1977, 17.

19. Michael Ruby, "Bert Lance's Bind," *Newsweek,* July 18, 1977, 69.

20. Michael Ruby, "What the Report Says," *Newsweek,* August 29, 1977, 18–19.

21. Schudson, *Watergate in American Memory,* 70–82; Zelizer, *Jimmy Carter,* 53–72.

22. "Lance's Loan," *Time,* August 15, 1977, 10; Carl T. Rowan, "Keeping Bert Lance Costly to President," *Spokane Daily Chronicle,* September 8, 1977, 4; "Lance Lashes Out at News Reporters," *Statesville* [N.C.] *Record and Landmark,* September 14, 1977, 1.

23. "Jimmy Carter's Job Approval Ratings Trend," Gallup Historical Statistics and Trends, http://www.gallup.com/poll/116677/presidential-approval-ratings-gallup-historical-statistics-trends.aspx. Based on declining public support, Congress became less inclined to work with the Carter administration. During the remainder of his administration, Carter encountered a divided Democratic party and the rise of the Religious Right. Zelizer, *Jimmy Carter,* 73–87.

24. The mediated image first emerged in reporting surrounding Carter's transition efforts. Barry Jagoda oral history interview, October 8, 1999, by Martha Joynt Kumar, Office of Presidential Libraries, National Archives and Records Administration; White House Interview Program, White House Transition Project, page 7, http://www.archives.gov/presidential-libraries /research/transition-interviews/pdf/jagoda.pdf.

25. Mary Head, "Public Relations, Polls, and Pundits: The Failure of Image Management in the Carter White House" (master's thesis, Columbus State University, 1988); Greenberg, *Republic of Spin,* 385–407.

26. Hedrick Smith, "Carter Move Climaxed Long Process," *Lakeland [Florida] Ledger,* July 22, 1979, 1; "Studio 54 Patron Swears Jordan Used Cocaine," *Lakeland [Florida] Ledger,* August 29, 1979, 6A.

27. Howell Raines, "Citizens Ask if Carter Is Part of the 'Crisis,'" *New York Times,* August 3, 1979, A1; Zelizer, *Jimmy Carter,* 88–110.

28. "Br'er Rabbit Tries to Sink Carter," *Baltimore Sun,* August 30, 1979, A1.

29. UPI, "Carter Describes Foe," *New York Times,* August 31, 1979, A12.

30. Brooks Jackson, "Bunny Goes Bugs—Rabbit Attacks President," *Washington Post,* August 30, 1979, 1. Carter did not address the incident again publicly until he released his book *White House Diary* in 2010. Cody Combs, "Jimmy Carter Explains 'Rabbit Attack,'" CNN.com, November 21, 2010, http://politicalticker.blogs.cnn.com/2010/11/21/jimmy-carter-explains -rabbit-attack/.

31. Editors at the *Baltimore Sun* and *Hartford Courant* also placed the AP story on page 1 in the August 30 edition. "Carter vs. 'Killer Rabbit'—A Hairy Tale," *Hartford Courant,* August 30, 1979, 1A; "Br'er Rabbit Tries to Sink Carter," *Baltimore Sun,* August 30, 1979, A1. Over the next month, reporters, pundits, and editorial cartoonists churned out hundreds of packages, columns, and drawings about the sensational incident. A ProQuest Historical Newspapers search of "Carter" and "killer rabbit" between August 30 and September 31, 1979, revealed more than forty articles and columns about the incident in eight prominent U.S. newspapers.

32. "Killer Rabbit and President Carter," *CBS Evening News,* 08/30/1979, VTNAC.

33. Germond and Witcover, "Ridicule: Cruelest of All," 35.

34. Jagoda, interview with the author, January 10, 2017.

35. Goldman and Clift, "Mr. Outside in Stride," 29; Glad, *Jimmy Carter,* 452.

36. Images more troubling than killer rabbits besieged Carter's administration. Americans encountered daily breaking news accounts of the Iran Hostage Crisis in newspapers and newsmagazines and on the nightly network news, particularly ABC's *America Held Hostage: The Iranian Crisis,* which evolved into *Nightline,* and eventually the twenty-four-hour Cable News Network (CNN). News images of the crisis initially buttressed and ultimately diminished Carter's presidential image. Zelizer, *Jimmy Carter,* 101–25.

37. Johnson, *Democracy for Hire,* 182.

38. Gerald Rafshoon, oral history interview, April 8, 1983, by Joseph Devaney et al., MCPA-POHP-CPP, page 50, http://web1.millercenter.org/poh/transcripts/ohp_1983_0408_rafshoon .pdf. Seifert, *The Politics of Authenticity in Presidential Campaigns,* 58–78.

39. Goldman and Clift, "Mr. Outside in Stride," 29; Cash, *The Mind of the South.*

40. Quoted in Woodruff, *"This Is Judy Woodruff at the White House,"* 130.

41. Goldman and Clift, "Mr. Outside in Stride," 29.

42. Ibid.; Schroeder, *Presidential Debates,* 50; Michael Weiler and Barnett Pearce, *Reagan and Public Discourse in America* (Tuscaloosa: Univ. of Alabama Press, 2006), 97.

43. Jeffrey Howison, *The 1980 Presidential Election: Ronald Reagan and the Shaping of the American Conservative Movement* (New York: Routledge, 2013); Brownell, *Showbiz Politics,* 196–97; Greenberg, *The Republic of Spin,* 408–15.

44. Baudrillard, *Simulacra and Simulation,* 47; Kenneth Holden, *The Making of the Great Communicator: Ronald Reagan's Transformation from Actor to Governor* (New York: Globe Pequot, 2013). Deaver built on this image in the coming years, perfecting Reagan's resolved yet optimistic persona through photo-ops at the cliffs of Normandy on the fortieth anniversary of D-Day, atop the Great Wall of China, in the midst of a montage to America at the 1984 Los Angeles Olympics, and before the Berlin Wall, demanding, "Mr. Gorbachev, tear down this wall." Seifert, *The Politics of Authenticity in Presidential Campaigns,* 79.

45. As quoted in Weiler and Pearce, *Reagan and Public Discourse in America,* 97, 136.

46. As quoted in Schroeder, *Presidential Debates,* 50.

47. The League of Women Voters did not invite independent presidential candidate John Anderson to participate in the event when he slipped under 15 percent in the polls. Schroeder, *Presidential Debates,* 149–50.

48. Reagan defeated Carter by more than 8 million votes, winning 50.7 percent of the popular vote and 489 electoral college votes. H.W. Brands, *Reagan: The Life* (New York: Random House, 2016), 230–37.

49. Steven Weisman, "Carter Aides Try to Develop Rousing, 'Positive' Themes for Campaign," *New York Times,* June 9, 1980, B11; Gerald Rafshoon, Oral History Interview, April 8, 1983, by Joseph Devaney et al., MCPA-POHP-CPP, page 50, http://web1.millercenter.org/poh /transcripts/ohp_1983_0408_rafshoon.pdf; James Glen Stovall, "Incumbency and News Coverage of the 1980 Presidential Election Campaign," *Western Political Quarterly* 37.4 (1984): 621–31; Timothy Stanley, *Kennedy vs. Carter: The 1980 Battle for the Democratic Party's Soul* (Lawrence: Univ. of Kansas Press, 2010), 1–298; Cary Covington et al., "Shaping a Candidate's Image in the Press: Ronald Reagan and the 1980 Presidential Election," *Political Research Quarterly* 46.4 (1993): 783–98; Howison, *The 1980 Presidential Election,* 87–113.

50. McCombs and Shaw, "The Agenda-Setting Function of the Mass Media," 176–87; Lewin, "Frontiers in Group Dynamics," 145; Maxwell McCombs and Donald Shaw, "Structuring the 'Unseen Environment,'" *Journal of Communication* 26.2 (1976): 18–22.

51. Broder once wrote: "There is no escaping that every time we do that job we inject ourselves into the campaign—into the central event of the campaign—and become players not observers." David Broder, "Real Presidential Debates," *Washington Post,* September 5, 1984, 1. Conservative news pundit George Will engaged in an ethical conflict of interest during the 1980 presidential debates by coaching Reagan and later heralding his "thoroughbred performance" on *Nightline.* Debate-gate, as it was called, further undermined the credibility of campaign journalists. Morton Kondracke, "Debategate," *New Republic,* July 18, 1983, https://newrepublic .com/article/89585/debategate-carter-reagan-debate-scandal; Zelizer, *Jimmy Carter,* 111–25.

52. Hemmer, *Messengers of the Right,* 270. Journalists reeled from a credibility crisis, contributing to the erosion of their audiences and the decline of media markets. John Nerone, *The Media and Public Life: A History* (New York: Wiley and Sons, 2015), 241–88.

53. Covington et al., "Shaping a Candidate's Image in the Press: Ronald Reagan and the 1980 Presidential Election," 783–98; Howison, *The 1980 Presidential Election,* 87–113; Adam Clymer, "Michael Deaver Dies," *New York Times,* August 19, 2007, http://www.nytimes.com/2007/08/19 /washington/19deaver.html?_r=2&.

54. Howison, *The 1980 Presidential Election,* 87–113.

55. As quoted in Flippen, *Jimmy Carter, the Politics of Family, and the Rise of the Religious Right,* 203; Greenberg, *The Republic of Spin,* 397–407; Blumenthal, *The Permanent Campaign.*

56. As quoted in Schroeder, *Presidential Debates,* 50.

57. Robert Kaiser, "Carter's Last Roll at a Big Media Audience Ricocheted into Ether," *Washington Post,* November 4, 1980, A7; Pressman, *Remaking the News,* 253–315.

58. Kaiser, "Carter's Last Roll at a Big Media Audience Ricocheted into Ether," A7.

59. Ibid.

60. Carter, interview with the author, October 17, 2014.

61. Woodruff, interview with the author, March 31, 2017.

62. Woodruff, *"This Is Judy Woodruff at the White House,"* 125–50. By 1976, broadcast coverage was an increasingly important factor in presidential election cycles, and Carter staged his campaign with the era's dominant medium in mind. "No administration in the television age has studied the methods of the medium more religiously than this one, and none designed its actions more accordingly," Wilkie wrote. As quoted in Greenberg, *Republic of Spin,* 405. Mears, whose career corresponded with the rise of television news, agreed. Mears, interview with the author, August 18, 2012.

63. Greenberg, *The Republic of Spin,* 405. "Reagan and his people started using television as an art form," Donaldson contended. Donaldson, interview with the author, January 13, 2017.

64. Schieffer, interview with the author, August 12, 2014.

65. Mears, interview with the author, August 18, 2012.

66. Woodruff, interview with the author, January 2017.

67. Witcover, interview with the author, January 18, 2017; Germond and Witcover, "Ridicule: Cruelest of All," 35; John Lacy, "The Rabbit Done It?" *Hartford Courant,* November 17, 1980, A15; Rafshoon, interview with the author, August 12, 2014; Gerald Rafshoon, "Washington Classroom with Gerald Rafshoon," C-SPAN, October 7, 2013, https://www.c-span.org /video/?315502-1/washington-classroom-gerald-rafshoon; Howison, *The 1980 Presidential Election,* 87–113.

68. Weisman, "The President and the Press," 34.

69. Auletta, "How Carter Plays the Press: Who'll Win," 17; Howison, *The 1980 Presidential Election,* 87–113; Covington et al., "Shaping a Candidate's Image in the Press: Ronald Reagan and the 1980 Presidential Election," 783–98.

70. Weisman, "The President and the Press," 34.

71. Ibid.

72. Witcover, interview with the author, January 18, 2017; Woodruff, *"This Is Judy Woodruff at the White House,"* 125–50.

73. Greenberg, *The Republic of Spin,* 408–15.

74. Woodruff, interview with the author, March 31, 2017. Cloud agreed: "Reagan was one of the first to use the Hollywood system to control access," and now it has come to dominate presidential politics. Cloud, interview with the author, August 11, 2014.

75. "In my earlier days . . . , a politician was able to so-called 'let his hair down,' and have a drink with a group of reporters," Witcover recalled. Witcover, interview with the author, January 18, 2017.

76. Weisman, "The President and the Press," 34; Pressman, *Remaking the News,* 315–25; Greenberg, *Republic of Spin,* 408–15.

EPILOGUE

1. As quoted in David Fahrenthold, "Trump Recorded Having Extremely Lewd Conversation about Women in 2005," *Washington Post,* October 8, 2016, https://www.washingtonpost.com /politics/trump-recorded-having-extremely-lewd-conversation-about-women-in-2005/2016 /10/07/3b9ce776-8cb4-11e6-bf8a-3d26847eeed4_story.html?utm_term=.db2725ad56ab

2. Ibid.; Paul Farhi, "A Caller Had a Lewd Tape of Donald Trump. Then the Race to Break the Story Was On," *Washington Post,* October 7, 2016, https://www.washingtonpost.com/lifestyle /style/the-caller-had-a-lewd-tape-of-donald-trump-then-the-race-was-on/2016/10/07/31d 74714-8ce5-11e6-875e-2c1bfe943b66_story.html?utm_term=.38cd0ca1c659

3. As quoted in Katy Tur, *Unbelievable: My Front-Row Seat to the Craziest Campaign in American History* (New York: Dey Street, 2017), 219.

4. Patterson, *The Mass Media Election*; Thomas Patterson, "Pre-Primary News Coverage of the 2016 Presidential Race: Trump's Rise, Sanders' Emergence, and Clinton's Struggle" (Cambridge, Mass.: Harvard Kennedy School, Shorenstein Center on Media, Politics, and Public Policy, 2016).

5. As quoted in Patterson, "Pre-Primary News Coverage of the 2016 Presidential Race"; Thomas Patterson, "News Coverage of the 2016 Presidential Primaries: Horse Race Reporting Has Consequences" (Cambridge, Mass.: Harvard Kennedy School, Shorenstein Center on Media, Politics, and Public Policy, 2016).

6. Julian Zelizer, "17 Democrats Ran for President in 1976. Can Today's GOP Learn Anything from What Happened," *Politico Magazine,* September 7, 2015, http://www.politico.com /magazine/story/2015/09/2016-election-1976-democratic-primary-213125; Kevin Kruse and Julian Zelizer, *Fault Lines: A History of the United States since 1974* (New York: Norton, 2019), 196–230.

7. "I have this theory that the candidate who masters the dominant medium of his time is the most successful politician," Schieffer contended. Schieffer, interview with the author, August 12, 2014.

8. Peter Francia, "'Going Public' in the Age of Twitter and Mistrust of the Media: Donald Trump's 2016 Presidential Campaign," in *The Internet and the 2016 Presidential Campaign,* ed. Jody Baumgartner and Terri Towner (New York: Lexington Books, 2017), 199–219; Pablo Boczkowsky and Zizi Papacharissi, *Trump and the Media* (Boston: MIT Press, 2017); Brian Creech, "Finding the White Working Class in 2016: Journalistic Discourses and the Construction of a Political Identity," *European Journal of Cultural Studies* 3.3 (2018): 386–402, DOI: 10/1177/1367549418786412.

9. Patterson, "Pre-Primary News Coverage of the 2016 Presidential Race"; Schulman and Zelizer, *Media Nation,* 126–44, 176–89; Pressman, *On Press,* 170–83.

10. Patterson, "News Coverage of the 2016 Presidential Primaries"; Thomas Patterson, "News Coverage of the 2016 National Conventions: Negative News, Lacking Context" (Cambridge, Mass.: Harvard Kennedy School, Shorenstein Center on Media, Politics, and Public Policy, 2016).

11. Patterson, "News Coverage of the 2016 Presidential Primaries."

12. As quoted in Matt Taibbi, *Insane Clown President: Dispatches from the 2016 Circus* (New York: Spiegel and Grau, 2017), 11; Francia, "'Going Public' in the Age of Twitter and Mistrust of the Media," 199–219; Patterson, "News Coverage of the 2016 General Election: How the Press Failed the Voters," 2–21; Boczkowsky and Papacharissi, *Trump and the Media.*

13. Taibbi, *Insane Clown President,* 9–12.

14. David Mindich, "For Journalists Covering Trump, a Murrow Moment," *Columbia Journalism Review,* July 15, 2016, https://www.cjr.org/analysis/trump_inspires_murrow_moment _for_journalism.php; cited in Pressman, *On Press,* 190, 229.

15. In the aftermath of the *Access Hollywood* controversy, Trump tweeted: "This election is being rigged by the media pushing false and unsubstantiated charges, and outright lies in order to elect Crooked Hillary!" As quoted in Jim Kuypers, ed., *The 2016 American Presidential Campaign and the News: Implications for American Democracy and the Republic* (New York: Lexington Books, 2018), 1.

16. Kruse and Zelizer, *Fault Lines,* 498.

17. Andrew Chadwick, *The Hybrid Media System: Politics and Power* (New York: Oxford Univ. Press), 240–85.

18. Reporters increasingly operated in a different mode and climate than they encountered during the consensus age of network television's fairness doctrine. Hemmer, *Messengers of the Right,* xi–xvi; Julian Zelizer, "How Washington Helped Create the Modern Media: Ending the Fairness Doctrine," in *Media Nation,* 176–89; Kruse and Zelizer, *Fault Lines,* 196–230; Susan Douglas, "Breaking the Rules of Political Communication: Trump's Successes and Miscalculations," in *Trump and the Media,* ed. Boczkowsky and Papacharissi, 133–43.

19. Taibbi, *Insane Clown President,* 11. Presidential candidates still were expected to develop rapport with reporters even after the rise of partisan news channels, which was accelerated by the demise of the fairness doctrine in 1987. Greenberg, *The Republic of Spin,* 416–26; Schulman and Zelizer, *Media Nation,* 126–44; 176–89; Pressman, *On Press,* 170–83. Moving in the direction first initiated in the mid-twentieth century, news channels seeking a competitive edge encouraged reporters to forsake objectivity for "fair and balanced [interpretative] reporting," privileging soft news and adversarial tones. Partisan punditry proliferated across mediums at the turn of the twenty-first century.

20. Broder warned of the continued influence of the cynicism triggered by the crises of confidence in showbiz politics and adversarial journalism, and his admonition came to fruition amid widening fault lines of presidential politics in 2016: "Cynicism is epidemic right now. It saps people's confidence in politics and public officials, and it erodes both the standing and standards of journalism. If the assumption is that nothing is on the level, nothing is what it seems, then citizenship becomes a game for fools, and there is no point in trying to stay informed." David Broder, "War on Cynicism," *Washington Post,* July 6, 1994, as quoted in Patterson, "News Coverage of the 2016 National Conventions: Negative News, Lacking Context," 2–23; Kruse and Zelizer, *Fault Lines,* 196–230. Once in office, Trump continued his Nixon-

inspired attack of the news media as the "enemy of the people," denouncing and rebutting "fake news" with "alternative facts" and tightening media access. As quoted in Kuypers, ed., *The 2016 American Presidential Campaign and the News,* 101; Pressman, *On Press,* 171. But, as temporarily muzzled newshounds of the Reagan-era feared, many Americans viewed attacks against the news media as "a defeat for the press" and not as an assault on our political system. Weisman, "The President and the Press," 34.

21. Boczkowsky and Papacharissi, *Trump and the Media,* 1.

22. Taibbi, *Insane Clown President,* 1–29; Kruse and Zelizer, *Fault Lines*; Boczkowsky and Papacharissi, *Trump and the Media*; Francia, "'Going Public' in the Age of Twitter and Mistrust of the Media," 199–219; Douglas Kellner, "Donald Trump and the Politics of the Spectacle," in *Media, Ideology, and Hegemony,* ed. Savas Coban (Leiden, Netherlands: Brill, 2018), 183–98; Corey Robin, "The Politics Trump Makes," *N+1,* https://nplusonemag.com/online-only/online-only/the-politics-trump makes/.

23. As quoted in Eric Alterman, "The Decline of Historical Thinking," *New Yorker,* February 4, 2019, https://www.newyorker.com/news/news-desk/the-decline-of-historical-thinking; Walter Lippman, *Liberty and the News* (New York: Harcourt, Brace, and Howe, 1920), 54.

24. Kruse and Zelizer, *Fault Lines,* 196–230; Corey Robin, "The Politics Trump Makes," *N+1,* https://nplusonemag.com/online-only/online-only/the-politics-trump-makes/.

25. Thomas Paine, *Major Works: Common Sense/The American Crisis/The Rights of Man/ The Age of Reason/Agrarian Justice* (New York: Bahribook, 2017), 214.

26. Donaldson, interview with the author, January 17, 2017.

INDEX